PRAISE FOR *EMPIRE OF THE SUMMER MOON*

"Mesmerizing . . . while this is a nonfiction book about war, it is equally a book about two nations trying to control their destinies by whatever means necessary. In Quanah Parker, Gwynne has found the perfect vehicle for telling that story." —*Chicago Tribune*

"*Empire of the Summer Moon* impresses indelibly. It's a must-read for anyone interested in Texas history, certainly, and absolutely for anyone searching for a deeper understanding of the American experience."
—*Austin American-Statesman*

"Sam Gwynne is a master storyteller and a dogged reporter, and in this book he makes history come to life in a way that everyone—not just students of the Texas myth—will find irresistible. I couldn't put it down."
—**Evan Smith, CEO and editor in chief of** *The Texas Tribune*

"Among the strengths of this powerful book are the author's novelistic skills, the unstoppable pace of the narrative, and the vivid delineation of its historical characters. . . . *Empire of the Summer Moon* is a skillfully told, brutally truthful, history." —*The Dallas Morning News*

P9-CCU-962

"Glorious . . . Readers are in for an eye-opening trek. . . . *Empire of the Summer Moon* expands our sense of what it has meant to be an American. Expect it on my list of the best books of the year."
—*The Plain Dealer*

"In *Empire of the Summer Moon*, Sam Gwynne has given us a rich, vividly detailed rendering of an important era in our history and of two great men, Quanah Parker and Ranald Slidell Mackenzie, whose struggles did much to define it."
—**Larry McMurtry**

ADDITIONAL PRAISE FOR
EMPIRE OF THE SUMMER MOON

A National Book Critics Circle Award Finalist
A *New York Times* Notable Book
A *Christian Science Monitor* Best Book of 2010

"Transcendent . . . *Empire of the Summer Moon* is nothing short of a revelation. Gwynne . . . doesn't merely retell the story of Parker's life. He pulls his readers through [the] American frontier. . . . This book will leave dust and blood on your jeans."

—*The New York Times Book Review*

"An outstanding addition to western-history collections."

—*Booklist*

"Gwynne's writing is crisp and well researched."

—*The Christian Science Monitor*

"An engrossing, rawboned history."

—*San Antonio Express-News*

"S. C. Gwynne's *Empire of the Summer Moon* is many things—a thrilling account of the Texas frontier in the nineteenth century, a vivid description of the Comanche nation, a fascinating portrait of Cynthia Ann Parker and her son, the mysterious, magnificent Quanah—but most of all it is a ripping good read. Gwynne writes history with a pounding pulse and a beating heart. In *Empire of the Summer Moon* he has given us an epic frontier peopled with real men and women, living and dying and hoping and dreaming at the bloody edge of civilization. I couldn't put it down."

—Jake Silverstein, editor, *Texas Monthly,* and author of
Nothing Happened and Then It Did

"Man for man, the Comanches were the fiercest and most resourceful warriors in North America, and they held on to their domain with an almost otherworldly tenacity. In this sweeping work, S. C. Gwynne re-creates the Comanches' lost world with gusto and style—and without sentimentality. After reading *Empire of the Summer Moon,* you'll never think about Texas, or the Great Plains, in quite the same way again."

—Hampton Sides, author of *Blood and Thunder* and *Hellhound on His Trail*

Also by the Author

Selling Money

The Outlaw Bank

EMPIRE

SUMMER MOON

Quanah Parker and the Rise and Fall of the
Comanches, the Most Powerful Indian
Tribe in American History

S. C. Gwynne

Scribner

New York   London   Toronto   Sydney

SCRIBNER

A Division of Simon & Schuster, Inc.
1230 Avenue of the Americas
New York, NY 10020

Copyright © 2010 by S. C. Gwynne

All rights reserved, including the right to reproduce this book or portions thereof
in any form whatsoever. For information, address Scribner Subsidiary Rights
Department, 1230 Avenue of the Americas, New York, NY 10020.

First Scribner trade paperback edition May 2011

SCRIBNER and design are registered trademarks of The Gale Group, Inc.,
used under license by Simon & Schuster, Inc., the publisher of this work.

For information about special discounts for bulk purchases, please contact
Simon & Schuster Special Sales at 1-866-506-1949 or
business@simonandschuster.com.

The Simon & Schuster Speakers Bureau can bring authors to your live event.
For more information or to book an event, contact the Simon & Schuster Speakers
Bureau at 1-866-248-3049 or visit our website at www.simonspeakers.com.

Book design by Kelvin P. Oden / Oh Snap! Design

Manufactured in Italy

40

Library of Congress Control Number: 2009049747

ISBN 978-1-4165-9105-4
ISBN 978-1-4165-9106-1 (pbk)
ISBN 978-1-4165-9715-5 (ebook)

Insert photograph credits: 1, 4, 12 courtesy of the Dolph Briscoe Center for American History, University of Texas, Joseph E. Taulman Collection; 3, 6–8, 10 courtesy of the Panhandle Plains Historical Museum; 9, 13, 15, 17 courtesy of the Fort
Sill Museum; 14, 16, 18 courtesy of the Oklahoma Historical Society; 2 courtesy
of the Library of Congress; 5 courtesy of the Baylor University Library, Waco Texas

To Katie and Maisie

＊ー　弍◆彐　ー＊

The desert wind would salt their ruins and there
would be nothing, no ghost or scribe, to tell any
pilgrim in his passing how it was that people had
lived in this place and in this place had died.

—Cormac McCarthy

CONTENTS

CONTENTS

EMPIRE OF THE SUMMER MOON

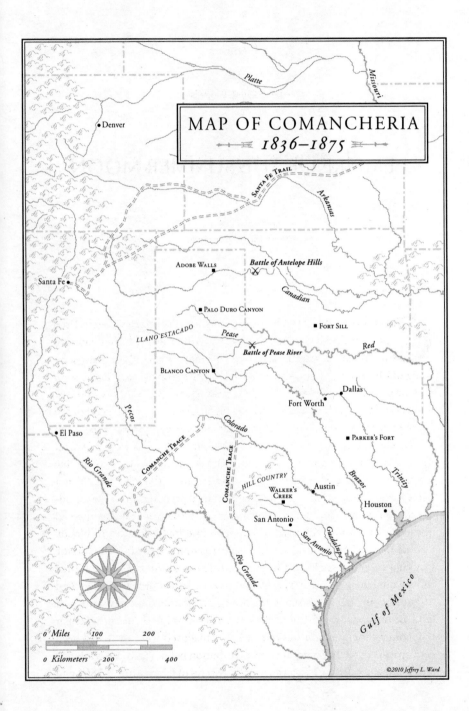

MAP OF COMANCHERIA
1836–1875

Denver

Platte

Missouri

SANTA FE TRAIL

Arkansas

ADOBE WALLS

Battle of Antelope Hills

Santa Fe

Canadian

PALO DURO CANYON

FORT SILL

LLANO ESTACADO

Pease

Battle of Pease River

Red

BLANCO CANYON

Dallas

Fort Worth

Pecos

COMANCHE TRACE

Colorado

El Paso

PARKER'S FORT

Rio Grande

COMANCHE TRACE

Brazos

Trinity

HILL COUNTRY

WALKER'S
CREEK

Austin

Houston

San Antonio

San Antonio

Guadalupe

Rio Grande

Gulf of Mexico

0   Miles   100   200

0   Kilometers   200   400

©2010 Jeffrey L. Ward

One

A NEW KIND OF WAR

CAVALRYMEN REMEMBER SUCH moments: dust swirling behind the pack mules, regimental bugles shattering the air, horses snorting and riders' tack creaking through the ranks, their old company song rising on the wind: "Come home, John! Don't stay long. Come home soon to your own chick-a-biddy!"[1] The date was October 3, 1871. Six hundred soldiers and twenty Tonkawa scouts had bivouacked on a lovely bend of the Clear Fork of the Brazos, in a rolling, scarred prairie of grama grass, scrub oak, sage, and chaparral, about one hundred fifty miles west of Fort Worth, Texas. Now they were breaking camp, moving out in a long, snaking line through the high cutbanks and quicksand streams. Though they did not know it at the time—the idea would have seemed preposterous—the sounding of "boots and saddle" that morning marked the beginning of the end of the Indian wars in America, of fully two hundred fifty years of bloody combat that had begun almost with the first landing of the first ship on the first fatal shore in Virginia. The final destruction of the last of the hostile tribes would not take place for a few more years. Time would be yet required to round them all up, or starve them out, or exterminate their sources of food, or run them to ground in shallow canyons, or kill them outright. For the moment the question was one of hard, unalloyed will. There had been brief spasms of official vengeance and retribution before: J. M. Chivington's and George Armstrong Custer's savage massacres of Cheyennes in 1864 and

1868 were examples. But in those days there was no real attempt to destroy the tribes on a larger scale, no stomach for it. That had changed, and on October 3, the change assumed the form of an order, barked out through the lines of command to the men of the Fourth Cavalry and Eleventh Infantry, to go forth and kill Comanches. It was the end of anything like tolerance, the beginning of the final solution.

The white men were grunts, bluecoats, cavalry, and dragoons; mostly veterans of the War Between the States who now found themselves at the edge of the known universe, ascending to the turreted rock towers that gated the fabled Llano Estacado—Coronado's term for it, meaning "palisaded plains" of West Texas, a country populated exclusively by the most hostile Indians on the continent, where few U.S. soldiers had ever gone before. The llano was a place of extreme desolation, a vast, trackless, and featureless ocean of grass where white men became lost and disoriented and died of thirst; a place where the imperial Spanish had once marched confidently forth to hunt Comanches, only to find that they themselves were the hunted, the ones to be slaughtered. In 1864, Kit Carson had led a large force of federal troops from Santa Fe and attacked a Comanche band at a trading post called Adobe Walls, north of modern-day Amarillo. He had survived it, but had come within a whisker of watching his three companies of cavalry and infantry destroyed.[2]

The troops were now going back, because enough was enough, because President Grant's vaunted "Peace Policy" toward the remaining Indians, run by his gentle Quaker appointees, had failed utterly to bring peace, and finally because the exasperated general in chief of the army, William Tecumseh Sherman, had ordered it so. Sherman's chosen agent of destruction was a civil war hero named Ranald Slidell Mackenzie, a difficult, moody, and implacable young man who had graduated first in his class from West Point in 1862 and had finished the Civil War, remarkably, as a brevet brigadier general. Because his hand was gruesomely disfigured from war wounds, the Indians called him No-Finger Chief, or Bad Hand. A complex destiny awaited him. Within four years he would prove himself the most brutally effective Indian fighter in American history. In roughly that same time period, while General George Armstrong Custer achieved world fame in failure and catastrophe, Mackenzie would become obscure in victory. But it was Mackenzie, not Custer, who would teach the rest of the army how to fight Indians. As he moved his men across the broken, stream-crossed country, past immense herds of buffalo and prairie-dog towns that stretched to the horizon, Colonel Mackenzie did not have a clear idea of what he was doing, where precisely he was going, or how to fight Plains Indians in their homelands. Neither did he have the faintest idea that he would be the one largely responsible for defeating the last of the hostile Indians. He was new to this sort of Indian fighting, and would make many mistakes in the coming weeks. He would learn from them.

For now, Mackenzie was the instrument of retribution. He had been dispatched to kill Comanches in their Great Plains fastness because, six years after the end of the Civil War, the western frontier was an open and bleeding wound, a smoking ruin littered with corpses and charred chimneys, a place where anarchy and torture killings had replaced the rule of law, where Indians and especially Comanches raided at will. Victorious in war, unchallenged by foreign foes in North America for the first time in its history, the Union now found itself unable to deal with the handful of remaining Indian tribes that had not been destroyed, assimilated, or forced to retreat meekly onto reservations where they quickly learned the meaning of abject subjugation and starvation. The hostiles were all residents of the Great Plains; all were mounted, well armed, and driven now by a mixture of vengeance and political desperation. They were Comanches, Kiowas, Arapahoes, Cheyennes, and Western Sioux. For Mackenzie on the southern plains, Comanches were the obvious target: No tribe in the history of the Spanish, French, Mexican, Texan, and American occupations of this land had ever caused so much havoc and death. None was even a close second.

Just how bad things were in 1871 along this razor edge of civilization could be seen in the numbers of settlers who had abandoned their lands. The frontier, carried westward with so much sweat and blood and toil, was now rolling backward, retreating. Colonel Randolph Marcy, who accompanied Sherman on a western tour in the spring, and who had known the country intimately for decades, had been shocked to find that in many places there were fewer people than eighteen years before. "If the Indian marauders are not punished," he wrote, "the whole country seems in a fair way of becoming totally depopulated."[3] This phenomenon was not entirely unknown in the history of the New World. The Comanches had also stopped cold the northward advance of the Spanish empire in the eighteenth century—an empire that had, up to that point, easily subdued and killed millions of Indians in Mexico and moved at will through the continent. Now, after more than a

century of relentless westward movement, they were rolling back civilization's advance again, only on a much larger scale. Whole areas of the borderlands were simply emptying out, melting back eastward toward the safety of
the forests. One county—Wise—had seen its population drop from 3,160
in the year 1860 to 1,450 in 1870. In some places the line of settlements had
been driven back a hundred miles.[4] If General Sherman wondered about
the cause—as he once did—his tour with Marcy relieved him of his doubts.
That spring they had narrowly missed being killed themselves by a party of
raiding Indians. The Indians, mostly Kiowas, passed them over because of a
shaman's superstitions and had instead attacked a nearby wagon train. What
happened was typical of the savage, revenge-driven attacks by Comanches
and Kiowas in Texas in the postwar years. What was not typical was Sherman's proximity and his own very personal and mortal sense that he might
have been a victim, too. Because of that the raid became famous, known to
history as the Salt Creek Massacre.[5]

Seven men were killed in the raid, though that does not begin to describe
the horror of what Mackenzie found at the scene. According to Captain
Robert G. Carter, Mackenzie's subordinate, who witnessed its aftermath, the
victims were stripped, scalped, and mutilated. Some had been beheaded and
others had their brains scooped out. "Their fingers, toes and private parts
had been cut off and stuck in their mouths," wrote Carter, "and their bodies,
now lying in several inches of water and swollen or bloated beyond all chance
of recognition, were filled full of arrows, which made them resemble porcu-
pines." They had clearly been tortured, too. "Upon each exposed abdomen
had been placed a mass of live coals. . . . One wretched man, Samuel Elliott,
who, fighting hard to the last, had evidently been wounded, was found
chained between two wagon wheels and, a fire having been made from the
wagon pole, he had been slowly roasted to death—'burnt to a crisp.' "[6]

Thus the settlers' headlong flight eastward, especially on the Texas frontier, where such raiding was at its worst. After so many long and successful
wars of conquest and dominion, it seemed implausible that the westward
rush of Anglo-European civilization would stall in the prairies of central
Texas. No tribe had ever managed to resist for very long the surge of nascent
American civilization with its harquebuses and blunderbusses and muskets
and eventually lethal repeating weapons and its endless stocks of eager, land-
greedy settlers, its elegant moral double standards and its complete disregard
for native interests. Beginning with the subjection of the Atlantic coastal

tribes (Pequots, Penobscots, Pamunkeys, Wampanoags, et al), hundreds of tribes and bands had either perished from the earth, been driven west into territories, or forcibly assimilated. This included the Iroquois and their enormous, warlike confederation that ruled the area of present-day New York; the once powerful Delawares, driven west into the lands of their enemies; the Iroquois, then yet farther west into even more murderous foes on the plains. The Shawnees of the Ohio Country had fought a desperate rearguard action starting in the 1750s. The great nations of the south—Chicasaw, Cherokee, Seminole, Creek, and Choctaw—saw their reservation lands expropriated in spite of a string of treaties; they were coerced westward into lands given them in yet more treaties that were violated before they were even signed; hounded along a trail of tears until they, too, landed in "Indian Territory" (present-day Oklahoma), a land controlled by Comanches, Kiowas, Araphoes, and Cheyennes.

Even stranger was that the Comanches' stunning success was happening amid phenomenal technological and social changes in the west. In 1869 the Transcontinental Railroad was completed, linking the industrializing east with the developing west and rendering the old trails—Oregon, Santa Fe, and tributaries—instantly obsolete. With the rails came cattle, herded northward in epic drives to railheads by Texans who could make fast fortunes getting them to Chicago markets. With the rails, too, came buffalo hunters carrying deadly accurate .50-caliber Sharps rifles that could kill effectively at extreme range—grim, violent, opportunistic men blessed now by both a market in the east for buffalo leather and the means of getting it there. In 1871 the buffalo still roamed the plains: Earlier that year a herd of four million had been spotted near the Arkansas River in present-day southern Kansas. The main body was fifty miles deep and twenty-five miles wide.[7] But the slaughter had already begun. It would soon become the greatest mass destruction of warm-blooded animals in human history. In Kansas alone the bones of thirty-one million buffalo were sold for fertilizer between 1868 and 1881.[8] All of these profound changes were under way as Mackenzie's Raiders departed their camps on the Clear Fork. The nation was booming; a railroad had finally stitched it together. There was only this one obstacle left: the warlike and unreconstructed Indian tribes who inhabited the physical wastes of the Great Plains.

Of those, the most remote, primitive, and irredeemably hostile were a band of Comanches known as the Quahadis. Like all Plains Indians, they were nomadic. They hunted primarily the southernmost part of the high plains, a place known to the Spanish, who had been abjectly driven from it, as Comancheria. The Llano Estacado, located within Comancheria, was a dead-flat tableland larger than New England and rising, in its highest elevations, to more than five thousand feet. For Europeans, the land was like a bad hallucination. "Although I traveled over them for more than 300 leagues," wrote Coronado in a letter to the king of Spain on October 20, 1541, "[there were] no more landmarks than if we had been swallowed up by the sea . . . there was not a stone, nor a bit of rising ground, nor a tree, nor a shrub, nor anything to go by."[9] The Canadian River formed its northern boundary. In the east was the precipitous Caprock Escarpment, a cliff rising somewhere between two hundred and one thousand feet that demarcates the high plains from the lower Permian Plains below, giving the Quahadis something that approximated a gigantic, nearly impregnable fortress. Unlike almost all of the other tribal bands on the plains, the Quahadis had always shunned contact with Anglos. They would not even trade with them, as a general principle, preferring the Mexican traders from Santa Fe, known as Comancheros. So aloof were they that in the numerous Indian ethnographies compiled from 1758 onward chronicling the various Comanche bands (there were as many as thirteen), they do not even show up until 1872.[10] For this reason they had largely avoided the cholera plagues of 1816 and 1849 that had ravaged western tribes and had destroyed fully half of all Comanches. Virtually alone among all bands of all tribes in North America, they never signed a treaty. Quahadis were the hardest, fiercest, least yielding component of a tribe that had long had the reputation as the most violent and warlike on the continent; if they ran low on water, they were known to drink the contents of a dead horse's stomach, something even the toughest Texas Ranger would not do. Even other Comanches feared them. They were the richest of all plains bands in the currency by which Indians measured wealth—horses—and in the years after the Civil War managed a herd of some fifteen thousand. They also owned "Texas cattle without number."[11]

On that clear autumn day in 1871, Mackenzie's troops were hunting Quahadis. Because they were nomadic, it was not possible to fix their location. One could know only their general ranges, their hunting grounds, perhaps old camp locations. They were known to hunt the Llano Estacado; they liked to camp in the depths of Palo Duro Canyon, the second-largest canyon in North America after the Grand Canyon; they often stayed near the headwaters of the Pease River and McClellan's Creek; and in Blanco Canyon, all within a roughly hundred-mile ambit of present-day Amarillo in the upper Texas Panhandle. If you were pursuing them, as Mackenzie was, you had your Tonkawa scouts fan out far in advance of the column. The Tonks, as they were called, members of an occasionally cannibalistic Indian tribe that had nearly been exterminated by Comanches and whose remaining members lusted for vengeance, would look for signs, try to cut trails, then follow the trails to the lodges. Without them the army would never have had the shadow of a chance against these or any Indians on the open plains.

By the afternoon of the second day, the Tonks had found a trail. They reported to Mackenzie that they were tracking a Quahadi band under the leadership of a brilliant young war chief named Quanah—a Comanche word that meant "odor" or "fragrance." The idea was to find and destroy Quanah's village. Mackenzie had a certain advantage in that no white man had ever dared try such a thing before; not in the panhandle plains, not against the Quahadis.

Mackenzie and his men did not know much about Quanah. No one did. Though there is an intimacy of information on the frontier—opposing sides often had a surprisingly detailed understanding of one another, in spite of the enormous physical distances between them and the fact that they were trying to kill one another—Quanah was simply too young for anyone to know much about him yet, where he had been, or what he had done. Though no one would be able to even estimate the date of his birth until many years later, it was mostly likely in 1848, making him twenty-three that year and eight years younger than Mackenzie, who was also so young that few people in Texas, Indian or white, knew much about him at the time. Both men achieved their fame only in the final, brutal Indian wars of the mid-1870s. Quanah was exceptionally young to be a chief. He was reputed to be ruthless, clever, and fearless in battle.

But there was something else about Quanah, too. He was a half-breed, the son of a Comanche chief and a white woman. People on the Texas frontier would soon learn this about him, partly because the fact was so exceptional. Comanche warriors had for centuries taken female captives—Indian, French, English, Spanish, Mexican, and American—and fathered children by them who were raised as Comanches. But there is no record of any prominent half-white Comanche war chief. By the time Mackenzie was hunting him in 1871, Quanah's mother had long been famous. She was the best known of all Indian captives of the era, discussed in drawing rooms in New York and London as "the white squaw" because she had refused on repeated occasions to return to her people, thus challenging one of the most fundamental of the Eurocentric assumptions about Indian ways: that given the choice between the sophisticated, industrialized, Christian culture of Europe and the savage, bloody, and morally backward ways of the Indians, no sane person would ever choose the latter. Few, other than Quanah's mother, did. Her name was Cynthia Ann Parker. She was the daughter of one of early Texas's most prominent families, one that included Texas Ranger captains, politicians, and prominent Baptists who founded the state's first Protestant church. In 1836, at the age of nine, she had been kidnapped in a Comanche raid at Parker's Fort, ninety miles south of present Dallas. She soon forgot her mother tongue, learned Indian ways, and became a full member of the tribe. She married Peta Nocona, a prominent war chief, and had three children by him, of whom Quanah was the eldest. In 1860, when Quanah was twelve, Cynthia Ann was recaptured during an attack by Texas Rangers on her village, during which everyone but her and her infant daughter, Prairie Flower, were killed. Mackenzie and his soldiers most likely knew the story of Cynthia Ann Parker—most everyone on the frontier did—but they had no idea that her blood ran in Quanah's veins. They would not learn this until 1875. For now they knew only that he was the target of the largest anti-Indian expedition mounted since 1865, one of the largest ever undertaken.

Mackenzie's Fourth Cavalry, which he would soon build into a grimly efficient mobile assault force, for the moment consisted largely of timeservers who were unprepared to encounter the likes of Quanah and his hardened plains warriors. The soldiers were operating well beyond the ranges of civilization, beyond anything like a trail they could follow or any landmarks they could possibly have recognized. They were dismayed to learn that their principal water sources were buffalo wallow holes that, according to Carter, were "stagnant, warm, nauseating, odorous with smells, and covered with green slime that had to be pushed aside."[12] Their inexperience was evident during their first night on the trail. Sometime around midnight, above the din of a West Texas windstorm, the men heard "a tremendous tramping and an unmistakable snorting and bellowing."[13] That sound, as they soon discovered, was made by stampeding buffalo. The soldiers had made the horrendous mistake of making camp between a large herd of buffalo and its water source. Panicked, the men emerged from their tents in darkness, screaming and waving blankets and trying desperately to turn the stampeding animals. They succeeded, but by the smallest of margins. "The immense herds of brown monsters were caromed off and they stampeded to our left at breakneck speed," wrote Carter, "rushing and jostling but flushing only the edge of one of our horse herds. . . . one could hardly repress a shudder of what might have been the result of this nocturnal visit, for although the horses were strongly 'lariated out,' 'staked,' or 'picketed,' nothing could have saved them from the terror which this headlong charge would have inevitably created, had we not heard them just in time to turn the leading herds."[14]

Miraculously spared the consequences of their own ignorance, the bluecoats rounded up the stray horses, broke camp at dawn, and spent the day riding westward over a rolling mesquite prairie pocked with prairie-dog towns. The latter were common in the Texas Panhandle and extremely dangerous to horses and mules. Think of enormous anthills populated by oversized rodents, stretching for miles. The troopers passed more herds of buffalo, vast and odorous, and rivers whose gypsum-infused water was impossible to drink. They passed curious-looking trading stations, abandoned now, consisting of caves built into the sides of cliffs and reinforced with poles that looked like prison bars.

On the second day they ran into more trouble. Mackenzie ordered a night march, hoping to surprise the enemy in its camps. His men struggled through steep terrain, dense brush, ravines, and arroyos. After hours of what Carter described as "trials and tribulations and much hard talk verging on profanity" and "many rather comical scenes," they fetched up bruised and battered in the dead end of a small canyon and had to wait until daybreak to find their way out. A few hours later they reached the Freshwater Fork of the Brazos, deep in Indian territory, in a broad, shallow thirty-mile-long valley that averaged fifteen hundred feet in width and was cut by smaller side canyons. The place was known as Blanco Canyon and was located just to the east of present-day Lubbock, one of the Quahadis' favorite campgrounds.

Whatever surprise Mackenzie had hoped for was gone. On the third day the Tonkawa scouts realized they were being shadowed by a group of four Comanche warriors, who had been watching their every move, presumably including what must have seemed to them the comical blunders of the night march. The Tonks gave chase, but "the hostiles being better mounted soon distanced their pursuers and vanished into the hills." This was not surprising: In two hundred years of enmity, the Tonkawas had never been close to matching the horsemanship of the Comanches. They *always* lost. The result was that, while the cavalrymen and dragoons had no idea where the Comanches were camped, Quanah knew precisely what Mackenzie was doing and where he was. The next night Mackenzie compounded the error by allowing the men the indulgence of campfires, tantamount to painting a large arrow in the canyon pointing to their camp. Some of the companies blundered yet again by failing to place "sleeping parties" among the horses.

At around midnight, the regiment was awakened by a succession of unearthly, high-pitched yells. Those were followed by shots, and more yells, and suddenly the camp was alive with Comanches riding at full gallop. Exactly what the Indians were doing was soon apparent: Mingled with the screams and gunshots and general mayhem of the camp was another sound, only barely audible at first, then rising quickly to something like rolling thunder. The men quickly realized, to their horror, that it was the sound of stampeding horses. *Their* horses. Amid shouts of "Every man to his lariat!" six hundred panicked horses tore loose through the camp, rearing, jumping, and plunging at full speed. Lariats snapped with the sound of pistol shots; iron picket pins that a few minutes before had been used to secure the horses now whirled and snapped about their necks like airborne sabres. Men tried to grab them and were thrown to the ground and dragged among the horses, their hands lacerated and bleeding.

When it was all over, the soldiers discovered that Quanah and his warriors had made off with seventy of their best horses and mules, including Colonel Mackenzie's magnificent gray pacer. In west Texas in 1871, stealing someone's horse was often equivalent to a death sentence. It was an old Indian tactic, especially on the high plains, to simply steal white men's horses and leave them to die of thirst or starvation. Comanches had used it to lethal effect against the Spanish in the early eighteenth century. In any case, an unmounted army regular stood little chance against a mounted Comanche.

This midnight raid was Quanah's calling card, a clear message that hunting him and his Comanche warriors in their homeland was going to be a difficult and treacherous business. Thus began what would become known to history as the Battle of Blanco Canyon, which was in turn the opening salvo in a bloody Indian war in the highlands of west Texas that would last four years and culminate in the final destruction of the Comanche nation. Blanco Canyon would also provide the U.S. Army with its first look at Quanah. Captain Carter, who would win the Congressional Medal of Honor for his bravery in Blanco Canyon, offered this description of the young war chief in battle on the day after the midnight stampede:

> A large and powerfully built chief led the bunch, on a coal black racing pony. Leaning forward upon his mane, his heels nervously working in the animal's side, with six-shooter poised in the air, he seemed the incarnation of savage, brutal joy. His face was smeared with black warpaint, which gave his features a satanic look. . . . A full-length headdress or war bonnet of eagle's feathers, spreading out as he rode, and descending from his forehead, over head and back, to his pony's tail, almost swept the ground. Large brass hoops were in his ears; he was naked to the waist, wearing simply leggings, moccasins and a breechclout. A necklace of beare's claws hung about his neck. . . . Bells jingled as he rode at headlong speed, followed by the leading warriors, all eager to outstrip him in the race. It was Quanah, principal warchief of the Qua-ha-das.[15]

Moments later, Quanah wheeled his horse in the direction of an unfortunate private named Seander Gregg and, as Carter and his men watched, blew Gregg's brains out.

Two

A LETHAL PARADISE

THUS DID QUANAH PARKER, the son of a white woman from an invading civilization, begin to fulfill an intricate destiny. He would soon become one of the main targets of forty-six companies of U.S. Army infantry and cavalry—three thousand men—the largest force ever dispatched to hunt down and destroy Indians. He was to become the last chief of the most dominant and influential tribe in American history. What follows is, in the largest sense, the story of Quanah and his family. It has its roots in both the ancient tribal heritage of the Comanches and in the indomitable, fate-cursed Parker clan, which came to symbolize for many nineteenth-century Americans the horrors and the hopes of the frontier. The two lineal streams came together in his mother, Cynthia Ann, whose life with the Comanches and fateful return to white civilization form one of the Old West's great narratives. Behind it all is the story of the rise and fall of the Comanches. No tribe in the history of North America had more to say about the nation's destiny. Quanah was merely the final product of everything they had believed and dreamed of and fought for over a span of two hundred fifty years. The kidnapping of a blue-eyed, nine-year-old Cynthia Ann in 1836 marked the start of the white man's forty-year war with the Comanches, in which Quanah would play a leading role. In one sense, the Parkers are the beginning and end of the Comanches in U.S. history.

The story starts, as it must, in Texas in the tumultuous and transformative year of 1836, twelve years before Cynthia Ann Parker gave birth to Quanah in a patch of prairie flowers on Elk Creek near the Wichita Mountains in southwestern Oklahoma.[1]

That year General Antonio López de Santa Anna made an epic blunder that changed the destiny of Texas, and thus of the North American continent. On March 6, while flying the blood-red flag of "no quarter given," some two thousand of his Mexican troops destroyed several hundred Texans at a small mission known as the Alamo in the town of San Antonio de Bexar. At the time it seemed like a great victory. It was a catastrophic mistake. He compounded it three weeks later at the nearby town of Goliad when he ordered his army to execute some three hundred fifty Texan soldiers after they had surrendered. The prisoners were marched out in columns, shot down, and their bodies burned. Wounded men were dragged into the streets of the presidio to be shot. These acts created martyrs and spawned legends. The murderous ferocity of the Alamo fighters was mere prelude to what happened next. On April 21, at the Battle of San Jacinto, a force of Texans under the command of General Sam Houston outmaneuvered Santa Anna's army, cornered it against a muddy bayou, and, with extreme bias, destroyed it. The victory marked the end of Mexican rule north of the Rio Grande, and the birth of a sovereign nation called the Republic of Texas.[2]

The news was cause for jubilation among the settlers, and in the spring of 1836 no citizens of the new republic had greater reason to celebrate than an extended family of religious, enterprising, transplanted easterners known to their neighbors as the Parker Clan. Drawn by the promise of free land, they had journeyed to Texas from Illinois in 1833 in a caravan of thirty oxcarts. The deal they were offered seemed almost too good to be true. In exchange for meaningless promises of allegiance to Mexico (of which Texas was still a part), several Parker family heads were each given grants of 4,600 acres of land in central Texas near the present town of Mexia. In perpetuity. No taxes or customs duties for ten years. Pooling their resources, they had aggregated adjacent lands totaling 16,100 acres (25.2 square miles), a veritable kingdom by the standards of their native Virginia. (They supplemented their grants with another 2,300 acres they bought themselves for $2,000.)[3] The land itself was magnificent, located at the edge of Texas's prodigiously fertile blackland prairie, timbered with forests of post oak, ash, walnut, and sweet gum, and crossed with broad, rolling meadowlands. There was a bubbling spring (a "gushing fountain"[4] in one description), several creeks, and the nearby Navasota River. Fish and game abounded. In 1835 about two dozen people representing six Parker families and relatives built a one-acre fort on the property containing four blockhouses, six log cabins, and a bulletproof front gate, all enclosed by sharpened, cedar-timber walls fifteen feet high. There were gunports everywhere, even in the floor of the blockhouses' second story, and benches on which shooters could stand. Parker's Fort was a small—and prodigiously fortified—pastoral utopia. It was exactly the sort of place most American pioneers dreamed of.

The fort had another distinction: In the year of Texas's independence it was situated on the absolute outermost edge of the Indian frontier. There were no Anglo settlements to the west, no towns, no houses, no permanent structures of any kind save for the grass huts of the Wichitas or the makeshift shacks of Comancheros and other Indian traders. (Between Parker's Fort and Mexican California stood Santa Fe and the small, scattered settlements of New Mexico.) And the fort was so far beyond the ordinary line of settlements that there were hardly any people *behind* it, either. In 1835, Texas had a population of less than forty thousand.[5] Though a few towns like Nacogdoches and San Antonio had both histories and bustling cultures, most of their residents lived on farms and plantations and in small settlements along river bottoms. Almost all were subsistence farmers, and most lacked any sort of government protection at all. Whatever small and unresponsive Mexican forces had existed were now gone, and the fragile Texas republic had better things to do than protect lunatic Anglo farmers who insisted on living beyond civilization's last outposts. Along with a handful of widely scattered neighbors, the Parkers were left to their own devices in a truly anarchic place ruled entirely by Indians.

But the Parkers were even more alone on the frontier than this description suggests. To say that their fort was near present-day Dallas might suggest that the entire Indian frontier in North America in those days ran northward toward Canada along that line of longitude. But in 1836 the only borderland where white civilization met hostile Plains Indians was in Texas. Oklahoma was pure Indian territory, a place where beaten tribes of the South and middle Atlantic states were being forcibly relocated, often right on top of warlike plains tribes. The Indian-dominated plains north of that—part of the future states of Kansas, Nebraska, and the Dakotas—were simply unreached yet by anything like civilization. The first fight between the U.S. Army and the

Lakota nation on the northern plains did not take place until 1854.[6] The Oregon Trail did not exist yet. All of the towns on the hostile frontier were in Texas. You can think of the Parkers' land as the tip of a blunt finger of Anglo-European civilization jutting out into the last stronghold of untamed Indians in America. That anyone, let alone families with babies and small children, would possibly want to settle there was scarcely imaginable to most people in the civilized east. In 1836 it was an extremely dangerous place.

Which does not explain why, on the warm and fragrant spring morning of May 19, less than a month after the Battle of San Jacinto had removed most of what passed for federal power from the territory, the Parker clan was behaving as though they were living on a settled, hundred-year-old farm west of Philadelphia. Ten of the sixteen able-bodied men were out working the cornfields. The eight women and nine children were inside the fort, but for some reason the massive, armored gate had been left wide open. The men who remained there were unarmed. Though the Parkers had been the prime movers behind the formation of the original companies of Texas Rangers[7]— designed specifically to deal with the Comanche threat[8]—local commander James Parker had, as he put it, recently "disbanded the troops under my command"[9] because he perceived little danger. Later he conceded that there may have been another reason: in his own words, "because the government was not in a condition to bear the expense of supporting troops"[10]—meaning he would not get paid. It remains unclear how he and his brother Silas, also a Ranger captain, could possibly have come to the conclusion that their settlement was, even temporarily, safe. They were almost certainly aware of recent Comanche raids in the area: In mid-April a caravan of settlers had been attacked and two women kidnapped; on May 1, a family named Hibbons had been attacked on the Guadalupe River. Two men had been killed and Mrs. Hibbons and her two children had been taken captive. She had somehow escaped, and later wandered battered, bleeding, and nearly naked into a camp full of astonished Rangers in the middle of the night. The Rangers managed to rescue the children from a Comanche camp.[11] Under normal circumstances, a small group of defenders at Parker's Fort could have held off a direct assault from a large body of Indians.[12] As it was, they were easy prey.

At ten o'clock in the morning a large band of Indians rode up to the fort, stopping in front of its main gate. Estimates of the number of warriors vary from one hundred to six hundred, but the smaller number is probably more accurate. There were women, too, mounted like the men. The riders carried a white flag, which might have reassured more naïve settlers. The Parkers were too new to the western frontier to know exactly who this painted-for-war group was—seventeen-year-old Rachel Parker Plummer guessed incorrectly, and perhaps wishfully, that they were "Tawakonis, Caddoes, Keechis, Wacos," and other sedentary bands of central Texas[13]—but they had encountered Indians before and knew immediately that they had made a disastrous error in leaving themselves so exposed. Had they fully understood whom they were confronting—mostly Comanches, but also some Kiowas, their frequent running mates—they might have anticipated the horrors that were about to descend on them. As it was, there was nothing to do but play along with the idea of a parlay, so forty-eight-year-old Benjamin Parker, one of the six men in the fort, walked out to meet the warriors.

What happened next is one of the most famous events in the history of the American frontier, in part because it came to be regarded by historians as the start of the longest and most brutal of all the wars between Americans and a single Indian tribe.[14] Most of the wars against Native Americans in the East, South, and Midwest had lasted only a few years. Hostile tribes made trouble for a while but were soon tracked to their villages where their lodgings and crops were burned, the inhabitants exterminated or forced to surrender. Lengthy "wars" against the Shawnees, for example, were really just a series of Indian defeats strung out over many years (and complicated by British-French alliances). Wars against the northern Plains Indians such as the Sioux started much later, and did not last nearly as long.

When Benjamin Parker reached the assembled Indians, alone, on foot and unarmed, they told him they wanted a cow to slaughter and also directions to a water hole. He told them they could not have the cow, but offered other food. He returned to the fort through the open gate, told his thirty-two-year-old brother, Silas, what the Indians had said, remarked on the absurdity of their request for directions to water when their horses were still dripping wet, then gathered up a few staples and bravely went back out, even though Silas warned him not to. Meanwhile, seventy-eight-year-old family patriarch John Parker, his elderly wife, Sallie, and Rachel Plummer's sister Sarah Parker Nixon were fleeing out the back exit, a low doorway—too low for a horse to pass through—that led to the spring.[15] Another Parker in-law, G. E. Dwight, did the same with his family, prompting Silas to say, scornfully: "Good Lord, Dwight, you are not going to run? Stand and fight like a man, and if we have to die we will sell our lives as dearly as we can." This was bad advice. Dwight ignored it. In spite of his bravado, Silas had left his shot pouch back in his cabin. He then made another mistake, failing to tell his niece Rachel to join the others and run away with her fourteen-month-old son, James Pratt Plummer. "Do you stand here," he said to her instead, "and watch the Indians' motions while until I run into the house for my shot pouch."

But events were moving much faster than Silas Parker had expected. As Rachel watched in horror, the Indians surrounded her uncle Benjamin and impaled him on their lances. He was clubbed, shot with arrows at extremely close range, and then, probably still alive, scalped. This all happened very quickly. Leaving Benjamin, the Indians turned and charged the fort. Rachel was already running with her son in her arms toward the back door. She was quickly caught. In her own detailed account "a large sulky Indian picked up a hoe and knocked me down."[16] She fainted, and when she came to was being dragged by her long red hair, bleeding profusely from her head wound. "I made several unsuccessful attempts to raise my feet before I could do it," she wrote. She was taken to the main body of Indians, where she saw her uncle's mutilated face and body up close. She saw her son in the arms of an Indian on horseback. Two Comanche women began to beat her with a whip. "I supposed," Rachel recalled, "that it was to make me quit crying."[17]

Meanwhile the Indians attacked the men who had remained in the fort, killing Silas and his relatives Samuel and Robert Frost. All three were scalped. Next, the warriors turned to a task especially suited to mounted, raiding Plains Indians: running down fleeing, screaming victims. Elder John Parker, his wife, Sallie, and her daughter Elizabeth Kellogg, a young widow, had managed to travel three-quarters of a mile when the Indians overtook them. All three were surrounded and stripped of all of their clothing. One can only imagine their horror as they cowered stark naked before their tormentors on the open plain. The Indians then went to work on them, attacking the old man with tomahawks, and forcing Granny Parker, who kept trying to look away, to watch what they did to him.[18] They scalped him, cut off his genitals, and killed him, in what order no one will ever know. Then they turned their attentions to Granny, pinning her to the ground with their lances, raping her, driving a knife deep into one of her breasts, and leaving her for dead.[19] They threw Elizabeth Kellogg on a horse and took her away.

In all the confusion, Silas Parker's wife, Lucy, and her four children had also run out the back gate of the fort in the direction of the cornfields. The

Indians caught them, too, forced Lucy to surrender two of her children, then dragged her, the two remaining children, and one of the men (L. D. Nixon) back to the fort, where they were somehow rescued by three men from the cornfields who had arrived with rifles. The two children who remained in captivity were soon to become household names on the western frontier: Silas and Lucy Parker's blue-eyed, nine-year-old daughter, Cynthia Ann, and her seven-year-old brother, John Richard.

Thus ended the main battle. It had taken barely half an hour and had left five men dead: Benjamin Parker, Silas Parker, Samuel and Robert Frost, and Elder John Parker. Two women were wounded, Cynthia Ann's mother, Lucy, and Granny Parker, who had miraculously survived. The raiders had taken two women and three children captive: Rachel Parker Plummer and her toddler son (the first child born at Parker's Fort),[20] Elizabeth Kellogg, and the two young Parker children. Before they left, the Indians killed a number of cattle, looted the place, and set fire to some of the houses. They broke bottles, slashed open the tick mattresses, threw the feathers in the air, and carried out "a great number of my father's books and medicines," in Rachel's description. She described what happened to some of the looters:

> Among [my father's medicines] was a bottle of pulverized arsenic, which the Indians mistook for a kind of white paint, with which they painted their faces and bodies all over, dissolving it in their saliva. The bottle was brought to me to tell them what it was. I told them I did not know though I knew because the bottle was labeled.[21]

Four of the Indians painted their faces with the arsenic. According to Rachel, all of them died, presumably in horrible agony.

In the aftermath of the raid, there were two groups of survivors, neither of which knew of the other's existence. Rachel's father, James Parker, led a group of eighteen—six adults and twelve children—through the dense wilderness of trees, bushes, briars, and blackberry vines along the Navasota River, terrified the whole time that Indians would find them. Parker wrote: "every few steps did I see briars tear the legs of the little children until the blood trickled down so that they could have been tracked by it."[22] Every time they came to a sandy part of the river bottom, Parker had them walk backward across it to confuse pursuers. Unfortunately this ploy also fooled the other group of survivors, who never found them, though both were headed to the same place: Fort Houston, near modern-day Palestine, Texas, roughly sixty-five miles away.[23] At one point James's group went thirty-six hours without food, finally eating only after he managed to catch and drown a skunk. They traveled for five days and finally gave up, too exhausted to continue. James went on alone to get help, covering the last thirty-six miles to Fort Houston, amazingly, in a single day. Four days later, the second group of refugees arrived at the same place. The survivors did not return to bury their dead until July 19, fully one month after the raid.

The preceding description may seem needlessly bloody in its details. But it typified Comanche raids in an era that was defined by such attacks. This was the actual, and often quite grim, reality of the frontier. There is no dressing it up, though most accounts of Indian "depredations" (the newspapers' favorite euphemism) at the time often refused even to acknowledge that the women had been victims of abuse. But everyone knew. What happened to the Parkers was what any settler on the frontier would have learned to expect, and to fear. In its particulars the raid was exactly what the Spanish and their successors, the Mexicans, had endured in south Texas, New Mexico, and northern Mexico since the late 1600s, and what the Apaches, Osages, Tonkawas, and other tribes had been subjected to for several centuries. Most of the early raids in Texas were driven by a desire for horses or whatever loot could be taken. Later, especially in the last days of the Indian wars, vengeance would become the principal motivation. (The Salt Creek Massacre in 1871 was an example.) The savagery of those raids would make the violence at Parker's Fort seem tame and unimaginative by comparison.

The logic of Comanche raids was straightforward: All the men were killed, and any men who were captured alive were tortured to death as a matter of course, some more slowly than others; the captive women were gang-raped. Some were killed, some tortured. But a portion of them, particularly if they were young, would be spared (though vengeance could always be a motive for slaying hostages). Babies were invariably killed, while preadolescents were often adopted by Comanches or other tribes. This treatment was not reserved for whites or Mexicans; it was practiced just as energetically on rival Indian tribes. Though few horses were taken, the Parker's Fort raid must have been deemed a success: There were no Indian casualties, and they had netted five captives who could be ransomed back to the whites for horses, weapons, or food.

The brutality of the raid also underscores the audacity of the Parker family itself. Though they had built themselves a sturdy fort, they quite obviously neither farmed nor hunted nor gathered water within its walls. They were of necessity often outside its stockades, constantly exposed to attack and under no illusions about the presence of warlike Indians or about what they did to their captives. There was no quality of self-deception in their undertaking. And yet they persisted, bred prolifically, raised their children, farmed their fields, and worshipped God, all in a place where almost every waking moment held a mortal threat.

As a breed they were completely alien to the Plains Indians' experience of Europeans. When the Spanish empire had moved ruthlessly north from Mexico City in the seventeenth and eighteenth centuries, dominating, killing, and subjugating native tribes along the way, it had done so in an extremely organized, centrally controlled fashion. Military presidios and Catholic missions were built and staffed first; soldiers arrived; colonists followed and stayed close to mother's skirts. The westward push of the Americans followed a radically different course. Its vanguard was not federal troops and federal forts but simple farmers imbued with a fierce Calvinist work ethic, steely optimism, and a cold-eyed aggressiveness that made them refuse to yield even in the face of extreme danger. They were said to fear God so much that there was no fear left over for anyone or anything else.[24] They habitually declined to honor government treaties with Native Americans, believing in their hearts that the land belonged to them. They hated Indians with a particular passion, considering them something less than fully human, and thus blessed with inalienable rights to absolutely nothing. Government in all its forms lagged behind such frontier folk, often showing up much later and often reluctantly. This was who the Parkers were. Elder John and his sons had lugged themselves westward out of the wet green forests of the east and toward the scorching treeless prairies of the country's heartland. They were militant predestinarian Baptists, severe in their religion and intolerant of people who did not believe as they did. John's eldest son, Daniel, the clan's guiding spirit, was one of the leading Baptist preachers of his generation and spent his life picking doctrinal fights with his fellow churchmen. He founded the first Protestant church in Texas. The Parkers were politically connected, too. Both James and Daniel were representatives to the political gathering in 1835 known as the "consultation" whose purpose was to organize a provisional government for Texas.

Though their lands were temporarily abandoned after the raid, parts of the extended Parker clan were soon pushing restlessly westward again. They, more than columns of dusty bluecoats, were what conquered the Indians. In that sense Quanah's own genetic heritage contained the seeds of his tribe's eventual destruction. His mother's family offers a nearly perfect example of the sort of righteous, hard-nosed, up-country folk who lived in dirt-floored, mud-chinked cabins, played ancient tunes on the fiddle, took their Kentucky rifles with them into the fields, and dragged the rest of American civilization westward along with them.

While the survivors of the Parker's Fort raid crawled and stumbled through the lacerating brush of the Navasota River bottom, the Indians they feared were riding resolutely north, as fast as they could go with their five captives. They pushed their ponies hard and did not stop until after midnight, when they finally made camp in the open prairie. Such flight was ancient practice on the plains. It was exactly what the Comanches did after a raid on Pawnee, Ute, or Osage villages: Pursuit was assumed, safety existed only in distance. The raid had begun at ten a.m.; if the Indians rode twelve hours with few breaks, they might have covered sixty miles, which would have put them somewhere just south of present-day Fort Worth, well beyond the last white settlements.

Under normal circumstances, one might have been able to only guess at the fate of the hostages as they disappeared into the liquid darkness of the frontier night. But as it turns out we know what took place, and what happened on the ensuing days. That is because Rachel Parker Plummer wrote it down. In two roughly similar accounts, she told the story of her thirteen-month captivity in excruciating detail. These were widely read at the time, in part because of their often astonishing frankness and brutal attention to detail, and in part because the rest of America was fascinated to hear what became of the first adult American females to be taken by the Comanches. The accounts form a key part of the Parker canon; they are a principal reason for the fame of the 1836 raid.

Rachel presents an interesting, and compelling, figure. At the time of the raid, she was seventeen. She had a fourteen-month-old son, which suggests that she married her husband, L. T. M. Plummer, when she was fifteen. This would have been normal enough on the frontier. As the account proves, she was also smart, perceptive, and, like many of the Parkers, quite literate. She was sensible, hardheaded, and remarkably resilient, considering what was done to her. Though she does not detail the sexual abuse she suffered, she also makes it painfully clear that that is what happened. ("To undertake to narrate their barbarous treatment," she wrote, "would only add to my present distress, for it is with the feelings of deepest mortification that I think of it, much less to speak or write of it. . . ."[25])

After the Indians stopped for the night, they picketed their horses, made a fire, then began a victory dance that reenacted the events of the day, displaying the bloody scalps of their five victims. The dance included striking the captives with their bows and kicking them. Rachel, who along with Elizabeth Kellogg had been stripped naked, describes the experience: "They now tied a plaited thong around my arms, and drew my hands behind me. They tied them so tight that the scars can be seen to this day. They then tied a similar thong around my ankles, and drew my feet and hands together. They now turned me on my face . . . when they commenced beating me over the head with their bows, and it was with great difficulty that I could keep from smothering in my own blood. . . ."[26] Along with the adults, Cynthia Ann and John were kicked, stamped, and clubbed. So was fourteen-month-old James Plummer. "Often did the children cry," wrote Rachel, "but were soon hushed by blows I had no idea they could survive."[27] The two adult women were raped repeatedly in full view of the bound children. It is impossible to know what the nine-year-old Cynthia Ann could possibly have made of this—brutally beaten, cut and chafed from the long ride, and now forced to watch the degradation of her adult cousins. Rachel does not speculate: She merely assumes their torment and misery.

The next day the Indians and their captives once again headed north, pushing at the same brutal pace.

Three

—◆— ◄◊► —◆—

WORLDS IN COLLISION

—◆— ◄◊► —◆—

THE PARKER RAID marked the moment in history when the western-most tendrils of the nascent American empire touched the easternmost tip of a vast, primitive, and equally lethal inland empire dominated by the Comanche Indians. No one understood this at the time. Certainly, the Parkers had no notion of what they were dealing with. Neither the Americans nor the Indians they confronted along that raw frontier had the remotest idea of the other's geographical size or military power. Both, as it turned out, had for the past two centuries been busily engaged in the bloody conquest and near-extermination of Native American tribes. Both had succeeded in hugely expanding the lands under their control. The difference was that the Comanches were content with what they had won. The Anglo-Americans, children of Manifest Destiny, were not. Now, at this lonely spot by the Navasota River, the relentless American drive westward had finally brought them together. The meaning of their meeting, and the moment itself, became completely clear only in hindsight.

Though the idea would have astonished Texas settlers of the time, the Comanche horsemen who rode up to the front gate of Parker's Fort that morning in May 1836 were representatives of a military and trade empire that covered some 240,000 square miles,[1] essentially the southern Great Plains. Their land encompassed large chunks of five present-day states: Texas, New Mexico, Colorado, Kansas, and Oklahoma. It was crossed by

23

nine major rivers, stair-stepped north to south across six hundred miles of mostly level plains and prairie. In descending order, they were: the Arkansas, Cimarron, Canadian, Washita, Red, Pease, Brazos, Colorado, and Pecos. If you counted the full reach of Comanche raiding parties, which ranged deep into Mexico and as far north as Nebraska, their territory was far bigger than that. It was not an empire in the traditional sense, and the Comanches knew nothing of the political structures that stitched European empires together. But they ruled the place outright. They held sway over some twenty different tribes who had been either conquered, driven off, or reduced to vassal status. In North America their only peers, in terms of sheer acreage controlled, were the western Sioux, who dominated the northern plains.

Such imperial dominance was no accident of geography. It was the product of more than 150 years of deliberate, sustained combat against a series of enemies over a singular piece of land that contained the country's largest buffalo herds. Those adversaries included the colonial Spanish, who had driven north into New Mexico in 1598 and later into the Texas territory, and their Mexican successors. They included a host of native tribes, and a dozen tribes who contested for supremacy on the buffalo ranges, among them Apaches, Utes, Osages, Pawnees, Tonkawas, Navajos, Cheyennes, and Arapahoes. The empire was not based solely on military supremacy. The Comanches were diplomatically brilliant, too, making treaties of convenience when it suited them and always looking to guarantee themselves trade advantages, particularly in that most tradeable of all commodities on the plains, horseflesh, of which they owned more than anyone. One sign of their domination was that their language, a Shoshone dialect, became the lingua franca of the southern plains, much as Latin had been the commercial language of the Roman Empire.

Considering all of this, it is just short of amazing that the Anglo-Americans, in the year 1836, knew so little about the Comanches. The Spanish, who fought them for more than a century,[2] knew a great deal, though even they did not suspect the full scope of the empire. As late as 1786, the Spanish governor of New Mexico still believed that the Comanche stronghold was in Colorado, when in fact they had established supremacy as far south as the San Saba country of Texas, some five hundred miles away.[3] This is partly because the European mind simply could not comprehend the distances the average Comanche could travel. The nomadic range of their bands was around eight hundred miles. Their striking range—this confused the insurgent populations as much as anything—was *four hundred miles*.[4]

That meant that a Spanish settler or soldier in San Antonio was in grave and immediate danger from a Comanche brave sitting before a fire in the equivalent of modern-day Oklahoma City. It took years before anyone understood that the same tribe that was raiding on the plains of Durango, Mexico, was also riding above the Arkansas River in modern-day Kansas. But by 1836, of course, the Spanish were long gone, replaced by Mexicans who had even less success dealing with Comanches, who contemptuously referred to them as their "stock-keepers."[5] It is one of history's great ironies that one of the main reasons Mexico had encouraged Americans to settle in Texas in the 1820s and 1830s was because they wanted a buffer against Comanches, a sort of insurance policy on their borderlands. In that sense, the Alamo, Goliad, San Jacinto, and the birth of the Texas republic were the product of a misguided scheme to stop the Comanches. No one knew this, either. Certainly not settlers like the Parkers who were, in effect, being offered up as meat for Comanche raiders.

Still, encounters at that point between whites and Comanches had been extremely rare. Lewis and Clark knew the tribe only by hearsay. Lewis wrote about the "great Padouca nation" (Padouca was believed to be another name for Comanche) that "occupied the country between the upper parts of the River Platte [present Nebraska] and the River Kanzas." He goes on to say that "of the Padouca there does not now even exist the name."[6] They were thus just a rumor, and perhaps not even that. In 1724 the French trader Étienne Véniard de Bourgmont visited the Padoucas and described them as "not entirely wandering—[they] are partially sedentary—for they have villages with large houses and do some planting."[7] Since there was never such a thing as a sedentary, village-dwelling Comanche, it is likely that the Padoucas were something altogether different (quite possibly plains-dwelling Apaches, though it is impossible to prove).

In the 1820s, Stephen F. Austin and his first group of Anglo Texas settlers encountered the Comanches, and Austin was even briefly held captive by them. They seemed otherwise friendly enough, and nothing came of it. The first pack trains moved down the Santa Fe Trail in 1821, connecting Missouri to New Mexico with a route that crossed Kansas, Colorado, and Oklahoma. Total traffic, however, averaged only about eighty wagons a year. Some were attacked by Indians, but in those years white people moving down a trail were not to be confused with settlers who actually wanted to hold land. The trail was merely a thin ribbon of commerce that jeopardized neither hunting

grounds nor traditional lands, and reports of Comanche attacks were probably exaggerated.[8] Contact was minimal, and in any case the traders found it
hard to tell one Indian from another.

In 1832, Sam Houston, then working as a trader with the Cherokees,
made an unsuccessful trip to Texas to try to make peace among Comanches,
Osages, and Pawnees.[9] In 1834, a troop of two hundred fifty mounted dragoons under Colonel Richard Dodge made contact with them above the
Red River. According to the description of George Catlin, a well-known
artist and chronicler of the west who was with Dodge, the Americans were
dazzled by Comanche horsemanship, their prowess from horseback with a
bow and arrow, and their ability to break wild mustangs. Catlin even specu-
lated—hilariously, in retrospect—that "it is probable that in a few days we
will thrash them."[10] He had no clue what he was talking about. In battle, the
Comanches would have likely cut the heavily mounted and musket-firing
dragoons to ribbons. (W. S. Nye wrote that the soldiers "were attired in cos-
tumes better suited to comic opera than to summer field service in Oklahoma.")[11] But these encounters offered little or no information about the
true nature of the tribe. "Their history, numbers, and limits are still in obscurity," wrote Catlin at the time. "Nothing definite yet is known of them."[12]
Just how obscure they were, as late as 1852, is apparent in the account of an
expedition to the headwaters of the Red River by Captain Randolph Marcy,
published in 1853. He describes the country—which was at the time the
core of the Comanche empire, fully sixteen years after Parker's Fort—as a
completely unexplored place "no white man [had] ever ascended"[13] and as
unknown to Americans as unexplored regions of Africa.

It should be noted that the Comanches and Kiowas who raided Parker's
Fort were *mounted*. Indians riding horses may seem obvious enough to us
now, but to Americans in the early nineteenth century the phenomenon was
quite new. In spite of the indelible image of whooping, befeathered savages
on horseback, most Indians in the Americas were footbound. There were
no horses at all on the continent until the Spanish introduced them in the
sixteenth century. Their dispersal into wild mustang herds was exclusively
a western event, confined to the plains and to the southwest, and accruing
almost entirely to the benefit of the aboriginal inhabitants of those areas. This
meant that no soldier or settler east of the Mississippi, going back to the first
settlers, *had ever encountered a mounted Indian warrior*. There simply weren't
any. As time went by, of course, eastern Indians learned to ride horses, but

that was long after they had surrendered, and no eastern, midwestern, or southern Native American tribe ever rode into battle.

The first settlers ever to see true horse Indians were the Texans, because it was in Texas where human settlement first arrived at the edges of the Great Plains. The Indians they encountered were primitive nomads and superb riders, nothing at all like the relatively civilized, largely agrarian, village-dwelling tribes of the East who traveled and fought on foot and presented relatively easy targets for white militias and armies. The horse Indians lived beyond the forests in an endless, trackless, and mostly waterless expanse of undulating grass that was itself terrifying to white men. They resembled less the Algonquins or the Choctaws than the great and legendary mounted archers of history: Mongols, Parthians, and Magyars.

They came from the high country, in the place we now call Wyoming, above the headwaters of the Arkansas River. They called themselves "Nermernuh," which in their Shoshone language meant, simply, "People." They were of the mountains: short, dark-skinned, and barrel-chested. They were descendants of the primitive hunters who had crossed the land bridge from Asia to America in successive migrations between 11,000 and 5,000 BC, and in the millennia that followed they had scarcely advanced at all. They grubbed and hunted for a living using stone weapons and tools, spearing rodents and other small game and killing buffalo by setting the prairies on fire and stampeding the creatures over cliffs or into pits. They used the dog-travois to travel—a frame slung between two poles, pulled by a dog—lugging their hide tipis with them. There were perhaps five thousand of them, living in scattered bands. They squatted around fires gorging themselves on charred, bloody meat. They fought, reproduced, suffered, and died.

They were in most ways typical hunter-gatherers. But even among such peoples, the Comanches had a remarkably simple culture. They had no agriculture and had never felled trees or woven baskets or made pottery or built houses. They had little or no social organization beyond the hunting band.[14] Their culture contained no warrior societies, no permanent priest class. They had no Sun Dance. In social development they were culturally aeons behind the dazzlingly urban Aztecs, or the stratified, highly organized, clan-based Iroquois; they were in all ways utterly unlike the tribes from the American southeast, who in the period from AD 700 to 1700 built sophisticated cultures around maize agriculture that featured large towns, priest-chiefs, clans, and matrilineal descent.[15] To the immediate east were tribes—including the Missouris, Omahas, Pawnees, and Wichitas—who excelled at pottery and basketry, spun and wove fabric, practiced extensive agriculture, and built semipermanent houses covered with grass, bark, or earth.[16] The Nermernuh knew none of those things. From the scant evidence we have, they were considered a tribe of little or no significance.[17] They had been driven to this harsh, difficult land on the eastern slope of the Rockies by other tribes—meaning that, in addition to everything else they were not good at, the Comanches were not very good at war, either.

What happened to the tribe between roughly 1625 and 1750 was one of the great social and military transformations in history. Few nations have ever progressed with such breathtaking speed from the status of skulking pariah to dominant power. The change was total and irrevocable, and it was accompanied by a complete reordering of the balance of power on the American plains. The tribes that had once driven the Comanches into the mountains of Wyoming would soon be either dim memories (Kansas, Omahas, Missouris) or, like the Apaches, Utes, and Osages, retreating to avoid extermination. The Nermernuh were like the small boy who is bullied in junior high school then grows into a large, strong, and vengeful high schooler. Vengeance they were good at, and they had extremely long memories for evils done to them. It should be noted that the dull boy became suddenly very clever, too, and he went from being the least clever boy to the cleverest of all.

The agent of this astonishing change was the horse. Or, more precisely, what this backward tribe of Stone Age hunters did with the horse, an astonishing piece of transformative technology that had as much of an effect on the Great Plains as steam and electricity had on the rest of civilization.[18]

The story of the Comanches' implausible ascent begins with the arrival of the first conquistadors in Mexico in the early sixteenth century. The invaders brought horses with them from Spain. The animals terrified the natives, provided obvious military superiority, and gave the Spaniards a sort of easy mobility never before seen by the inhabitants of the New World. The Spanish horses were also, by the purest of accidents, brilliantly suited to the arid and semiarid plains and mesas of Mexico and the American West. The Iberian mustang was a far different creature from its larger grain-fed cousin from farther north in Europe. It was a desert horse, one whose remote ancestors had thrived on the level, dry steppes of central Asia. Down the ages, the breed had migrated to North Africa by way of the Middle East, mixing blood with other desert hybrids along the way. The Moorish invasions brought it to Spain.[19] By that time it had become, more or less, the horse that found its way to America: light, small, and sturdy, barely fourteen hands high, with a concave Arabian face and tapering muzzle. This horse didn't look like much, but it was smart, fast, trainable, bred to live off the grasses of the hot Spanish plains and to go long distances between watering holes. Possessed of great endurance, the animal could forage for food even in winter.[20]

Thus the mustang immediately prospered in Mexico and enabled the Spanish, in haciendas around Mexico City, to become horse breeders on a grand scale. Barely twenty years after Cortés landed, Coronado was able to amass fifteen hundred horses and mules for his great northern expedition.[21] As the Spanish conquest spread, so did their horses. Since they were fully aware of what might happen if indigenous tribes learned to ride, one of the very first ordinances they passed prohibited natives from riding any horse. They could not enforce such laws, of course. Ultimately they needed Indians and mestizos to work their ranches. This meant that knowledge of how to groom, saddle, bridle, and break horses gradually passed from Spanish control into the hands of the locals. This transmission of Spanish horse culture began in Mexico in the sixteenth century and continued steadily as the Spaniards drove north to New Mexico in the seventeenth century.

That was the first part of the horse revolution. The second was the dispersal of the horses themselves. This happened very slowly at first. The first real herd of horses in North America arrived with the expedition of Don Juan de Oñate to New Mexico in 1598. He brought with him seven hundred horses. The Spanish defeated, converted, and then enslaved the local Pueblo Indians, who built their forts and missions for them. The Indians also tended the horses, though they never showed any interest in using them for anything besides food.

But the Pueblos were not the only Indians in New Mexico. By giving shelter and aid to them, the Spanish had incurred the wrath of local Athapaskan bands—Apaches—who had conducted raids against settlements almost since they began. Now something quite interesting and, in the Spanish history of the Americas, unprecedented happened. The Apaches began to adapt themselves to the horse. No one knows exactly how this happened, or precisely how they came into possession of the elaborate Spanish understanding of horses. But it was an amazingly swift transfer of technology. The Indians first stole the horses, then learned how to ride them. The horse culture was entirely copied from the Spanish. Indians mounted from the right, a practice the Spanish had taken from the Moors, and used crude replicas of Spanish bits, bridles, and saddles.[22]

The horse gave them astounding advantages as hunters. It also made them doubly effective as raiders, mainly because it afforded them an immediate and swift method of escape. According to Spanish records, mounted Apaches were conducting raids into New Mexican settlements as early as the 1650s. In spite of this auspicious start, the Apaches were never a great horse tribe: They did not fight on horseback, and never learned the art of breeding or particularly cared to learn it. They used their Spanish mustangs mainly for basic travel and had an inordinate fondness for cooked horseflesh, eating most of the ones they had and saving only the choicest for riding.[23] They were also, always, a semiagricultural tribe, which meant that their applications of the horse would always be limited—in ways that would later accrue entirely to the benefit of their greatest foes, the Comanches. But for now they had what no other tribe in the Americas had.

And they managed to cause an enormous amount of trouble. They began a relentless and deadly series of raids against the peaceful Pueblos, who were scattered in settlements from Taos to Santa Fe and south along the Rio Grande. The Apaches would attack and then disappear quickly into the western landscape, and the Spanish could neither stop them nor track them down. With each raid, too, they became richer in horses. In one raid alone in 1659, they took three hundred.[24] It became clear to the Pueblos, eventually, that the Spanish could not protect them. This was very likely the main reason for the great Pueblo revolt in 1680. There were other reasons, too, like the forced labor, the imposition of Catholicism, and the suppression of Pueblo culture and tradition. Whatever the cause, the Pueblos rose, and in a grisly, blood-soaked rebellion drove the Spanish out of New Mexico. For ten years. Their imperial nemesis gone, the Indians lapsed into their old ways, which included pottery-making and farming but not horses, for which they had no use. Abandoned by the Spanish, thousands of mustangs ran wild into the open plains that resembled so closely their ancestral Iberian lands. Because they were so perfectly adapted to the new land, they thrived and multiplied. They became the foundation stock for the great wild mustang herds of the Southwest. This event has become known as the Great Horse Dispersal. The dissemination of so many horses to a group of thirty plains tribes permanently altered the power structure of the North American heartland. The Apaches had been the first North American Indians to understand what hunters and raiders could do with a horse; the other tribes would soon learn.

The horse and the knowledge of how to use it spread with astonishing speed through the midcontinent. In 1630, no tribes anywhere were mounted.[25] By 1700, all Texas plains tribes had them; by 1750, tribes of the Canadian plains were hunting buffalo on horseback. The horse gave them what must have seemed to them an astonishing new mobility. It allowed them, for the first time, to fully master the buffalo. They could now migrate with the herds. They could now travel faster than a buffalo at full gallop, and they quickly learned to ride the huge creatures down on the open plains, thrusting their fourteen-foot lances between the animals' ribs or shooting them on the run with arrows. Hunting skills quickly became martial skills, too. Tribes who learned to hunt on horseback gained an almost instant military dominance over nonhorse tribes, and for a time over everyone else who dared challenge them. It turned them into expansive traders, providing both the thing to be traded and the mobility to reach new markets.

What the horse did not do was change their fundamental natures. Before the arrival of the horse, they were peoples whose lives were based almost entirely on the buffalo. The horse did not change this. They merely became much better at what they had always done. No true plains tribes fished or practiced agriculture before the horse, and none did so after the horse. Even their limited use of berries and roots went unchanged.[26] They remained relatively primitive, warlike hunters; the horse virtually guaranteed that they would not evolve into more civilized agrarian societies. Still, the enhancements were breathtaking to see. War could now be made across immense distances. Horses—the principal form of wealth on the plains—could now be gathered and held in large numbers. And there was the simple, fundamental, spiritual power of the animal itself, which had transformed these poor foot Indians into dazzling cavalrymen. And the new technology turned tribes who had lagged behind their peers in culture and social organization into newly dominant forces. These included names that would soon be famous throughout the country: Sioux, Cheyenne, Kiowa, Arapaho, Blackfoot, Crow, and Comanche.

No one knows exactly how or when the Comanche bands in eastern Wyoming first encountered the horse, but that event probably happened somewhere near the midpoint of the seventeenth century. Since the Pawnees, who lived in the area we now call Nebraska, were known to be mounted by 1680, the Comanches almost certainly had horses by that time. There were no witnesses to this great coming together of Stone Age hunters and horses, nothing to record what happened when they met, or what there was in the soul of the Comanche that understood the horse so much better than everyone else did. Whatever it was, whatever sort of accidental brilliance, whatever the particular, subliminal bond between warrior and horse, it must have thrilled these dark-skinned pariahs from the Wind River country. The Comanches adapted to the horse earlier and more completely than any other plains tribe. They are considered, without much debate, the prototype horse tribe in North America. No one could outride them or outshoot them from the back of a horse. Among other horse tribes, only the Kiowas fought entirely mounted, as the Comanches did. Pawnees, Crows, even the Dakotas used the horse primarily for transport. They would ride to the battle, then dismount and fight. (Only in the movies did the Apaches attack riding horses.)[27] No tribe other than the Comanches ever learned to breed horses— an intensely demanding, knowledge-based skill that helped create enormous wealth for the tribe. They were always careful in the castration of the herd; almost all riding horses were geldings. Few other tribes bothered with this. It was not uncommon for a Comanche warrior to have one hundred to two hundred mounts, or for a chief to have fifteen hundred. (A Sioux chief might have forty horses, by comparison.)[28] They were not only the richest of all tribes in sheer horseflesh, their horses were also the main medium through which the rest of the tribes became mounted.[29]

The first Europeans and Americans to see Comanche horsemanship did not fail to notice this. Athanase de Mézières, a Spanish Indian agent of French descent, described them thus:

> They are a people so numerous and haughty that when asked their number they make no difficulty of comparing it to that of the stars. They are so skill-ful in horsemanship that they have no equal; so daring that they never ask for or grant truces; and in the possession of such a territory that, finding in it an abundance of pasturage for their horses and an incredible number of [buffalo] which furnish them all the raiment, food, and shelter, they only just fall short of possessing all the conveniences of the earth.[30]

Other observers saw the same thing. Colonel Richard Dodge, whose expedition made early contact with Comanches, believed them to be the finest light cavalry in the world, superior to any mounted soldiers in Europe or

America. Catlin also saw them as incomparable horsemen. As he described it, the American soldiers were dumbfounded at what they saw. "On their feet they are one of the most unattractive and slovenly looking races of Indians I have ever seen, but the moment they mount their horses, they seem at once metamorphosed," wrote Catlin. "I am ready, without hesitation, to pronounce the Comanches the most extraordinary horsemen I have seen yet in all my travels." He went on to write:

> Amongst their feats of riding there is one that has astonished me more than anything of the kind I have ever seen or expect to see, in my life:—a stratagem of war, learned and practiced by every young man in the tribe; by which he is able to drop his body on the side of his horse at the instant he is passing, effectively screened from his enemies' weapons, as he lays in a horizontal position behind the body of his horse, with his heel hanging over the horses's back. . . . in this wonderful condition, he will hang whilst his horse is at fullest speed, carrying with him his bow and shield and also his long lance 14 feet in length.[31]

Thus positioned, a Comanche warrior could loose twenty arrows in the time it took a soldier to load and fire one round from his musket; each of those arrows could kill a man at thirty yards. Other observers were amazed at the Comanche technique of breaking horses. A Comanche would lasso a wild horse, then tighten the noose, choking the horse and driving it to the ground. When it seemed as if the horse was nearly dead, the choking lariat was slacked. The horse finally rose, trembling and in a full lather. Its captor gently stroked its nose, ears, and forehead, then put his mouth over the horse's nostrils and blew air into its nose. The Indian would then throw a thong around the now-gentled horse's lower jaw, mount up, and ride away.[32] The Comanches, as it turned out, were geniuses at anything to do with horses: breeding, breaking, selling, and riding. They even excelled at stealing horses. Colonel Dodge wrote that a Comanche could enter "a bivouac where a dozen men were sleeping, each with a horse tied to his wrist by the lariat, cut a rope within six feet of the sleeper, and get away with the horse without waking a soul."[33]

No other tribe, except possibly the Kiowas, so completely lived on horseback. Children were given their own horses at four or five. Soon the boys were expected to learn tricks, which included picking up objects on the ground at a gallop. The young rider would start with light objects and move to progressively heavier objects until finally, without assistance and at a full gallop, he could pick up a man. Rescuing a fallen comrade was seen as one of the most basic obligations of a Comanche warrior. They all learned the leather thong trick at a young age. Women could often ride as well as men. One observer watched two Comanche women set out at full speed with lassoes and each rope a bounding antelope on the first throw.[34] Women had their own mounts, as well as mules and gentle horses for packing.

When they were not stealing horses, or breeding them, they were capturing them in the wild. General Thomas James told a story of how he had witnessed this in 1823, when he had visited the Comanches as a horse buyer. He watched as many riders headed bands of wild horses into a deep ravine where a hundred men waited on horseback with coiled lariats. When the "terrified wild horses reached the ambush" there was a good deal of dust and confusion as the riders lassoed them by the neck or forefeet. But every rider got an animal. Only one horse got away. The Comanches pursued him and in two hours he came back "tamed and gentle." Within twenty-four hours one hundred or more wild horses had been captured "amid the wildest excitement" and appeared to be "as subject to their masters as farm horses."[35] They would chase a herd of mustangs for several days until the animals were exhausted, making them easy to capture. Comanches waited by water holes for parched horses to gorge themselves so they could barely run, then captured them. While the Comanches had a limited vocabulary to describe most things— a trait common to primitive peoples—their equine lexicon was large and minutely descriptive. For color alone, there were distinct Comanche words for brown, light bay, reddish brown, black, white, blue, dun, sorrel, roan, red, yellow, yellow-horse-with-a-black mane-and-tail; red, sorrel, and black pintos. There were even words to describe horses with red, yellow, and black ears.[36]

Comanche horsemanship also played a leading role in another Comanche pastime: gambling. Stories of Comanche horse hustles are legion. One of the more famous came from the Texas frontier. A small band of Comanches showed up at Fort Chadbourne, where the army officers challenged them to a race. The chief seemed indifferent to the idea, but the officers were so insistent that he agreed to it anyway. A race was arranged over a distance of four hundred yards. Soon a large, portly brave appeared on a long-haired "miserable sheep of a pony." He carried a heavy club, with which he hit the horse. Unimpressed, the officers trotted out their third-best horse, and bet the Comanches flour, sugar, and coffee against buffalo robes. Swinging the club "ostentatiously," the Indian won. For the next race, the soldiers brought out their second-best horse. They lost this race, too. Now they insisted on a third race, and finally trotted out their number-one horse, a magnificent Kentucky mare. Bets were doubled, tripled. The Comanches took everything the soldiers would wager. At the starting signal, the Comanche warrior whooped, threw away his club, and "went away like the wind." Fifty yards from the finish, the Comanche rider turned fully around in his saddle, and with "hideous grimaces" beckoned the other rider to catch up. The losers later learned that the same shaggy horse had just been used to take six hundred horses away from the Kickapoo Indians.[37]

In the late 1600s, Comanche mastery of the horse had led them to migrate southward out of the harsh, cold lands of the Wind River and into more temperate climates. The meaning of the migration was simple: They were challenging other tribes for supremacy over the single richest hunting prize on the continent: the buffalo herds of the southern plains.

In 1706 they rode, for the first time, into recorded history. In July of that year a Spanish sergeant major named Juan De Ulibarri, on his way to gather Pueblo Indians for conversion in northern New Mexico, reported that Comanches, in the company of Utes, were preparing to attack Taos pueblo.[38] He later heard of actual Comanche attacks.[39] This was the first the Spanish or any white men had heard of these Indians who had many names. One name in particular, given to them by the Utes, was Koh-mats, sometimes given as Komantcia, and meant "anyone who is against me all the time." The authorities in New Mexico translated this various ways (Cumanche, Commanche) but eventually as "Comanche."[40] It would take the Spaniards years to figure out exactly who these new invaders were.

Four

HIGH LONESOME

> With these remarks, I submit the following pages to the perusal of a generous public, feeling assured that before they are published, the hand that penned them will be cold in death.[1]

Those are the words of twenty-year-old Rachel Parker Plummer, written probably sometime in early 1839. She was referring to her memoir of captivity, and predicting her own death. She was right. She died on March 19 of that year. She had been dragged, sometimes quite literally, over half of the Great Plains as the abject slave of Comanche Indians, and then had logged another two thousand miles in what amounted to one of the most grueling escapes ever made from any tribe by any captive. To the readers of her era, the memoir was jaw-dropping. It still is. As a record of pure, blood-tinged, white-knuckled adventure on America's nineteenth-century frontier, there are few documents that can compare to it.

On the morning after that harrowing first night, the five Parker captives—Rachel and her fourteen-month-old son, James, her aunt Elizabeth Kellogg (probably in her thirties), nine-year-old Cynthia Ann Parker, and her seven-year-old brother, John, were strapped to horses behind Comanche riders again and taken north. For the next five days the Comanches pressed hard, passing Cross Timbers, the forty-mile-wide patch of woods on the otherwise open prairie west of modern Dallas, "a beautiful faced country," as Rachel put it, with "a great many fine springs." Not that she was allowed to drink from them. During that time, the Indians gave their captives no food at all, and only a single small allowance of water. Each night they were tied tightly with leather thongs that made their wrists and ankles bleed; as before, their hands and feet were drawn together and they were put facedown on the ground.

Rachel does not tell us much about what happened to Cynthia Ann—beyond the blows, the blood, and the trussing of the first night—but it is possible to make an educated guess about what happened to her. Though Comanches were mercurial about these things, their treatment of a nine-year-old girl would usually have been different from that accorded the adult women. Cynthia Ann's first few days and nights were no doubt horrific. There was the shrieking panic of the Indian attack, the uncomprehending horror of the moment her mother, Lucy, set her on the warrior's horse, her own father's bloody death, the astonishing sight of her cousin and aunt being raped and abused. (In spite of her strict Baptist upbringing, as a farm girl she would have known about sex and reproduction; still, it would have shed little light on what she witnessed.) There was the hard ride through the prairie darkness of northern Texas to the camp where she was tied and bludgeoned, then the five subsequent days on the trail without food.

Considering what happened to her later, however, it is likely that the beatings and harsh treatment stopped. There are plenty of records of children being killed by Comanches, and of young girls being raped, but in general they fared far better than the adults. For one thing, they were young enough to be assimilated into a society that had abysmally low fertility rates (partly caused by the life on horseback, which induced miscarriages early in pregnancy) and needed captives to keep their numbers up.[2] They were also valuable for the ransom they might bring. In several other unusually violent Comanche raids, young female captives had been conspicuously spared and quickly accepted into the tribe. Girls had a decent chance, anyway. Certainly that was true compared to adult male captives, who were automatically killed or tortured to death. The strongest argument for her humane treatment was the presence at the Parker raid of the man who would later become her husband and a war chief: Peta Nocona. Indeed, Peta may well have led the raid, and it may have been his horse upon which Lucy Parker had put the screaming, protesting Cynthia Ann.[3]

On the sixth day the Indians divided their captives: Elizabeth Kellogg was traded or given to a band of Kichai Indians, a sedentary tribe from north-central Texas that raised crops and enjoyed something like vassal status with the Comanches; Cynthia Ann and John went to a band of middle Comanches, probably the Nokonis; Rachel and James went to another Comanche band. She had assumed that they would let her son, bruised and bloody but somehow still alive, stay with her. She was wrong. "As soon as they found out I had weaned him," she wrote, "they, in spite of all my efforts, tore him from my embrace. He reached out his hands toward me, which were covered with blood, and cried, "'Mother, Mother, oh, Mother!' I looked after him as he was borne from me, and I sobbed aloud. This was the last I ever heard of my little Pratt."[4]

Rachel's band pushed on to the cooler elevations in the north, probably into what is now eastern Colorado. She found herself on the high, barren plains. "We now lost sight of timber," Rachel wrote. "We would travel for weeks and not see a riding switch. Buffalo dung is all the fuel. This is gathered into a round pile; and when set on fire it does very well to cook by, and will keep fire for several days."[5] They were in the heart of Comancheria, an utterly alien place that was known to mapmakers of the time as the Great American Desert. To anyone accustomed to timbered lands, which describes almost everyone in America prior to 1840, the plains were not just unlike anything they had ever seen, they were, on some fundamental level, incomprehensible, as though a person who had lived in the high mountains all his life were seeing the ocean for the first time. "East of the Mississippi civilization stood on three legs—land, water, and timber," wrote Walter Prescott Webb in his classic *The Great Plains*. "West of the Mississippi not one but two of those legs were withdrawn—water and timber—and civilization was left on one leg—land. It is a small wonder that it toppled over in temporary failure."[6]

If there existed an implacably hostile human barrier to Spanish, French, and American advance in the form of the Plains Indians, there also existed an actual, physical barrier. For people living in the twenty-first century this is hard to imagine, because the land today is not as it was in the nineteenth century. Almost all of the American landscape has now been either farmed, ranched, logged, or developed in some way, and in many parts of the country the raw distinctions between forest and prairie have been lost. But in its primeval state, almost all of North America, from the eastern coast to the 98th meridian—a line of longitude that runs north to south roughly through the modern cities of San Antonio, Oklahoma City, and Wichita—was densely timbered, and the contrast between the dense eastern woodlands and the "big sky" country of the west would have been stark. A traveler going west would have seen nothing like open prairie until he hit the 98th meridian, whereupon, in many places, he would have been literally staring out of a dark, Grimm Brothers forest at a treeless plain. It would have seemed to him a vast emptiness. At that point, everything the pioneer woodsman knew about how to survive—including building houses, making fire, and drawing water—broke down. It was why the plains were the very last part of the country to be settled.

The main reason was rainfall. Or lack of it. Just west of the 98th, the annual rainfall dropped below twenty inches; when that happens trees find it hard to survive; rivers and streams become sparse. The ecology of the plains was, moreover, one of fire—constant lightning- or Indian-induced conflagrations that cut enormous swaths through the plains and killed most saplings that did not live in river or stream bottoms. A traveler coming out of humid, swampy, rain-drenched, pine-forested, river-crossed Louisiana would have hit the first prairie somewhere south of present-day Dallas, not very far from Parker's Fort. Indeed, one of the reasons Parker's Fort marked the limit of settlement in 1836 was that it was very near the edge of the Great Plains. That land consisted of rolling, creased plains dotted with timber; there was thicker timber in the bottoms of the Navasota River. (From the Parkers' point of view this was quite deliberate; they built a stockade fort, after all, of cedar.) But a hundred miles west there would have been no timber at all, and by the time the traveler reached modern-day Lubbock and Amarillo, he would have seen nothing but a dead flat and infinitely receding expanse of grama and buffalo grasses through which only a few gypsum-laced rivers ran and on which few landmarks if any would have been distinguishable. Travelers of the day described it as "oceanic," which was not a term of beauty. They found it empty and terrifying. They also described it as "trackless," which was literally true: All traces of a wagon train rolling through plains grass would disappear in a matter of days, vanishing like beach footprints on an incoming tide.

Not only were the High Plains generally without timber and water, they were also subject to one of the least hospitable climates in North America. In the summer came brutal heat and blowtorch winds, often a hundred degrees or hotter, that would later destroy whole crops in a matter of days. The winds caused the eyes to burn, the lips to crack, and the body to dehydrate with alarming speed. In fall and winter there was the frequent "norther"—a sudden strong wind from the north, often at gale force, accompanied by a solid sheet of black clouds and enormous billowing clouds of blown sand. A norther could send the temperature plunging by fifty degrees in an hour. A "blue" norther had the additional feature of freezing, driven rain. This was routine weather on the plains.

Worst of all was the blizzard. People from the east or west coasts of America may think they have seen a blizzard. Likely they have not. It is almost exclusively a phenomenon of the plains, and got its name on the plains. It entailed wind-driven snow so dense and temperatures so cold that anyone lost in them on the shelterless plains was as good as dead. In the years after the plains were settled it was not unusual for people to become lost and die while walking from their barns to their houses. Howling winds blew for days. Forty- to fifty-foot snowdrifts were common, as were "whiteouts" where it no longer became possible to tell the ground from the air. Plains blizzards swallowed whole army units, settlements, and Indian villages. This, too, was Comancheria, the beautiful and unremittingly hostile place they had chosen, the southernmost and richest range of the American buffalo. This was the very last part of the continent conquered and held by the U.S. Army. The last part anyone wanted, the last part civilized. The land alone stood a good chance of killing you. The fact that it was inhabited by Comanches and other mounted Indians made death something of a certainty.

This is where Rachel Plummer was now, very likely five hundred miles beyond the nearest settlement, in a place where only a few white men had ever been. From a settler's viewpoint, this was just empty territory, part of the United States by dint of the Louisiana Purchase (1803) but without forts or soldiers or even human beings beyond the odd trapper or explorer or occasional mule train along the nearby Santa Fe Trail. The first caravans would not roll across the Oregon Trail for four years. This was Indian land; lived on by Indians, hunted by Indians, and fought over by Indians. In Rachel's account, she spent much of her thirteen months of captivity on the high plains, though she also describes a journey through the Rocky Mountains, where "I suffered more from cold than I ever suffered in my life before. It was very seldom I had anything to put on my feet, but very little covering for my body."[7]

She was a slave and was treated like one. Her job was to tend the horses at night and to "dress" buffalo skins by day, with a quota that she had to fill every full moon. This process involved painstakingly scraping all the flesh off the skin with a sharp bone. Lime was then applied to absorb grease, then the brains of the buffalo were rubbed all over it until it became soft.[8] To make the quota and avoid a beating she often took her buffalo skins with her while she tended the horses. She had been given to an old man, and thus had become the servant of his wife and daughter, both of whom mistreated her.

Rachel's kidnapping may seem the somewhat random product of a random raid on a Texas settlement. There were, in fact, important reasons for what had happened to her, all related to the highly specialized buffalo economy of the plains. Hides and robes had always been useful trading items. (Comanche trade rested on horses, hides, and captives.) The hides were rising in value, so much so that, while an individual Comanche might eat only six buffalo per year, he would now kill an average of forty-four per year, and the number grew every year. The women, of course, did all the value-added work: preparing the hides and decorating the robes. The men of the plains soon realized that the more wives they had, the greater their production of hides would be, thus the more manufactured goods they could trade for.[9] This simple commercial fact had two important effects: first, an increase in polygamy among Indian men; and second, a desire to seize and hold more women captives. These changes were perhaps more instinctive than deliberate among the Comanches. But it meant that Rachel's days would always be long and hard, and that she would always have to meet her quotas.

She was also, unfortunately, pregnant. She had been four months pregnant at the time of the Parker raid, and had borne all of this misery in advancing stages of pregnancy. In October 1836 she gave birth to her second son. She knew immediately that the child was in danger. She spoke the Comanche language well enough to, as she put it, "expostulate with my mistress to advise me what to do to save my child."[10] To no avail. Her master thought the infant too much trouble, and feeding him meant that Rachel was not able to work full-time. One morning, when the baby was seven weeks old, half a dozen men came. While several of them held Rachel, one of them strangled the baby, then handed him to her. When he showed signs of life, they took him again, this time tying a rope around his neck and dragging him through prickly pear cactus, and eventually dragged him behind a horse around a hundred-yard circuit. "My little innocent one was not only dead, but literally torn to pieces," wrote Rachel.[11]

The tribe moved on. In spite of what she had been through, Rachel somehow kept up her daily routines. She managed to note details of the flora, fauna, and geography that she saw. She wrote about prairie foxes, mirages of cool blue lakes that would appear magically in front of her, and shell fossils on the open plains. In what amounted to the first ethnography of the tribe, she noted details of Comanche society. The group moved every three or four days;

the men danced every night; some worshipped pet crows or deerskins; before going into battle the men would drink water every morning until they vomited; taboos included never allowing a human shadow to fall across cooking food. When she had free time, she climbed to the top of mountains and even explored a cave. With her new grasp of the language, she was able to eavesdrop on a large Indian powwow near the headwaters of the Arkansas River. Since women were not allowed in tribal councils, "I was several times repulsed with blows," she wrote, "but I cheerfully submitted to abuse and persevered in listening to their proceedings."[12] She overheard a plan for a large-scale, multitribe invasion of Texas. After taking Texas, and driving out the inhabitants, they would attack Mexico. The attack was to come either in 1838 or 1839.

In spite of Rachel's amazing resilience, she began to lose hope. She believed that her son, James, was probably dead, and that her husband, father, and mother had probably not survived the attack at Parker's fort. She had almost no hope of escaping, or of ever changing her status in the tribe. Despondent, suicidal, but unable to kill herself, she decided to provoke her captors into doing the job for her. After being ordered by her captor's daughter ("my young mistress") to get a root-digging tool from the lodge, she refused. The young woman screamed at her, then ran at her. Rachel threw her onto the ground, held her down "fighting and screaming," and began beating her over the head with a buffalo bone, expecting "at every moment to feel a spear reach my heart from one of the Indians."[13] If they were going to kill her, she was determined at least to make a cripple of her captor. As this unfolded, she realized that a large crowd of Comanche men had gathered around them. They were all yelling, but no one touched her. She won the fight. "I had her past hurting me and indeed nearly past breathing, when she cried out for mercy," wrote Rachel. She let go of her adversary, who was bleeding freely, then picked her up, carried her back to the camp and washed her face. For the first time, the woman seemed friendly.

Not so her adoptive mother, who told Rachel she intended to burn her to death. (She had burned Rachel before with fire and hot embers.) Now Rachel and the old woman fought, in and around the roaring fire. Both were badly burned; Rachel knocked the woman into the fire twice and held her there. During the fight they broke through one side of the tipi. Again, a crowd of men assembled to watch them. Again, no one intervened. Again, Rachel won. The following morning twelve chiefs assembled at the "council house" to hear the case. All three women testified. The verdict: Rachel was sentenced to replace the lodge pole she had broken. She agreed, provided that the young woman helped her. After that, Rachel says, "all was peace again."

It is impossible to read Rachel Plummer's memoir without making moral judgments about the Comanches. The torture-killing of a defenseless seven-week-old infant, by committee decision no less, is an act of almost demonic immorality by any modern standard. The systematic gang rape of women captives seems to border on criminal perversion, if not some very advanced form of evil. The vast majority of Anglo-European settlers in the American West would have agreed with those assessments. To them, Comanches were thugs and killers, devoid of ordinary decency, sympathy, or mercy. Not only did they inflict horrific suffering, but from all evidence *they enjoyed it.* This was perhaps the worst part, and certainly the most frightening part. Making people scream in pain was interesting and rewarding for them, just as it is interesting and rewarding for young boys in modern-day America to torture frogs or pull the legs off grasshoppers. Boys presumably grow out of that; for Indians, it was an important part of their adult culture and one they accepted without challenge.

A story from the early 1870s illustrates the larger point. According to the account of a former child captive named Herman Lehmann, who later became a full-fledged warrior, a group of Comanches had attacked some Tonkawa Indians, in their camp. They had killed some of them and run off the rest. In the abandoned camp, they found some meat roasting in the fire. It turned out to be the leg of a Comanche. The Tonkawas, known for their cannibalism, had been preparing a feast. This sent the Comanches into a fury of vengeance, and they pursued the Tonkawas. A fierce battle followed, in which eight Comanches were killed and forty were wounded. Still, they were victorious, and now, in the battle's aftermath, they turned to deal with the enemy's wounded and dying. "A great many were gasping for water," wrote Lehmann, who was there,

> but we heeded not their pleadings. We scalped them, amputated their arms, cut off their legs, cut out their tongues, and threw their mangled bodies and limbs upon their own campfire, put on more brushwood and piled the living, dying and dead Tonkaways on the fire. Some of them were able to flinch and work as worms, and some were able to speak and plead for mercy. We piled them up, put on more wood, and danced around in great glee as we saw the grease and blood run from their bodies, and were delighted to see them swell up and hear the hide pop as it would burst in the fire.[14]

This sort of cruelty is a problem in any narrative about American Indians, because Americans like to think of their native aboriginals as in some ways heroic or noble. Indians were, in fact, heroic and noble in many ways, especially in defense of their families. Yet in the moral universe of the West—in spite of our own rich tradition of torture, which includes officially sanctioned torments in Counter-Reformation Europe and sovereign regimes such as that of Peter the Great in Russia—a person who tortures or rapes another person or who steals another person's child and then sells him cannot possibly be seen that way. Crazy Horse was undoubtedly heroic in battle and remarkably charitable in life. But as an Oglala Sioux he was also a raider, and raiding meant certain very specific things, including the abuse of captives. His great popularity—a giant stone image of him is being carved from a mountain in South Dakota—may have a great deal to do with the fact that very little is known about his early life.[15] He is free to be the hero we want him to be.

Thus some chroniclers ignore the brutal side of Indian life altogether; others, particularly historians who suggest that before white men arrived Indian-to-Indian warfare was a relatively bloodless affair involving a minimum of bloodshed, deny it altogether.[16] But certain facts are inescapable: American Indians were warlike by nature, and they were warlike for centuries before Columbus stumbled upon them. They fought over hunting grounds, to be sure, but they also made a good deal of brutal and bloody war that was completely unnecessary. The Comanches' relentless and never-ending pursuit of the hapless Tonkawas was a good example of this, as was their harassment of Apaches long after they had been driven from the buffalo grounds.

Such behavior was common to all Indians in the Americas. The more civilized agrarian tribes of the east, in fact, were far more adept at devising lengthy and agonizing tortures than the Comanches or other plains tribes.[17] The difference lay in the Plains Indians' treatment of female captives and victims. Rape or abuse, including maiming, of females had existed when eastern tribes had sold captives as slaves in the seventeenth and eighteenth centuries. But that practice had been long ago abandoned. Some tribes, including the giant Iroquois federation, had never treated women captives that way.[18] Women could be killed, and scalped. But not gang-raped. What happened to the Parker captives could only have happened west of the Mississippi. If the Comanches were better known for cruelty and violence, that was because, as one of history's great warring peoples, they were in a position to inflict far more pain than they ever received.

Most important, the Indians themselves saw absolutely nothing wrong with these acts. For westering settlers, the great majority of whom believed in the idea of absolute good and evil, and thus of universal standards of moral behavior, this was nearly impossible to understand. Part of it had to do with the Comanches' theory of the nature of the universe, which was vastly different from that of the civilized West. Comanches had no dominant, unified religion, or anything like a single God. Though in interviews after their defeat they often seemed to go along with the idea of a "Great Spirit," Comanche ethnographers Ernest Wallace and E. Adamson Hoebel were extremely skeptical of any creation myths that involved a single spirit or an "evil one."[19] "We never gave much consideration to creation," said an old Comanche named Post Oak Jim in an interview in the 1930s. "We just knew we were here. Our thoughts were mostly directed toward understanding the spirits."[20]

The Comanches lived in a world alive with magic and taboo; spirits lived everywhere, in rocks, trees, and in animals. The main idea of their religion was to find a way to harness the powers of these spirits. Such powers thus became "puha," or "medicine." There was no dogma, no priestly class to impose systematic religion, no tendency to view the world as anything but a set of isolated episodes, with no deeper meaning. There were behavioral codes, to be sure—a man could not steal another man's wife without paying penalties, for example. But there was no ultimate good and evil: just actions and consequences; injuries and damages due.

Enemies, meanwhile, were enemies, and the rules for dealing with them had come down through a thousand years. A Comanche brave who captured a live Ute would torture him to death without question. It was what everyone had always done, what the Sioux did to the Assiniboine, what the Crow did to the Blackfeet. A Comanche captured by a Ute would expect to receive exactly the same treatment (thus making him weirdly consistent with the idea of the Golden Rule), which was why Indians always fought to their last breath on battlefields, to the astonishment of Europeans and Americans. There were no exceptions. Of course, the same Indians also believed, quite as deeply, in blood vengeance. The life of the warrior tortured to death would be paid for with another torture-killing if possible, preferably even more hideous than the first. This, too, was seen as fair play by all Indians in the Americas.

What explains such a radical difference in the moral systems of the

Comanches and the whites they confronted? Part of it has to do with the relative progress of civilizations in the Americas compared to the rest of the world. The discovery of agriculture, which took place in Asia and the Middle East, roughly simultaneously, around 6,500 BC, allowed the transition from nomadic, hunter-gatherer societies to the higher civilizations that followed. But in the Americas, farming was not discovered until 2,500 BC, fully four thousand years later and well after advanced cultures had already sprung up in Egypt and Mesopotamia. This was an enormous gap. Once the Indians figured out how to plant seeds and cultivate crops, civilizations in North and South America progressed at roughly the same pace as they had in the Old World. Cities were built. Highly organized social structures evolved. Pyramids were designed. Empires were assembled, of which the Aztecs and Incas were the last. (As in the Old World, nomadism and hunter-gatherer cultures persisted alongside the higher civilizations.) But the Americas, isolated and in any case without the benefit of the horse or the ox, could never close the time gap. They were three to four millennia behind the Europeans and Asians, and the arrival of Columbus in 1492 guaranteed that they would never catch up. The nonagrarian Plains Indians, of course, were even further behind.

Thus the fateful clash between settlers from the culture of Aristotle, St. Paul, Da Vinci, Luther, and Newton and aboriginal horsemen from the buffalo plains happened as though in a time warp—as though the former were looking backward thousands of years at premoral, pre-Christian, low-barbarian versions of themselves. The Celtic peoples, ancestors of huge numbers of immigrants to America in the nineteenth century, offer a rough parallel. Celts of the fifth century BC were described by Herodotus as "fierce warriors who fought with seeming disregard for their own lives."[21] Like Comanches they were savage, filthy, wore their hair long, and had a hideous keening battle cry. They were superb horsemen, inordinately fond of alcohol, and did terrible things to their enemies and captives that included decapitation, a practice that horrified the civilized Greeks and Romans.[22] The old Celts, forebears of the Scots-Irish who formed the vanguard of America's western migrations, would have had no "moral" problem with the Comanche practice of torture.

To their enemies, the Comanches were implacable buffalo-horned killers, grim apostles of darkness and devastation. Inside their own camps, however, where Rachel Parker Plummer, Cynthia Ann Parker, and the others now found themselves, they were something entirely different. Here, wrote Colonel Richard Irving Dodge, one of the first Americans to observe them closely, the Comanche "is a noisy, jolly, rollicking, mischief-loving braggadoccio, brimful of practical jokes and rough fun of any kind . . . rousing the midnight echoes with song and dance, whoops and yells."[23] He loved to gamble and would bet on anything—absolutely anything—but especially on horses and games of chance, and would happily wager his last deerskin. He loved to sing. He especially loved to sing his personal song, often written expressly for him by a medicine man. He often woke up singing and sang before he went to bed. He adored games of any kind, but more than anything else in the world he liked to race horses. He was vain about his hair—often weaving his wife's shorn tresses in with his own to create extensions, as modern women do. He would roll those extensions in beaver or otter skin. He was an incurable gossip and had, according to Dodge, a "positive craving to know what is going on around him."[24]

He would dance for hours, or days. He doted on his family, especially on his sons, and spent winters snug and indolent, wrapped in thick buffalo robes by the fire in his tipi, a brilliant piece of architectural design that required only a small fire to keep him warm even during the frigid, wind-lashed plains winters. And he loved to talk. "He will talk himself wild with excitement," wrote Dodge, "vaunting his exploits in love, war, on the chase, and will commit all sorts of extravagances while telling."[25] His fellow tribe members had names like "A Big Fall by Tripping," "Face Wrinkling Like Getting Old," "Coyote Vagina," "Gets to Be a Middle-aged Man," "Always Sitting Down in a Bad Place," "Breaks Something," and "She Invites Her Relatives."[26] To others, they were the personification of death. To themselves, they were simply "People."

They were in most ways typical Plains Indians. The culture of all true plains tribes was built around the buffalo, which provided life's essentials: food, lodging (tipis made of hides), fuel (dried dung), tools (bone implements, water pouches made from the paunch), tack (bridles, thongs, and saddles made of hide), ropes (from twisted hair), clothing (buckskins, moccasins, and fur robes), and weapons (bowstrings made from sinews and clubs). Before the arrival of the buffalo hunters in the 1870s, the huge, swift animals were literally too numerous to count. The larger part of this population lived on the southern plains—Comancheria. They were the reason the newly mounted tribe had fought for that land in the first place.

The buffalo was a dangerous creature to hunt. A healthy buffalo could run nearly as fast as an ordinary horse for two miles. Because it was the Indian practice to ride up on it from behind, shooting or lancing it, the wounded buffalo was thus an immediate threat to the rider. The danger, as Texas Ranger Rip Ford wrote, was "to be caught and lifted, horse and all, upon the horns of so huge a beast, tossed like a feather so many feet in the air, to fall all mixed up with your four-footed companion."[27] Indian ponies were trained to turn instantly away from the buffalo at the twang of the bowstring.

Buffalo was the food the Comanches loved more than any other. They ate steaks cooked over open fires or boiled in copper kettles. They cut the meat thin, dried it, and stored it for the winter and took it on long trips. They ate the kidneys and the paunch. Children would rush up to a freshly killed animal, begging for its liver and gallbladder. They would then squirt the salty bile from the gallbladder onto the liver and eat it on the spot, warm and dripping blood. If a slain female was giving milk, Comanches would cut into the udder bag and drink the milk mixed with warm blood. One of the greatest delicacies was the warm curdled milk from the stomach of a suckling calf.[28] If warriors were on the trail and short of water, they might drink the warm blood of the buffalo straight from its veins. Entrails were sometimes eaten, stripped of their contents by using two fingers. (If fleeing pursuers, a Comanche would ride his horse till it dropped, cut it open, removed its intestines, wrap them around his neck, and take off on a fresh horse, eating their contents later.)[29] In the absence of buffalo, Comanches would eat whatever was at hand: dry-land terrapins, thrown live into the fire, eaten from the shell with a horned spoon;[30] all manner of small game, even horses if they had to, though they did not, like the Apaches, prefer them. They did not eat fish or birds unless they were starving. They never ate the heart of the buffalo.

The Comanches were also true Plains Indians in their social structure. Nermernuh were organized in bands, a concept white men never quite understood. They insisted on looking at the Comanches as a *tribe,* meaning a single political unit with a head chief and, presumably, a cadre of civil and military subchiefs to do his bidding. This was never true. Nor was it true of the Cheyennes or the Arapahoes or anyone else on the plains. Comanches all spoke the same language, dressed roughly in the same way, shared the same religious beliefs and customs, and led a common style of life that distinguished them from other tribes and from the rest of the world. That life, however, according to ethnographers Wallace and Hoebel, "did not include political institutions or social mechanisms by which they could act as a tribal unit."[31] There was no big chief, no governing council, no Comanche "nation" that you could locate in a particular place, negotiate with, or conquer in battle. To whites, of course, this made no sense at all. It resembled no governing system they recognized. Across the plains, they insisted on making treaties with band headmen—often very colorful, strong-willed, and powerful ones—assuming incorrectly that the headmen spoke for the entire tribe. They would make this mistake again and again.

The bands were always difficult for outsiders to understand. It was difficult to distinguish between them, or even to know how many bands there were. They occupied different, vaguely defined pieces of Comanche territory, and were distinguished by small cultural nuances that eluded the unpracticed eye: one liked a particular dance, another an item of clothing, one liked to eat pemmican, another pronounced its words more slowly than the other bands. The Spanish, seeing the world from the far western edge of Comanche country, thought there were three bands. They were wrong, though they were right that they had probably had contact with only three. Texas Indian agent Robert Neighbors, one of the keenest observers of the tribe, said in 1860 he thought there were eight. Other observers counted as many as thirteen, some of which eventually disappeared, were absorbed, or were exterminated.[32]

Historians generally agree that there were five major bands at the turn of the nineteenth century. Most of the discussion in this book will focus on them. Each contained more than a thousand people. Some perhaps had as many as five thousand. (At its zenith, the entire nation was estimated at twenty thousand.) They were: the Yamparika (Yap Eaters), the northernmost band, who inhabited the lands to the south of the Arkansas River; the Kotsoteka (Buffalo Eaters), whose main grounds were the Canadian River valley in present-day Oklahoma and the Texas Panhandle; the Penateka (Honey Eaters), the largest and southernmost band, whose territory stretched deep into Texas; the Nokoni (Wanderers), "middle" Comanches, who occupied the lands in north Texas and present-day Oklahoma between the Penateka and the northern bands; finally, the Quahadis (Antelopes), Quanah's band, which haunted the headstreams of the Colorado, Brazos, and Red rivers in far northwest Texas. Each band played a different part in history. The Penatekas were the ones largely responsible for driving the Lipan Apaches into the Mexican borderlands and fought most of the first battles against the Texans; the Kotsotekas were the main raiders of the Spanish settlements in New Mexico; the Yamparikas battled the Cheyennes and Arapahoes on the northern borderlands of Comancheria. The Nokonis attacked Parker's Fort; the Quahadis fought the last battles against the U.S. Army. All cooperated with one another on the friendliest of terms. All had, almost invariably, the same interests at heart. They hunted and raided together on an informal, ad hoc basis, and frequently swapped members. They never fought one another.[33] They always had common interests, common enemies, and in spite of their decentralization acted with remarkable consistency when it came to diplomacy and trade. (Other tribes had band structures that were even harder for whites to understand. Sitting Bull, for example, was a member of the Sioux tribe, but his affiliation was with the Lakota, or western division, also known as Teton, and his specific band was Hunkpapa.)

The Comanches, as a tribe, were thus without a center. But even within the band, their political structures were remarkably nonhierarchical, and their headmen wielded only limited power. There were usually two main chiefs in each band, one peace or civil chief, and one war chief. Though the former was usually superior to the latter, he exercised nothing like absolute control over individual band members, and there was nothing institutional about his power. There were indeed some very strong Comanche chiefs who commanded great allegiance, but they retained their power only so long as people went along with them. The civil chief's main job was that of a billeting officer—the man who said when the tribe would move and where it would go.[34] He sat with a council that would rule on individual cases of theft, adultery, or murder, or whatever crime might come before them. But there was no consistent body of traditional law, no police, and no judges. It was, in effect, a system of private law. If a wrong was committed, then it was up to the wronged party to litigate it. Otherwise there would be no enforcement. Payment for damages usually came in the form of horses.[35]

The head war chief, meanwhile, was a grand and glorious warrior but was not actually in charge of many of the war or raiding parties that went out, nor could he determine who joined them or where they went. These were gathered by individual warriors with individual notions about where they wanted to go. In Comanche society, anyone could be a war chief; it meant simply that you had an idea to raid, say, Mexican ranchos in Coahuila, and were able to gather a sufficient number of warriors to do it. Head war chiefs got that way because they were good at recruiting war parties. They would inevitably lead the most important sorties, and would lead the most important expeditions against powerful enemies. But they did not control, nor would they have wanted to, the martial plans of individual braves.

Since discipline and authority were lacking at the tribal and band levels, one might expect that the power of the families or clans made up for this. But here, too, the Comanche was remarkably free of the usual social fetters. Though the family unit was the clearly the basis of the band, the bands were never organized around a family group, nor were families even the main force in the regulation of marriage. There were no clan organizations of any kind. A family could not prevent a daughter or son from marrying outside his or her band, and could not even prevent a family member from leaving the band.[36] There was no principle of heredity in leadership, which was based entirely on merit.

The Comanche male was thus gloriously, astoundingly free. He was subject to no church, no organized religion, no priest class, no military societies, no state, no police, no public law, no domineering clans or powerful families, no strict rules of personal behavior, nothing telling him he could not leave his band and join another one, nothing even telling him he could not abscond with his friend's wife, though he certainly would end up paying somewhere between one and ten horses for that indulgence, assuming he was caught. He was free to organize his own military raids; free to come and go as he pleased. This was seen by many people, particularly writers and poets from James Fenimore Cooper onward, as a peculiarly American sort of freedom. Much was made of the noble and free life of the American Savage. It was, indeed, a version of that freedom, especially from onerous social institutions, that drew many settlers west to the primitive frontier.

This was the culture in which Rachel Plummer found herself. If there was much joy, laughter, singing, and gaming among the men, there was little left for her. As a woman, she was a second-class citizen, a member of a caste whose lot it was to do most of the hard work, including herding, skinning, butchering, drying beef, making clothing, packing and repairing tipis. And of course tending to children and all family matters. As a *captive* woman she had even fewer rights, and having been taken as an adult, she was never likely to get any more than she had. She bore the scars of her initial captivity and from punishments she had received. (Those who saw her later said she was quite visibly scarred.) She was the sexual slave of her master and of anyone he chose to share her with, which would have included members of his family. Considering what else she put up with, including the torture of one child and the murder of another, this would have been among the least of her worries. She was, as we have seen, the maltreated servant of her master's women.

In other ways, Rachel became entirely Comanche. She shed her pioneer clothing for Indian buckskins, and, though she does not comment on it, would have been as filthy and bug-ridden as any of the Comanches, who were notable even among Indians for their lack of hygiene. She would have chopped off her long, lovely red hair. In addition to buffalo meat, which she loved, she developed a taste for prairie dogs ("fat, and fine to eat"), beaver ("the tail only"), and bear ("very fat and delicious food"). It is doubtful that she participated in the universal Comanche habit of picking lice off themselves and cracking them with their teeth, a practice that disgusted white observers. Like other women, she probably served the men during the entertainments, fetching water for them while they danced. If she played any of the games that women and children played (shinny, double-ball), she does not mention it. She knew that she was no longer in danger of being killed. She also knew that, if she remained with the tribe, her life would never change.

Having failed in her plan to goad the Indians into killing her, she resolved now to persuade someone to purchase her from her captor. On the high plains she encountered a group of Mexicans. "I tried to get one of them to buy me," she wrote. "I told him that even if my father and husband were dead, I knew I had enough land in Texas to fully indemnify him; but he did not try to buy me, although he agreed to do it."[37] She did not give up hope. Later, while she was tending the band's horses, she encountered what she called "Mexican traders"—almost certainly Comancheros from New Mexico. They asked her to take them to her master, which she did. Then, in her presence, they asked him if he would sell her. Her master's shocking answer: "Sí, señor."

Five

THE WOLF'S HOWL

── ✦ ──

T HE UNHERALDED ARRIVAL of mounted Comanche warriors in Spanish New Mexico in 1706 marked the beginning of their first long war against white men. The fight took place entirely on the Indians' terms. The Comanches did not defeat a Spanish army on a broad field of battle in a single, final combat, or see its imperial ranks reeling in inglorious retreat across the Rio Grande. Massed armies in ceremonial formations fighting pitched battles on open ground were not the way of the American West. Instead there were raids and counterraids and a sort of bedouin warfare people would later call guerrilla, conducted by small, mobile forces in a gigantic landscape that swallowed human beings as though they had never existed. What happened to the Spanish at the hands of the Comanches was not conventional military defeat but a century and a half of brutal, grinding aggression that soaked their northern frontier in blood and left them, ultimately, with an empire emptied of meaning. They had arrived in the New World as conquistadors, powerful beyond measure, triumphantly secure in their own peculiar style of militarized Catholicism. In the north they ended up as virtual prisoners in their own missions and presidios, trapped inside a failed system that neither attracted colonists nor succeeded in converting Indians, and in any case could not protect either group from the horse tribes. The Comanches did not beat the Spanish so much as render them irrelevant—onlookers in an immense struggle for control of the center of the North American continent in which they no longer played a decisive role.

This shift in the balance of power changed the history of the American West and the fate of the North American continent. The Spanish conquest of the Americas had begun in the early sixteenth century with sweeping, and startlingly easy, victories over the powerful Aztecs (Mexico) and Incas (modern-day Peru). Much of the aboriginal population of Latin America had been subsequently defeated by arms, or disease, or both. The price, in Native American terms, was ghastly. In Central Mexico the Indian population in 1520, the year after Hernán Cortés arrived in his galleons, was eleven million; by 1650 that number had plummeted to one million. The Indians who survived were enslaved under an economic system known as *encomienda* in which the conquistadors were authorized to occupy Indian lands, tax the inhabitants, and force them to perform labor. In return, the *encomenderos* provided the teaching and ministrations of Catholicism, instruction in the Spanish language, food, and defense. It was, in short, imported feudalism, in which the *indios* played the role of serfs. The same pattern had been followed in the vast Spanish holdings in South America. As a premise for colonization, subjugation, and forced assimilation, this system had worked with cruel precision.

But as the Spanish pushed their frontier northward from Mexico City, toward what they believed would be the conquest of all of North America, their carefully calibrated system began to break down. Their style of colonialism worked best on sophisticated, centrally ruled tribes like the Aztecs and Incas. It did not work at all on the low-barbarian, precivilized, and non-agrarian tribes of northern Mexico. Long, bloody wars in the sixteenth and seventeenth centuries against the Chichimec and Tarahumare tribes proved the somewhat distasteful point that in order to fully assimilate such Indians they had to virtually exterminate them. In the late sixteenth century, after fifty years of intermittent warfare, the Chichimecs disappeared from the face of the earth.[1] Other less violent tribes proved uninterested in and ill adapted to what the brown-robed padres promised, which was food and shelter in exchange for labor in the fields and a strict adherence to Catholic morality.

The latter included what the Indians saw as bizarre and inexplicable changes in their sexual habits. (Monogamy was generally not an Indian notion.) The poor *indios* would often run away. They would be caught and punished, sometimes by a priest wielding a lash, and this in turn sometimes led to revolt. The days of easy conquest were over, and even harder days lay ahead. As savagely tough as the Chichimecs were, they were nothing compared to what the Spanish would come up against north of the Rio Grande. The Indians there were also low-barbarian, precivilized, mostly nonagrarian, and similarly uninterested in bowing submissively to the Most Catholic King. But these *indios* had a lethal new technology. None of the conquistadors had ever fought mounted Indians.

When that small band of Comanches showed up in Taos in July of 1706, New Mexico was the seat of the Spanish empire in the north. Its biggest town and territorial capital was Santa Fe, established in 1610 when the Spanish had, in effect, leapfrogged over several thousand miles of unconquered terrain to plant their flag in the far north. (It took a long time for the actual frontier to catch up with it.) The rest of the population—a few thousand white Spaniards, mestizos (people of mixed Indian and Spanish blood), and the Pueblo Indians they had subjugated—lived in settlements that were strung like beads along various streams and the narrow valleys of the Rio Grande. The Spanish had learned a few things from their unpleasant conquest of northern Mexico: The forts now would be built with high, palisaded walls; the *encomienda* was abandoned. Their imperial system here consisted of presidios packed with well-armed soldiers, missions tended by Catholic priests bent on the conversion of heathen Indians, and ranchos tended by the colonists who came north—mostly mestizos. Its success depended ultimately upon its ability to make Indian converts and attract colonists; forts in the middle of nowhere staffed by demoralized soldiers meant nothing at all.

This plan may have looked good on paper, even more so since Spain had no real rivals in the continent's yawningly empty midsection. But in the plains and mesalands of the American West it failed miserably. The trouble started around 1650. That was when various bands of the Apache tribe, newly mounted on Spanish horses and bristling with hostility, began raiding the New Mexican settlements. Nothing the Spanish had seen or experienced in Mexico prepared them for these attacks. That was not because they were defenseless. Their soldiery consisted of heavily mounted dragoons equipped with steel-plated armor; large-caliber, muzzle-loading harquebuses and miquelets, pikes, and gleaming sabers. Though to our modern eyes they may have looked a bit comical, they were in fact perfectly equipped to fight European wars against similarly equipped European combatants. In pitched battle, they could be quite deadly.

But the Indians did not fight that way—not by choice, anyway. They did not advance in regimental ranks across open fields. They never took a direct charge, scattering and disappearing whenever one was made. They never attacked an armed fort. They relished surprise, insisted on tactical advantage. They would attack whole villages and burn them, raping, torturing, and killing their inhabitants, leaving young women with their entrails carved out, men burned alive; they skewered infants and took young boys and girls as captives. Then they used the speed of their Spanish mustangs to get away, leaving the elaborately equipped dragoons to rumble ponderously after them. It was a style of fighting later perfected by even more aggressive plains tribes, who were far better horsemen. For fifty years the raiding continued, and while the Spanish had certainly killed their share of Apaches, nothing really changed. The settlements were as vulnerable as ever to Indian attack.

Then something remarkable happened. Starting around 1706, the Spanish authorities in Santa Fe began to notice a striking change in the behavior of their hated adversaries.[2] They were, it seemed, *disappearing,* or at least moving off, generally to the south and west. Raiding had virtually stopped. It was as though a treaty of peace had been signed, but nothing of the sort had happened. The Spanish civil and military establishments began to realize that some sort of catastrophe had befallen the Apaches, though the extent of it would not be clear for years to come. In 1719 a military expedition to the northeast of Santa Fe had found several populous and formerly dangerous bands of the Apaches—the Jicarillas, Carlanes, and Cuartelejo—in what appeared to be full retreat from their old grounds.[3]

What was happening? The Spanish were not entirely unaware of geopolitical realities. They understood that the Comanches and Apaches were at war. But they had difficulty enough telling one Indian from another, let alone figuring out the status of a war between tribes that fought unseen battles with unknown outcomes over hundreds of square miles of land. All they were sure of was that their enemies were vanishing.

What they were sensing from afar, however, amounted to the wholesale destruction of the Apache nation. This was no small undertaking. Apacheria was, in the human and geographical terms of the era, a vast entity. It consisted of perhaps half a dozen major bands and stretched from the mountains of New Mexico to the plains of present-day Kansas and Oklahoma, and clear down to the Nueces River in southern Texas.[4] It was the product of another sweeping southward migration—this one by Athapaskan tribes starting in the 1400s, who moved from Canada down the front range of the Rockies, destroying or assimilating other hunter-gatherer tribes.[5] While this was most likely not an attempt to kill off the entire tribe, neither was it a simple question of moving the Apaches off their hunting grounds. The Comanches had a deep and abiding hatred of Apaches, and what they did to them also had a good deal to do with blood vengeance. Either way, the Comanches were in the middle of a relentless southward migration, and the Apaches were in their way.

Almost all of this violence is lost to history. It generally took the form of raids on the villages of the Athapaskans, whose fondness for agriculture—ironically a higher form of civilization than the Comanches ever attained—doomed them. Crops meant fixed locations and semipermanent villages, which meant that the Apache bands could be hunted down and slaughtered. The fully nomadic Comanches had no such weakness. The details of these raids must have been horrific. The Apaches, who fought on foot, became easy marks for the mounted, thundering Comanches in their breechclouts and black war paint. (They wore black because it was the color of death and because it was in keeping with their minimalist wardrobe. Later they would adopt feathered headdresses, colorful war paint, and tattoos from others, especially the northern plains tribes; in these years they were unadorned and elemental; a stripped-down war machine.)[6] Prisoners were rarely taken. Whole villages were routinely burned. Children were taken captive. Torture of survivors was the norm, as it was all across the plains.

The Spanish saw this only in flashes. In 1723 they recorded a bloody attack against an Apache *rancheria*. In 1724 the Comanches made a raid so brutally effective against the Jicarilla band that they ended up carrying off half of the women and killed all but sixty-nine members of the band.[7] The Jicarillas were soon begging for, and received, Spanish protection. Other Apaches, including the Mescaleros, were similarly retreating westward from the Comanche onslaught. In 1724, according to Texas governor Domingo Cabello, the Lipan Apaches were completely vanquished from the southern plains in a bloody nine-day battle at a place the Spanish called El Gran Cierro de La Ferro ("Great Mountain of Iron"), thought to be on the Wichita River in what is now southwestern Oklahoma.[8] By the end of the 1720s, the savagery of the attacks on the Apaches had become so pronounced, and so widespread, that some Apaches even sought the shelter of the Spanish pueblo at Pecos, not far from Santa Fe. The Comanche response was to attack the pueblo.

The Spanish actually tried to save what was left of the Apaches—a policy not entirely out of keeping with their self-interest. In 1726 they gave the tribe lands near Taos, hoping that this would amount to a barrier against the Comanches. In 1733 a mission for the Jicarilla Apaches was founded on the Rio Trampas. None of these strategies really worked. The action was all rearguard. By 1748 the sweep was complete. The Jicarillas had been driven from their native lands, as had the other bands who had occupied the buffalo grounds in West Texas, and the present-day western Kansas, western Oklahoma, and eastern Colorado; they had even fled from the protection of the mission at Taos. Almost all the Apache bands had by then been cleared from the southern plains, and all of the bands that the Spanish kept records of moved southwest into what would become their new homeland: the deserts and mesas of Arizona and New Mexico and the Mexican borderlands. (These included the Chiricahua, the bands of Geronimo and Cochise; the two chiefs would become famous fighting in these marginal lands in the latter nineteenth century.) Those bands who were not driven westward, including the Lipans, ended up in the bone-dry scrublands of the Texas Trans-Pecos. Many Apache bands simply vanished from history, including the plains-dwelling Faraones, Carlanes, and Palomas.[9] By the 1760s the Comanches were driving the Apaches before them across the Rio Grande into Mexico.

The Apaches were not their only victims. As the Comanches streamed south across the Arkansas River, flush with their astonishing mastery of the horse and their rapidly evolving understanding of mounted warfare, they discovered something else about themselves: Their war parties could navigate enormous distances using only natural landmarks. They could also do it *at night*. They were better at this, too, than anyone else. Before leaving, a war party would assemble and receive navigational instruction from elders, which included drawing maps in the sand showing hills, valleys, water holes, rivers. Each day of the journey was planned, and the novices would commit this to memory. Dodge reported that one such group of raiders, none older than nineteen, and none of whom had ever been to Mexico, was able to travel from Brady's Creek, Texas, near modern San Angelo, to Monterrey, Mexico—three hundred fifty–plus miles—without making a wrong turn and with nothing more than the instructions they had received.[10]

Thus the various Comanche bands could launch strikes in any direction, at any time, anywhere on the plains or their hinterlands. They attacked the Pawnees in Kansas, the Utes in eastern Colorado and eastern New Mexico, the Osages in Oklahoma, the Blackfeet in Wyoming, the Kiowas and Kiowa Apaches in Kansas and Colorado, the Tonkawas in Texas. By 1750 few tribes dared to set foot on the southern plains unless the Comanches permitted them to. The powerful northern tribes, including the Cheyenne, stayed north of the Arkansas. (This boundary would be fiercely contested again in the late 1830s.) As always with the Comanches, diplomacy was mixed with war: A key peace treaty was made in 1790 with the Kiowas that gave the Comanches a powerful ally with whom they shared their hunting grounds. Peace with the Wichitas opened huge trading opportunities linked to the French in Louisiana. There were some tribes, such as the Wacos and Tawakonis from central Texas, who simply managed to exist in harmony with the Comanches, and in any case did not make war on them. And then, of course, some enmities—like those with the Tonkawas, Apaches, and Utes—never seemed to die. Such muscular migrations had happened before in North America—one thinks of the powerful Iroquois league moving inexorably west in the seventeenth century, destroying the Huron and Erie tribes, and driving the Algonquian peoples before them as they occupied the Ohio River valley.[11]

It was not at all clear to anyone in the middle and later eighteenth century that these important shifts in military power were taking place. (Nor was it completely clear a century later.) The Spanish, virtually the only chroniclers of the Comanche nation prior to the nineteenth century, usually saw only its effects,[12] and in any case could not then have pieced together a coherent military map of their northern provinces. But by 1750 the Comanches had in fact carved out a militarily and diplomatically unified nation with remarkably precise boundaries that were patrolled and ruthlessly enforced. They had done it with extreme violence, and that violence had changed their culture forever. In the decades that followed, the Comanches would never again be satisfied with hunting buffalo. They had quickly evolved, like the ancient Spartans, into a society entirely organized around war, in which tribal status would be conveyed exclusively by prowess in battle, which in turn was invariably measured in scalps, captives, and captured horses. The Comanche character, as perceived by the Spanish, was neatly summarized in the following report from Brigadier Pedro de Rivera y Villalón's 1726 inspection tour of the northern provinces of New Spain.

Each year at a certain time, there comes to this province a nation of Indians very barbarous and warlike. Their name is Comanche. They never number less than 1,500. Their origin is unknown, because they are always wandering in battle formation, for they make war on all the Nations. . . . After they finish the commerce which brought them here, which consists of tanned skins, buffalo hides, and those young Indians which they capture (because they kill the older ones), they retire, continuing their wandering until another time.[13]

Thus did Comancheria—a land long known to the Spanish only as Apacheria—announce itself. And thus did the Comanches, in the scope of a few decades, become the new chief enemies of the Spanish regimes in New Mexico and Texas. (Apaches continued to prove a nuisance in the borderlands, but were never again a major threat.) It proved to be a far more complex relationship than the one with the Apaches. For one thing, the Spanish authorities were the first to recognize both the existence of the "Comanche barrier" and its usefulness to them. The Spanish still had large territorial ambitions and greatly feared French expansion west from Louisiana as well as the unremitting westward flow of the English settlements.

In that sense the Comanche country, already a huge expanse of the American plains, became more valuable to Spain than all of her troops north of the Rio Grande.[14] If the Comanches stood as a seemingly impenetrable obstacle to Spanish expansion, they also offered a guarantee that the French and English would not pass, either. The French had pursued an entirely different colonial policy, eschewing outright conquest in favor of influence-peddling, alliance-making, and a sort of mercantile diplomacy—most importantly involving weapons but other commodities, too—by state-sponsored traders, often with great effect. The French were behind the 1720 massacre of an entire Spanish expedition at the hands of the Pawnees, even though no Frenchman fired a weapon.[15] Now they longed to open markets up to Louisiana trading companies, and their traders had pushed westward along the Red River as early as 1718. Unfortunately, they made the mistake of arming the enemies of the Comanches, the Apaches and the Jumanos, in effect betting on the wrong horses.[16] They thus soon became unwelcome in Comanche lands. That meant the virtual cessation of French intrigue in Texas. English settlements would not arrive in Texas until 1820 or so; yet even then it would take them half a century to break the Comanche barrier. The other component of the new Comanche relationship was trade. In addition to their prowess in war, the Comanches were great merchants and traders. They had more raw wealth in the form of horses, skins, meats, and captives than any tribe on the plains. Bartering and selling went on for years unofficially; so strong was this current that in 1748 the tribe was officially admitted to the Taos trade fair.

But trade relationships did not mean that the fighting stopped. In the 1720s, Spain's Comanche wars were just beginning. The pattern was always the same: constant raiding would lead the Spanish to launch punitive expeditions. These soldiers often got lost, especially when they wandered too far to the East, too far into Comancheria itself, and thus into the trackless, treeless high plains. Some never returned. On a number of occasions the Comanches simply ran off their horses, leaving the men to die of thirst or starvation. More often the soldiers would ride out of the presidio, kill the first Indians they found, and return home. Many could not tell one Indian tribe from another, and often did not care to. They recorded many such attacks, including a 1720 raid in which Comanches stole fifteen hundred horses. In 1746 there was a major attack on the Taos pueblo, and another against Abiquiu in 1747; at the relatively large Pecos pueblo in 1748 they killed 150 people.[17] Large counter-raids were mounted in 1716,[18] 1717, 1719, 1723, 1726, and 1742.[19]

Not all were failures. In 1751, after three hundred mounted Comanches attacked the New Mexican pueblo of Galisteo, provincial governor Vélez Cachupin dispatched soldiers that pursued the Indians down the Arkansas River, possibly into modern-day Kansas. They caught up with them in a wood, set the wood on fire, killed one hundred one of them, and took the rest prisoners. The Spanish province of Texas, which was subjected to Comanche raids beginning in the 1750s, followed a similar pattern, though with even rarer success. Indian raids continued. Expeditions were launched. Comanches became ever more powerful. One measure of their growing power was the route Spanish expeditions took from Santa Fe to San Antonio· in the eighteenth century. It crossed the Texas border and dived deep into Mexico before turning northward again. The point: The Spanish did not dare cross Comancheria, even with soldiers. To travel was to circumnavigate Comanche lands, as though they were sovereign. This never changed. By the time Spain finally ceded its New World possessions to Mexico in 1821, the Comanches were firmly in possession of the field. Their empire had grown, their Indian foes had been driven deep into Spanish territories. Most Texas missions and many in New Mexico had been shuttered; the once-vaunted Spanish soldiery rattled its sabers and stayed close to home.[20]

The Spanish made many mistakes in their northern provinces. They made them with metronomic consistency and they made them over a colonial period that spanned two centuries. Though they were not always cruel and incompetent, they were cruel and incompetent enough of the time to cause great problems for themselves, and they were inevitably hamstrung by European-style military and civilian bureaucracies attempting to operate in a savage land of barren mesas and infinite horizons. The entire premise of their northern expansion—essentially a headlong and blindly optimistic dive into lands dominated by culturally primitive, mounted, and irremediably hostile Indians—was fatally flawed. But in an era of grave misjudgments the greatest miscalculation of all took place in the year 1758. It happened on a lovely bend of a limestone river, amid fields of wildflowers in the hill country of Texas, about one hundred twenty miles northwest of San Antonio, and resulted in a grisly, era-defining event that became known as the San Saba Massacre. The massacre, in turn, would draw Spain into its greatest military defeat in the New World. Both came at the hands of the Comanches. There were many reasons for what took place, and many Spanish officials played a part. But the man to whom history assigns responsibility was an officer named Don Diego Ortiz de Parrilla. That he was ill-fated, unlucky, and undeserving of much of the blame for what happened did not make it any easier for him. Parrilla's story offers one of history's clearest windows into what it was like in embattled, Comanche-tormented New Spain in the middle of the eighteenth century.

The story begins in 1749. That year several Apache bands, including the numerous Lipans, rode into San Antonio to sign a peace treaty. They also proclaimed, to the somewhat flabbergasted padres, their earnest desire to enter into mission life and become humble and duty-bound subjects of the king of Spain.[21] This was marvelous, astonishing news. These men were the same remorseless killers who had been raiding the Texas settlements with a fury ever since San Antonio's founding in 1718, finding ever more imaginative ways to torture, maim, and eviscerate Spanish subjects. They appeared to be sincere. Over the next few years they would continue to approach the "brown robes" with the same deeply compelling idea: They wanted peace; they wanted their own mission and presidio; and they wanted them to be built in their homeland, which they said was in the vicinity of the San Saba River, near the present-day town of Menard, Texas.

The idea took root. Even though soldiers and settlers in the area were suspicious of Apache motives, the priests, who were beside themselves with happiness at their good fortune, moved resolutely forward. Everyone agreed that peace with the Apaches was highly desirable. Their conversion to Catholicism, on the other hand, was a sort of mystical dream. No mission had ever been planted among the Apaches. A successful mission would represent a sort of imperial twin killing: a rare spiritual coup accompanied by hard, secular evidence of the soundness of Spanish colonial policy in the north. Though it was the subject of considerable debate, the idea moved slowly forward through the political and religious minefields of eighteenth-century New Spain. Expeditions were sent to scout locations in 1753 and 1755.[22] Politics were played; skepticism was expressed concerning sullen and uncooperative Apaches who showed up only occasionally but always demanded gifts. The doubting civil authorities were slowly won over, in part because they had heard stories from prospectors of fabulous gold and silver lodes in the hill country.[23] These had gone unexploited because of the presence of hostile Indians. The priests also hammered hard at the idea that without the missions the cunning and insidious French would attempt to advance their own interests in Texas. The French ploy always worked. By 1756 the idea had even found a champion—a prodigiously rich philanthropist from Mexico named Don Pedro Romero de Terreros, who offered to pay for all costs of two missions for the Apaches for a period of three years. His conditions: The missions must be built in Apache country, and they had to be run by his cousin, the ingratiating and boundlessly optimistic Father Alonso Giraldo de Terreros.[24] With Terreros's contracts in hand, and visions of gold mines and docile Apaches dancing in their heads, the viceregal office approved the project.

The man appointed to oversee it was Colonel Parrilla. As far as anyone could tell, he was perfect for the job: a soldier with far more experience and frontier savvy than most of the neophytes and perfumed noblemen sent over the years from Spain to track Indians. Parrilla was a man of considerable ability. He had been governor of the provinces of Sonora and Coahuila, and had led successful campaigns against Apache bands in the Gila country of western New Mexico. He understood frontier conditions and was under no illusions about the Indian style of warfare. It was a measure of the importance of these missions that a man like Parrilla was put in charge of them. An even greater sign was that Parrilla reported not to the governors of Texas or New Mexico but directly to the viceroy in Mexico City.[25] He proved himself immediately competent, supervising construction of a mission and presidio, arranging for the transport of fourteen hundred head of cattle and seven hundred head of sheep, planting of crops, and also the transport of a number of Tlascaltecan Indians from northern Mexico to help with the hoped-for Apache converts.

. In spite of this, Parrilla was deeply skeptical of the entire enterprise. As time went by, his suspicions had only gotten worse. Even before he left for San Saba, he had written the viceroy that he believed the Apaches were as treacherous as ever, and that they had shown few signs of making good on their promises. He was not reassured when, every so often, a few Lipans would appear at San Antonio to reassert their desire to become loyal subjects of the king, always requiring generous gifts that included cattle, horses, beans, salt, sugar, tobacco, hats, blankets, knives, bridles, kettles, ribbons, and beads.[26] For the most part.the Indians stayed away. On the eve of the move to the mission, when they should have been swooning in anticipation of simultaneously receiving Jesus and pledging allegiance to the Spanish king, none could be found. Parrilla had delayed the move as long as he could, finally bowing to pressure from the ebullient Father Terreros. He had then balked at actually building the mission, but again succumbed to political pressure. On April 18, 1757, four priests reported for duty at the mission on the south bank of the San Saba River. Across the river, several miles away, one hundred soldiers were garrisoned in a stockade-fence presidio.

All was finally in place, except for one problem: there were still no Apaches. One of the padres was sent out into the wilderness to recruit them, but once more there were none to be found. Then in June it seemed to the hopeful fathers that the miraculous moment had finally arrived. That month they discovered some three thousand Indians camped near the mission. This was more than they could have dreamed possible. But as the missionaries prepared to welcome their new charges, they learned the real reason for the gathering: the annual buffalo hunt. There was some talk of going north to fight other Indians, too, but no talk at all of coming into the mission. The Indians soon vanished.

Parrilla, now certain that he had been duped, wrote the viceroy: "Your Excellency will understand what a difficult undertaking is the formation of missions for the heathen Apache nation, and will see that the favorable reports that were sent in to that Captaincy General concerning the matter were direct results of the unreliability that has always characterized the missionaries and inhabitants of the province of Texas in every occurrence that has concerned them."[27] Meanwhile, three of the four priests had also lost confidence in the venture, leaving Father Terreros as its sole supporter. "We find no reason," wrote the dissenting padres, "why we should remain with this enterprise, which we consider ill-conceived and without foundation from the beginning. . . . Having fully learned the wishes of the Indians, we find no other motive [for friendship] than the hope of receiving gifts."[28] Parrilla tried to abandon the mission project altogether, proposing that the presidio alone be moved north to protect the mines, with no success. Though he was bitterly frustrated, and not a little nervous about manning an outpost so far beyond the frontier, he had his viceregal orders.

In any event, it was already too late. That fall a few passing Apache bands told the padres that a great invading army of *norteños* was on the way to do battle with them, a force so great that the Apaches could not even trust the Spanish to protect them. ("Northerners" was what the Apaches called the Comanches, because they invariably came at them from the north.) While this must have seemed to Parrilla as far-fetched as everything else the Apaches had said and promised, this time they were telling the truth. It was a truth that would soon reveal the real reason for the Apaches' odd behavior.

The San Saba Mission proposal was indeed, as Parrilla had suspected, a sham. The Lipans and other bands never had any intention of converting to Christianity. But what neither Parrilla nor any Spanish official had understood was the *reason* for the deception, and thus they had no idea of the extent of the treachery that had been perpetrated upon them. What had in fact happened, while the padres were busy shining up their sacramental vessels, was that the Comanche empire—an area far, far larger than any Spaniard suspected in those years—had arrived precisely on their doorstep.[29] The Spanish had been cleverly lured well beyond the actual boundaries of the Apache lands. The San Saba country was not their homeland at all: It was Comancheria proper, and a Spanish fort there amounted to a declaration of war on the Comanches. This was exactly what the Apaches wanted: They wanted their dire enemy destroyed. Or at least stopped in its relentless southward sweep.

It was, in most ways, an excellent plan. But it did not work. Spring of 1758 brought cool rains and abundant wildflowers to the San Saba country. As the Apaches expected, it also brought Comanches, riding hard under a full moon. (So many raids were made by moonlight that in Texas a full, bright spring or summer moon is still known as a Comanche Moon.) On the morning of March 2, the priests in the mission noticed that the Apaches had disappeared. Then came yells from beyond the mission walls. A group of Indians on horseback had stolen all sixty-two of their horses. Suspecting that he was dealing only with horse thieves, Parrilla dispatched fifteen soldiers to pursue them. The soldiers quickly realized that the trouble was much bigger than they had thought, and returned fearfully to the fort. They reported that the hills were alive with enemies.

Parrilla now rode to the mission, where three priests and a handful of Indians and servants were protected by five soldiers, to beg Father Terreros to leave for the far greater security of the fort. Terreros refused, insisting that the Indians would never harm him. He was wrong. On the morning of March 16, 1758, mass was interrupted by the noise of whooping Indians. When the padres ran to the parapets, they saw a jaw-dropping sight: On all sides of the mission were gathered some two thousand warriors, many painted black and crimson, Plains Indians in the full regalia of war. They were mostly Comanches. As with many Comanche raids, there were also outriders, in this case Wichitas, with whom the Comanches had recently made peace. (In later years, the outriders tended to be Kiowas; in both cases they usually rode under Comanche leadership.) They were armed with bows, lances, and muskets. For a short time, they pretended to be friendly, insisting they had come to offer their allegiance to the Spaniards; the tall, stolid Comanche chief even accepted gifts, though he did so disdainfully, as though the givers were not worth his consideration. Then the looting and killing started.

The first to die was Father Terreros, shot with a musket. He was followed by a soldier who was guarding him. Others were shot or hacked to death. The Indians set fire to the buildings of the mission. The dead priests were stripped, their bodies mutilated. One of them, Padre Santiesteban, was decapitated. Meanwhile, the attackers busied themselves plundering the rich storerooms, killing cattle, and creating mayhem. When Parrilla heard of the attack, two miles away in the fort, he sent out a squad of nine soldiers to reinforce the mission. With more than three hundred people at the presidio, mostly women and children (families of the soldiers), he dared not send more. But his soldiers never reached the mission. They were almost immediately attacked, and all were shot or lanced. Two were killed outright, and the rest dragged themselves, wounded and terrified, back to the fort. That was the last rescue attempt Parrilla would make. The padres, who had chosen to stay in the mission against his orders, were on their own. Of the mission's inhabitants, only a handful survived, taking shelter inside one of the buildings that was not burned. The Indians, meanwhile, carried on a three-day orgy fueled by the provisions of the mission, while Parrilla and his soldiers remained timidly and powerlessly inside the presidio's high timber walls, which the Indians never attacked. On the fourth day, Parrilla finally judged it safe to investigate the damage. It was a scene of total desolation. Almost the entire mission was destroyed. Ten people, including three priests, had been killed.

What happened next amounted to a sort of wholesale panic on the northern frontier of New Spain, set off by the previously unthinkable notion that Spanish presidios and missions were now vulnerable to Comanche attack. This was especially true of the people in San Antonio, who believed that Indians were now headed to the provincial capital and who quickly barricaded themselves even though they had only a week's provisions. So terrified were they that they abandoned all of the cattle the residents owned—some two thousand head in all—because they could find no one brave enough to guard them. It was the same or worse in other settlements. After the massacre, Parrilla requested immediate relief from other forts. None came. He protested to the viceroy, who sent orders to Spanish forts in Mexico to send help. Still, nothing happened. Fully three sets of viceregal orders had little or no effect. The most Parrilla ever got was a few soldiers. By that time the invaders were far away.

News of the attack on San Saba Mission and the killing and mutilation of the priests spread rapidly through the Spanish settlements. If the first reaction was largely blind fear, it was quickly replaced with cold fury, and a desire for bloody revenge. This was especially true in the viceroy's office in Mexico City. The garrisons in Texas that had refused to send troops to relieve San Saba were now summarily ordered to supply men and arms to a punitive expedition that would be headed by Parrilla himself. A force of 600 men was soon raised, consisting of Spanish regulars plus a host of Indian auxiliaries, including Coahuiltecans and 134 Apaches. It was, quite deliberately, the greatest expedition that Spanish money and might could buy. Never had such a large number of men been dispatched to punish Indians. It marched north in August 1759 in search of Comanches. Like most Spanish officers before him, especially those who knew what they were doing, Parrilla refused to venture out into the heart of the Comanche lands on the Great Plains, though his Indian scouts assured him that this is where the Comanches were. Instead he hung to the east, in the timbered country on the fringes of the plains. He marched for many days, and finally found an Indian encampment.

They were Tonkawas. Even though Parrilla almost certainly knew this— from his Indian scouts—he did what so many of his predecessors had done. He attacked anyway. Vengeance was vengeance, and Indians, to some extent, were Indians. So he surrounded the Tonkawa village and attacked with his six hundred soldiers and killed seventy-five of them and took one hundred fifty women and children prisoners, to be taken back to San Antonio for "reduction"—conversion to Christianity and forced assimilation. He may or may not have understood that the Tonkawas were bitter enemies of the Comanches. (In the nineteenth century they would be used with lethal effect by white soldiers against Comanches, especially as trackers.) The army continued north.

In October 1759, Parrilla's force found itself about eighty miles northwest of present Fort Worth, near the Red River, which marked the northern boundary of Texas. There, near the present town of Ringgold, he encountered yet another prodigious assemblage of Indians. Though the typically paranoid Spanish had suspected French collusion in the attack on the San Saba Mission, there is no evidence to support it. But this fearsome group, consisting of an ad hoc alliance of several thousand Comanches, Wichitas, Osages, Red River Caddoans, and other tribes, and dug into breastworks in the enemy's path, almost certainly had some assistance from French intrigue. That the Comanches were the dominant power in this part of the world did not mean they did not make alliances of convenience, especially where Apaches and Spanish were concerned. They were at war with the Osages, but happy to ride with them against Parrilla.

What happened next might have been one of the greatest slaughters in the history of the American West, except for the fact that Parrilla's forces almost immediately turned tail and ran. Though his Spanish regulars had charged on his command, the rest of the army proved utterly feckless. Most of it melted away. Retreat turned into panic, and panic turned into headlong flight. For some reason—perhaps because they were so pleased to capture all of the provision wagons of a large Spanish army—the Indians did not pursue Parrilla's terrified, fleeing army. Because of this, his forces suffered few casualties, an inconvenient fact that he was hard-pressed to explain to his skeptical superiors back in San Antonio and later in Mexico City.

It was a stunning defeat, the worst inflicted on the Spanish in the New World. The Spanish had thrown everything they had at the Comanches and their allies and had been humiliated. No expeditions would ever again be sent against the Comanches in Texas; no missions were ever again established in hostile country. More important, both the Indians and Spanish of the day were interested in what happened in the same way. In the fog of war, it was a clear consensus. The fight at Spanish Fort was evidence of a major swing in the balance of power, one that heralded the beginning of a long period of violence against both Texas and northern Mexico. Within a few years Comanche power in Texas would become almost absolute. Though Spain maintained some of its missions and presidio for another sixty years, they were powerless to do anything except defend themselves. Parrilla himself was sent to Mexico to face court-martial. He lied. He said he had faced six thousand Indians under the command of French officers flying French flags. The court found no evidence of Frenchmen under arms or in positions of command. Parrilla was disgraced.

New Spain's leaders were not always incompetent in their handling of the Comanche problem. There were several governors and several generals who showed themselves to be shrewd and resourceful leaders, and Spain produced at least one governor of real genius who managed to do what two centuries of such governors and scores of later politicians, Indian agents, and American armies could not: make a genuine peace with the Comanches. His name was Don Juan Bautista de Anza. He was governor of the province of New Mexico from 1777 to 1787, and he was perhaps the most brilliant of all the men who ever faced the problem of hostile Indians. If the postrevolution Texans or the post–Mexican War federal Indian authorities had studied Anza, the history of the opening of the American West might have been quite different, indeed.

Anza, a hardened Indian fighter who had met with success on the California and Sonora frontiers, inherited the same intractable Indian problem every other governor had faced. The Comanches were ascendant, the Apaches were skulking in the hinterlands but were still lethal, and the Navajos and Utes were restive in the west. All were troublesome but the most notorious Indian of all in those years was a Comanche chief known as Cuerno Verde

("Green Horn"), leader of the Kotsoteka band, whose father had been killed in battle with Spaniards and whose vengeance was legendary.[30] He was, as Anza wrote to the commander-general of the interior provinces of New Spain, "a scourge of the kingdom, who had exterminated many pueblos, killing hundreds and making as many prisoners whom he afterwards sacrificed in cold blood."[31] As soon as Anza became governor, he proposed a bold and previously unthinkable strategy to defeat the Comanches: Attack them in their own country at the same moment when they were coming to attack New Mexicans. The Spanish had always thought defensively, or at least in terms of punitive expeditions. Anza aimed aggressively for the root cause of the problem.

On August 15, 1779, the new governor gathered an army of six hundred men, including 259 Indians, and set off in search of Cuerno Verde. To avoid detection, he took a different and more mountainous route than the one used by all previous Spanish expeditions,[32] crossing the front range of the Rockies near South Park. He went ultimately north and east, onto the elevated plains in present-day eastern Colorado, where he found the Indian camp. Though most of its warriors and the chief were absent, Anza attacked anyway; the Indians fled. It took the Spanish nine miles to ride them down, and another three miles to subdue them. They killed eighteen—presumably old men, boys, and women—and took thirty women and thirty-four children prisoner. They got all five hundred horses. From the prisoners, Anza learned that Cuerno Verde was off raiding in New Mexico but was returning soon for a grand feast and celebration.

Anza waited for him, surprised him on the trail in Colorado near a place that is still known as Greenhorn Peak, and in a piece of brilliant battlefield strategy, engineered one of the great Spanish victories in North America. He had ventured into the heart of Comancheria, to the very homeland of the Comanche, where countless others had perished, and where they had never been beaten in a major fight, and he had triumphed. Anza wrote later that he believed he owed his victory in part to Cuerno Verde's arrogance. After Cuerno Verde attacked the six-hundred-strong Spanish battle line with his bodyguard of fifty warriors, Anza theorized that "his death was caused by his own intrepidity and the contempt he wished to show our people, being vaunted by the many successes that they have always obtained over us because of the irregularities with which they have always warred. . . . From this should be deduced the arrogance, presumption and pride which characterized this barbarian, and which he manifested until the last moment in various ways, disdaining even to load his own musket. . . ."[33] Only a handful of warriors escaped capture or death. The Spanish suffered only one casualty. Anza and his lancers launched other attacks into Comancheria, and though none was nearly as effective as the one against Cuerno Verde, he soon had their full attention.

What Anza did next was equally unconventional. Other governors, flush with such success, would likely have tried to destroy the rest of the Comanches, in spite of the fact that there were more than twenty thousand of them on the plains[34] (or, according to Anza's own inflated estimate, thirty thousand). But Anza was not trying to beat the Comanches, just scare them enough so that a diplomatic accommodation could be made. Considering what had happened in New Mexico and what was even now happening in Texas, he had what sounded like a wildly implausible goal: He wanted to make friends and allies of them.

This he did. He gathered Comanche chiefs for peace talks, insisting that he speak with all of the bands that touched the western perimeter of the plains, and eventually insisting on appointing a single chief to speak for all the bands, something that had never happened before. Anza treated the Comanches as equals, did not threaten their hunting grounds, and refused to try to declare sovereignty over them. He offered them trade. They liked and respected him. In one of the more remarkable diplomatic pirouettes ever seen on the border, Anza then managed to concoct an overweening solution to all his problems. He somehow managed not only to get the Comanches to sign a peace treaty, but also to bind them with their enemies the Utes in an alliance with Spain against their bitterest foes, the Apaches. Then, for the coup de grâce, he took this combined force of Spanish, Ute, and Comanche and used it to force the Navajo into the compact.

Odder still, Anza's treaty worked. In the entire history of the American West, few treaties between whites and Indians have ever held up more than a few years. Most were invalid the day they were signed. History is full of hundreds of Indian treaties concocted by governments who could not enforce them. This is the rare exception. It was only with the province of New Mexico, and it probably saved New Mexico from the long terror of Comanche raiding that was even then being unleashed on Texas and northern Mexico. The truce with the Utes was broken soon enough, but the treaty with New Mexico actually held up. It did so in part because it was in the

Comanches' own best interests. New Mexico was a mother lode of trade, a place where they could sell their horses and captives. The Anza peace gave rise to a new, and quite special form of mercantile relationship between the western Comanches and New Mexico. Instead of terror there was simply trade, conducted by an entirely new breed, hard-bitten mestizo middlemen who went by the name of Comancheros.

Six

BLOOD AND SMOKE

MIRABEAU BUONAPARTE LAMAR was a poet. His best-known works—they were apparently popular in certain literary corners of nineteenth-century America—were "Thou Idol of My Soul" and "An Evening on the Banks of the Chatahoochee." He was also an expert fencer, a superb horseman, an amateur historian, and an oil painter of some accomplishment and sensibility. When he was elected president of the sovereign nation known as the Republic of Texas in 1838, his critics derided him for making a better poet than president.

That may or may not have been true. But the one thing everyone could agree on, in that violent and unsettled year, was that he was, even by frontier standards, a dangerous, mean, and uncompromising son of a bitch. There is a famous photograph of him from sometime in the 1840s in which he looks less like a poet than a button man for the mob. His arms are crossed defiantly and defensively, enhancing the wrinkles in an already deeply creased broadcloth suit. His hair, swept back from his forehead, looks like it needs washing and combing. His thin lips are curled ever so slightly back into something that looks like the beginning of a snarl. It is unclear just how the poet and painter came to be housed in the body of a truculent Indian-annihilator and would-be empire builder.[1]

He owed his elevation to the presidency both to his heroism at the battle of San Jacinto—his rescue of two fellow soldiers was so breathtakingly brave that it drew a salute from enemy lines—and to the utter failure of his predecessor, the brilliant alcoholic statesman Sam Houston, to solve the Indian "problem." In the years since San Jacinto and the raid at Parker's Fort, white men had been pouring into Texas by the thousands, crashing headlong into the eastern boundary lands of Comancheria, and as a result the frontier had exploded in violence, most of it at the hand of the Comanches. Houston had taken a conciliatory approach. He refused to implement congressional troop authorizations. He refused to authorize frontier forts. He had spent time with Indians, both as an agent and as the ambassador for the Cherokee nation in Washington. He liked them and believed he understood them. He often sided with them, and he invariably defended their right to territory. When a Comanche chief asked him to set a boundary on white settlement, he answered in frustration: "If I could build a wall from the Red River to the Rio Grande, so high that no Indian could scale it, the white people would go crazy trying to devise a means to get beyond it."[2] He had held peace talks with Comanches, without result.

Meanwhile the settlers rushed in like a moon tide from the East, bearing their ingenious instruments that "stole the land," and spurred on by the Texas Congress's opening of all Indian lands to white settlement (over Houston's veto). As homesteads crept up the valleys of the Colorado, Guadalupe, and Brazos rivers, Comanche attacks escalated. In just the first two years of Houston's administration more than one hundred captives were carried off. Most, like little nine-year-old Cynthia Ann Parker, were simply, heartbreakingly gone. There was no appeal to the government, no redress, just wrenching, empty grief for hundreds of families who could not know the fate of their loved ones in the high, windy plains of Comancheria. After the raid at Parker's Fort, Cynthia Ann's uncle—and Rachel's father—James had pleaded on two occasions with Sam Houston to finance a rescue expedition to retrieve the five hostages.[3] Houston had turned him down flat. There was violent death everywhere along the bleeding edge of this westernmost frontier—a great deal more than historians ever recorded—and Houston could not afford to throw his scant resources at the rescue of one set of captives, however touching their story.

By late 1838 the new republic had reached a boiling point. And just at that moment, Mirabeau Buonaparte Lamar was elected president. The hard-edged Lamar was the perfect counterpoint to the measured, diplomatic Houston, whom he despised as much as he hated the new city on a bayou in east Texas that bore his name. One of Lamar's first acts was to move the capital from the swamps of east Texas one hundred fifty miles west to a new town named Austin at the very foot of the Balcones Escarpment—in other words, right up against the edge of Comanche country.[4] The move westward was in keeping with the views of this pro-slavery fire-eater who wanted nothing to do with union with the United States. His dream was to push the borders of his young republic all the way to the golden shores of the Pacific Ocean. Austin would be at the confluence of key western trade routes, a sort of Constantinople of the primitive West, the seat of a sprawling empire called Texas that would vie for continental supremacy with the agglomeration of eastern states known as the United States of America. Though the majority of Texans had expected that they would be annexed almost instantly by the United States after their victory at San Jacinto, Lamar had plenty of fellow dreamers. One of them was James Parker, who proposed to the Congress that he lead four thousand men gloriously to capture Santa Fe and New Mexico, and that each of the men be given three hundred sixty acres as a reward. Congress declined to approve the plan.[5]

In spite of an empty treasury and currency that was almost worthless,[6] Lamar saw no reason why he could not build his empire of the West. The first step, of course, was getting rid of the Indians. He believed that Indians should be either expunged from Texas or killed outright. This included all Indians, from the Comanches on the west to the Wacos in the middle, and the Shawnees and Delawares and Cherokees in the east. In his inaugural address he put this quite succinctly, in case anyone was not clear about where he stood. Citing the Indians' cruelties, he called for an "exterminating war" against them that would "admit of no compromise, and have no termination except in their total extinction, or total expulsion."[7] The Congress of the Republic of Texas heartily agreed. That month they voted to create an eight-hundred-forty-man regiment of fifty companies to serve for three years; they also voted a million-dollar appropriation.

Thus Lamar's rallying cry: extinction or expulsion. It sounds a good deal like a public appeal for genocide, certainly among the very few in modern history. But as appalling as it might sound, in fact Lamar, a man who had experience with Creek Indians in Georgia, was just being brutally candid in a way that almost no white men had ever been on the subject of Indian rights. His was a policy of naked aggression, as usual, but without the usual lies and misrepresentation. He demanded the Indians' complete submission

to the Texans' terms—there would be no endless renegotiation of meaningless boundaries—and stated quite clearly what would happen to them if they
did not agree. "He proposed nothing and presided over nothing that was not
already fully established in Anglo-American precedent and policy," wrote
historian T. R. Fehrenbach. "The people and the courts had decided that
true peace between white men and red men was impossible, unless either
the Indians gave up their world, or the Americans eschewed the nation they
were determined to erect upon this continent."[8] Since two hundred years of
duplicity and bloodshed had proved that neither of those things would ever
happen, Lamar was just stating what was to him obvious.

What he had done that no high-ranking government official in the neighboring United States of America had ever done before was to explicitly deny
that Indians in Texas had rights to *any territory at all*. Every treaty ever signed
assumed that Indians would get at least some land on their terms. Indeed, in
1825 the U.S. government had created an Indian Country (modern Oklahoma) in order to guarantee that, in the words of Secretary of War James
Barbour, "the future residence of these peoples will be forever undisturbed."[9]
Lamar and most of the residents of their new sovereign nation opposed the
very principle. In some sense, what he proposed was better than the piecemeal
destruction that had been meted out to the eastern tribes. In another sense,
it was an invitation to the outright slaughter of native peoples. The Texas
Congress loved the new Indian policy. In 1839 two thousand revved-up,
patriotic, adventure-hungry Texans signed up to fight Indians.[10]

And fight them they did. The upshot of the Lamar presidency was an
almost immediate war against all Indians in Texas. The summer of 1839
witnessed one of the most savage campaigns ever unleashed against Native
Americans. The first target was the Cherokees, who had been pushed relentlessly westward over many decades from their homelands in the Carolinas.
Many had landed in the piney woods and sandy riverbanks of east Texas,
near the Louisiana border, where they had largely lived in peace with whites
for almost twenty years. They were one of the five "civilized tribes," and were
indeed quickly absorbing the white man's culture, dressing like whites, farming or running businesses, speaking English. The excuse for getting rid of
them was a trumped-up charge that they were part of a Mexican-backed plot
to drive the whites from Texas. It was almost certainly false, but it was all that
Lamar and his secretary of war needed.

Faced with the demand for his immediate departure from the state, Chief

Bowles of the Cherokees agreed to leave if the government compensated his tribe for improvements they had made on the land. The Texans agreed in principle, but offered little, and talks soon broke down. Then, by plan, the soldiers moved in. Nine hundred of them. On July 15, 1839, they attacked a Cherokee village.[11] On July 16 they cornered five hundred Cherokees in a dense thicket and swamp and proceeded to kill most of the men, including Chief Bowles. Two days later, the soldiers burned their villages, homes, and fields.

The war was just beginning. Flush with his victory over the Cherokees, Texas commander Kelsey Douglass requested permission to clean out the "rat's nest" of other, mostly peaceful, tribes in east Texas. Now there was more killing, and more fire. By the end of July, the cornfields and villages of all the Cherokees, Delawares, Shawnees, Caddoans, Kickapoos, Creeks, Muskogees, and Seminoles in east Texas were burned to the ground. Their innocence was beside the point. Whether a particular murder was committed by a Kiowa, Caddo, Wichita, or Creek seemed to Texans to make less and less difference. Most of the dispossessed Indians took their ragged, starving families and headed north to the designated Indian Territory, where some twenty thousand officially relocated Indians[12] now jostled with one another and with the native plains tribes—the last stop on what came to be known as the "trail of tears." Some of the Cherokees, including Chief Bowles's son, tried to flee to Mexico. As though to make sure there was absolutely no misunderstanding at all about the new Indian policies, the Texans hunted them down over several hundred miles and shot them, then took their women and children prisoner.[13] Only two tribes, the Alabamas and the Coushattas, were permitted to stay—though they were moved from their own fertile fields to much less desirable lands. Thus were tens of thousands of acres of superb farmland in east Texas opened to white farmers, who immediately, happily, and presumably with immaculately clean consciences, moved in.

Those were the sedentary, somewhat civilized, relatively nonwarlike, beaten-down, relocated, unmounted, agrarian Indians of east Texas, anyway. There were other sedentary tribes who lived beyond the frontier and were thus safe for the moment from this cleansing by fire: Wichitas, Wacos, Tawakonis, Kichais, Tonkawas, and a few others. But while it might be entertaining and rewarding to massacre and exile the relatively harmless and broken Muskogees and Seminoles, the real trouble, most of the "depredations," came not from the east but from the west. Everyone knew it. For all of their bravado and puffed-up war talk and insatiable greed for new territory, there was very little the Texans could do in the immense expanse of land, constituting most of Texas itself, that was ruled by the Comanches.

To understand their dilemma, look at a map of modern Texas. Draw a line from San Antonio through Austin and Waco, ending at Dallas at the forks of the Trinity River. That is roughly the western, meaning Comanche, frontier as it existed in the late 1830s, though there was very little settlement near present-day Dallas. Most of it was spread around Austin and San Antonio. That line also follows the 98th meridian almost exactly—meaning that this is where the trees start to thin out; by the 100th meridian, in the neighborhood of modern Abilene, they are mostly gone. In the region of Austin and San Antonio it marks the edge of the Balcones Escarpment, a fault zone where the big, rolling, timbered limestone hills rose from the fertile coastal plain. (They rose so abruptly that their stone ramparts reminded the Spanish of balconies in a theater, hence the name.) Piercing this line at three points were the Brazos, Colorado, and Guadalupe rivers. Imagine them as raiders' highways, sweeping down the state from the Northwest, aimed directly at the heart of the Texas frontier.

These rivers were also, of course, highways into the uplands of Comancheria, for anyone brave or stupid enough to ascend them. The problem was that, to the west of the line, from a white man's perspective, there was a vast, mysterious, frightening, bone-dry world inhabited by a fierce and primitive people who could outride, outshoot, and out-track them, and who could navigate enormous distances with alarming ease. The Indians fought mounted, too, which put the westerners, with their heavy horses, their practice of fighting on foot, and their cumbersome, muzzle-loading rifles, at a huge disadvantage. Because the Indians did not have permanent villages, they were usually impossible to locate; if you located them you were likely to wish you hadn't.

That did not stop the Texans from trying. In those early years of the republic, a motley assortment of militias, ranger companies, volunteers, and state companies trooped out regularly after Comanches following raids. They killed some Comanches, and they got lucky a few times, but mostly they did not. Mostly they were schooled by the superior Indians in plains warfare, and many of them died hard and lingering deaths. More than the Texans ever cared to admit.

One of the best examples of these early conflicts took place in February

1839 between Comanches and a state militia under Colonel John Moore. Moore was blessed with the same character trait that made pioneers want to settle the wildest and most hostile regions of the country, where their families were likely to be raped and disemboweled: heedless, unwarranted optimism. He viewed Indians as subhumans who were in need of destruction. He was known for standing next to the preacher during sermons at his church, casting a severe eye upon the congregation to make sure they did not fall asleep.[14] He had been told by the Comanches' arch-foes, the Lipan Apaches, that a band of Comanches was camped in the prairie north of Austin. The Lipans, victims of near extermination by the Comanches, could always be counted on to betray their old tormentors, to sniff them out and go running to the authorities. Afraid to fight Comanches alone, the Lipans invested much time goading the white man to chase their enemy. They also volunteered to join an expedition against them. Moore, who would not have known the first thing about how to find Comanches in the live oak thickets and limestone mesas of the Texas hill country, took them on. It should be noted that, with very few exceptions, white soldiers would have had very little chance of finding Comanches without the help of their old enemies, usually the Tonkawas or the Lipan Apaches. This was true for all of the years of the Comanche conflict. Moore's expedition was one of the first to use Indian scouts. Later it became the policy of Texas and the practice of all white soldiers. (Custer made the mistake of not heeding the warnings of his Indian trackers at Little Bighorn.) There were some able trackers among the whites—Ranger Ben McCulloch was one, Kit Carson another—but generally speaking white soldiers were unable to read signs effectively in the wilderness, even if they had received instruction. It was Indian trackers, as much as white soldiers under famous generals like George Crook, Nelson Miles, and Ranald Mackenzie, who were responsible for the destruction of the Plains Indians. The cinematic image of the dusty, standard-bearing cavalry riding out from stockade forts is often missing one key component: the Indian scout.

Thus did Colonel Moore depart, with sixty-three hastily recruited volunteers and fourteen Lipan Apaches under their chief, Castro, for the limestone breaks of the San Gabriel River north of Austin, probably near the present town of Georgetown.[15] When they reached the encampment, the Comanches had already departed, leaving a trail that headed upriver. Before they could follow, a prairie storm came howling in from the north. The men hunkered down in a grove of post oak in the fierce, penetrating cold, and waited out the driving snow and sleet. For three days. "Some of the horses froze to death," wrote Noah Smithwick, one of the captains of the expedition, "and the Indians, loth to see so much good meat go to waste, ate the flesh."[16] When the weather cleared, they pursued the Comanches northwest to the junction of the Colorado and San Saba rivers, at the site of the present town of San Saba, some seventy-five miles inside the frontier. This was, by the standards of 1839, deep inside Comanche territory. There the Lipan scouts spotted the lodge fires. Smithwick, who was with them, describes what it felt like to be a white man tracking Indians in the heart of Comancheria:

> While riding along about dark we heard a wolf howl behind us. My [Lipan] guide stopped short and assumed a listening attitude. In a few moments another answered, way to the right. Still the Indian listened so intently that his form seemed perfectly rigid. Then another set up a howl on our left. "Umph, lobo," said the Lipan, in a tone of relief. I can't say that I admired the music of the wolf at any time, but it certainly never had a more unmusical sound than on that occasion, and when I saw that even an Indian's ears were uncertain whether it was a wolf or a Comanche, I felt the cold chills creeping over me.[17]

What they had found was a village of more than five hundred people. These were Penatekas—Honey Eaters—southern Comanches so arrogantly secure in the fastness of their ancient lands that they had posted no sentinels, so comfortably oblivious to any threat from the outside that in the chill early morning of February 15 they were all asleep in their tipis, wrapped warmly in their buffalo robes. Meanwhile the volunteers—they were all starting to call themselves "rangers"—were shivering in the icy darkness, loading and priming their old single-barrel, muzzle-loading muskets, waiting for daybreak.

The events of the next hour offered a stunning illustration of what happened when white men who had no idea how to fight Plains Indians came up against a tribe that had no idea that white men would ever attack them in their heartland. Their meeting was a precursor of years of grinding frontier war between the two. From the whites' point of view, the ensuing battle amounted to a series of glaring, and nearly fatal, mistakes.

The first was when Moore, the incurable optimist, ordered his men to dismount about a mile from the Comanche camp and approach quietly on foot. This was a perfectly good surprise tactic, had it been executed in the Appalachian mountains of Kentucky one hundred years before. But this was the West. And these were Comanches. He had left his horses unguarded—perhaps the single most disastrous mistake a commander could make on the Great Plains.

He would soon pay for it. At daylight the soldiers rushed the camp, blasting directly into the tipis, firing blindly at everyone who emerged. The peaceful winter scene gave way to pure chaos with women and children shrieking, Texans "throwing open the doors of the wigwams or pulling them down and slaughtering the enemy in their beds," dogs barking, men yelling, and shots ringing out. One ranger, Andrew Lockhart, who believed his teenage daughter Matilda was being held captive, raced ahead screaming, "Matilda, if you are here, run to me!" He never found her. (It later turned out that she *was* there and she did hear him, but her cries were swallowed by the noise and gunfire.)[18]

Instead of standing and fighting, as white men might be expected to do, the Comanches did what they always did in similar circumstances: They scattered like quail and rushed for their horses. This was Moore's second mistake, again unthinkable in a surprise attack on Plains Indians: He had overlooked the Comanche horse herd. He had forgotten to stampede it. This meant that many Comanches were almost instantly mounted. Then they did what all plains tribes did automatically when given the chance: They circled back behind the soldiers and stampeded the Texans' horses. With that, the entire tenor of the battle changed.

Moore now found himself with his troopers and Indians, wandering around an empty camp with nothing to shoot at as the realization dawned on him that almost all of his men were afoot in the wilderness and that they were greatly outnumbered by mounted Indians. And now Moore got scared. In the words of Texas Ranger historian Mike Cox, he "realized that he had cut a bigger plug of tobacco than he could chew."[19] He ordered a retreat to the protective cover of a wooded ravine.[20] The Comanches now rallied and charged, but were repulsed several times by accurate and lethal long-bore rifle fire. Though he had found an effective redoubt in the rocks and trees of the ravine, Moore's brilliant surprise had suddenly turned into a desperate defensive action. With their superior numbers, the Indians could have annihilated the soldiers.[21] But no Indian plan of battle in American history ever included sacrificing large numbers of lives to take a position. That was what white men did, exemplified in attacks later on at places like Little Round Top, Iwo Jima, and Gallipoli. The Plains Indians' almost universal reluctance to press advantage was, from a tactical standpoint, one of their biggest weaknesses. It saved countless thousands of white lives.

Thus the Indians eventually withdrew. Castro, disgusted with Moore's

blundering tactics, his bizarre and cowardly order to retreat, and his failure
to destroy the Comanche village, deserted with all of his Lipans. Moore was
now forced to make a long and humiliating retreat, on foot, one hundred
fifty miles down the Colorado to Austin, carrying six wounded men, frightened the entire way of an Indian attack.[22] He believed, with his irrepressibly
optimistic self-confidence, that he had won the battle. All he had done was
to sidestep a disaster. The Comanches he had attacked retaliated immediately with a bloody raid against the settlements on the Colorado.

If the Comanches had taken a lesson from what happened on the San Saba—
and apparently they had not—it would have been that the nature of the
game had changed completely. The Texans were not the Spanish or the Mexicans. They were tougher, meaner, almost impossible to discourage, willing
to take absurd risks to secure themselves a plot of dirt, and temperamentally
well suited to the remorseless destruction of native tribes. They did not rely
on a cumbersome, heavily mounted, overly bureaucratized, state-sponsored
soldiery; they tended to handle things themselves, with volunteers who not
only were not scared of Indians but actually *liked* hunting them down and
killing them. Their president did not drone on as most government officials from time immemorial had about dreary, overly technical treaties that
granted Indians boundaries and homelands in exchange for promises to
return hostages or to refrain from harming whites. Lamar was talking about
extinction. Extermination. That was the meaning of the Moore raid, as inept
as it was. It was also the meaning of the extraordinary events that took place
in the spring and summer of 1840 in San Antonio and south Texas. They
amounted to the first big, reverberating collision between the westward-
booming Texans and the Lords of the South Plains.

On January 9, 1840, the tolling of the San Fernando cathedral bell in
San Antonio signaled the arrival of three Comanche chiefs. San Fernando is
one of the great Spanish churches in North America. Its bell is the archetypal
mission bell of the old American West. It rang matins for the Spanish and
later Mexican padres, announced attacks by Apaches and Comanches dating
from 1749. It was from its limestone tower that Mexican general Santa Anna
hung his brilliant red "no quarter" flag that signaled the start of the Battle of
the Alamo. In the Texan era, its peals dispatched minutemen to fight Mexicans and Indians.

On the bright, clear morning of January 9 there was no apparent threat, just something quite out of the ordinary. The Comanches had come to talk peace. They were alarmed at the encroachment on their old grounds, and they wanted it to stop. They had never made a treaty before with the Texans, but during Sam Houston's presidency he had constantly badgered them about it. Now they were thinking maybe this was not such a bad idea. They were especially worried by surveyors, determined men who practiced a dark and incomprehensible magic intended to deprive the Indians of their lands. Even worse, the dark magic seemed to work. The Comanches killed them in horrible ways whenever the opportunity arose.

They were received civilly by the local army commander, Colonel Henry W. Karnes, who was still recovering from the wound he received when he had been shot in the hip with an arrow in a battle with Comanches in the summer of 1838.[23] He told them bluntly that he would not discuss peace with them unless they returned all of their captives. The chiefs, apparently understanding what Karnes was saying, nodded agreeably and left, promising to return. Karnes, meanwhile, soon received a very special set of orders, unprecedented in Texas and very likely American history. They came from Secretary of War Albert Sidney Johnston, a tall, dashing soldier with a finely chiseled nose who would later be killed, heroically, while leading Rebel troops in a devastating charge against Grant's army at the Battle of Shiloh in 1862.[24] Johnston instructed Karnes, in no uncertain terms, that "the government assumes the right with regard to all Indian tribes . . . to dictate the conditions of such residence." This was rhetoric straight from Lamar. In the same vein, he then asserted that "our citizens have the right to occupy any vacant lands of the government, and they must not be interfered with by the Comanche."[25] This meant their lands were forfeit. Period. Moreover, said Johnston, if the Indians did not bring in prisoners *they were to be held hostage*—by most civilized standards an appalling way to treat an enemy who comes by invitation to negotiate peace.

The Comanches arrived on March 19. There were thirty-five warriors. They were in a festive, happy mood. They had brought thirty-two women, children, and old men with them. They were expecting no trouble. They were perhaps thinking of the old days, when the cowed and cautious Spanish and then Mexicans had allowed them free run of the town. Both the men and women were painted elaborately and attired in their finest beads, feathers, and skins. They had brought with them huge stacks of furs and a small herd of horses, apparently expecting to do a good deal of trading. The presence of these tradeable goods suggests that they may have completely misunderstood what Karnes had told them. They squatted in the street and waited. Young Indian boys played with toy bows and arrows, and white men affixed coins to trees for them to shoot.[26] A crowd of townspeople had gathered. They were not hostile, just curious.

They could not help noticing, though, that the Indians had brought only one captive with them. This was Matilda Lockhart, the same girl whose father had called to her during Colonel Moore's fight on the San Saba a year before. She had been taken in a raid in 1838 along with her younger sister, during which other family members had been killed. She was fifteen, and her appearance in the plaza in San Antonio shocked the people who saw her. As one observer—Mary Maverick, wife of a prominent local merchant—put it, Matilda's "head, face and arms were full of bruises, and sores, and her nose was actually burnt off to the bone—all the fleshy end gone with a great scab formed on the end of the bone. Both nostrils were wide open and denuded of flesh."[27] She said she had been tortured by the Comanche women. It was not just her face that had been disfigured. Her entire body bore scars from fire. In private Matilda informed the white women that what she had suffered was even worse than that. She had been "utterly degraded," she said, using the code word for rape, "and could not hold her head up again."

The Comanches were completely oblivious to the effect this had on the Texans. Many of the latter were familiar with the tortures practiced by the eastern tribes such as the Choctaws and Cherokees, which included the use of fire. But it was almost always practiced on *men*. Those tribes rarely abducted, raped, and tortured white women, as the plains tribes did.[28] Even to people accustomed to Indian violence, the sight of Matilda came as a shock. As if to make things worse, Matilda was an intelligent, perceptive girl who had learned the Comanche language quickly and thus knew that there were other captives in Indian camps. She estimated fifteen. She told the Texans about these captives.

This was all prelude to the meeting, which took place in a one-story courthouse that would go down in history as the Council House. The building was made of limestone and had a flat timber roof and dirt floor.[29] Twelve Indians, all Penatekas and variously described as "chiefs" or "principal men," were ranged across from three appointed Texas commissioners. Their spokesman was Spirit Talker (his Comanche name was variously given as "Muguara" or "Mukewarrah"), a good-humored and apparently peaceable type with a taste for whiskey who had recently hosted ranger Noah Smithwick for three months in his camp, at one point facing down a group of Wacos who wanted to kill Smithwick.[30] Smithwick had liked him and found him intelligent and sincere, and had "many long, earnest talks" with him. He had spoken eloquently to Smithwick about the white man's destruction of his hunting grounds, saying

> The white man comes and cuts down the trees, building houses and fences, and the buffalos get frightened and leave and never come back, and the Indians are left to starve, or if we follow the game we trespass on the hunting ground of other tribes and war ensues. . . . If the white men would draw a line defining their claims and keep on their side of it the red men would not molest them.[31]

If he sounds like a white man's sort of Indian, it must be noted that he was also headman of the band that had made the raid on the Lockhart homestead, thus the same group that had killed her family members, taken her and her younger sister, and tortured her and raped her. It was Spirit Talker's village that Colonel Moore had attacked on the San Saba.

Inside the courthouse, the Texans got right to business. They demanded to know why the Comanches had brought only one captive. Spirit Talker replied that there were indeed more captives, but they were in camps over which he had no control. He was very likely telling the truth, but no one believed him. He then explained that he believed that all of the captives could be ransomed. Of course, he added helpfully, they would require a high ransom in the form of goods, ammunition, blankets, and vermillion. But that could all be worked out. Then he surveyed his guests and concluded, with a grand gesture: "How do you like that answer?"

He may have thought he was being clever, or reasonable, or just plain chatty. Or maybe he was mistranslated. In any case, he grossly misunderstood his audience. He and his people considered themselves honorable warriors. To them, abduction of captives was honorable warfare. So was rough treatment of captives. To Spirit Talker, Matilda was an item of plunder, something not quite fully human, something to be bargained for. The Texans, meanwhile, considered the Indians vicious, conscienceless killers. Their treatment of the pathetic, noseless girl was gruesome and irrefutable evidence of that. Whatever Spirit Talker had in mind, or meant to say, those were the last words he ever spoke.

Colonel William Fisher, one of the Texas commissioners, replied sharply:

"I do *not* like your answer. I told you not to come here again without bringing in your prisoners. You have come against my orders. Your women and children may depart in peace. . . . When those prisoners are returned, your chiefs here present may likewise go free. Until then we hold you as hostages."[32] As he spoke, a detachment of soldiers marched into the courthouse and took up positions in the front and back. When the astonished Comanches finally figured out, through the terrified translator, what had been said, they panicked and rushed for the doors.

The soldiers closed ranks. Spirit Talker, who got to the door first, drew his knife and stabbed a soldier. Then the soldiers opened fire, dropping Spirit Talker and other Indians as well as several of their own people. They fired again. The room was filled with noise and smoke and blood and ricocheting rifle balls. One soldier, Matthew "Old Paint" Caldwell, took a stray bullet in the leg. Hobbled, he grabbed a musket from one of the chiefs, blew his head off, then used it to bludgeon another Indian to death. The fight spilled outside, and now a full-scale, Hollywood-style melee erupted in the plaza. The Indians who had waited outside—men, women, and children—turned on the onlookers, many of whom were armed, and the fighting spread. People who saw it said the Indian women and boys fought as hard as the men.[33] One Indian boy shot a district judge through the heart with a "toy" arrow, killing him. The Comanches never really had a chance. Though it started as a street fight, it turned quickly to massacre, and then, soon enough, into something that resembled a turkey shoot in which the Comanches played the unaccustomed role of fleeing, terrified victims.

Within half an hour the "fight" was over. Now there was just a large, bloodthirsty, vengeful mob hunting Comanches through the streets of San Antonio. It was not pretty. A group of Indians who made it to the river were picked off, one by one, as they swam across.[34] Every Indian was hunted down. The house-to-house hunt was grim, and cruel. Some Indians took refuge in stone houses and locked the doors.[35] In Mary Maverick's firsthand account, several white men climbed to the top of a building and set it on fire with a "candlewick ball soaked in turpentine." Two Comanche men soon emerged from the smoke and fire. One had his head split open with an ax; the other was shot dead.

When it was over, thirty warriors, three women, and two children lay dead. Thirty-two were taken prisoner, many of them badly wounded. Seven Texans were killed, and ten wounded. (The town's sole surgeon, a German immigrant, worked through the night to save the whites; the Indians were unattended.)[36] The soldiers threw the remaining thirty-two Comanches in the dirt-floored jail behind the courthouse. The next day a woman who had not been wounded was given a horse and rations and told to ride to her people with the news of what happened. She was also to deliver an ultimatum: The survivors would be put to death unless the Comanche bands released the fifteen captives that Matilda Lockhart had told them about. If the woman did not return in twelve days, during which time there would be a full truce, "these prisoners shall be killed, for we will know that you have killed our captive friends and relatives."[37] If the Texans felt good about their bargaining position, they would soon learn otherwise.

Under normal circumstances, we would never have found out how this news was received in the Comanche villages. But in this case a young captive named Booker Webster, who was later released, left a harrowing account. When the woman arrived with her news, the Comanches reacted with a mixture of horror, despair, and cold fury. More or less in that order. The women screamed and wailed in mourning. They slashed their arms, and faces, and breasts, and lopped off fingers. Some even injured themselves fatally. The men moaned and rocked back and forth and some chopped off their hair. So large was the horse herd belonging to the dead chiefs that it took two days to kill and burn them all (a Comanche custom).

Then, through the smoke of burning horseflesh, they unleashed their feelings of depthless grief and anger on the hostages. In Booker Webster's account, "they took the American captives, thirteen in number, and roasted and butchered them to death with horrible cruelties."[38] One can only imagine what drawn-out horrors were perpetrated on them. The captives included children, one of whom was the six-year-old sister of Matilda Lockhart.

The Indians never responded to the ultimatum. They were in fact terribly demoralized, leaderless, and unsure what to do. In the nuanced world of the Comanches, where signs and spirits and magic and medicine were important decision-making tools, such an event was a profound spiritual blow, a completely mystifying shift in the *puha* of the band's headmen. With a white man's mentality, they might have simply destroyed San Antonio by fire or at least wreaked terrible havoc. They did not do that. Instead, several days later, three hundred warriors led by Isimanica rode to the San Jose Mission, just south of town, where they demanded the return of the prisoners and challenged the Texans to a fight. The Texans refused to give up the prisoners and insisted, bizarrely, that because the twelve-day truce was still in effect, they could not fight. Or perhaps the commanding officer was simply afraid of leaving the mission walls. Many of the white soldiers thought so. It was a strange scene, one that was rarely if ever repeated on the plains: a large force of Indians trying, unsuccessfully, to goad white soldiers into combat. One of the officers, Lysander Wells, accused the commanding officer, Captain William D. Redd, of cowardice. They promptly fought a duel, and killed each other. Though the Indians remained in prison, most eventually escaped. The women, some of whom were given to San Antonio citizens as slaves, also escaped. Oddly, there was, eventually, another exchange of captives that brought a boy—Booker Webster—and a young girl back to civilization. The girl was almost as badly scarred as Matilda Lockhart. They were spared because they had been adopted into the tribe.

Thus ended what became famous in the annals of Texas as the Council House Fight. Many Texans saw this as a sign that Texas, in the Lamar era, would brook no compromises with Indians. They were right. But the Texans had also made a terrible blunder that resulted immediately in the torture-killing of the rest of the hostages, set off a massive wave of retaliatory raids against settlements that ended up taking dozens of white lives, and destroyed for years whatever confidence the Comanches had in the integrity of the Texas government. One can only wonder what William Lockhart, whose lovely six-year-old daughter was slowly roasted alive to avenge the massacre, thought of the strategy. And though the whites crowed that they had killed twelve "leading chiefs," there is no evidence to support that claim.[39] From Smithwick's account, Spirit Talker was the leader of a relatively small group within the Penateka band. Isimanica, the most dangerous of the chiefs and far more powerful than Spirit Talker, was not there, nor was Isawaconi, who claimed to be the main chief of the Penatekas. Nor were prominent chiefs Pah-hah-yuco, Old Owl, Little Wolf, and Buffalo Hump.[40] The men who were killed were without a doubt leaders, but not big chiefs. Finally, as it turned out, there was little evidence that the Comanches at the Council House were involved in any recent raids on Texas settlements.[41] At the time of the attack, in fact, Isimanica had apparently been abroad among the lodges hawking the idea of peace.[42]

Now, instead of securing the peace, white men in south Texas were about to be targets of the greatest mobilization in Comanche history.

Seven

✦━═◈═━✦

DREAM VISIONS AND APOCALYPSE

✦━═◈═━✦

IN LEGEND AND history, the Penatekas (Pen-'ah-took-uhs) were the largest and most powerful of all the Comanche bands. They had swept the Apaches into Mexico and fought the Spanish to a standstill in Texas. They raided, at will, deep into Mexico, and dominated the tribes of central Texas. They were also the one large Comanche band that had come into close and constant contact with the invaders and colonizers. The other main bands—Yamparika, Kotsoteka, Quahadi, and Nokoni—still held themselves largely aloof from settlements and soldiers, from their cultures and their invisible white man's diseases. They stayed farther out on the Great Plains, following the buffalo herds. The Quahadis dealt extensively with the merchants of Santa Fe, but only through the Comanchero intermediaries.

This proximity to whites had changed the Penatekas. Profoundly. As Spirit Talker pointed out, they had seen the buffalo depart, never to come back to the southernmost reaches of the plains. They were thus forced to hunt different sorts of increasingly smaller game. And eventually, as the game thinned out, into trading for food with the white man or with farmers like the Wichitas or Wacos. As years passed, they had more and more contact with whites, not all of it unfriendly. They cadged food and stole small useful or ornamental things. Most had learned to speak Spanish and some had even learned English. They discovered that clothing made of cotton or wool was warmer in winter and cooler in summer than their traditional skins.

They began, like the members of the Five Civilized Tribes, to adopt white clothing. Metal kettles were more practical than clay jars, and when they wore out could be used to make arrow points. Ready-made glass beads were brighter than handcrafted shell beads.[1] With every raid they accumulated the white man's artifacts—his utensils and tools and weapons. It was a sort of cultural pollution that could not be stopped. There developed a casual intimacy between the cultures that was somehow interwoven with all the blood and violence and hostility.

Such intimacy could be seen in a story from the hill country a few years later. A woman who was part of a German settlement recalled a typical Comanche encounter. "One day while I was home," she said, "in walked a big buck indian. I had just made a successful bake of bread and was exceedingly proud of it. . . . The big scamp sized up everything, spied my bread, picked it up and walked off with it. . . ." There is an interesting and almost funny offhandedness here: It would not have been surprising if she had picked up a rolling pin and beaned him with it. Other people in her town complained that Comanches would show up at mealtime expecting generous hospitality and would steal small items from around the house.[2] To a Yamparika, living in a village far to the north on the Arkansas River, such a scene would have been beyond imagining.

Texans, too, were beginning to understand this change. The following account was published in the *Houston Telegraph and Texas Register* on May 30, 1838, after a delegation of Comanches had visited President Sam Houston, at his invitation.

All expected to meet a band of fierce, athletic warriors with sinewy limbs and gigantic frames, but what was their astonishment on arriving at the President's House, to behold paraded there about 25 diminutive, squalid, half-naked, poverty stricken savages, armed with bows and arrows, and mounted on wretched horses and mules! Every feeling of admiration was dispelled at once, and our citizens viewed them with mingled feelings of pity and contempt . . . their squaws and children were scattered in all directions through the city picking up old tin plates, iron hoops, clippings of tin, glass bottles, and similar rubbish which they appeared to consider extremely valuable. . . .

Mr. Legrand, who has resided several years among the Comanches, states that this party belongs to a portion of the tribe called "Comanches of the Woods"—who inhabit the hilly country northeast of Bexar [San Antonio]. They are a poor, degraded, sorry race and hardly have any resemblance to the Comanches of the prairie.[3]

This is a remarkable account in many ways. First, in its sneering, overtly racist dismissal of the Indians, and in its frank astonishment that real Indians were not like James Fenimore Cooper Indians. Second, in the fact that, minus the Anglocentrism, the writer is substantially correct in his observations. Comanches *were* short, and they *were* unimpressive physically, as almost all observers had noted. They *were* half-naked (it was summer in Houston, so they wore simple breechclouts), they *did* ride mustangs that were small, unshod, scrawny, and unattractive by European standards. They used bows and arrows as their main weapons. They were undoubtedly poor in the eyes of the average Texan, having no houses or real estate or bank accounts. And they of course loved to scavenge tin and iron: That was how they made arrows, knives, and lances.

The reporter got the larger sense of it right, too. The Penatekas, by virtue of years of cross-cultural pollination, were a decayed and degenerative version of the truly wild Comanches of the plains. The proximity had its physical effects as well. Smallpox epidemics had killed huge numbers of Penatekas in 1816 and 1839 (cholera would destroy most of what was left in 1849). Their hunting grounds had become so depleted by the influx of settlers that soon many in the band would be on the verge of starving to death. They had indeed become the Comanches of the Woods, dependent now on the alien culture for their livelihood, while the rest of the bands still rode free and wild on the high plains. In fact, while the Penatekas were being cross-pollinated out of existence and reeling from white man's diseases, you could argue that the Comanches of the high plains were still at the peak of their historical power.[4] Where the reporter was wrong was in the implied assumption that this decadent version of the pure plains warrior would not amount to much of a military threat. He was quite wrong about that. The pathetic little half-naked folks still constituted the greatest light cavalry on earth; no more than a handful of American or Texan soldiers were yet a match for them.

Buffalo Hump had a vision. It had come to him in the night. It was a violent, mystical, all-encompassing, apocalyptic sort of dream vision in which the lying and treacherous Texans, perpetrators of the massacre at the Council House, were attacked and driven into the sea. Buffalo Hump was a Penateka chief. Until recently he was a lower sort of chief, the type that could recruit warriors for this or that raid but did not enjoy the jefe status of the big civil and war chiefs. But now many of the *paraibos* were dead. Some had been killed in the disastrous 1816 smallpox epidemic that swept through Comanche, Wichita, and Caddo villages and killed as many as four thousand Comanches,[5] taking fully half of the estimated eight thousand band members at the turn of the nineteenth century. At least four headmen were lost during another smallpox epidemic in 1839; twelve more war chiefs were killed at the Council House Fight. Buffalo Hump was a survivor, a charismatic leader who spoke fluent Spanish and would live to fight many campaigns, even after most of his band had been destroyed. He happened to be Spirit Talker's nephew.[6] He had first encountered white colonists, *taibos,* at the Barton Springs settlement in Austin in 1828, where he conversed with them in Spanish and charmed them and was described as "a magnificent specimen of savage manhood."[7] That was before the Comanches had figured out how unfriendly and acquisitive the Anglo-Texans were. A German scientist who met him in the 1840s described him this way:

> The pure, unadulterated picture of a North American Indian, who, unlike the rest of his tribe, scorned every form of European dress. His body naked, a buffalo robe around his loins, brass rings on his arms, a string of beads around his neck, and with his long, coarse black hair hanging down, he sat there with the serious facial expression of the North American Indian which seems to be apathetic to the Europeans.[8]

Though no photograph of Buffalo Hump exists, there is one of his son, who was said to look like him. It shows a strikingly handsome young man of perhaps twenty with shoulder-length hair; wise, calm eyes; epicene features; and the thousand-yard stare that Indians always assumed for the camera. Buffalo Hump had one of those Comanche names—there were a large number of them—that the prudish whites could not quite bring themselves to translate. His Nermernuh name, properly transliterated, was Po-cha-na-quar-hip, which meant "erection that won't go down."[9]

Buffalo Hump's dream vision was uncommonly powerful. In the weeks of rage and mourning that followed the massacre in San Antonio, in the crushing heat of the high Texas summer, when riders spread the news throughout Comancheria, it held enormous, raw appeal. The vision, like many visions experienced by war chiefs, was, at its core, an idea for a raid. But this would not be just any raid. Driving the Texans into the sea would take a military expedition such as the Comanches seldom ever mounted.

Throughout July, Buffalo Hump gathered his forces. He sent messengers to the distant bands—Yamparika, Kotsoteka, Nokoni—but succeeded in getting only a few recruits. The northern bands were leery of the idea, both because of the magically powerful disease that had just swept through their southern brethren and because of the deaths of so many war chiefs. There was far too much bad medicine in the South. They also had their own troubles in the North: Cheyennes and Arapahoes had pushed southward into the buffalo ranges between the Arkansas and Canadians rivers, a direct assault on Comancheria. And perhaps they understood, too, what they would understand so well later on, which was that the Penatekas, in their proximity to the white man, were no longer traditional Comanches. They were becoming something different, something degraded.

But most of the other Penateka chiefs, including Isimanica, Little Wolf, and Santa Anna, agreed to follow. Some Kiowas came, too. Kiowas had trouble refusing a good fight; they had some mystical kinship with the Comanches even though they spoke a different language and had a culture that was more complex than anything the Comanches had. By midsummer Buffalo Hump had more than four hundred warriors and some six hundred camp followers. The latter—boys and women—were necessary, because driving all of the Texans into the sea and watching their blood spill into the blue waters of the Gulf of Mexico was going to take longer than a few weeks. This was going to be a war against the Tejanos, and Buffalo Hump needed logistical support.

On August 1, they rode, one thousand of them, down from the hard, stream-crossed limestone battlements of the Balcones Escarpment, down along the gorgeous cypress-lined banks and crystalline pools of the Blanco River, down to its confluence with the spring-fed San Marcos and out onto the blackland prairie of south-central Texas.[10] Their destination: the towns and settlements strung out along the rivers and creeks that swept southward toward the grassy plains and shallow bays of Texas's coastal bend. As they got farther south they moved by night. On August 4 they rode by the light of the rising Comanche moon, penetrating beyond the line of the frontier and deep into the settlements of Anglo-Texas.

When Texas Ranger Ben McCulloch crossed their trail two days later near the town of Gonzales, he could scarcely believe his eyes. One thousand riders had passed almost completely unnoticed through territory that, while not thickly populated, contained many homesteads and settlements.

No one in south Texas had ever seen anything like this. The people who had spotted the invaders were mostly dead. One of them was a man named Tucker Foley, who had encountered a screen of twenty-seven warriors. They cornered him at a water hole, roped him and dragged him out, cut the bottoms of his feet off, made him walk around the burned prairie for a while for their entertainment, then shot and scalped him.[11] McCulloch and a small force of volunteers shadowed the Indian force. There were far too many to fight.

What followed is known to Texans as the Great Linnville Raid. In history it is often twinned with the event that it precipitated, famous as the Battle of Plum Creek. They happened within the span of two weeks. Together they form a singular and often surreal piece of Texas history, a spasm of anger and violence on a scale rarely seen in the West. It was Buffalo Hump's greatest—and worst—moment, and it was one of the first moments of true greatness for the men who were beginning to call themselves Texas Rangers and who would soon, in those very same hills and prairies, having learned how to fight from the Comanches themselves, change the nature of frontier warfare in North America.

At four p.m. on August 6, 1840, just short of five months after the Council House Fight, Buffalo Hump's army slammed into the town of Victoria, about one hundred miles southeast of San Antonio and twenty-five miles from the coast. The town had received no warning, and the Indians entered easily. They killed a dozen people, swirled through the streets as the citizens fled to rooftops and windows, and opened up with rifle fire. Here, as usual, Comanche medicine detoured what might have been a wholesale slaughter. The Comanches did not close in for the kill and simply proceed, house by house, to kill all of Victoria. Instead, they circled the town as though it were a herd of buffalo, stole horses and cattle, carried off a small black girl, and generally made mischief. The sheer number of horses, which you can think of in modern terms as sequences of one-thousand-dollar bills deposited instantly into your checking account, distracted them. They were not materialistic except when it came to horses. Horses they valued, for themselves and for what they would bring in trade. Meanwhile, the residents of Victoria had time to build barricades. The Comanches attacked again in the morning, but were discouraged by rifle fire. They buzzed like hornets on the outskirts of town for a while, stole somewhere between fifteen hundred and two thousand horses, and, leaving thirteen corpses and many wounded behind, spurred on for the coastal road. They did not have any special idea where they were going, but they were following Buffalo Hump's vision. They were riding to the sea, with as many as three thousand horses.

The tribe cut a bloody swath of violence across the coastal lowlands, looting, killing, and burning on their way to Matagorda Bay, and sweeping the entire country of horse stock as they went.[12] They took captives, too, including a Mrs. Nancy Crosby, the granddaughter of Daniel Boone, and her baby. Since she could not quiet the child, they killed it, spearing it in front of her.[13] On August 8 the army rode in a spectacular crescent formation into the coastal town of Linnville, instantly enveloping it. Now, quickly, Buffalo Hump's vision seemed to be fulfilled. The panicked inhabitants fled before the thundering Comanches in the only direction they could—toward the sea, and into the only possible safe haven—sailboats, several of them, anchored in shoal water about a hundred yards from shore.[14] Many fleeing townspeople were cut down in the water, including one Major H. O. Watts, the young customs inspector, who had just gotten married. His wife, described by one witness as "a remarkably fine looking woman,"[15] was captured. When the Indians tried to strip her, the usual first move with any captive, they encountered the mysterious and formidable obstacle of her whalebone corset, which they could not undo. Frustrated, they strapped her to the back of a horse and took her along with them. Many residents saved themselves by boarding a large schooner that was also anchored just offshore.

The Indians, meanwhile, had discovered the miraculous contents of the warehouses: cloth and fabric, umbrellas, hats, fine clothing, and hardware. Linnville was an important shipping center; the merchandise was destined for San Antonio and the Mexican trade. The Indians removed all they could carry from the warehouses, then set them on fire. The townspeople watched from the boats—there was not a breath of wind that day, so their boats were becalmed—as their homes, their business offices, and all but one of the warehouses went up in flames.[16] As the town burned, the Indians whooped and danced and herded cattle into pens where they hacked and shot them to death. This description comes from John J. Linn, a resident of Victoria at the time of the raids:

> These Indians made free with, and went dashing about the blazing village, amid their screeching squaws and "little Injuns," like demons in a drunken sat-

urnalia, with Robinson's [a local merchant] hats on their heads and Robinson's umbrellas bobbing about on every side like tipsy young balloons.[17]

After burning the town, which was so thoroughly destroyed that it was never rebuilt, the Indians departed, heading back the way they had come.[18] If their antics in the town seemed like a bad dream, what happened next suggested a full-scale hallucination. The truth was that Buffalo Hump had lost control of his army. Vengeance had dissolved into something that more closely resembled pure fun. It had started with the orgy of horse-thieving in Victoria—even for Comanches, three thousand horses was an immense haul. Then came the astonishing discovery of the Linnville warehouses, stuffed with the accoutrements of bourgeois life. The Nermernuh had arrived in town in buckskins and breechclouts. They left wearing stovepipe hats, high leather boots, and expensive pigeon-tailed coats with bright brass buttons worn backward and buttoned up from behind.[19] They had taken the calicoes and bright ribbons from the warehouses and festooned their lances with them and plaited them into the tails of their horses. The group that moved off down the Victoria road was not just picturesque, a splash of brilliant color in the thornscrub of south Texas, but heavy with all the swag they could carry, which included iron hoops and less frivolous hardware for making weapons. It was all packed on horses and mules. Whether Buffalo Hump believed that his vision had been fulfilled is not known. Whatever he thought, the plan for a glorious extended war against the Tejanos had been replaced by a singular urge to get back home with a previously unimaginable quantity of loot.

The Texans were completely aware of this. Such a huge train, packed with stolen goods and tipis and containing women and children and even a few old men, moving so ponderously across the wide-open, dun-colored prairie, was not something easily missed. Nor was it an opportunity to be squandered. Three separate companies of men were formed to fight the invaders. One of them, consisting of 125 recruits from the Guadalupe River settlements under Captain John J. Tumlinson, intercepted the army near Victoria. They did what most *taibo* soldiers of the era had been taught to do: They dismounted and prepared to fight. In a fight with Comanches, dismounting on open ground was like signing your own death warrant. Men on foot against mounted men moving at 20 or 30 miles per hour who could shoot twelve arrows in the time it took to reload a rifle and fire it once was not a fair fight. It was only a question of how long the men on foot might live, and how lucky they might get in shooting a few Comanches out of the saddle.

Tumlinson's men were quickly surrounded by swirling, circling Comanches. They should have been slaughtered where they stood. But on this day the Comanches had other interests. Mainly, the defense of their groaning caravan. Tumlinson's men retreated as quickly as they could, and the Indians drew off, more concerned with their women and packhorses than with Tumlinson's pathetic attack.

The army continued north, toward the hill country, in the searing heat that had turned most of the prairie brown. In a normal raid, especially a big one, Comanches would attack, then split up into small groups and ride hard for the hinterlands. This was old, established practice among mounted Plains Indians. Now they did neither; in their arrogance they lumbered up the most obvious trail home. Having absconded with such prodigious poundage of material goods, perhaps they had no choice. On August 12 they were spotted by scouts near present-day Lockhart, moving in a northwesterly direction through the long grasses and dark loam of one of Texas's loveliest prairies. Eyewitness John Henry Brown describes the sight. They had

a full view of Indians passing diagonally across our front, about a mile distant. They were singing and gyrating in divers grotesque ways, evidencing their great triumph, and utterly oblivious of danger. Up to the time they had lost but one warrior; they had killed 20 persons.[20]

They had been expected. In addition to his other errors of command, Buffalo Hump had committed the sin of being perfectly predictable. The white men knew where he would cross the Guadalupe and other rivers. Awaiting him, thus, were an assortment of two hundred men who had arisen spontaneously from the towns of Gonzales, Lavaca, Victorai, Cuero, and Texana. (Tumlinson's men would not make the battle.) None were soldiers in the normal sense of the word. They included in their ranks many young men who had arrived in Texas after the Battle of San Jacinto looking specifically for adventure, violence, and glory. They were not sodbusters who shouldered long rifles only when danger approached. They were sharp-eyed, audacious, and fearless twenty-four-year-olds with little sense of their own mortality and a distinct taste for combat. "They were drawn to the West by the wildness and danger and daring of the frontier life," wrote Mary Maverick in her memoir.[21] They were highly motivated to track Indians and kill them and happily did it without pay or reward. Comanches, of course, had never seen anything like this breed of men. There were Tonkawa Indians, too, spoiling as always for revenge. All were under the command of Major General Felix Huston, the head of the state militia, a soldier of the old school who had once fought a duel over military promotion with Secretary of War Albert Sidney Johnston.[22]

Huston now proceeded to make his own large blunder. Perhaps predictably, it was the same one Tumlinson had made two days before: He ordered his men to dismount on the open plain, and form a "hollow square" battle line. As before, mounted warriors encircled them, firing arrows and using their thick, buffalo hide shields to deflect bullets (which they did quite effectively). Dismounted men were wounded, horses were killed. According to Brown

> This was the fatal error of the day. There we remained for thirty or forty precious minutes, during which time the warriors were dexterously engaging us, while their squaws and unarmed men were pressing the immense cavalcade of pack animals and loose horses forward to the mountains of the Rio Blanco and San Marcos. At the same time, their sharpshooters were inflicting on us and our horses serious damage.[23]

As things got worse, Major General Huston was implored by his more experienced Indian fighters, notably Ben McCulloch and Matthew Caldwell, to order a mounted charge. While Huston was pondering his deteriorating situation, something remarkable happened: One of the Comanche war chiefs, who had charged very close to the Texans, using his shield with great skill, was hit by a bullet and fell from his horse. He was soon seized by two comrades and carried away. There was a moment when the frenzy of the Comanche attack seemed to abate. From their ranks came an eerie, wolflike howling sound. Something had gone wrong with the medicine; perhaps, as was sometimes the case, the Indians believed that the warrior's *puha* would make him invulnerable to bullets.

Caldwell, fully grasping the moment, yelled to Huston, "Now, General! Charge 'em! They are whipped!" And for perhaps the first time in history, a large group of nonuniformed, mounted, lightly armed men galloped forward to confront a mounted Plains Indian tribe on its own terms and in its own style of combat. Even more important, the attack marked the first time that a representative of traditional fighting—General Huston—had given way in military tactics to the buckskin-clad Indian fighters of the frontier, represented by McCulloch and Caldwell. The Battle of Plum Creek, as it would go down in history, signified the beginning of the shift in fighting style that would find its true form in the next few years in the Texas Rangers. It is noteworthy that one of the men fighting for Texas at Plum Creek was John Coffee Hays—one of those fearless young men who had come looking for adventure. He was destined to become the most legendary Ranger of them all.[24]

Mounted now, and screaming like Comanches, the Texans spurred forward and crashed into the long column, holding their fire until the last moment, and unleashing a volley that dropped fifteen Indians. They stampeded the herd of loose horses, which then slammed broadside into the packhorses, many of whom were carrying heavy loads of iron and were bogged down on muddy ground. The pandemonium was such that Comanche warriors, already spooked by the bad medicine of the chief's death, now found themselves unable to maneuver. They panicked and began to flee. What ensued was a fight between retreating Comanches and advancing Texans that straggled on over fifteen miles of ground. It was a bloody fight. The Indians stopped long enough to kill their captives, including Daniel Boone's granddaughter Nancy Crosby, who was tied to a tree and drilled with arrows. Mrs. Watts was more fortunate. She, too, was tied to a tree and shot, but her whalebone corset deflected the arrow. She escaped the murderous events of the day with a flesh wound and terrible sunburn.[25] White soldiers could be equally unforgiving. One of them who came upon a dying Comanche woman was seen stamping her with his boot, then impaling her on an Indian lance.

The Texans considered the battle a major victory. Whether it was or not remains, to this day, very hard to tell, mainly because, as usual, the Indians never offered their own version of events. While historians agree that the Texans charged and the Indians fled and that one Texan was killed and seven wounded, there is little agreement on how many Indians died, or how successful their escape was. Estimates of Indian dead were variously given as 25, 50, 60, 80 and 138, though the number of bodies actually recovered was somewhere between 12 and 25.

But there is evidence that the Indian retreat was, in fact, tactically quite brilliant. The Comanches were most concerned with protecting their wives and children. This they seem to have done. Though they lost much of their loot, they held on to many of the horses. According to Linn, who was entirely of the glorious-victory-for-the-whites school of history, only "several hundred head of horses and mules were recovered."[26] Out of three thousand. What this points to is a victory that was possibly not quite as magnificent as it is portrayed in Ranger histories and other accounts sympathetic to the Texans. In the view of historians Jodye and Thomas Schilz, the Comanche strategy during the battle consisted of a number of feints, executed on horse-back at high speed, that confused the whites, screened their camp followers, and thus allowed them to escape.

> The display of color and equestrian skill made for a dazzling distraction that gave the women and children time to begin herding the stolen livestock toward the northwest to get it out of Huston's reach. . . . Despite suffering heavy losses, Buffalo Hump had led a raid all the way to the Texas coast and had brought most of his people safely home. . . . The Battle of Plum Creek was a tactical draw.[27]

When the battle was over the Tonkawas, who by most reports had done a good deal of the heavy fighting, thus paying off their ancient blood debts, gathered around a big fire they had built. They began singing. Several men then dragged a dead Comanche toward the fire. They cut small fillets from his body, skewered them on sticks, thrust them into the fire, cooked them, and ate them. After a few mouthfuls, according to Robert Hall, who witnessed this, "They began to act as if they were very drunk. They danced, raved, howled and sang, and invited me to get up and eat a slice of Comanche. They said it would make me very brave."[28]

If some doubt lingers as to the magnificence of the Texans' victory at Plum Creek, there is no disagreement at all about what happened two months later on the Upper Colorado River. Having convinced his superiors that the Comanches had not suffered enough for their atrocities of the Victoria and Linnville raids, Colonel John Moore, still smarting from his humiliation on the San Saba in 1839, drummed up a squad of volunteers for another punitive expedition. On October 5 he left with ninety white men and twelve Lipan Apaches and marched northwest up the Colorado River. By mid-October he had gone farther west than any Anglo-Texan had ever gone before, some three hundred miles west of Austin. There the Lipans found a Comanche camp of sixty lodges (eight to ten people in a lodge was normal). According to some accounts, this was Buffalo Hump's camp.[29] The soldiers camped a few miles away. It was a clear, cold October night; the earth was white with frost.

They attacked at dawn, and because Moore had learned his lesson on the San Saba, they came on horseback. Once again, the Indians, who did not believe that *taibos* could possibly attack them so far inside Comancheria, were completely unprepared. What followed, as the Texans plunged into the village, was more butchery than battle. The Indians who managed to

escape their burning tipis found that they were cornered against the Colorado River. Many died crossing it. Those who managed to crawl up the other
bank were pursued, some for up to four miles, and shot down.[30] Many were
left to die in burning tipis. Only two soldiers were killed, evidence that most
of the Comanches never even got to their weapons. Moore himself dispensed
with the usual niceties about trying to avoid killing women and children
(a staple of western military reports), saying that he had left "the bodies or
men, women and children—wounded, dying and dead on every hand." He
claimed to have killed one hundred thirty people in about half an hour and
there is no reason to doubt him. He took thirty-four prisoners, captured five
hundred horses, and destroyed the village by fire. Thus were the sins of Linnville and Victoria avenged. But the big war had just begun.

Eight

WHITE SQUAW

HERE IS HISTORY that is based on hard, documented fact; history that is colored with rumor, speculation, or falsehood; and history that exists in what might be termed the hinterlands of the imagination. The latter describes many of the nineteenth-century accounts of the captivity of Cynthia Ann Parker, the legendary "White Squaw" who chose the red man over the white man and a life of unwashed savagery over the comforts of "civilization." Most are informed by a sort of bewildered disbelief that anyone, but especially a woman, could possibly want to do that. The result, as in this 1893 telling by a former federal Indian agent, is often a weirdly incongruous attempt to graft European romantic ideals on to Stone Age culture:

> As the years rolled by, Cynthia Ann developed the charms of captivating womanhood, and the heart of more than one dusky warrior was pierced by the Ulyssean darts of her laughing eyes and the ripple of her silvery voice, and laid at her feet the trophy of the chase.[1]

There is plenty of literature like this, and much of it amounts to a denial that there was any such thing as Indian culture. It's all Tristan and Isolde. Cynthia Ann is seen falling in love, wandering through fragrant, flower-strewn fields, discussing the prospects of connubial bliss with her warrior swain, and so forth. (In another completely made-up "historical" account that appeared in many places, her younger brother and fellow captive, John Parker, courts a "night-eyed" "Aztec" beauty, a captive herself, whiling away the idle hours in amorous talk. She later risks her own life to nurse him through smallpox, and they ride off into the sunset together.)² Other versions of her life assumed the reverse: a harsh reality in which Cynthia Ann was suffering terrible hardship and "degradation." But in this case it was happening *entirely against her will.* The idea, expressed in delicate Victorian code, of course, was that she was forced to have sex with greasy, dark-skinned, subhuman Indians because she could not possibly have chosen to do so on her own. "No situation can be depicted to our minds," sighed the *Clarksville Northern Standard* in northeast Texas, "replete with half the horrors of that unfortunate young lady's."³

Both approaches grew out of the same fundamental problem: No one really knew what happened to her, and no one ever knew what she thought. People were thus free to indulge their prejudices. Though she became, in lore, legend, and history, the most famous captive of her era, the fact was that, at the age of nine, she had disappeared without a trace into the incomprehensible vastness of the Great Plains. Most captives were either killed or ransomed within a few months or years. The White Squaw stayed out twenty-four years, enough time to forget almost everything she had once known, including her native language, to marry and have three children and live the full, complex, and highly specialized life of a Plains Indian. She was seen twice, and only briefly: The first sighting happened ten years after her capture; the second, five years after that. Almost every other moment of that time is, in conventional historical terms, completely opaque. Plains Indians did not write letters or journals or record their legal proceedings, or even keep copies of treaties—history meant nothing to them.

That does not mean, however, that she has gone entirely into legend. Understanding her life requires a bit of digging about in the Indian affairs of the middle century, some historical sleuthing with the benefit of one hundred sixty years of hindsight. It is possible to ascertain which Comanche bands she lived with, where those bands lived, when and where epidemics of white man's diseases struck them, when they won or lost battles, the identity of her husband and the names and approximate birth dates of her three children.

Perhaps most important, we know the general behavior of the tribe toward what might be called a "loved captive." To victims of Comanche brutality, it was almost impossible to believe that such a phenomenon existed.

Yet it did, and it was not uncommon. The infertile Comanche women and statistically death-prone Comanche men were undiscriminating in whom they invited into the tribe. Their captives included Mexicans, Spanish, members of many other tribes (including hated foes like the Utes and Apaches), whites of all descriptions, and slave children. Their bloodline, as twentieth-century studies would show, was extremely impure compared to other tribes. The ones they adopted were usually prepubescent children. Adult women were either killed or, like Rachel Plummer, destined for hard lives as slaves, sexual and otherwise. Some, like Matilda Lockhart, were terribly abused. Loved captives were something entirely different. They were embraced and cherished and treated as full family members. This was Cynthia Ann.

Fortunately, in view of Cynthia Ann's resonating silence on the subject, there exist several parallel accounts. The best comes from Bianca "Banc" Babb, taken captive by Comanches at the age of ten in September 1866 in Decatur (northwest of present-day Dallas), and ransomed seven months later. She was taken by the same band—Nokonis—that took the Parker captives. Her written chronicle remains the only first-person narrative of a girl's captive time with a southern plains tribe.[4] There are great similarities with the captivity of Cynthia Ann Parker, starting with the horrific circumstances under which Banc was taken. Her mother was stabbed four times with a butcher knife while Banc held her hand.[5] Then the little girl watched as her mother was shot through the lungs with an arrow and scalped while still alive. (She was later found with her blood-smeared baby daughter, who was trying to nurse at her dying mother's breast.)[6] Banc also watched as Sarah Luster, a beautiful twenty-six-year-old who was captured with her, became, in Banc's brother's words, "the helpless victim of unspeakable violation, humiliation, and involuntary debasement."[7]

Like the Parker captives, Banc, her brother, and Mrs. Luster were strapped behind Indians on horses and taken on a furious ride north. They had little food and were not allowed to dismount their horses. At one point Banc was given a chunk of bloody meat cut from a cow that wolves had killed. She ate it, and liked it. She lost control of her bowels while on the back of the horse, and thus acquired her unfortunate Indian name: "Smells Bad When You Walk." After four days of chafe and dire thirst and muscle ache and blistering sunburn, they arrived at the Indian village. Here the Comanche with whom she had ridden gave Banc to his sister, whose husband had been killed the morning before the raid on the Babb house. The widow had no children of her own.[8]

And then everything changed. Banc was taken into a close-knit family group that consisted of thirty-five people who camped together in eight buffalo-hide tipis. She and her Comanche mother, Tekwashana, shared a tipi. According to Banc's memoir:

> This woman was always good to me, that is she never scolded me, and seldom ever corrected me. . . . Our bed consisted of a pile of dead grass, with blankets and dressed buffalo robes spread over the grass. On cold winter nights my Squaw Mother would have me stand before the fire, turning [me] round occasionally, so I could get good and warm, then she would wrap me up in a buffalo robe and lay me on the bed over near the outer edge, next to the tentwall and tuck me in good and warm. . . . She . . . seemed to care as much for me as if I were her very own child.[9]

The world Banc describes sometimes sounds like a child's paradise. Indeed, she recalled that "every day seemed to be a holiday." She played happily with other children. She loved the informality of meals that usually involved standing around a boiling kettle and spearing meat with skewers. She liked the taste of the meat, though she said it took a long time to chew. Tekwashana taught her to swim, pierced her ears, and gave her long silver earrings with silver chains and brass bracelets for her arms. The Comanche women mixed buffalo tallow and charcoal and rubbed it into her bright blond hair to make it dark. She loved the war dances. She learned the language quickly and so well that, after only seven months of captivity (which she believed was two years), it was hard for her to "get my tongue twisted back so I could talk English again to my folk and my friends."[10] She had two dresses, and neither was buckskin: One was made of calico, and one made of blue-and-white-striped bed ticking.

Banc also describes hardship and days that were not like holidays at all. Her captors were, after all, nomadic hunter-gatherers; life was at best uncertain. There was not always enough food to eat. Sometimes her family group would get only small rations of dried meat; on other occasions they would not give her any and she sometimes went two days without food. "When our supply of dried meat was gone we lived on boiled corn," she wrote, "and when that was exhausted and everybody hungry, they would kill a fat horse or mule and then we would have a feast as long as that lasted." She said her family owned three hundred horses, which suggests that they detested horse meat and ate it only as a last resort. Or perhaps they detested the idea of eating such a useful and tradeable commodity. The band moved its camp every three weeks—typical of nomads who required a good deal of horse pasturage—which meant hard work for everyone, including Banc. She carried water, gathered wood, and packed the horses and mules on moving days, and helped see to all the logistics of the move, including the care of the dogs. At one point she violated a taboo by passing in front of the men's tipis while fetching water. In punishment, an old woman set her dogs on her. Later that same woman attacked her with an ax, managing instead to kill a young Indian girl who happened to intervene. The woman, Banc noted, was summarily executed.

In April 1867, Banc was ransomed for $333. That night a heartbroken Tekwashana shut her out of the tent. Later she relented and convinced Banc to try to escape with her, carrying the girl on her back. This was extreme behavior, punishable by violence, and clear evidence of how much Tekwashana loved her adopted daughter. The two were tracked down and caught the next day. Banc was soon returned to her family. At their reunion, she realized that she had forgotten how to speak English.

Another account, less complete but similar in many ways, came from a girl who lived in central Texas. One of the bloodiest raids ever carried out by Comanches took place in Legion Valley, near modern-day Llano, Texas, in 1868. They took seven captives but killed five of them in the first few days—including a baby and a three-year-old—leaving only lovely, long-haired Malinda Ann "Minnie" Caudle, eight, and a boy named Temple Friend, seven. Minnie was immediately adopted by a fat Comanche woman, with whom she rode back to the Indian camp. Her new mother slept with her to keep her warm and tried to shelter her from the events of the first night, when Minnie's two aunts were raped and tortured as they wept and prayed aloud.[11] The next day her captors decided the two aunts were too much trouble. When they seized them and killed them, Minnie's Comanche mother threw a blanket over her head so she would not have to watch.[12] Like Banc Babb, Minnie Caudle was treated with great kindness. Her new mother told her stories by the fire. The Comanche women would not let the Indian men harm her. They cooked meat for her the way she liked it, and when they passed salt licks they made sure to get some salt to season her food. They dressed her in buckskin and greased her body with tallow to keep her dry in rain and snow.[13] Like Banc, too, Minnie was held captive half a year, then ransomed and returned. Her story survived in one published interview and in later interviews with her descendants.[14]

Thus two experiences that were very likely similar, except for the ransoming and return, to Cynthia Ann Parker's. One can only speculate. As long as both of them lived, Banc and Minnie defended the Comanche tribe. Minnie Caudle "would not hear a word against the Indians," according to her great-granddaughter. Her great-grandson said, "She always took up for the Indians. She said they were good people in their way. When they got kicked around, they fought back."[15] This is asserted against the brute facts of her own experience, which involved watching her captors rape and kill five members of her family. Banc Babb, against all reason and memory, felt the same way. In 1897 she applied for official adoption into the Comanche tribe. Both girls had seen something in the primitive, low-barbarian Comanches that almost no one else had, not even people like Rachel Plummer with long experience of tribal life. Banc's brother Dot Babb described it as "bonds of affection almost as sacred as family ties. Their kindnesses to me had been lavish and unvarying, and my friendship and attachment in return were deep and sincere."[16] The children all had the sense that, at the core of these most notorious and brutal killers, there existed a deep and abiding tenderness. Perhaps that should be obvious, since they were, after all, human beings. But it was absolutely not obvious to white settlers on the western frontier in the mid-nineteenth century.

In April 1846 an Indian agent from Texas named Leonard H. Williams was dispatched by the U.S. Indian Commissioners to find a Comanche headman named Pah-hah-yuco. This was not just any *paraibo*. Pah-hah-yuco was, along with the cunning, diminutive Mopechucope (Old Owl), the greatest of the Penateka peace chiefs.[17] In 1843 he had intervened to stop the torture and killing that had been planned for three Texas commissioners who had been sent to make amends for the Council House massacre. Most of his tribe had supported the idea of burning the white men. Pah-hah-yuco had that sort of power. He was a large, portly man, weighed more than two hundred pounds, had several wives, and what one observer described as "a pleasing expression of countenance, full of good humor and joviality."[18] His name has been translated as "The Amorous Man," but one suspects a more priapic meaning in the Comanche original.[19] Colonel Williams, whose expedition consisted of eleven men, was instructed to invite the chief to treaty talks, the first ever with the United States, of which Texas had just become part. He was also told to find out if there were any captives in the camp, and to purchase them if he could.

Williams found Pah-hah-yuco on the Washita River, in what is now
Oklahoma, probably not far from where it flows into the Red River, about
seventy-five miles north of modern-day Dallas. It is unclear how Williams
found the village in the great, wild beyond of the unsurveyed Indian territories, but he undoubtedly used Indian guides who were friendly with Comanches, very likely Delawares or Wichitas. It must have been a heart-pounding,
adrenaline-pumping moment when his small band first rode, unannounced,
into the huge Comanche village with its lodges and campfires and racks of
drying buffalo meat that snaked for miles along the banks of the river. The
arrival of the Williams party created an immediate uproar in the camp. Some
of the younger warriors plotted immediately to kill them. Luckily, Williams
found out about this from a Mexican boy captive, and claimed the protection of Pah-hah-yuco, who, according to Williams, "with difficulty succeeded in pacifying and restraining his men."[20]

Having narrowly escaped assassination, Williams now discovered, to his
astonishment, that the Indian village contained the blue-eyed, light-haired
Cynthia Ann Parker, the last unaccounted-for victim of the infamous massacre at Parker's Fort, the little blond girl who never returned. It is unclear
exactly how he learned of this, because she certainly did not tell him, and
because being rescued from her grim and horrible fate was entirely the white
man's idea and not hers. She was nineteen. Colonel Williams had met her
before, having been acquainted with the Parker family in their early days in
Texas. Such was her notoriety, even then, that Williams immediately dispatched a runner with the news back to the governor's office in Austin.

Then Williams set about trying to purchase her from the Indians. Buying
and selling captives was normal enough commerce in those days. It had been
a source of profit to the Comanches since the earliest days of their ascendancy on horseback. They had done a brisk trade in Apache and Mexican
captives, often using the elaborately tattooed Wichitas of north-central Texas
as brokers. The captives often ended up, transshipped like bales of cotton, in
Louisiana markets. Nowadays the business seemed to be centered in various
Red River depots, where mercenary traders and other louche types from the
outer borderlands with few scruples ran a sort of human arbitrage business,
ransoming captives from the Indians then reselling them to their families at a
profit. It was a highly speculative business, and involved a good deal of lying
and misrepresentation. There were captives whose "saviors" turned out to be
the worst sort of swindlers.

But, as Williams soon discovered, this case was different. The Indians simply would not negotiate. In one account, he offered "12 mules and 2 mule loads of merchandise" for her, a princely sum for a single hostage. That was refused by the Indians who, according to a newspaper story, "say they will die rather than give her up."[21] Another had him offering "a large amount of goods and $400 to $500 in cash."[22] Still, the Indians refused. There were several reported versions of Cynthia Ann's behavior. In one, she ran off and hid to avoid Williams and the others. In another, she "wept incessantly," presumably at the thought of being returned. In a third version, Colonel Williams was granted permission to speak to her. She approached him, then sat down under a tree and stared in front of her, refusing to speak or even to indicate whether she understood him. In James T. DeShields's nineteenth-century telling, almost certainly embellished for the tender sensibilities of his readers: "the anxiety of her mind was betrayed by the perceptible quiver of her lips, showing that she was not insensible to the common feelings of humanity."[23]

A letter written four months later from commissioners Pierce Butler and M. G. Lewis to the commissioner of Indian affairs in Washington cleared up the mystery. They suggested that the problem was not with Pah-hah-yuco or with the other headmen, who were more than willing to sell her for the right price. It was rather that "The young woman is claimed by one of the Comanches as his wife. From the influence of her alleged husband, or from her own inclination, she is unwilling to leave the people with whom she associates."[24] This was love, apparently, as difficult as that was for the white world to swallow. Either way, she wasn't going anywhere, for any amount of money. On the mercenary frontier, this was in itself shocking news.

At some point Cynthia Ann and Peta Nocona began living with the Penatekas, though the exact date will never be known. The Comanches responsible for the Parker's Fort raid were allegedly Nokonis. But the evidence for this is sketchy at best, as was the *taibos'* general understanding of Indian bands. They may well have been Penatekas. Or even Tennawish, a lesser band that camped, hunted, and raided with the Penatekas. Or even a combination of bands. One report had Cynthia Ann with the Yamparikas from the distant north, which was almost certainly not true. But the band distinction is important. Based on the available evidence, the band Cynthia Ann was associated with throughout most of the 1840s were Penatekas: Pah-hah-yuco's southern Comanches.

That was bad luck. However she landed with them, it meant that she was thrown into the middle of a social and cultural disaster of epic proportions. To use a later historical parallel, it would have been like being adopted into a Jewish family in Berlin in 1932. There was not much future in it. She thus became the helpless victim of huge, colliding historical forces utterly beyond her control. What happened to the Penatekas in the 1840s destroyed them as a coherent social organization. They did not go down quickly and they did not go down without a fight—in their death throes they were in some ways more lethal than ever, particularly in their Mexican raids—but they never recovered. Much of what was left of them, starving and demoralized, limped on to a tiny reservation in 1855, despised even by other Comanches.

Only ten years before, such a thing would have been unimaginable. At the moment of the raid on Parker's Fort, the moment when a weeping Lucy Parker placed her terrified daughter on the rear flank of a Comanche mustang, the Comanches, and the Penatekas in particular, had been at the peak of their historical power and influence. They had defeated the Europeans, cowed the Mexicans, and had so thoroughly mastered the far southern plains that they were no longer threatened by other tribes. They had enough enemies to keep them entertained and supplied with a surfeit of horseflesh. But none to really worry about. Their source of food and sustenance, the buffalo, roamed the plains in record numbers and still ranged into every corner of Comancheria. The tribe's low birth rates virtually guaranteed that their nomadic life following buffalo herds was infinitely sustainable. Their world was thus suspended in what seemed to be a perfect equilibrium, a balance of earth and wind and sun and sky that would endure forever. An empire under the bright summer moon. For those who witnessed the change at a very intimate and personal level, including Cynthia Ann and her husband, the speed with which that ideal world was dismantled must have seemed scarcely believable. She herself, the daughter of pioneers who were hammering violently at the age-old Comanche barrier that had defeated all other comers, now adopted into a culture that was beginning to die, was the emblem of the change.

Somehow she and her husband, Peta Nocona, survived the cataclysm. As nomads, they moved constantly. One imagines her on one of these migrations, on horseback, moving slowly across the open grassy plain with hundreds of others, warriors in the vanguard, toward a wide, hazy horizon that would have looked to white men like unalloyed emptiness. There were the long trains of heavily packed mules and horses and the ubiquitous Comanche dogs. There were horses dragging travois that carried the huge tent poles and piled buffalo hides and scored the earth as they went along—perfectly parallel lines drawn on the prairie, merging and vanishing into the pale-blue Texas sky. All trailed by the enormous horse remuda, the source of their wealth. It must have been something to behold. Cynthia Ann lived a hard life. Women did all of the brutally hard work, including most of the work that went into moving camp. They did it from dawn till dark, led brief difficult lives, and did not complain about it; they did everything except hunt and fight.

Her camp locations show just how far she roamed. Pah-hah-yuco's camps were found in 1843 north of the Red River and south of modern-day Lawton, Oklahoma, on Cache Creek (the encampment was on a creek bank on the open prairie and stretched for half a mile).[25] In 1844 he was camped on the Salt Plains of present-day north-central Oklahoma, on the Salt Fork of the Arkansas River,[26] well north of the Washita, where Williams found him in 1846. In 1847 his band was spotted a hundred miles north of Austin, in rolling, lightly timbered prairie, camped in a village of one hundred fifty lodges,[27] and again that same year in a village in the limestone hills and mesas west of Austin. She was identified as being with the Tennawish band in 1847, who often camped with the Penateka (with whom Pah-hah-yuco was often associated), and for all practical purposes after 1845 may have been the same band. Those camps were in far west Texas on the headwaters of the Red River. Some accounts had her wearing "calico borne from the sacking of Linnville" and fleeing "with the discomfited Comanches up the Guadalupe and Colorado,"[28] suggesting she had been with Buffalo Hump on his raid. But these things cannot be proved.

Such migrations are in keeping with what we know of the Penateka. In the wake of the Council House Fight, they had moved their camps north, away from the extreme hostilities of the Lamar regime. In the middle of the decade, after changes in the political climate, they began to drift back southward to their usual ranges. Cynthia Ann went with them. She moved in a three-hundred-mile radius. Wherever she was, it was her bad luck to be with the Comanches whose villages and hunting grounds were first in line to be jostled by the impatient and grimly determined onrush of white civilization.

The Penatekas had borne the brunt of the Mirabeau Lamar years (1838–1841). They had been defeated at the Council House, at Plum Creek, and on the upper Colorado River. Two of those had been massacres. They had won military engagements, too, to be sure—including the San Saba and Bird's Creek fights—and they had won plenty more against militia and ranging companies that were never recorded. But they must have had the sense that they had lost more than they had won, especially to a foe that seemed to have limitless resources, human and financial, at its disposal. Between 1836 and 1840 alone, the Penateka were thought to have lost a quarter of all their fighting men.[29]

With such small numbers, it would normally take years to recover from such setbacks. But the Penatekas were already out of time. What was killing them steadily and surely was not the warlike policies of Lamar, as harsh as they were. Or even the catastrophic disappearance of game from their eastern ranges. The agent of destruction was the same one that had destroyed the majority of the population of almost every Indian tribe in the Americas, starting with the Aztecs: white man's disease. This was not the first time that horse tribes had been hit by disease. Prior to 1820 it is thought that some thirty epidemics of varying scales moved through the Plains Indians: measles, malaria, whooping cough, and influenza, taking an unknown toll on their numbers.[30] But the Penatekas were hit harder than any other band or tribe on the plains. Their Mexican raiding had brought back smallpox in 1816 along with another horrifying and easily transmitted disease they had never seen before: syphilis. In 1839 smallpox had swept through them again, this time brought by Kiowas from the Mandan Indians on the Missouri River. Thousands had died.

They had no defense against this terrifying, invisible magic. While the Comanches' abilities to treat simple medical conditions could be fairly sophisticated—they treated toothaches successfully with heated tree fungus, filled cavities by stuffing dried mushrooms in the hole; they made laxatives by boiling the cambium layer of the willow tree; they used mechanical tourniquets and even primitive surgery on gunshot wounds[31]—the best they could muster against these marauding spirits were prayers and incantations, magical markings on the body, and purification rites. One example of the latter was the presumed cure for smallpox: The sufferer took a sweat bath and then immersed himself in a cold stream, a treatment that often proved fatal.

Then, in 1849, came the most devastating blow of all: cholera. The disease had first appeared on earth in India's Ganges River delta in the early nineteenth century. It broke out in Europe in 1830, crossed the ocean to America in 1832, and spread rapidly from there. It came west on the wagon trains with thousands of Forty-niners who were traveling to the gold fields of California. They traveled by old trails like the Santa Fe, but they cut new trails, too, including a route along the Canadian River, which passed through Oklahoma and Texas, and thus through the very heart of Comanche country. In 1849 alone three thousand pioneers traveled that route. They were a dirty, scurvy lot themselves, with hygiene scarcely better than the Indians, gold-crazed hilljacks from the poorer parts of the East and trans-Appalachia. They carried death with them (they had smallpox, too), and spread it in hundreds of Indian villages.

Cholera was not subtle; it killed fast and explosively. Its incubation period was from two hours to five days, which meant that, from the moment of infection, it could and often did kill a healthy adult in a matter of hours. The disease is marked by severe diarrhea and vomiting, followed by leg cramps, extreme dehydration, raging thirst, kidney failure, and death.[32] It was a horrible way to die, and a horrible thing to watch. The disease was transmitted by the ingestion of fecal matter, either directly or in contaminated water or food. Imagine a village of five hundred primitive people with poor or nonexistent sanitary habits in which several hundred of them have violent, uncontrollable diarrhea. The water sources would soon be infected, and then everything else would be infected, too, creating a sort of microbial nightmare. Unable to understand what was causing it, the People had no chance. Because the Nermernuh viewed illness superstitiously, the sick were often left to die alone, layering one kind of horror on another. Grief-stricken families left their dying mothers or fathers or children to flee to the "safety" of another village, only to infect them, too. The disease ripped through the rest of the plains as well. Half of the entire Kiowa tribe perished; five decades later Kiowas remembered it as the most terrible experience in tribal memory.[33] Half of the southern Cheyennes died—an estimated two thousand had perished, a number that included *entire* bands. There was evidence of disease-driven suicide among Kiowas and Arapahoes.[34]

No one knows how many thousands of Comanches died in the cholera epidemic of 1849. Some of the northern bands, including the Kotsoteka, were devastated by it as well. It is believed that *half* of the still-surviving Penateka died. That would mean that the band's members dropped from eight thousand to two thousand in less than thirty years, though no hard estimate is possible. Most of the important camp headmen died in 1849. What started as gradual disintegration now looked like dissolution. Pah-hah-yuco managed to live through it, though he soon withdrew to far northern ranges.

The band chose Buffalo Hump to succeed him, but the title lacked any meaning, since from now on the band had no common leader.[35] What was left of them found that the buffalo no longer came south to their ranges, and that much of the other game had disappeared, too. They had signed a few treaties, meanwhile, which of course did nothing to protect them. The agreements drew lines that the Indians could not cross, even to hunt, while white men sent surveying parties scurrying westward across those same imaginary lines into Indian lands. By the early 1850s many of the Penatekas were starving. In the words of one of their chiefs, Ketumseh,

> Over this vast country, where for centuries our ancestors roamed in undisputed possession, free and happy, what have we left? The game, our main dependence, is killed and driven off, and we are forced into the most sterile and barren portions of it to starve. We see nothing but extermination left before us, and we await the result with stolid indifference. Give us a country we can call our own, where we may bury our people in quiet.[36]

We can see this all now: the complete narrative of the Honey Eaters, the roots of their power, their long migrations south, their wars with Apaches and Mexicans, their rise to dominance on the southern plains, the curse of their proximity to the settlements, and what the cholera did to them. We can see their degradation, their decay, their suffering, the arc of their fall. But that is all hindsight.

No one on the frontier or in Houston or in Washington understood any of this at the time. There was little doubt that the Texans had won the fights at Council House and Plum Creek and the Colorado. But no one knew exactly what that meant or what portion of the Comanche tribe had been involved. A fierce and independent group numbering in the thousands with a remuda of fifteen thousand horses and camping in Palo Duro Canyon—the Quahadis—was beyond anything they knew or could guess at. Nor did the Texans have any idea how many Comanches died from cholera, or from the smallpox in 1839. They were invisible catastrophes; they would not be fully understood for decades. Comancheria still loomed before them, as dark, impenetrable, and lethal as ever. The last thing on anyone's mind was mounting a large force of soldiers to ride far into the Northwest and try to conquer it. The *taibos* knew that much, anyway.

In this shadowy world of half knowledge and vague assessments, it was also impossible to see the principal side effect of Lamar's war policy. Though he had driven the southern Comanches north of the Red River and thus produced a temporary peace, he had not changed the nature of the Comanches. The culture was based on war: Young men still had to fight and kill and return with horses. Instead of riding for the Texas frontier, which was now seen as a dangerous place, the Penateka looped to the west, down the old Comanche Trace, which opened into the Mexican states of Tamaulipas, Coahuila, Nuevo León, and Chihuahua. There was little effective government here, the legacy of the long, slow decline of Spanish Imperial power and Mexico's lack of will to hunt down marauding Indians in its northern provinces. Its eighty-thousand-man army stayed in the south, and was mainly used against the Mexican people. The only real threat were the armed vaqueros. The result was a sort of raider's paradise.

And now Buffalo Hump and Santa Anna and other Penateka chiefs cut a wide arc of bloody terror through the eastern provinces of Mexico. They left a long trail of bloated and charred corpses and burned-out villages. They tortured hundreds or thousands to death, no one would ever know how many. They took captive children by the dozen and cattle and horses, and in the summer months people reported seeing this remarkable procession heading back north along the Trace, through current Fort Stockton, a long dusty line of cattle and horses and captives, the spoils of a season's raiding. Comanche raiders killed thousands more people south of the Rio Grande than they ever killed in Texas; much of this was done by Penatekas, and much of it was done in what history now sees as their dying days.

Peace in Texas was an illusion, too. How deeply the whites misunderstood the Comanches was evident in the peace treaty of 1844, the product of three years' work by Sam Houston, who had returned to the presidency in 1841, bringing his pacifist notions back with him. Though the Texans were dealing with only a fraction of the Penateka—the treaty's signers were only Old Owl and Buffalo Hump (Pah-hah-yuco and Santa Anna were not there)—they persisted in referring to the "Comanche tribe" and the "Comanche nation" as though all of the bands had been part of the negotiations. Sam Houston himself, old Indian hand that he was, persisted in the mistaken belief that Comanche chiefs wielded power over other bands and Kiowas.[37] In this formulation, they could thus sign a treaty that all Comanches from eastern Colorado and western Kansas to the Mexican border would dutifully obey. The idea was preposterous. The camp headmen within the Penateka band were barely able to agree among themselves. The dangerous Comanches, the Comanches still riding free and unbeaten and unencumbered on the more remote prairies, as yet undestroyed by war or disease, hadn't signed anything.

But no one in Texas in the middle century could have told you that. Nor could they have imagined that getting rid of the Comanches was going to take another thirty years of war.

Colonel Williams's visit to the Comanche camp put the Parker family back in the headlines—as much for the discovery that Cynthia Ann's bones were not bleaching in an alkali creek somewhere as for her refusal to return. On June 1, 1846, the *Houston Telegraph and Texas Register* ran a story about the meeting. "Miss Parker has married an Indian chief," it said, with the matter-of-factness of a social notice, "and is so wedded to the Indian mode of life that she is unwilling to return to her white kindred." The story added that every possible effort had been made to reclaim her, but they had all been unsuccessful. "Even if she should be restored to her kindred here," the story concluded ruefully, "she would probably take advantage of the first opportunity and flee away to the wilds of northern Texas."

Not everyone was willing to accept this state of affairs. Robert Neighbors, a talented Indian agent who was Texas commissioner of Indian affairs at the time, was foremost among them. Believing that Cynthia Ann was the only white captive still alive among the plains tribes, he mounted a concerted effort in the summer of 1847 to get her back. That meant sending messengers to the villages bearing gifts and money. He had no more luck than Colonel Williams had. "I have used all means in my power during the last summer to induce those Indians to bring her in by offering large rewards," he wrote in a November 18, 1847, report to the U.S. commissioner of Indian affairs, "but I am assured by the friendly Comanche chiefs that I would have to use force to induce the party that has her to give her up."

He also said something interesting. He noted that she was "with the Ten-na-wish band of Comanches . . . with whom we hold little or no intercourse. They reside on the headwaters of the Red River."[38] If he was right, and he very likely was, then Cynthia Ann and her husband had jumped bands, and in so doing had traveled well west of the normal Penateka ranges. Pah-hah-yuco himself was sometimes affiliated with the Tenawish,[39] which might explain the jump. Whatever the cause, it was a clear move away from trouble, away from the death throes of the Penatekas. Cynthia and Peta Nocona were fleeing the Texas frontier. They were refugees. Within a year, the couple changed bands again. They camped even farther north, on Elk Creek south of the Wichita Mountains in Indian Territory (Oklahoma).

There, with the world crashing down around the southern Comanches, a son was born to Cynthia Ann and Peta Nocona. According to later interviews with his descendants, they named him Kwihnai, "Eagle." If that is true, then the name Quanah is a nickname. Its meaning, too, is far from clear. According to his son Baldwin Parker in a later interview, the name comes from the Comanche "kwaina," meaning "fragrant."[40] Though this name is usually translated as "smell," "odor," "fragrance," or "perfume," the Shoshone root word *kwanaru,* meaning "stinking," may suggest the real source of the name. In this theory, people modified his original name to mean "stink."[41] Within the next two years, Cynthia Ann gave birth to a second son whom she named "Peanuts." From later interviews with Quanah, the name originated in his mother's fond childhood memory of eating peanuts around the fireside at Parker's Fort.[42] Both names are unusual and suggest that Cynthia Ann, who family legend said was a "spirited squaw," and her husband had defied Comanche custom by naming the children themselves.[43]

The first anyone knew of these events was in 1851, when a group of traders led by a man named Victor Rose, who would later write histories of the era, saw her in a Comanche village. When they asked her if she wanted to leave, she shook her head and pointed to her children, saying, "I am happily married. I love my husband, who is good and kind, and my little ones, who, too, are his, and I cannot forsake them." Rose described Peta as a "great, greasy, lazy buck."[44] The account has an odd ring to it: Rose undoubtedly saw Cynthia Ann, because he was the first to report the existence of children. But it is unlikely that she uttered those grammatically perfect sentences. The timing is worth noting. The existence of the two brothers playing at her feet would seem to confirm that Quanah was born before 1850, and possibly as early as 1848. In any case, she was sincere. She was "Nautdah" now, "Someone Found," the name given to her by Peta Nocona, whose name means "He Who Travels Alone and Returns."[45]

The last anyone on the frontier heard of Cynthia Ann in the 1850s came in a report from the intrepid explorer Captain Randolph Marcy, a reliable chronicler of the frontier. "There is at this time a white woman among the Middle Comanches, who, with her brother, was captured while they were young children from their father's house in the Western part of Texas," he wrote, confirming that she had changed bands and placing her with the Nokonis or the Kotsotekas, who were known as Middle Comanches. "This woman has adopted all the habits and peculiarities of the Comanches; has an Indian husband and children, and cannot be persuaded to leave them."[46]

For the moment she was free again in the way that Comanches had always been free. In the way that the hapless Penateka no longer were. She was on the open plains, where the buffalo still roamed in their millions and Comanche power stood inviolate. Where the white man still did not dare to go.

Nine

CHASING THE WIND

THE REST OF the Parker hostages—Rachel Plummer, Elizabeth Kellogg, John Richard Parker, and James Pratt Plummer—suffered very different fates. All were intertwined in some way with Rachel's father and Cynthia Ann's uncle James W. Parker, the man whose breathtaking lack of judgment had been largely to blame for the disaster that had befallen the clan in May of 1836. Like many other members of the Parker clan, James was a colorful figure. But he was much more than that. He was one of the most outrageous, extreme, obsessive, ambitious, violent, dishonest, morally compromised, reckless, and daring characters ever to stake a claim on the early Texas frontier. He was a man of more contradictions than anyone could keep track of: a prominent citizen who was accused at various times of being a murderer, counterfeiter, liar, drunk, horse thief, and robber. He was kicked out of two different churches for lying and drunkenness. And yet during his lifetime he was an elected justice of the peace, one of the original Texas Rangers, a representative at the legendary "consultation" that set the stage for the Texas revolution, and a friend of Sam Houston and Mirabeau Lamar. He was a preacher who once had his own church, a successful businessman who owned a sawmill and thousands of acres of land. Though an odor of impropriety, untruth, and general malfeasance haunts his life, he was never convicted of anything. Some of his neighbors believed that the raid itself had been the result of his shady business dealings. They alleged that he had bought stolen horses from Indians with counterfeit money, and that the true purpose of the attack had been to avenge the fraud.[1] Nothing was ever proven, and James himself mounted a spirited defense of his honor in a self-published pamphlet.[2] He admitted to killing five people, but they were all Indians and there were no criminal penalties in the Republic of Texas for murdering redskins.

And yet that was not how James Parker was mainly known. For all of the obloquy and misadventure, he was famous throughout the West as *the man who searched for the Parker captives*. The man who refused to give up. He made five trips, alone, into Indian lands between 1836 and 1837, mostly acting on tips about young white women—like his daughter Rachel—who had been carried off by Indians. He made another four or five excursions from 1841 to 1844, based on information he believed would lead him to his niece Cynthia Ann Parker, his nephew John Richard Parker, or his grandson James Pratt Plummer.[3] He logged perhaps five thousand miles, much of it alone. The only remotely comparable captive hunter in American history was a former slave named Britt Johnson, who made five trips into the wilderness starting in 1864 searching for his wife and children, who were also captured by Comanches.[4] (If James's story begins to sound familiar, it was the basis for John Ford's magnificent western *The Searchers* starring John Wayne in the James Parker role and Natalie Wood as his niece, the screen version of Cynthia Ann.)

Parker's first trip in search of his relatives, to Nacogdoches in East Texas, was a stunning and unexpected success. His sister-in-law Elizabeth Kellogg had been purchased by Delaware Indians and brought in to that city to trade. The Delawares, presumably marking up what they had paid the Kichais (who got her from the Comanches), wanted $150 for her. James was both overjoyed and, as would be the case at various times in his life, "penniless." He somehow managed to convince his old friend Sam Houston to put up the money.

Thus was Elizabeth ransomed on August 20, 1836, three months after the raid. History does not record what happened to her after that, though the social position of returned female captives in nineteenth-century America was deeply compromised. People were under no illusions about what had happened to them. They knew with great specificity what Plains Indians did to adult women, and thus repatriated captives were usually objects of pity. If they were married, their husbands often would not take them back. In several cases unmarried women captives were wealthy enough to attract husbands in spite of what had happened to them. Elizabeth probably lived out a life of quiet shame in the shadows, perhaps in the home of a Parker relative. She would have been an embarrassment: That may be why James says so little about her.

Between August 1836 and October 1837, Parker spent most of his time in the wilderness searching for the captives. He was mainly tracking his daughter Rachel, because in those early years his informants—traders along the Red River, Texas's northern boundary—had heard stories only of young women and nothing about children being held by Indian tribes. His journeys are chronicles of hardship and near disaster. On his first trip, he found his horse could not swim across the swollen Red River so he abandoned it, crossed the river on his own, and headed off into the Indian territories on foot, an action that people of the day considered tantamount to suicide. He weathered a driving rainstorm that flooded the prairie to a depth of two feet and was followed by a blue norther that howled down out of the Canadian plains and froze it all. He was almost certainly going to die, in his own estimation, when he managed to start a fire by stuffing some cotton from his shirt into his pistol and firing it at a log that had somehow stayed dry in the torrent. On his next trip he ventured into the wilderness unarmed—again, tantamount to suicide—and this time went six days without food, breaking his fast by strangling and eating a skunk. On the next he spent a full month lurking around a Comanche camp, leaving messages in English by nearby streams. He knew that Indians forced captives to fetch water, and was hoping, though there would seem to be less than a chance in a million of this ever happening, to get his daughter's attention. All his suffering was in vain. None of the stories he heard got him any closer to his daughter.

In October 1837 he returned home for the fourth time, discouraged and in poor health. While he recuperated, he dispatched his son-in-law Lorenzo Nixon (who was married to Rachel's sister) to the Red River trading posts to see if there was any news of women captives. Now, finally, his luck turned. At one of the posts, Nixon was tipped that a Mrs. Plummer had arrived in Independence, Missouri, outside of modern-day Kansas City. He found her there a few weeks later. Her first words to him were: "Are my husband and father alive?" Nixon said they were. Then she asked: "Are mother and the children alive?" The answer to that, too, was yes.

Like everything else that happened to the Parker family in those early days, the story of Rachel Parker Plummer's return is a strange and epic tale that stretches across several thousand miles of frontier. She was purchased from her Comanche captor in August of 1837 by a group of Comancheros. At the time she was probably somewhere on the high plains of eastern Colorado. She was put on a horse and taken on what she described as a "very hard" seventeen-day ride to Santa Fe, which was then still a part of Mexico. The Comancheros, who would actually not acquire that name for another five or six years, were one of the West's most interesting subcultures. They owed their existence to the 1786 peace made by New Mexico governor Juan Bautista de Anza and the Comanches, after his defeat of Cuerno Verde in Colorado. From that year forward, Comanches could freely enter Spanish settlements to trade for horses, and New Mexican traders could operate safely on the plains of Comancheria. American accounts often described Comancheros as "renegades" or "half-breeds,"[5] the latter referring to what was supposed to be Comanche blood. In fact they were half-breeds, or mixed blood, but so was almost the entire population of New Mexico. They were mestizos, of mixed Spanish and Indian blood, as most Mexicans are today. They were less renegades than businessmen, though they were famously hard-bitten characters and occasionally rode with Comanches and Kiowas on horse- and cattle-stealing raids. The Comanches traded livestock, hides, and captives to the Comancheros in exchange for beads, knives, paint, tobacco, pots and pans, calico and other cloths, metal spikes for making arrows, coffee, flour, and bread. The trading took place in specific locations such as Palo Duro Canyon in the Texas Panhandle and various places in northeastern New Mexico.

As years went by, more and more of the Comanchero trade was in guns, ammunition, and whiskey, and they dealt increasingly in stolen cattle, which they fenced to merchants who in many cases sold them back to their original owners, often the military.[6] They were important to the Comanches for many reasons, but perhaps the most important was that they allowed the still-wild bands—the Quahadis, Yamparikas, Nokonis, and Kotsotekas—to stay out of the white man's settlements, away from the blandishments of white civilization, away from the diseases that were destroying their southern brethren. (On the east, a comparable trading network evolved among the Kickapoos, Delawares, and Shawnees in the Indian country, offering the Comanches the same opportunities.)[7] Comancheros also gave the People a way to trade and profit from captives. In the late eighteenth and early nineteenth centuries the Comancheros had dealt mainly in captive Indians from a variety of tribes for use as mine workers or servants. But starting in 1821 the Anglo settlement in Texas changed all that. Once it became clear that Texans would pay generously for captives, an active market sprang up. (When U.S. general Zachary Taylor announced in 1842 that the U.S. government would pay for any captives brought into Fort Gibson, in what is present-day eastern Oklahoma, the market went wild, as did the takings.)[8] The Comancheros were soon doing a brisk business in white captives as well.

The men who ransomed Rachel Plummer were not speculators; they had been operating under specific instructions from William and Mary Donoho, a wealthy Santa Fe couple, who had told them to pay any price for white women. The Donohos were remarkable people, especially Mary. She was thought to be the first woman ever to travel the Santa Fe Trail, doing so in 1833. She was the first female U.S. citizen to live in Santa Fe; two of her children were the first Anglo children born there.[9] They took Rachel in and put her up at the best hotel in town, which had dirt floors, where she enjoyed her first night in a bed in fifteen months. The Donohos were exceptionally kind to her, assuring her that everything would be done to return her to her relatives. The people of Santa Fe welcomed her, too, in spite of her deeply compromised status. They raised $150 for her to help her get back home.

But Rachel's run of bad luck was not quite over. Her $150 was immediately stolen by the dishonest clergyman who had been entrusted to hold it. And then a violent rebellion broke out in the streets of Santa Fe. Two thousand Pueblo Indians ambushed two hundred government militiamen. A massacre followed. The rebels beheaded the governor, placed his head on a pole, and paraded it through the streets. They put a district judge in stocks, cut his hands off, and waved them in his face.[10] The Pueblos installed their own governor.

This was enough for the Donohos, who were now fearful for their own safety. They fled east, with the hapless Rachel in tow, back to their Missouri home—a two-month journey of some eight hundred miles straight through the heart of Comancheria. In her memoir, Rachel dismisses the trip, which very few white Americans had made at that point, as a minor inconvenience:

> The road led through a vast region of prairie, which is nearly one thousand miles across. This, to many, would have been a considerable undertaking, as it was all the way through an Indian country. But we arrived safely at Independence, where I received many signal favors from many of the inhabitants.[11]

Reunited with her brother-in-law, together they departed, in the dead of winter, for Texas. The trip was long, cold, and miserable—yet another thousand miles. On February 19, 1838, Rachel arrived at her father's home near Huntsville, Texas, north of Houston. She had made a nearly unbelievable nineteen-month odyssey across a huge portion of the continent, and it had taken a fearful toll on her. James describes her as being "in very bad health," and observes:

> She presented a most pitiable appearance; her ematiated [sic] body was covered with scars, the evidences of the savage barbarity to which she had been subject during her captivity.[12]

Curiously, he says nothing about her life back home. Instead, he describes a "protracted illness," during which she prayed for her son James Pratt, and then her peaceful death.

> She often said that this life had no charms for her, and that her only wish was that she might live to see her son restored to his friends. . . . In about a year from the time she returned to her paternal home, she calmly breathed out her spirit to Him who gave it, and her friends committed her body to the silent grave.

This strangely bowdlerized account leaves out most of the important events of the last part of her life. James does not mention Rachel's pregnancy, for example, which was in itself a remarkable event. Her third child was conceived soon after she had returned, which meant that her husband, L. T. M. Plummer, had gotten over what so many others could not: the fact of her violation by Indians. They were starting another family. Nor does James mention another remarkable fact: Toward the end of Rachel's pregnancy, his family was forced to flee their home because it was threatened by a gang of vigilantes who had vowed to kill him.

The vigilantes believed that he had murdered a Mrs. Taylor and her daughter, apparently in connection with a robbery. According to a letter James sent to Governor Lamar requesting relief, the same gang had staged mock trials and had hanged people.[13] They had written James a note saying they were going to kill him and L.T.M. and destroy their property. James went into hiding, and insisted that his family, which numbered perhaps a dozen people, travel to Houston, some seventy miles away. Fearing that the vigilantes might try to kill them, too, they avoided the dirt road and instead made their way, in freezing rain and bitter cold, through thick brush and pine forest, often cutting their own trails. It probably took them a week.

They slept out in the open with only the clothing they had hurriedly gathered before leaving. Rachel was very likely nine months pregnant at the time.

James does not mention this episode in his published narrative. He merely says that Rachel died of a "protracted illness," and most historians have tended to let it go at that. But what killed her was the flight from Huntsville to Houston. In a letter he wrote to his friend Mirabeau Lamar on or about the date of Rachel's death, James gave the fullest explanation of what happened.

> I directed my family to move to the citty of Houston while at thare urgent solicitation I was induced to keep out of the way of those outlaws; but with such malignant Vigilance did these usurpers of the law watch us, that my familty to evade them was so exposed to the cold rain and inclemency of the weather as not only to endanger all thare lives but has actually taken Four of my beloved to thare long home; (among whom was my daughter Mrs. Plummer).[14]

Rachel died on March 19. Her infant son, Wilson P. Plummer, born on January 4, 1839, outlived her by two days.[15] It is ironic that, after all she had suffered, and the thousands of miles she had traveled, her death was caused, indirectly, by her own father in what ought to have been the safety of her own home.

In 1841, James started searching again, now focused on the captives still at large: his niece Cynthia Ann, his nephew John, and his grandson James. His account of the next four years is again full of derring-do and near calamity. In late 1842 he heard that two boys had been brought in to Fort Gibson. He arrived there in January 1843 to find his grandson and his nephew. James Pratt Plummer was now eight; John Richard Parker was thirteen. They spoke no English. James's first reaction was to run away, and he had to be persuaded to come back. The three somehow made their way home, in cold and wet weather, partly on foot and without proper winter gear (nothing was ever easy with James), through the Indian territory and back to Texas.

In his narrative, James suggests a simple, happy ending for the boys, but it was more complicated than that. John seems to have been returned to his mother, Lucy, who had remarried in 1840 and divorced soon afterward and who had been mired in the settlement of her dead husband Silas Parker's estate for four years. John was dispatched by her sometime around 1850 or

1851 (Lucy died in 1852) to try to find Cynthia Ann and bring her back. Somehow he managed to find her—an astounding story in its own right—though he had no more luck than Colonel Williams, Robert Neighbors, or Victor Rose.

In his report on his expedition to the headwaters of the Red River in 1852, Captain Randolph Marcy wrote that he had met John Parker around this time and spoken with him:

> The brother of the woman, who had been ransomed by a trader and brought home to his relatives, was sent back by his mother for the purpose of endeavoring to prevail upon his sister to leave the Indians and return to her family; but he stated to me that on his arrival she refused to listen to the proposition, saying that her husband, children and all that she held most dear were with the Indians, and there she should remain.[16]

No one knows what happened to John. There were many stories. Cynthia Ann believed, as she later told interviewers, that he had died of smallpox. She was wrong, at least on the timing of his death. He was reported to have served in the Civil War under a colonel in the Texas Rifles. The most popular story was that John returned to live with the Comanches. In this version, he came down with smallpox, was abandoned, and nursed back to health by a Mexican woman who had been a captive herself (the "night-eyed" "Aztec" beauty). He became a rancher in Mexico, lived to a ripe old age, and died in 1915. Several newspaper accounts of the day suggested as much. Such are legends of the West.

James Pratt Plummer had a more prosaic fate. By the time of his capture, his father, L.T.M., had remarried, and had two children. When they arrived back in Texas, the elder James did something that was both bizarre and fully in keeping with his mercurial character. He refused to let L.T.M. have James Pratt. The reasons are not entirely clear but were most likely financial: James wanted money. He claimed at one point that he paid $1,000 for the two children, an apparent lie for which he was later banished from his church. He tried to hold L.T.M. up for some of that. He may have been trying simply to keep his grandson, who looked disarmingly like his beloved daughter Rachel. Unable to gain custody of his son, L.T.M. Plummer petitioned Sam Houston, who was again president of the Republic of Texas. Houston responded angrily:

Sir,

Your communication in reference to the detention of your son by Mr. James W. Parker, came duly to hand. . . .

In case of this kind, the attempt to swindle a distressed father on account of his long lost child is in every way deserving of the severest reprehension. Though I had some reason to suspect the professions of Mr. Parker, yet, until this case was presented, I had not supposed him capable of practicing such scandalous fraud upon his kindred and connexions. . . . His pretensions about his liability for two hundred dollars, etc., are utterly groundless. You will, therefore, take your child home.[17]

Little more is known of James Pratt's life. He married twice, fathered four children, and died on November 17, 1862, of pneumonia while serving in the Confederate Army in Little Rock, Arkansas.[18]

James Parker's last trip in search of Cynthia Ann took place in 1844. He presumably learned of Colonel Williams's meeting with her and gave up. He was kicked out of another church, this time for drunkenness. He prospered. He was elected justice of the peace in Houston County. He died in 1864 at the age of sixty-seven, having outlived most of his children and siblings. By then the Parkers were one of the most affluent and influential clans in Texas. His brother Daniel had founded nine churches before his death in 1845, making him the leading Protestant clergyman in Texas. His brother Isaac was a prominent politician, an original member of the Texas Congress in 1836. He later served as a state representative and a state senator. Yet another brother, Joseph Allen, was a large landowner and prominent citizen in Houston. For all of their prosperity and success, they never returned to Parker's Fort, which soon disappeared. Some said it was dismantled within a few years, its stout cedar posts used to build other homesteads farther to the east, where life was less dangerous.

Ten

DEATH'S INNOCENT FACE

EW HISTORIANS WOULD argue that the Treaty of Guadalupe Hidalgo, which a defeated Mexican republic signed on February 2, 1848, in the wake of a lopsided war, was as momentous an event in American history as the signing, seventeen years later, of the surrender at Appomattox Courthouse. Yet in its own way it was quite as definitive. Appomattox stitched the nation back together. It asserted that this oddball disaggregation of warring states was in fact a single nation with eternal common interests—a unified political idea that now included both a federal government with powers the founders could never have imagined, as well as millions of freed slaves whose welfare and freedom were now its assumed burden and responsibility.

But Guadalupe Hidalgo created the physical nation itself. Before the treaty the American West consisted of the old Louisiana Purchase lands that rose in ladderlike fashion from the mouth of the Mississippi, climbed the courses of the Missouri, and touched the rocky, fog-shrouded shores of the Northwest. It was a tentative, partial fulfillment of the national myth. Guadalupe Hidalgo, in which Mexico gave up its claims north of the Rio Grande, made the dream suddenly, and completely, real. It added the old Spanish lands that lay, enormous and sun-drenched, athwart the Southwest. They included the modern states of Arizona, Colorado, Utah, New Mexico, California, and Nevada. There was Texas, too, in a sense, though it had been subsumed in 1845. U.S. annexation of Texas was what the war against Mexico was about, and the American victory settled the question forever. In all, the United States of America acquired 1.2 million square miles of real estate, an instant 66 percent increase in its total landmass. In terms of land gained, on a percentage basis, it was as though France had acquired Germany. Thus was the nation entirely recast. Its singularity of purpose, its raw and conquistador-like desire to possess and dominate all lands it touched and to dispossess or destroy all of its aboriginal peoples, its burgeoning will to power could now stretch, untrammeled, from sea to shining sea. It was manifest destiny made manifest.

The treaty changed everything in the West. It changed the world beyond the 98th meridian for everyone and for all time but perhaps most radically for the native peoples who inhabited the stark, open middle of the continent. At the time of the Mexican war this was still mysterious, dangerous, untraveled land. Much of it—from Canada to south Texas—had never been explored by white men, especially the headwaters of the big rivers that ran through the heart of Comancheria. The continent's heart was pierced in two places: the Oregon Trail, which started in Missouri and scaled the continent along the North and South Platte Rivers to reach the Columbia, and the Santa Fe Trail, starting in the same place but then snaked from western Missouri to New Mexico, hugging the Arkansas River part of the way. But these were merely highways down which relatively small numbers of pioneers traveled. They did not draw settlement; westering pioneers did not stop in the middle of the Oregon Trail and decide they wanted to build a cabin. That was never their purpose and would have been suicidal anyway. The higher plains, including the 240,000 square miles of Comancheria, remained inviolate, their buffalo herds, horse tribes, trade routes, and rough boundaries still intact.

The problem for the Comanches was that, where once they existed as a buffer between two huge land empires, they now stood directly in the way of American nationhood. They were now surrounded by a single political entity. With the annexation of Texas, they were no longer dealing with a quirky, provincial republic with few resources, devalued currency, and a patchwork citizen soldiery; they were now a principal concern of the federal government, with its visions, blue-coated armies, vaults full of tax money, and complex, usually misguided, politically charged Indian policies. In the immediate aftermath of the Mexican war, none of this would have been apparent. In fact, a weird status quo reigned. Until the late 1840s, Texas was still the only part of civilized America that was in range of the horse tribes. In the Indian Territory, the relocations of eastern tribes had played out, depositing some twenty thousand Indians from a dozen tribes across modern-day Oklahoma; they jostled with one another and with plains tribes. But not with white men. Not yet. On the northern plains, in Sioux, Arapaho, and Cheyenne country, Indians had dealings with the military and occasionally confrontations, but there were no human frontiers in those lands.

The status quo would not hold much longer. In the 1830s and 1840s white civilization had shouldered its way slowly up the Colorado, Guadalupe, Trinity, and Brazos rivers in Texas, moving inexorably into the Comanche borderlands. Soon those settlements would be replicated in the North, too, ascending the Kansas, Republican, and Smoky Hill rivers, directly onto Cheyenne hunting grounds. It was moving even into the Indian Territories, which the federal government had specifically set aside for Indians. In 1849 the floodgates opened. The Gold Rush was the first great exercise of America's new spatial freedom. People poured giddily into the West in numbers that would have been unthinkable just a year before.

But pilgrims, land-grabbers, sodbusters, Forty-niners, and a nation with galloping expansionist urges were not the only problems for the Comanche nation in those years. Something else had happened during the years of the Texas Republic to change the fundamental nature of their relationship with the white man. Comanche power had long resided in sheer military superiority: the ability, man for man, to outride and outshoot the Anglo-Europeans. This had been true from the earliest days of Spanish rule. Now for the first time, came a serious challenge. It came in the form of dirty, bearded, violent, and undisciplined men wearing buckskins, serapes, coonskin caps, sombreros, and other odd bits of clothing, who belonged to no army, wore no insignias or uniforms, made cold camps on the prairie, and were only intermittently paid. They owed their existence to the Comanche threat; their methods, copied closely from the Comanches, would change frontier warfare in North America. They were called by many different names, including "spies," and "mounted volunteers," and "gunmen," and "mounted gunmen."[1] It was not until the middle of the 1840s that they finally had a name everybody could agree on: Rangers.

To understand who they were and why they were necessary, it is important to grasp the extremely difficult, nearly untenable situation in which the new Republic of Texas found itself in the late 1830s.

Texas was never supposed to be its own sovereign country. After their victory at San Jacinto the vast majority of Texans believed that their territory would be immediately annexed by the United States. There were a few would-be empire builders like Mirabeau Lamar and James Parker (who volunteered to fulfill Lamar's grandiose vision by conquering New Mexico) who had other ideas. But mostly everyone else wanted statehood. They were soon disappointed. There were two main reasons it did not happen. First, Mexico had never recognized the independence of its renegade northern province. If the United States added Texas it risked war with Mexico, something that, in 1836, it was not prepared to do. Nor could it easily admit a slave territory.

Texas was thus left alone, broke and militarily punchless, for ten years to confront two implacable enemies: Mexico on the south, and the Comanche nation on the west and north. The fledgling country would never know peace. Mexican incursions persisted; the city of San Antonio was captured twice by large Mexican armies in 1842. Raids were constant, as was the predation of itinerant bandits from across the border. And Texas's western frontier was the scene of continuous attacks by Comanches. It is interesting to note Texas's peculiar position here: Neither of these enemies would have accepted peace on the terms the new republic would have offered them. Even more remarkably, *neither would accept surrender*. The Mexican army consistently gave no quarter, most famously at the Alamo. All Texan combatants were summarily shot. The Nermernuh, meanwhile, did not even have a word for surrender. In plains warfare there was never any such thing; it was always a fight to the death. In this sense, the Texans did not have the usual range of diplomatic options. They *had to fight*.[2]

But while the Mexicans hovered, sent war parties north of the Nueces, and waited for their chance to reclaim their lost province, the constant, lethal, and unstoppable threat still came from the Comanches, who killed thousands more Texans than the Mexicans ever did. As ornery, stubborn, and fearless as the Texans were, they found themselves completely unprepared and ill equipped to deal with Comanches. So much so that, in the early days of the Republic, it looked very much as though the Texans were doomed to suffer the same fate as the Spanish and Mexicans. In the first phase of the Comanche wars, the Indians held all the advantages.

Their superiority started with weaponry. When the Texans arrived from Tennessee, Alabama, and other points east, they brought with them their main firearm, the Kentucky rifle. It was, in many ways, a fine piece of technology. Long, heavy-barreled, short-stocked, and extremely accurate, it could be devastatingly effective when fired from cover by a shooter at rest. It was an excellent hunting rifle. But it was ill suited to combat, and especially ill-suited to mounted combat. It required a good deal of time to load. Powder had to be measured and poured, and the ball had to be rammed down the barrel with a long rod. Then the tube had to be primed and the flint properly adjusted so that it would strike.[3] This all took at least a minute, which amounted to a death sentence against mobile, bow-wielding Comanches. Worse still for anyone fighting Comanches, the shooter had to dismount to use the long rifle. From the saddle, the weapon lost its only real advantage, which was its accuracy. The Texans had pistols, too, old-fashioned, single-shot dueling weapons,[4] equally cumbersome to load and fire, and equally impractical in the saddle.

All of which meant that Texans, in the early days of the Republic, usually fought on foot. From that position, facing a furious mounted attack by a bow-wielding foe, they had exactly three shots, and two of those had to be made at close range. They then either had to be covered by their comrades' fire, or take their chances reloading. The old Indian trick, and the classic wagon-train tactic, was to wait until the whites emptied their weapons, then charge before they could reload. For close-range fighting, the whites had hatchets or tomahawks that were of limited use at best.

Comanches, meanwhile, carried a far more effective and battle-tested assortment of weapons: a disk-shaped buffalo-hide shield, a fourteen-foot plains lance, a sinew-backed bow, and a quiver of iron-tipped arrows. Their abilities with bow and arrow were legendary. In 1834, Colonel Richard Dodge, who was skeptical of the stories of their prowess, nonetheless observed that the Comanche "will grasp five to ten arrows in his left hand and discharge them so rapidly that the last will be on its flight before the first has touched the ground, and with such force that each would mortally wound a man at 20–30 yards."[5] He also noted that, while for some reason the Indians had trouble shooting conventional targets, "put a five cent piece in a split stick, and by giving a dexterous twist he will make the arrow fly sideways and knock down the money almost every time."[6] Their accuracy from the back of a moving horse was, to most white men, astonishing.

The most destructive arrow wounds often came from the iron tips—basically just rough-cut triangles fashioned from barrel hoops or other sheet iron acquired from traders. They often bent or "clinched" when they hit bone, creating great internal damage and making extraction excruciatingly painful.[7] The Plains Indians' shields, made of thick, layered hide, were surprisingly effective against bullets, and at the right angle could stop any bullet from a musket and even, later, a rifle.[8] Their flexible lances were especially deadly; Indians used them to spear three-thousand-pound buffalo from behind—always on the right side, between the last rib and the hip bone[9]— at full gallop, which meant that they got lots of practice. The lances were unmatched by anything the white men had at close range and, as Dodge observed, "exceedingly destructive to life."[10]

Indians had guns, too, though their use in combat against whites, prior to the advent of repeating rifles in the 1860s, has been greatly overstated. Most of what the Indians had were cheap trade muskets that were inaccurate, fragile, and used inferior gunpowder that produced low muzzle velocities and often did not work in humid or rainy weather.[11] When they broke down, which they often did, Indians could not fix them. (In treaties, Indians often asked for gunsmithing services.) In the eastern woodlands, where it was possible to take cover, aim carefully, and fire, such weapons were marginally more valuable. On the plains, muskets were usually fired, by the relatively few Indians who had them, in an initial volley, then immediately replaced by arrow and lance.[12]

The Texan's greatest disadvantage lay in his horse and his horsemanship. American horses tended to be work plugs, plodding and incapable of running with the fleet, tough, and nimble Indian ponies. Frontier people did possess some finely bred horses, but most of them were too fragile to be ridden over many miles of hard terrain.[13] Over short distances, it was impossible for any white horseman to outdistance a Comanche mustang. Over long distances, Indian horses had the advantage of eating forage (cottonwood bark, among other things) and grass as opposed to the grain the settlers' horses ate.

Even properly mounted, though, the whites were not the riders the Indians were. In the woodlands of the East they had not ridden much, because the distances between places were nowhere near what they were in Texas, and they certainly had no idea how to fight in the saddle or to shoot accurately from a moving horse. Comanches fought entirely on horseback and in a way no soldier or citizen in North America had ever seen. Consider the classic attack on a stationary enemy. The warriors formed themselves into a wedge-shaped mass, which then morphed with great precision and at high speed into the shape of a huge wheel without spokes, whose rim consisted of one or more moving lines of warriors: wheels within wheels. As described by Wallace and Hoebel:

> The ring, winding around with machinelike regularity, approached nearer and nearer with each revolution. As a warrior approached the point on the circle nearest the enemy, he dropped into the loop around his horse's neck and shot arrows from beneath the neck. If his horse was shot down, he generally landed on his feet.[14]

No American or Texan on a work plug could ever be a match for that sort of attack; few Indian tribes ever were. The Comanches had been fighting this way for two hundred years. They engaged in this sort of combat as a way of life, against lethal and highly mobile opponents. War was what they did, and all of their social status was based on it. The conquest of the Apaches over a generation had caused a profound change in Comanche life. Before, hunting meat had been the transcendent purpose of their existence. Now it was making war, and the People had developed a hunger for it.[15] Most of their warfare was unseen by white men. But we have a few accounts from the era to remind us of what the Comanches were doing when they were not raiding white settlements. Former captive Herman Lehmann tells of a battle, probably typical in many ways of Indian fights, between Apaches and Comanches that raged for a full day, with great carnage on both sides. The Apaches lost twenty-five braves on the first day, the Comanches probably more than that. The next day the Comanches mounted another furious attack on horseback, this time killing forty more warriors and slaughtering all of the Apache women and children.[16] In another account by a former captive, eighteen hundred mounted Blackfeet clashed with twelve hundred mounted Comanches in a six-hour battle that featured ferocious hand-to-hand combat. The Comanches "whipped" their opponents and reclaimed the three thousand horses the Blackfeet had stolen.[17]

This was the sort of war-without-quarter they were now raining down on the hapless white farmers of the western frontier. The only real chance they had was to circle the wagons or the horses and hope they could kill enough Indians to make it too costly for them to continue. Mostly the settlers did not stand a chance.

The Texan solution to these problems—ranging companies—was unique in western military history. That was largely because, by anyone else's standards, the companies made no sense at all. They violated every rule of military organization and protocol; every standard of hierarchy that allowed a traditional army to function. They fit no known category: They were neither police nor regular army nor militia. They had been officially organized, in 1835 and 1836, behind the thunderous oratory of Cynthia Ann's uncle Daniel Parker, who became the prime mover in their establishment.[18] They were meant to step into the void left by the army that had fought at San Jacinto, almost all of which had been furloughed by 1837. The plan had looked good on paper. Six hundred mounted gunmen—Parker's legislation referred to them as "rangers," the first official use of the word—were commissioned to hunt Indians and defend the frontier.[19]

But in reality, the tiny, resourceless government provided neither guns nor men nor mounts.[20] It provided no uniforms, provisions, or barracks. There were never anywhere near six hundred men that could be classified as Rangers; often fifty was more like it; sometimes one hundred. And because there was no formal, political organization around them, no one was designated to appoint officers. They arose casually and by acclaim and solely on merit; the rank and file gave them their commissions. In the absence of provisions, Rangers hunted for themselves, often going into the field with only water and a mixture of sugar and parched corn they called "cold flour";[21] sometimes they were given food by the communities they defended. Sometimes they stole chickens. The only thing the government reliably provided, in its wisdom, was ammunition.

Oddly, considering the fact that almost nothing was given them, there seems to have been no real problem with recruitment: The western part of Texas in those years was awash in young, reckless, single men with a taste for wide open spaces, danger, and raw adventure.[22] They were almost all in their twenties, and they came to San Antonio looking for something other than a comfortable, sedentary life on a farm. They liked the idea of killing Comanches and Mexicans. Most of the famous Ranger captains had completed their careers by the time they were thirty-two. They had no property other than their horses and often no steady jobs. Without them, the idea of ranging companies would never have worked. They were happy to stay in the field for three to six months, the usual length of a Ranger commission. (It was this semipermanence that made them different from militia.) On this seemingly nonsensical model, Texas's primitive Indian fighting organizations developed in the years 1836 to 1840. The Rangers were simply what was needed, and they grew organically from that premise.

They began to patrol the frontier, looking for Comanches to kill. Since they were untried young men and did not know any better, they adapted quickly to this lethal new world of horses and weapons and Indian tactics. But they did not learn quickly enough to prevent appalling losses. The story of these first informal attempts to fight the Comanches will never be fully understood. That is because almost all of them went unrecorded. The new frontier folks, especially the Ranger types, were not literate, and they were not thinkers. They would rarely even acknowledge their victories (as whites were always falling all over themselves to do in the West, even when all they did was avoid disaster), let alone their defeats. The Rangers were just a dirty, ill-clad, underfed squad of irregulars anyway. They didn't write letters and didn't keep diaries. They rarely issued reports of any kind; often they didn't tell anyone at all what they had done. Nor were there any journalists around of the sort who would later chronicle, with detail and considerable fanfare, the Indian battles of the 1870s. The few reporters in east Texas towns like Houston, Richmond, and Clarksville would not begin to grasp who the Rangers were or what they had accomplished or how they had changed American warfare until after the outbreak of the Mexican war in 1846. The little that is known about what happened on the frontier during the years of the Republic comes from a handful of memoirists who participated in it and wrote it down only later.

From the evidence that does exist, however, it is apparent that many young men died fighting Comanches in battles that must have been cruelly one-sided. Ranger John Caperton estimated that "about half the rangers were killed off every year" and that "the lives of those who went into the service were not considered good for more than a year or two."[23] He also wrote that, of the one hundred forty young men in San Antonio in 1839, "100 of them were killed in various fights with Indians and Mexicans."[24] (Most would have been killed by Indians.) Those are very large numbers in a town with a population of only two thousand. There is a sense, when one reads histories of the Battle at Plum Creek, or of the bloody Moore raid that followed it, that the Texans quickly mastered the art of anti-Comanche warfare. This was not true. Plum Creek was a fiasco brought on as much by Buffalo Hump's failure to control his army and to stop them from looting as it was by the bravery of Texas fighters. Moore's success on the Colorado was entirely the result of surprise: The Comanches did not yet believe the white man would come after them in their homelands.

Colonel Moore's first, near-disastrous, attack on a Comanche camp offers a better look at what most of those early engagements might have looked like. So does Captain John Bird's scouting expedition, which left Fort Milam on the Brazos River (near Belton, Texas) on May 27, 1839, with thirty-one Rangers. Hunting for "depredating" Indians, they came upon a group of twenty-seven of them skinning buffalo. Pleased at their marvelous good luck, the white men spurred toward them, and the Comanches of course fled because it was not their way ever to receive any sort of charge.[25] The Rangers then gave chase and pursued them for three miles. Their horses, as usual, were no match for the Comanche ponies. So they gave up and headed back to the fort. Now, however, they began to notice that the Comanches had turned, too. Suddenly, the Comanches were pursuing *them*. In the words of one officer, they were "hurling their arrows upon us from every direction."[26] And there were forty of them. Bird then made the sort of error that experienced Comanche fighters would later never make: He fled like a scared jackrabbit. On the open prairie, that might have been the end of his company, especially since the Indian force, led by none other than Buffalo Hump, had now grown to some three hundred.[27]

But Bird got lucky. He and his fleeing company came upon a ravine that offered cover. What followed was typical of Ranger battles of the day: The white men took cover, the Indians charged, men on both sides died, and the Indians finally withdrew, unwilling to take the losses it would require to pry the white men, with their fire-spitting Kentucky rifles, from their positions. Also typical was the way the white man spun it: Bird actually managed to claim victory, even though he was dying when he did so. Six of his soldiers died, too. Others were wounded. He had taken 30 percent or more casualties. The reality was that the ravine had saved him and his men from outright slaughter. One can imagine many such moments on the prairie, every one of them lost to history, in which gallant, pursuing Rangers became desperate, fleeing Rangers, and in which no ravine was found and they all died quickly, or if they were unlucky enough not to die quickly, were slowly tortured to death by fire and other means. They were learning about that, too. (Veteran Indian fighters were widely believed to save one bullet for themselves, though there is only one recorded instance of it: In 1855, U.S. Infantry officer Sam Cherry's horse fell on him in a fight with Comanches. Pinned, he calmly shot five times at his attackers, then, surrounded by exulting Indians, he turned the gun to his temple for the last shot.)[28]

The Rangers were a rough bunch. They drank hard and liked killing and fistfighting and knife-fighting and executing people they deemed criminals or enemies. As time went by, and so many of them were killed, creating a sort of natural selection in their ranks, they got even rougher, more brutal, and more aggressive. They looked the part, too. Though the idealized Ranger wore a leather hat with its brim turned up, a kerchief, cotton shirt, and plain britches, the reality was something else. They wore whatever pleased them. Sometimes that meant colorful Mexican serapes and wide-brimmed sombreros. Sometimes fur hats, bobtailed coats, or dirty panamas. Often it meant head-to-toe buckskins or bits and pieces of buffalo robes. Some went about naked to the waist, wearing the equivalent of Indian breechclouts over leggings.[29] Many were large, physically imposing men with thick, brawny arms, long hair, and full beards. They had names like "Bigfoot" Wallace (who was truly huge, and a savage fighter), "Alligator" Davis (because he had wrestled one to a draw on the Medina River), and "Old Paint" Caldwell (because his skin was so mottled it looked like peeling paint). Seen from the more civilized parts of nineteenth-century America, they occupied a place in the social order just this side of brigands and desperados. They were not whom you wanted to pick a fight with in a frontier saloon.

And so it was remarkable that this group of violent, often illiterate, and unmanageable border ruffians should give its full and unswerving allegiance to a quiet, slender twenty-three-year-old with a smooth, boyish face and sad eyes and a high-pitched voice who looked younger than his years. His name was John Coffee Hays. He was called Jack. The Comanches, who feared him greatly, called him "Capitan Yack,"[30] as did the Mexicans, who put a high price on his head. He was the über-Ranger, the one everyone wanted to be like, the one who was braver and smarter and cooler under fire than any of the rest of them. He was one of the finest military commanders America has ever produced, a fact that San Antonians suspected as early as the late 1830s but the rest of the world would not learn until the Mexican war, when he became a national hero and his terrifying Rangers passed almost instantly into myth. Though he fought on the Texas frontier and Mexico for less than twelve years, he personally put an indelible stamp not only on the Texas Rangers—an organization that might be said to have arisen in imitation of him—but also the American West.

There is a photograph taken of him in 1865, when he was forty-eight, and it tells you everything about him. The face is still boyish, the hair thick and swept back, the features regular and moderately handsome and generally unexceptional except for one absolutely striking characteristic: his eyes. They are deep, wise, dead calm, a bit sad, and, even from a distance of 140 years, riveting. They are the eyes of a man who is not afraid of anything.[31] He was the first great Indian fighter on the plains frontier; he was the legend that spawned a thousand other legends, dime novels, and Hollywood movies.

He was born in Little Cedar Lick, Tennessee, in 1817 into a prosperous family of soldiers. His grandfather served with Andrew Jackson during the Indian Wars and later sold Jackson his famous home, the Hermitage. Hays's father also served under Jackson and named his son for one of Jackson's most trusted officers, John Coffee.[32] Like many other young men looking for adventure, especially Tennesseans, young Jack migrated to Texas after the battle of San Jacinto, arriving in San Antonio probably in 1838, where he soon found work as a surveyor. Surveying in those years was the actual mechanism by which the settlers pushed their way westward into Indian lands. After independence Texas gave to new settlers a sort of land grant known as a "head right." In order to give people clear title to the land, someone had to go out with levels, chains, and surveyors' compasses and certify the claim. The Penateka Comanches, predictably, hated them and went out of their way to hunt them down. It was probably the most dangerous job in North America. The year Hays arrived, most of the men who did it were killed by Indians.[33]

Still, the job appealed to Hays, who was after adventure as much as wages. Surveying parties began to include not only the surveyors, but armed guards for the surveyors, as well as adventuresome types who just felt like tagging along, exploring the land, doing some hunting, and possibly shooting an Indian.[34] For the fearless, the unattached, and the rough-and-ready, it was a good time to be living in San Antonio, Texas. The land on the edge of the Balcones Escarpment was strikingly beautiful. There were gentle live-oak savannahs, and in the spring they exploded into a rainbow spectrum of wildflowers. Game abounded: buffalo, bear, deer, antelope, wild turkeys, sandhill cranes, coyotes, wolves, and deer by the tens of thousands. The crystal clear limestone rivers like the Llano, the Guadalupe, the Pedernales, and the San Marcos were jumping with fish.[35]

Plenty of these young men died hard deaths in their new paradise, including Hays's own cousin. Hays was undeterred. He did quite a bit of surveying: In 1838 he successfully surveyed seventy-six head rights.[36] He also began to make a name for himself as an Indian fighter, especially one who knew how to keep his men alive. According to one writer who knew him, "The little Tennessean would seem to be another man when the cry 'Indians' was raised. He would mount a horse and assume the appearance of a different being. With him it was charge, and war to the knife, and the Indians were whipped every time they attacked his party."[37] Like Grant in the Civil War, Hays worried less about what his adversaries could do to him than about what damage he could inflict on them. Like Grant, too, he was all about offense. In conversation he was soft-spoken and well-mannered; in a fight he was cold as ice and firmly in command of men who quickly deferred to him. Having made his name keeping surveyors alive, he began to ride with the new ranging companies, who were often the same people who went out to guard surveying teams. We know that he fought at the Battle of Plum Creek, and that he was part of the ill-fated Moore expedition of 1839 that returned ignominiously home on foot.[38] We do not know much more about his first years.

But he had clearly distinguished himself. In 1840, at the age of twenty-three, Hays became captain of the San Antonio station of the Rangers, a force that had been officially established by the Texas Republic but was still required to furnish its own arms, equipment, horses, and even food. There was no pay at first; later it would be set at $30 a month, when it arrived at all.[39] Some of the funds in the early days came from donations from ordinary citizens. (The Rangers as an organization existed only intermittently, living from congressional authorization to authorization, often disbanding then reforming.) Considering the life expectancy of the new Indian fighters—two years at the outside—it was a job not everyone would have wanted. And yet changes were already taking place that were shifting the odds. No one knew this better than Hays. For one thing, the new breed of Ranger—the Hays Ranger—knew how to ride. And he was mounted on an agile and fast horse, the product of local breeding of mustangs with Kentucky, Virginia, and Arabian strains. Those horses were heavier than the Indian mounts, but they could run with mustangs and keep up with them over long distances. It was said that Hays would not accept any recruit whose horse was worth less than $100.

Under Hays the ranging companies, rarely numbering more than fifteen or twenty men—began to behave more and more like the people they were hunting. "They moved as lightly over the prairie as the Indians did," wrote Caperton, "and lived as they did, without tent, with a saddle for a pillow at night."[40] Hays, in particular, paid a good deal of attention both to his Comanche foes and to his Lipan Apache scouts, learning from them how to ride, fight, track, make camp. Each man had a rifle, two pistols, and a knife; he had a Mexican blanket secured behind his saddle, and a small wallet in which he carried salt and cold flour and tobacco.[41] That was all. Like Comanches, the Rangers often traveled by moonlight, navigating by river courses and the north star, and dispensing with fires altogether, making "cold camps" and eating hardtack or other uncooked rations.[42] Hays's men would sleep fully clothed and fully armed, ready to fight at a minute's notice. They crossed rivers even in freezing weather, swimming by the side of their horses.[43] None of this behavior had any precedent in American military history. No cavalry anywhere could bridle and saddle a horse in less time than the Rangers.

Some of this came naturally to these young men, but some was the result of training. Hays insisted that his men practice both shooting and riding. One drill involved setting two six-foot-high posts in the ground forty yards apart. The Ranger would ride toward them at full speed, firing his rifle at the first post and his pistols at the second. Before long they were able to hit a ring on the post that was the size of a man's head.[44] Note that these men were charging and shooting *on horseback,* a concept taken entirely from Plains Indians. They probably started to do this sometime between 1838 and 1840; whenever the transition took place, it was done in direct imitation of the Comanches' own style and represented an enormous advance in anti-Indian warfare. The Rangers were the only ones in America who could do anything like that from the saddle, and they were absolutely the only ones who could do it in battle. It came from pure necessity: No one who had fought Comanches could possibly believe that there was any advantage to fighting them dismounted, on open ground.

Riding drills were even more elaborate. In a contemporary description by one of Hays's men:

> After practising for three or four months we became so purfect that we would run our horses half or full speede and pick up a hat, a coat, a blanket, or rope, or even a silver dollar, stand up in the saddle, throw ourselves on the side of our horses with only a foot and a hand to be seen, and shoot our pistols under the horses neck, rise up and reverse, etc.[45]

What Hays mainly understood was the value of pure audacity, of striking fear and panic in his opponents' hearts. He was still at a great disadvantage in weaponry: Each of his men had only three shots before they had to stop and reload, an activity that could not be done easily on horseback. Thus his Rangers struck quickly and hard, often from ambush, and often at night, overcoming their odds with a pure and reckless charge. "The one idea rules," wrote contemporary Victor Rose. "Make a rapid, noiseless march—strike the foe while he was not on the alert—punish him—crush him!" In the fall of 1840, Hays and twenty men encountered a party of two hundred Comanches at a crossing of the Guadalupe River near San Antonio. The Comanches had stolen a large number of horses. Hays put it this way to the men: "Yonder are the Indians, boys, and yonder are our horses. The Indians are pretty strong. But we can whip them. What do you say?"

"Go ahead," the men replied. Their assumption, as always, was that Hays would lead. "And we'll follow if there's a thousand of them."[46] The Indians, very likely in disbelief that white people would be crazy enough to take ten-to-one odds against mounted Comanches in the wilderness, drew themselves into a battle line and waited for the small band to attack. The Texans charged furiously and discharged their three shots; the line of battle was "thrown into confusion." In the scuffle, the headman was hit and killed; the Indians fled.

In this way Hays and his small companies slammed into the Penateka in central Texas, in engagements that were mostly unrecorded. Hays preferred surprise—killing them, just as the Comanches preferred to do, in their villages while they slept. He had learned the fundamental lesson of plains warfare: It was either victory or death. The Indians gave no quarter, and the Rangers rarely did, either. There was no expectation of honorable surrender. Hays did not always win, though he was astoundingly successful in preserving the lives of his men. In one fight he took one hundred twenty men and fifteen to twenty Lipan Apaches into battle against a vastly larger force of Comanches, losing twenty to thirty.[47] In another he took fifty Texans and ten Lipans, engaged a larger force in a running fight for an hour and a half. Hays's horses faltered, then broke down, unable to stay with the Comanche ponies. Several of his men were wounded. According to his own report, "Hays was now out of provisions and was forced to subsist on his broken down horses, until he reached Bexar [San Antonio]."[48]

He also learned quickly what would soon become his main advantage: Comanches were extremely predictable. They never changed their methods.

They were deeply custom-bound and equally deeply mired in their notions of medicine and magic. They reacted to a given situation—such as the killing of their war chief or medicine man—in exactly the same way, every time. In white man's terms, they were easily spooked. What Hays did appeared to be unbelievably brave to men who did not have his ability to calculate odds; he was also, it must be said, unbelievably brave.

Hays had other attributes as well; he was extremely cautious where his men's safety was concerned, and almost motherly in his care of them when they were wounded. He was remarkably industrious in camp, hauling wood and water, staking and hobbling horses, cooking food. But "when it was a mere question of personal danger his bravery bordered closely on rashness." He had an iron constitution that made him seemingly impervious to discomfort, bad weather, or sleep deprivation: "I have frequently seen him sitting by his campfire at night in some exposed locality," wrote J. W. Wilbarger,

> when rain was falling in torrents, or a cold norther with sleet or snow was whistling about his ears, apparently as unconscious of all discomfort as if he had been seated in some cozy room of a first class city hotel, and this, perhaps, when all he had eaten for supper was a handful of pecans or a piece of hard tack.[49]

Though Hays's exploits in battle were known along the border before his appointment to captain in 1840, two battles in 1841 established his fame on the frontier. The first involved Mexicans. With twenty-five men Hays routed a superior force of cavalry near Laredo, took twenty-five prisoners, and captured twenty-eight horses. He did it on sheer nerve, ordering his men to dismount, advance on the enemy, and to hold their fire well beyond where any normal skirmishers would have dared. Hays, as always, led the charge. At sixty yards—forty yards within the range of their accurate Kentucky rifles—they finally opened up. The Mexicans fled, and the Rangers, without waiting to reload, drew their pistols, jumped on the horses the Mexicans had abandoned, and pursued them.[50] The defeat caused a panic in Laredo, many of whose residents "jumped" the Rio Grande in fear of their lives. When Hays approached the city, its alcalde came out with a white flag to beg the Rangers to spare the town.[51] They did. They would not always be so kind. In Mexico City in 1847 they once executed eighty men in reprisal for the death of one Ranger.[52]

The second involved, as most of his fighting did, Comanches. In the summer of 1841 a Comanche war party came down on the settlements around San Antonio, raiding and killing and stealing horses. Hays, with one of the

Texas Congress's intermittent appropriations in hand, raised a company of thirteen men and rode after them, trailing them about seventy miles westward from San Antonio to the mouth of Uvalde Canyon. Hays found the Indians by using a trick he had learned from the Lipans: He simply followed the large flock of vultures that circled in a towering spiral over the Comanches' bloody middens. Near the camp, Hays spotted and engaged a dozen Comanches. The Rangers charged, and the Indians took cover in a woody thicket.

Hays immediately understood the implications of what his opponents had done: Their arrows would be of little or no use to them in such dense brush. He then ordered his men to surround the thicket and shoot anyone who came out. Though he was wounded in the hand, he took two men with him and went into the thicket—he was later joined by a third—where they fought a four-hour battle with the Indians, killing ten of them. Hays himself made a rare, and casually chilling, report on it to the Texas secretary of war:

> The Indians had but one gun, and the thicket being too dense to admit their using their arrows well, they fought under great disadvantage but continued to struggle to the last, keeping up their warsongs until they were all hushed in death. Being surrounded by horsemen, ready to cut them down if they left the thicket, and unable to use their arrows with much effect in their situation their fate was inevitable—they saw it and met it like heroes.[53]

It was an astonishing display of warrior prowess. For it, Hays was promoted to major. He was not yet twenty-five.

Despite his success fighting Comanches, Hays still faced one very large and intractable problem: his single-shot, hard-to-reload rifles and old-style pistols put him at a severe disadvantage against Comanches who carried twenty arrows in their quivers. There was no way around it. He had tried to adapt the long rifle to mounted use—and had actually worked minor miracles—but it was still a clumsy weapon that was best fired and reloaded on the ground. It was still the old backwoods rifle from Pennsylvania via Kentucky. Its shortcomings accounted, in large part, for the berserk aggressiveness of Hays's Rangers in battle. To stand pat was to be soon peppered with iron-tipped arrows. Headlong attack, for all of its risks, remained a far safer idea.

Meanwhile, back in the civilized, industrializing East, an enterprise was under way that would soon solve Hays's problem, and in so doing change the world, but for now was mired in failure and obscurity. In 1830 a sixteen-year-old with big ideas and a knack for intricate mechanics named

Samuel Colt had carved his first model of a revolving pistol out of wood. Six years later, he took out a patent on it. In 1838 a company in Paterson, New Jersey, began to manufacture Colt's patented firearms. Among them was a .36-caliber, five-chambered revolving pistol with an octagonal barrel and a concealed trigger that dropped down when the gun was cocked. It was not the first such idea, but it was believed to be the first that was put into production for general use.

There was just one problem with the new gun. No one wanted it. The weapon's natural market, the U.S. government, could not see any application and refused to subsidize it. The weapon had the feel of a cavalry sidearm, but just then the U.S. Army did not have a cavalry. Nor did the new pistol seem to interest private citizens. It was a nifty, if somewhat impractical, product. Oddly, the only people who wanted it were in the exotic and faraway Republic of Texas. In 1839, President Mirabeau Lamar directed the Texas navy, of all things, to order 180 five-shot Colt revolvers from the Patent Arms Manufacturing Company in Paterson. Later the Texas army ordered another forty.[54] The pistols were shipped and paid for. There is no particular evidence that they were ever used by sailors or anyone else in the service of the Texas government. It seemed to be an obscure and impractical weapon destined for an obscure and irrelevant branch of the Texas military. Such as it was. And there they languished.

No one knows exactly how these revolvers came into the hands of Jack Hays and his Rangers. But they most certainly did. In later correspondence with Colt, Samuel Walker, one of Hays's most celebrated lieutenants, placed the date sometime in 1843.[55] This is probably accurate, since that was the same year Sam Houston disbanded the navy.[56] Whenever the event took place, the Rangers immediately grasped the significance of such weapons. To them, Colt's contraption was a revelation: a multishot weapon that could be used from horseback and thus, at long last, even the odds. Though there is no record of it, Hays and his men must have spent long hours practicing with the new weapons and figuring out what they could do. And they must have spent many nights around the campfire discussing the revolver's strengths and weaknesses.

The new Colt revolver had many weaknesses. It was fragile. The bullets it fired were of a light caliber when a heavier load—.44 caliber or larger—was needed. It was not terribly accurate except at close range. It employed preloaded cylinders, which meant that a Ranger armed with two pistols and four cylinders had forty shots. But the cylinders were difficult to change, and when they were empty a man in the field could not reload them. That, however, did not change the basic, astounding fact of a *revolving* chamber. Hays and the rest of his Rangers, notably Ben McCulloch and Samuel Walker, were convinced of its potential. By the spring of 1844 they were ready to give Colt's unpopular, oddball revolver its first combat test.

That test came to be known as the Battle of Walker's Creek, a minor military engagement that became one of the defining moments in the history of Texas and of the American West. Indeed, it can be argued that before Jack Hays arrived in San Antonio, Americans in the West went about largely on foot and carried Kentucky rifles. By the time he left in 1849, anybody going west was mounted and carrying a holstered six-shooter. Walker's Creek was the beginning of that change.

In early June 1844, Hays and fifteen men were scouting the upper courses of the Pedernales and Llano. They were in the hill country, west of Austin and San Antonio, the Penateka heartland. Finding nothing, they headed back toward home. On June 8, they stopped to gather honey from a bee tree on Walker's Creek, a tributary of the Guadalupe River about fifty miles north of San Antonio. Hays, meanwhile, had dispatched two of his men to lag behind the group, and see if they were being followed. This was an old Indian practice. Hays had learned many old Indian practices. The two men soon dashed into camp and breathlessly reported that they had found ten sets of Indian horse tracks behind them. The company quickly saddled up and countermarched in the direction of the Indians. As they approached, three or four Indians made a great show of alarm, and then an even greater show of fleeing for their lives. Another old Indian trick. Hays did not fall for it, and he did not pursue them.[57]

Soon the rest of the body of Penatekas—seventy-five of them—showed themselves. The Texans advanced slowly, while the Indians fell back to the top of a steep hill, a superb defensive redoubt in the broken, rocky country timbered with live oak. From there they taunted the Rangers, yelling in Spanish and English, "Charge! Charge!"

Hays obliged them, though not exactly in the way they had imagined. Realizing that he and his fourteen men were temporarily concealed at the base of the hill, he turned his little band and galloped at full speed some two hundred to three hundred yards, circled the bottom of the hill, emerged behind the Indians, and charged their flank.[58] Taken by surprise, the Comanches still managed to recover quickly. They split their forces and wheeled on the Texans on both flanks, yelling loudly. Under normal circumstances, their assault would have broken the Ranger battle line. It would have routed them. But in a remarkable display of horsemanship and raw, bone-rattling courage, the Rangers formed a circle with their horses and thus, rump to rump, received the charge.

What happened next—seventy-five Penateka Comanches on fifteen Rangers, arrows and lances against repeating pistols—sounds like pure bloody pandemonium. Several Rangers were badly wounded. Their pistols, meanwhile, were dropping Indians from the saddle at an alarming rate. This stage of the fight lasted fifteen minutes. Then the Indians broke and fled. It became a running fight, and went for more than an hour on over two miles of rough terrain. Urged on by their heroic chief, the Indians kept rallying, regrouping, and attacking, only to be overwhelmed by the Rangers' fire-spitting Colt revolvers. Forty Indians were now dead or wounded. One Ranger was dead and four were wounded. Still, the fight went on, as the Indian leader rallied his men again and again.

Then, as though to illustrate the five-shooter's main weakness, Hays's men ran out of ammunition. More precisely, they had run out of preloaded cylinders, which could not be reloaded in the field, and no one had anything but five-shooters. They were now at the mercy of the thirty-five remaining Indians. Or at least they would be when the Indians figured out their ammunition had run out. Hays then coolly called out to see if anyone had any bullets left. One man, Robert Gillespie, rode forward and said he did. "Dismount and shoot the chief," ordered Hays. This Gillespie did: At a range of "thirty steps" he dropped the chief from his saddle. The remaining Indians "in wild affright at the loss of their leader . . . scattered in every direction in the brushwood."[59]

When the smoke had cleared, twenty Comanches were dead, and another thirty were wounded. Hays had suffered one man killed and three seriously wounded. One of his main lieutenants, Samuel Walker, was pinned to the ground with a Comanche lance. The Rangers made camp there, to care for their wounded. Three days later four Comanches showed up, perhaps to reclaim their dead. Hays attacked once more, killing three of them.

Though it would take awhile for everyone else on the frontier to understand what happened at Walker's Creek, and it would take the Mexican War to make the U.S. government understand what it meant, a fundamental, paradigm-shattering change had occurred. The Indians now faced the prospect of being blasted from horseback by guns that never emptied; the whites could now fight entirely mounted against their foes with weapons whose frequency of firing nearly matched that of the Comanches. The odds had been evened up. Or better. "Up to this time," Samuel Walker wrote in a letter to Samuel Colt in 1846, "these daring Indians had always supposed themselves superior to us, man to man, on horse. . . . The result of this engagement was such as to intimidate them and enable us to treat with them."[60]

Still, no one outside the Republic of Texas understood what Sam Colt had done. In 1844, fully six years after he had begun to produce his repeating pistols, his invention was a failure. The Paterson, New Jersey, factory had gone into bankrupcty in 1842. Colt managed to keep his patents but little else. The models, prototypes, and plans for his six-shooters were all lost or destroyed. He spent five years in poverty.

But there was hope, and Colt knew it. Word of what Hays and his men were doing with the revolver had reached him in the East. He was so excited that in the fall of 1846 he wrote Samuel Walker in Texas,

> with a few inquires regarding your expereance in the use of my repeating fire arm & your opinion as their adoptation to the military service in the war against Mexico—I have hard so much of Col Hayse and your exploits wit the arms of my invention that I have long desired to know you personally & get from you a true narrative of the vareous instances where my arms have proved of more than ordinary utility.[61]

Walker wrote back immediately and enthusiastically with a description of how effective the revolvers had been at the Battle of Walker's Creek. "With improvements," he concluded, "I think they can be rendered the most perfect weapon in the world for mounted troops."[62] From here on Sam Colt's prospects began very quickly to improve.

The war in Mexico had started and the Texas Rangers had volunteered for it and had been accepted by General Zachary Taylor. They were soon fighting south of the border. They made an extraordinary impression on the U.S. Army in Mexico. They were like nothing anyone had ever seen. They wore no uniforms, provided their own weapons and equipment, and went everywhere mounted. Unlike almost everyone else in the army, they preferred to fight mounted. They served mainly as scouts—effectively transferring the style of warfare they had learned from the Comanches to the lands south of

the border—and tales of their bravery, toughness, and resourcefulness spread
from the Mexican War around the world. Samuel Walker's swashbuckling
dash with seventy-five men through a field held by fifteen hundred Mexican
cavalry and Colonel Jack Hays's savage efficiency in clearing the roads of
Mexican guerrillas were told and retold in salons from Chicago to New York.
General Taylor complained of their lawlessness, but the fact of the matter
was that the enemy was terrified of them. Everyone was terrified of them.

The most striking thing of all about them was their weaponry. Their five-
shot Colts, and their ability to wield them with deadly accuracy from horseback, were the wonder of the army. So much so that the army now wanted
more. One thousand of them, to be exact, enough to supply all of the Rangers and other Texans in Mexico. There was just one problem. Colt had not
made a revolver of any kind for five years. He had no money, and he had
no factory to make them. He did not even have a working model of one of
his pistols. He even advertised in the New York newspapers, without success, trying to find one. Still, he offered to sell the army a thousand of them
for $25 apiece. With a contract in hand, in January 1847 he convinced his
friend Eli Whitney to make the pistols. Now all he had to do was design a
brand-new weapon.

And then something remarkable happened. Colt asked Samuel Walker,
who happened to be temporarily stationed in Washington, to help him with
the design. Colt wrote:

> I have sergested the propriaty of your coming to see me before I commence
> the construction of thes arms. . . . Get from the department an order to cum to
> New York & direct in the construction of thees arms with the improvements
> you sergest.[63]

Thus the two men—the hardened Ranger from the Texas frontier and the
ambitious young Connecticut Yankee—became collaborators. Walker was
full of ideas. He explained to Colt that he needed a bigger caliber, and that
the gun had to be heavier, more rugged, with a longer barrel and a longer and
fuller "handle." His refinements could be quite specific, too: In a letter to
Colt on February 19, 1847, he recommended making the "hind sight much
finer and the front sight of German silver and of a shape altogether different."[64] It was Colt's idea to use six chambers instead of five.

The result, the Walker Colt, was one of the most effective and deadly
pieces of technology ever devised, one that would soon kill more men in

combat than any sidearm since the Roman short sword.[65] It was a small cannon. It had an enormous nine-inch barrel and weighed in at four pounds nine ounces. Its revolving chambers held conical .44-caliber bullets that weighed two hundred twenty grains each. The powder charge—fifty grains of black powder—made the new Colt pistol as deadly as a rifle up to a hundred yards.[66] Engraved on its barrel—this was Sam Colt's gift to the Rangers—was an etching of the Battle of Walker's Creek, as Samuel Walker had described it to him. The sight of a Ranger on horseback, flashing Walker Colt in hand, is one of the indelible images from the Mexican War. It of course saved Colt. Though he lost a few thousand dollars on this deal, he later became one of the richest men in the country. Samuel Walker died, a hero, on October 9, 1847, in Huamantla, Mexico, from a sniper's bullet.

Eleven

WAR TO THE KNIFE

IN THE PLEASANT, cool October air, in a lovely prairie upland by a clear spring in a place no *taibo* had ever been, the woman called Nautdah set about the very hard work of dismantling fifteen-hundred-pound buffaloes. This was women's work, as was almost anything to do with a buffalo that did not involve tracking it and killing it. Comanche women cut the meat into strips for drying. They tanned the hides and made the robes and harvested the paunch and the sinew and the marrow from bones and the ground-up brains and every other part of the huge beasts that were, collectively, the foundations of Nermernuh existence. Women did everything else, too, it seemed: They cooked and tended to the children and horses, and did the packing when the pasturage ran out or the enemies got too close. They fought, too, usually only defensively; they went along with raiding parties. Nautdah did this.

It is impossible to say if Nautdah was happy, or if happiness had any place in her expectations of life, which amounted to an endless and unyielding progression of hard tasks. There were occasional joys. Children were joys. She had three of them. The oldest, a large, strong boy named Quanah, was twelve. His brother, Peanuts, was a few years younger. And there was the beautiful little girl, Toh-tsee-ah, "Prairie Flower," who was just a toddler. If there was such a thing as happiness on the crude frontier, she was very likely happy with her marriage, too. Her husband, Peta Nocona, was an enormous, muscular, dark-skinned man and a prominent war chief. She enjoyed his elevated social status. She enjoyed the fruits of his hunting. He was a great raider and had many horses, which made them, in plains terms, rich. She had to share him with only one other wife, a full-blood Comanche woman.

This was October 1860. Though the United States of America was a month away from electing Abraham Lincoln and thus setting in motion political events that would break the nation apart and spill the blood of a million men, none of this was apparent to Nautdah or her family. She and her people could read the presence of white men. They were extraordinarily tuned to the presence or absence of military power, to the pulse and increase of settlement, or to the presence or absence of military will. They understood when the game did not return to the hunting grounds. But they saw everything from the remoteness of the plains, still a vast piece of the American continent's midsection where much of life continued, amazingly, as it had before. Nautdah lived a life with her family that was not unlike the life of a Comanche woman in 1760. Or, in many ways, 1660. There were still buffalo. The Comanches still made war. They were still unchallenged in 95 percent of the old homelands.

The reader may well wonder how it is possible to see into a Comanche camp on the remote plains in a place where no white men lived or traveled. But the preceding account is not fictional in any sense. Though Cynthia Ann Parker was hard to track—and as time went by she was becoming an ever more distant memory on the fast-changing frontier—in October 1860 her whereabouts are known precisely. We know exactly where she was, who she was with, and what she was doing, and where she was camped within a few hundred yards. Her circumstances are known because of the events of the next two months, and because of the bloody catastrophe that was about to befall her, a fate that, twinned with her capture in the 1836 raid, made the woman born as Cynthia Ann Parker one of the least lucky people in the world.

She herself had no inkling of what was going to happen. She was doing what she had always done, and had a few months yet to enjoy the immemorial life of a Nermernuh woman. She was living in a large Comanche camp, one that contained as many as five hundred people. It was something more than a nomadic camp, though. It was more like an operations base and supply depot for many different raiding parties, a sort of swing station through which supplies moved as well as plunder, cattle, and horses on their way to markets elsewhere. The camp was also a relay for stolen horses.[1] This was

Indian logistics on a large scale; there were prodigious amounts of everything, from horses to shoes and sausages, suggesting a degree of planning
and orchestration that the Comanches were not known to possess. Here is
what was later found at the camp:

> a large amount of dried beef and buffalo meat, buffalo skins . . . an enormous
> amount of buffalo rugs, cooking utensils, axes, knives, tomahawks, tools for
> dressing skins, wooden bowls, moccasins, whetstones, leather bags filled with
> marrow out of bones and brains, little sacks of soup, sausages, guts stuffed with
> tallow and brains, and various other things . . . [2]

The Comanche camp was located near the Pease River, which originates
in the Texas Panhandle and snakes westward along the northern corridor of
Texas and joins the Red River. Before that confluence, south of the present-
day town of Quanah, and ten or twelve miles northeast of the town of Crowell, a clear, spring-fed stream called Mule Creek enters the Pease in a long
valley framed by rugged hills and oak and cottonwood and hackberry trees.
Nautdah's village was a mile back from where the crystalline Mule Creek met
the salty, gypsum-laced waters of the Pease, strung out for a few hundred yards
in a cottonwood grove along the creek. The country was pretty, spare. Wide,
high prairie plains were broken by the river and the hills and the steep ridges
that rose from the creek. The village was roughly 125 miles west of the line of
settlement, which in the autumn of 1860 ran just west of Fort Worth.

What Nautdah did was bloody, messy work. Sometimes she was covered
from head to toe in buffalo fat, blood, marrow, and tissue, so much so that it
turned her naturally light hair and light skin almost black.[3] So much so that
it would have been hard to spot her as the white woman in the Indian camp.
While she worked, she watched her children. She was still nursing her daughter, Prairie Flower. Her boys played. They were old enough to hunt now, too,
and sometimes they went out with their father. Peta Nocona, meanwhile,
spent his time hunting and raiding.

His raiding habits are known, too. Through the summer and early fall, he
led a series of sweeping, devastating raids into the counties between present-
day Fort Worth and Wichita Falls, Texas. There is more than a bit of irony in
the fact that one of his chief targets, Parker County, was named for his wife's
uncle Isaac Parker, yet another prominent Parker who lived in the county
seat of Weatherford.[4] Parker had arrived in Texas in 1833 with his father,
Elder John, and brothers Daniel, Silas, and James and the rest of the Parker
clan. He had served Texas as an elected representative or state senator almost

continuously from 1837 to 1857. He had been instrumental in passing the bill for the new county in 1855.[5] He was wealthy, exceedingly handsome, with chiseled features. He was widely known as a storyteller. Peta Nocona of course did not know any of this.

And now he had come to plunder his in-law's creation. From all local accounts, most of Nocona's raids came at night, by the light of what was already widely referred to in Texas as a Comanche moon. According to Parker County resident Hilory Bedford, "People on moonlit nights were in perfect dread. I well remember the time when the beautiful nights of the full moon, instead of being a source of pleasure, were, on the contrary, to be dreaded as the worst of evils."[6] Whole families and settlements were wiped out. Families with the names Youngblood and Rippy, lost forever to history, ceased to exist, leaving as monuments smoking, burned-out cabins, and bodies mutilated beyond recognition. The raiders stole cattle and horses. Most of the raiding in those days involved stealing. Bedford attributed the raids to Peta Nocona. Because this area was their old hunting ground, Nocona and his warriors knew the land intimately. Moving by night, they were almost impossible to apprehend.[7]

The raids were remarkable, too, because the panicked whites in that arc of settlement west of Fort Worth did not seem to be able to do anything to stop them. In March of 1860, Governor Sam Houston had authorized Colonel Middleton T. Johnson to raise a regiment of Rangers to punish the Indians on the state's northern and northwestern frontiers.[8] Though Rip Ford had won a splendid victory on Antelope Creek two years before, and had wanted to continue to pursue Comanches in their heartland, his funding had been cut off. Now Johnson raised five companies. They rode north to Fort Belknap, where they installed themselves. It is not clear exactly whom Johnson recruited, or what his standards were. But these men were very clearly not the old Hays Rangers. While they waited hopefully for Indian raids, they were engulfed in boredom. They drank. They fought each other with fists and knives, played poker, and hunted buffalo. Colonel Johnson at one point took a long leave of absence to get married in Galveston. In June one drunken Ranger shot another and wounded him. Another was said to have been murdered by local desperados, or deserted, it was hard to tell which. The men held dances at which they took both male and female parts.[9] They hunted buffalo.

When they finally took to the field, three hundred strong, they could not find any Indians. During the summer Johnson and his men were outfoxed, outrun, and generally humiliated in ways that would have amazed the old Rangers. According to one account, after one of their unsuccessful forays, they had started for home. Though they could not find Peta Nocona, he apparently had no trouble finding them. At night the Indians charged the Ranger camp, stampeded the horses, and drove them away, leaving the white men to return home across the plains on foot.[10] On another occasion, while the Rangers were riding north toward Oklahoma, Indians swept around south of them, stealing seventy-five horses and killing several settlers during a four-day spree. The Rangers turned, vowing to "wipe them out." Instead, the Indians set the prairie on fire, destroying horse forage and causing the white men to return to Fort Belknap.[11] The failure of Johnson's unit illustrated an old truth in the West: that knowledge of how to fight Comanches spread, at best, sporadically and unevenly along the frontier. There were things that Jack Hays knew in 1839 that Rangers in general still had not learned twenty years later.

The people on the frontier were furious. John Baylor, the flamboyant, vehemently anti-Indian editor of the Weatherford paper, *The White Man,* insulted the Rangers by calling them "perfectly harmless," declaring that their hiring was "the most stupendous sell practiced on the frontier people" and that all of their expectations "have resulted only in the rangers's eating twice their weight in beef at 11 cents a pound . . . drinking bad water, and cursing the day they were induced to soldier for glory, in a campaign that has resulted in the killing of two citizens, and the marriage of the Colonel of the regiment." It further stated that if he and his people found one of them, especially Johnson, they would hang him."[12] Johnson, meanwhile, seemed more interested in his blossoming love affair with the lovely socialite Louisa Power Givens.[13] His unsuccessful expeditions that summer offer a good example of what happened when white men wrote the history of the Indian wars. Johnson gets scant mention in Ranger histories. There is very little detail on his expeditions. He is dismissed with a shrug. No one is much interested in the abject humiliation of the institution of the Texas Rangers. If Indians had been writing about the northwest frontier of Texas in 1860, they might have characterized Peta Nocona's attacks as tactically brilliant guerrilla warfare, in the same way historians would later speak of the daring exploits of Confederate raider Nathan Bedford Forrest.

Flush with victory, scalps, cattle, and horses, Nocona returned to his camp on Mule Creek and rejoined his wife and three children. In late November he rode eastward again to the frontier, this time at the head of fifty-five warriors. This time the raiding was worse, crueler, more vengeful even than it had been in the early fall. His war party swung west of Mesquiteville (now Jacksboro), and rode hard into the line of settlements, killing everyone they saw. Near Weatherford they attacked the ranch of John Brown, stealing his horses, killing him by driving lances through every part of his body, and cutting off his nose. They rode across open country in a torrential rain and arrived at a place called Stagg Prairie, on the western edge of Parker County.[14] Here, on the very outermost edge of the bleeding frontier, in the most hazardous place in the state of Texas, a greenhorn name Ezra Sherman, who did not even own a gun, had decided to move his wife, Martha, and three children. On November 26, a group of seventeen braves from Nocona's force arrived at the Sherman home. The Shermans were having dinner at the time. The Indians entered the cabin, actually shook hands with the family, then asked for something to eat.[15] The Shermans, nervous and unsure what was happening, gave the Indians their table. Once they had eaten, the Indians turned the family out, though with continuing professions of goodwill. "Vamoose," they said. "No hurt, vamoose." The Shermans' seven-year-old son fled and hid himself. The others got away as fast as they could, stumbling in the driving rain across their fields toward a nearby farm.[16]

They weren't fast enough. Half a mile from their house, the Indians reappeared. Now they seized Martha, who was nine months pregnant. While Ezra and his two children continued on, they dragged Martha back to a point about two hundred yards from the cabin. There she was gang-raped. When they were finished, they shot several arrows into her and then did something that was unusually cruel, even for them. They scalped her alive by making deep cuts below her ears and, in effect, peeling the top of her head entirely off. As she later explained, this was difficult for the Indians to do, and took a long time to accomplish. Bleeding, she managed to drag herself back inside her house, which the heavy rain had prevented the Indians from burning, where her husband found her. She lived four days, during which time she was coherent enough to tell the story to her neighbors. She gave birth to a stillborn infant. She probably died of peritonitis: Comanches knew what it was and often aimed their arrows at a victim's navel. Half a century later, a Palo Pinto County rancher recalled that her scalping left her a "fearful sight."[17] She was one of twenty-three people who died by the hand of Peta Nocona's raiders over a span of two days, November 26 to November 28.

Frontier people saw Martha Sherman's death as the random and senseless slaughter of a Christian woman by a tribe whose primitive, godless, and subhuman nature it was to do such things. Mrs. Sherman hadn't hurt anyone. She had committed no acts of war. But her death was neither random nor senseless. She was as much a victim of colliding political and social forces as she was of the arrows and knives of Peta Nocona's raiders. Her death did mean something. It was a consequence of the unprecedented invasion of Comancheria by white settlers that had taken place at the end of the 1850s. The land she lived on was not the hardscrabble hills of Edwards Plateau west of Austin and San Antonio where the buffalo herd rarely roamed. This was lush, open, long-grass prairie beyond the Cross Timbers in northern Texas, and encompassed the rich and ancient buffalo ground that Comanches had been fighting for since the early eighteenth century. Pioneers had been gradually pushing westward behind a line of federal forts that had been built in the early 1850s. But the big rush came at the end of the decade, when white settlement leapfrogged fifty miles to a line of longitude that passes through present-day Wichita Falls: *way* beyond where the white people had ever gone before.

The newly chinked cabins in Parker County were part of this swelling presence. And though Martha Sherman was undoubtedly a well-intentioned and God-fearing woman, she and Ezra were part of that clamorous, chaotic, and brazenly aggressive lunge into the enemy's territory. The Comanches saw it that way, because there was no other way for them to see it. That fall the buffalo had moved south, bumping up against the white man's homesteads, meaning that Comanches who stayed away from the frontier were going hungry. Peta Nocona's brutal sweep through northern Texas was thus a political act, with political objectives. So was the Shermans' decision to build their cabin in western Parker County, though less self-consciously so. Both coveted the same land, both wanted the other side to stop contesting it, and neither was willing to give anything meaningful in exchange. By comparison, what happened at Parker's Fort was minor contact between picket lines. The raids of Peta Nocona in 1860 constituted outright war for territory. Everything was at stake now. Everything was changing.[18]

Exploding might be a better word. When Cynthia Ann Parker was taken from her family in 1836, the population of Texas was around 15,000. By 1860 it had grown to 604,215.[19] In the 1850s alone, some 400,000 new people had arrived. Fully 42,422 of Texas's residents that year were foreign born;

182,921 of them were slaves. San Antonio was a bustling town of 8,235.[20] Galveston, Houston, and Austin were all booming, transforming themselves from mudtraps where pigs roamed the streets into something that began to look like urban civilization. In 1836 there were only a few rutted dirt wagon roads in Texas; by 1860 there were thousands of miles of such roads, plus 272 miles of railroad tracks.[21] There were three newspapers when the Parker captives disappeared into the plains; now there were seventy-one.[22] Still, the state's population was mostly rural, and most of its citizens were subsistence farmers. On the outer frontier they built primitive dog-run cabins or sod huts, made everything themselves except for tools and weapons, and scratched out a hard and meager living from the land. They endured many of the horrors that settlers on the Appalachian frontier had endured a century before. And they kept coming on in spite of this, from Alabama and Tennessee and other points east, piling up by the thousands on the edge of the plains barrier that had stood inviolable for so long.

The problem, as Peta Nocona's raid illustrated, was that they were still being eviscerated, tortured, raped, and made captive by Comanches, and there was little evidence that anyone in the Office of Indian Affairs in Washington, D.C., had the remotest idea of what to do about it. It seemed impossible that, twenty-one years after Jack Hays and the Rangers started fighting Indians in new ways, this could be the case. Every so often troops would be sent forth with the glorious task of breaking Comanche power forever. Every so often they would actually find Comanches and kill a significant number of them. But these expeditions never added up to anything. They didn't stop anything. There was no concerted will to pursue the adversaries into their dark heartland, to destroy them.

And so the attacks continued, increasing in severity after 1857. Most came from the Yamparika, Kotsoteka, Nokoni, and Quahadi bands, who remained as free as ever in their strongholds in the far north or far west. Kiowas, equally untouchable above the Canadian River, were raiding, too, often in tandem with Comanches. The old patterns reasserted themselves, only slightly altered, and nothing really changed. The great wave of American settlement had swept forward from the eastern coastlands through the trans-Appalachian country and on past the Mississippi. It had had a brief moment of hope and optimism, sailing across the 98th meridian with the Shermans and other settlers. And suddenly it had crashed and burned yet again on the same vast and deadly physical barrier that had stopped the Spanish, the French, the Mexicans, and the original Texans: the Great Plains. There, stretching clear to Canada, remained the formidable war machines of the Sioux, Arapaho, Comanche, Kiowa, and Cheyenne.

By the time he left Texas to seek his fortune in California in 1849, Jack Hays had proved a point. He had shown, many would have said incontrovertibly, that Comanches could be hunted, pursued to their villages, fought on their own terms, and beaten. He had invented a new form of warfare, and he had invented its implausible agent of destruction: a lightly armed and lightly mounted man on a fast horse who wore an old slouch hat and scraggy beard and spit tobacco and defied absurd numerical odds against him. Hays had adapted a weapon no one else had wanted and had turned it into the ultimate frontier sidearm, one that soon changed the very nature of the experience of the American West. By the time the Mexican War ended, a casual observer might have concluded that the tide had already turned against the Indians and that the Comanches, encased as they now were inside the pulsing American empire and facing a determined people who understood how to fight them, were going to meet their doom rather faster than one might have expected.

Nothing of the sort happened. It was as though the Rangers had never happened, as though no one remembered what they had spilled the blood of so many young men to learn. No Rangers were consulted by anyone in Washington. Hays, who had gone west with the Gold Rush and soon became sheriff of San Francisco County, was largely forgotten, at least for a time, as were his hard-riding comrades. The Rangers were disbanded, replaced by U.S. Army units. They were periodically re-formed, which usually meant that a single captain recruited a band of men for an expedition with limited state funding, in 1850, 1852, 1855, 1857, and 1858. But most of these companies did little Indian fighting. Some fought small skirmishes with Lipan Apache raiders in far south Texas. A few fought Comanches. One of them went renegade, joining an ill-fated expedition under the command of an infamous adventurer to overthrow the government of Mexico. They ended by burning the Mexican border town of Piedras Negras and covering themselves with shame.[23] The 1857 recruits, wrote Walter Prescott Webb, "left practically no record of their presence on the frontier." One of their companies managed to find a small group of Indians, "but was completely deceived and worsted by them."[24] The notable exception to this was Rip Ford's 1858 expedition north of the Red River, of which more will be said later.

But the inefficiency of the post-Hays Rangers paled next to the U.S. Army, which over a decade managed to engineer a retrogression of astounding scale and proportion. The cruel, lingering death of Martha Sherman in the fall of 1860 had another meaning as well: It was the harvest of a decade of federal incompetence, stupidity, and willful political blindness.

The failure took many forms. In 1848 and 1849 the army sent its engineers forth to build a line of five forts, stretching from Fort Worth (which was one of them) to San Antonio. They were obsolete the minute they were finished. The line of settlement had already engulfed them.

There was also the problem of the men who were sent to occupy them. When it had withdrawn its forces from Mexico, the United States had sent seven companies of regulars to replace the Texas state troops. These consisted of *infantry* in various forms. Considering the advances in Indian warfare on the Texas frontier in the previous ten years, this was a remarkable decision. It could only have been made by people in cravats and waistcoats who lunched at fancy hotels and lived two thousand miles from the border; people, moreover, who did not want Indian wars and therefore did not want professional killers like Bigfoot Wallace out hunting redskins in their home ranges. In almost every way, the new Indian fighters were the antithesis of Hays's men.

The best examples were the army's new "elite" fighters in the West: the dragoons. They were a heavily mounted infantry who rode horses to the scene of battle, but fought dismounted. They were undoubtedly effective against comparably mounted and armed opponents, but on the Texas frontier they were a shocking anachronism, like something out of Louis XIV's court. They were clad in "French-inspired blue jackets, orange forage caps, white pantaloons, and sweeping mustaches."[25] Like Louis's old musketeers, too, they were self-consciously gallant, in ways that would soon seem nearly comical.

They were armed with weapons that the Spanish and Mexicans had long ago discovered to be useless against horse tribes: single-shot pistols (apparently the army, unlike its Mexican War victims, had not quite grasped the meaning or value of the Walker Colt), gleaming swords that had no particular application against Indians with fourteen-foot lances and rapid-fire arrows, and, oddest of all, the Springfield Arsenal Musketoon, Model 1842, a truly atrocious weapon that was unreliable at any distance. Heavy in the saddle, and not a real cavalry anyway, the splendidly arrayed horse infantry could barely manage twenty-five miles a day in pursuit of Indians. They often had to walk by their horses, so as not to exhaust them. The warriors they pursued—pursuit being something the army in the West did not do very much of—could ride fifty miles in seven hours, and one hundred miles without stopping, abilities the plodding, weighed-down dragoons simply refused to believe. The only way the Indians could ever be in danger from these soldiers, observed one Texas Ranger, was if their ridiculous appearance and ungainly horsemanship caused the Indians to laugh themselves to death.[26] "It was rather an unfortunate experiment to mount infantry soldiers," wrote a Ranger captain, "many of whom had never been on horse in their lives, to operate against the best horsemen in the United States—the Comanche. Yet the United States Army tried it."[27] One can only speculate on how long it would have taken Rangers under Hays or Walker or McCulloch to leave such soldiers in pieces on the ground. It is not surprising that they never caught any Indians.

They were still far more efficient than the infantry, which made up the largest part of the troops then stationed on the frontier. The choice was a curious one, since the best an infantryman could do in such a vast and wide open country, against a fleet, mounted opponent, was to shoot his weapon from the gun portals of a stockade fence. Such a defensive notion was reasonable enough in places more civilized than the western frontier. But it had nothing to do with fighting horse Indians, who were never stupid or desperate enough to attack federal forts. They quickly learned to bypass them. Even before the posts were complete, citizens in some towns were calling for protection by Rangers. In 1849 one Texas newspaper stated that "The idea of repelling mounted Indians, the most expert horsemen in the world, with a force of foot soldiers, is ridiculous."[28] It did not help that most of these men were foreign-born German and Irish, that many of them were criminals, led miserably demoralizing lives, and suffered greatly from disease, poor sanitation, and alcoholism.

Yet this was the policy that seeped forth from Washington. That policy was deeply ambivalent. In 1849 the Home Department (later to become the Department of the Interior) had taken over the Office of Indian Affairs from the army. In principle, this was a reasonable idea. But it set up two conflicting authorities. The Office of Indian Affairs was deeply committed to avoiding Indian wars in the West. It distrusted the army, and tended to disbelieve cries of wolf from the settlements, believing that the whites' problems with the Indians were of their own doing. They liked the idea of treaties, the more the better. They liked the notion of an enduring peace, in spite of the headlong rush of settlers into Indian territory who wanted peace only if it meant complete capitulation by Indians. The army knew better, but could do nothing about it. The Indian office was moreover deeply corrupt, full of agents who saw nothing wrong with cheating Indians of gifts or annuities or food allotments—acts that often led to bloodshed. The result was a policy of breathtaking passivity that lasted from 1849 to 1858. Soldiers were not to fight Indians unless attacked, or unless they had clear evidence that the Indians had been involved in a criminal act.

The government's approach was purely defensive. Thus the new line of forts, built one hundred miles to the west and finished by 1852,[29] were not much more effective than the first ones. Not at first, anyway. Though they had been built at great expense, they were typically understaffed and underfunded. Infantrymen could do little more than drill and march about the parade ground. Pursuit of mounted Comanches by foot troops was pointless. The forts were built to stop Indian raids on both the Texas frontier and northern Mexico, yet through most of the 1850s they were ineffective. As Wallace and Hoebel wrote, "Officers and troops were strangely ignorant of the rudiments of warfare as carried on by the Indians of the plains."[30]

The failure at the federal level also extended to treaties, which were no different from any of the failed treaties signed by the government of the United States from its earliest days. One historian has estimated the number of treaties made and broken by the government at 378.[31] The outcome of nearly every treaty was the same: White civilization advanced, aboriginal civilization was destroyed, subsumed, pushed out. The government made claims it could never enforce and never intended to enforce, and Indians died. This is a dreary history. The Five Civilized Tribes were chased westward by a series of treaties, each of which guaranteed that this time government promises would be kept, that this time the trail of tears would end. Some of this treaty-making was pure hypocrisy; some of it, as in the case of Texas Indian agent Robert Neighbors, was earnest and well-meaning naïveté. Indians always wanted agreements that would last for all eternity; no white man who ever signed one could have possibly believed that the government could make such promises.

An enormous amount of energy was expended making pointless treaties with Comanches. A brief summary will suffice to make the point. The first treaty was made in 1847, with the Penatekas, who of course could not enforce any of its provisions on the other bands. Its terms were typical: Indians were to give up captives and restore stolen goods, accept the jurisdiction of the United States, and trade only with licensed traders. In exchange, the government promised that no whites would be permitted to go among the Indians without a pass signed personally by the president of the United States, that they would give them blacksmiths to repair guns and tools, and would give them gifts worth $10,000.[32] The whites, of course, never upheld the treaty. One wonders who came up with the ridiculous idea of making President James K. Polk approve passes for every settler who wanted to cross into the Indian country. As usual, the Indians were not allowed beyond a certain established line. Whites, meanwhile, clamored forward. Another similar treaty followed in 1850, which the Senate would not ratify, making all of the promises of the Indian office meaningless.

The treaty of 1853 was pure fraud, on both sides. This agreement, signed by "representatives" of the northern Comanches, Kiowas, and Kiowa Apaches that had no tribal power to agree to anything, allowed the United States to build roads in Indian territory, establish depots and posts, and protect immigrants passing through. As compensation for this, the agents promised goods in the amount of $18,000 annually. The Indians pledged to cease their attacks both in the United States and Mexico, and to give back all of their captives.[33]

Neither side abided by the agreement, nor had they any intention of doing so. The annuity goods were not delivered, though someone in the Indian office undoubtedly made a tidy profit. The Indians, wise perhaps now to the ways of the white man, never had any intention of honoring their promises. They liked the idea of gifts, and wanted to see how much they could get. The whites inevitably got something out of these treaties: The Indians could be painted as treaty-breakers. They had after all signed a document saying they would not raid and would give up captives, and then they had, treacherously, refused to keep it, notwithstanding that settlers ignored it as they ignored every other treaty. Manifest Destiny, as a notion and as a blueprint for expanding empire, meant that the land, all of it, belonged to the white man. And white men did what they had done ever since they landed in Virginia in the seventeenth century: They pushed as far into Indian country as their courage, or Indian war parties, would let them. Imagine the alternative:

the U.S. government sending troops to shoot down God-fearing settlers who simply wanted a piece of the American dream. It never happened.

The best idea the U.S. government could muster was to put four hundred starving Penatekas and a thousand other mostly Wichita-Caddoan remnants on to reservations on the Brazos River in 1855. The plan was hatched by Jefferson Davis, the new secretary of war in the Franklin Pierce administration. The Penatekas, decimated by waves of diseases, their hunting lands emptied of game, and their culture polluted by the white invaders, were literally starving to death; the other Indians who remained were simply being overrun.

This plan backfired, too. The Comanches were given about twenty thousand acres on the Clear Fork of the Brazos between present-day Abilene and Wichita Falls. For nomadic hunters, this was an absurdly small plot, too small to raise stock and mostly impossible to farm. Only about four hundred of the remaining twelve hundred Penatekas came in; the rest, scared off by rumors that they would be killed, fled north of the Red River with the ubiquitous Buffalo Hump. For those who stayed, the idea was that they would become happy, well-adjusted farmers. But no Comanche had ever wanted to plant seeds. The Indian agent, Robert Neighbors, was forced to give them cattle. The reaction of Sanaco, one of the chiefs who came in, sums up the bitter resignation of the Penatekas:

> You come into our country and select a small patch of ground, around which you run a line, and tell us the President will make us a present of this to live on, when everybody knows that the whole of this entire country, from the Red River to the Colorado, is ours and always had been from time immemorial. I suppose, however, if the President tells us to confine ourselves to these narrow limits, we shall be forced to do so.[34]

But the main problem with the Texas reservations was the white people who lived next to them. By 1858 white farms and ranches surrounded the reservations. And soon the whites were blaming the reservation Indians for raids that were being carried out by northern bands. In the fall of 1858 there were a series of savage raids all along the frontier—a settlement twenty-five miles from Fredericksburg was completely annihilated. Under the leadership of the Indian-hating newspaper editor John Baylor, settlers organized themselves and threatened to kill all of the Indians on both reservations. On December 27, 1858, a party of seventeen peaceful Indians from the reservation—Anadarkos and Caddoans—were attacked by white men while they slept. The white men fired on them, killing four men and three women. The six men who were guilty of the murders were identified but never charged. The feeling was that no jury would ever convict them, and that their arrest might stir the border into full-scale revolt. Meanwhile Baylor continued to stir up trouble, even going so far as to say that he would kill any soldier who tried to stand in his way. By the spring of 1859 the area around the reservations was in full panic. Groups of whites went about armed and looking for Indians. In May, some whites opened fire on a group of Indians. There was little doubt now that if the Indians stayed there, there would a full-scale war. Or, more likely, a full-scale slaughter.

On July 31, Agent Neighbors and three companies of federal troops led a long, strange, and colorful procession of Indians out of the Brazos reservations, never to return. The sight was at once magnificent and pathetic. There were 384 Comanches and 1,112 Indians from the other tribes.[35] They moved in a slow procession in the shimmering heat of the prairie, dragging their travois behind them as they had for hundreds of years; they crossed the Red River on August 8, and on August 16 arrived at their new reservation on the Washita River near present-day Fort Cobb, Oklahoma. The next day agent Neighbors returned to Texas to file a report. While he was at Fort Belknap, a man named Edward Cornett, who disagreed with his Indian policies, walked up to him and shot him in the back.

By almost any measure, John Salmon "Rip" Ford was one of the West's most remarkable characters. He was at various times a medical doctor, a newspaper editor, a state representative and state senator, a flamboyant proponent of the Confederacy, and an explorer who blazed the San Antonio to El Paso trail, which later bore his name. He served as mayor of Brownsville, delegate to the 1875 Constitutional Convention, and superintendent of the state's Deaf and Dumb School. He was a peacekeeper, too. He once protected the Brazos Reservation Indians against false accusations from the local whites, but later refused to arrest the men responsible for killing the innocent Caddoans and Anadarkos, in spite of an order by a state district judge to do so.[36] Rip Ford was a man of many opinions, all of them strong.

But he was most famous as a fighter of Indians and Mexicans. He had joined Jack Hays's upstart Rangers in 1836, rising to the rank of first lieutenant. He served under Hays again as his adjutant during the Mexican War, where he earned his nickname. It was his job to send death notices to soldiers' families, and he often included the postscript "Rest in Peace." Since he ended up writing so many such reports, he shortened the message to "R.I.P." Many people believed the initials stood for all of the Indians he had killed. After the war he rejoined the Rangers, was promoted to captain, and spent time on the border hunting Mexican bandits and Indians. Though he was literate and cultured, he was a hard-looking man; you could imagine him in a cold camp in the limestone breaks of the hill country with Hays and McCulloch and the others, waking in a frozen dawn to track and kill Comanches. He had a broad face with deep-set eyes, a crooked nose, jug-handle ears, and a thin, hard mouth. He liked to wear buckskins and a long and narrowly cut beard. Sometimes he wore a stovepipe hat. He was known to be a hard drillmaster.

In January 1858, as Texas reeled from a fresh wave of Comanche attacks in Erath, Brown, and Comanche counties, Ford became the duly appointed savior of the frontier. Texas had had enough of the federal government's staggering incompetence, and of its utter failure to stop Indian attacks. The last straw had been the army's decision in 1857 to ship a large part of the federal troops in Texas, most of the Second Cavalry, north to Utah to quell a Mormon revolt.[37] The Comanches had understood this perfectly, and had stepped up their raids.

That was enough. Texans would take matters into their own hands. The sum of $70,000 was appropriated, and a hundred men were recruited for six-month terms of service. Ford, who accepted a commission as senior Ranger captain, would command them. Their mission was highly unusual. In recent years every significant military expedition against the Comanches had been mounted in response to specific attacks. The idea had been to pursue the raiders and punish them for what they had done. It was pure retribution. Ford and his men were to simply launch themselves north of the Red River, penetrate deep into Comanche territory, and strike an *offensive* blow. "I impress upon you the necessity of action and energy," Texas governor Hardin Runnels told Ford. "Follow any and all trails of hostile or suspected hostile Indians you may discover, and if possible, overtake and chastise them, if unfriendly."[38] Runnels's words sounded simple enough. In fact he was calling for open war against Indians, in direct defiance of federal policy. The orders harkened back to what Jack Hays had done twenty years earlier when he roamed the hill country looking for Indians, attacking whatever Indians he found. It no longer mattered to Texans if the Rangers had caught any Indians in criminal acts. The point was to strike them hard and preemptively; the point was that they could and would be pursued to deep within their homelands, to their very lodges.

Thus was Ford unleashed. He recruited the best men he could find, armed them each with two revolvers and a rifle, and drilled them on marksmanship and tactics.[39] They were going to do things the old Ranger way, the unpleasant, hard, and uncomfortable way. The Hays way. He added 113 friendly Indians to his force, mostly Tonkawas under their chief Placido and Caddos and Anadarkos under Jim Pockmark. There were even some Shawnees. Like Hays, Ford made extensive use of Indians, writing later that they "were men of more than ordinary intellect who possessed minute information concerning the geography and topography of that country."[40] On April 29, 1858, riding behind a wide screen of Indian flankers and scouts ("spies" in the vernacular of the day), Ford and his cohort splashed across the Red River, threading their way through large stretches of pure quicksand. The fact that they had absolutely no lawful authority outside of Texas did not seem to bother them.[41] On May 10 their scouts brought in two arrowheads, which were quickly identified by the Indians as Kotsoteka Comanche. On May 11 they discovered a small Comanche camp on the Canadian River. Ford had moved like a Ranger: quietly, building few or no campfires, sending scouts out for twenty miles in four directions. And in the Ranger company there was, of course, none of the fuss and feathers and repeated bugling that characterized the army expeditions. The army was learning the old Ranger lessons, but only slowly. The federal troopers still moved with startling obviousness across the prairie.

On May 12, Ford's Tonkawas attacked and quickly destroyed the camp, killing several Indians and taking others prisoner. Two Comanches escaped at full gallop, heading toward the Canadian River. The Rangers and reservation Indians followed, chasing the Indians at high speed for three miles. They galloped across the Canadian River, and soon drew up in front of a large Kotsoteka camp that ran for a mile along a creek. It was a lovely piece of ground, a pure, clear stream flowing into a river valley; beyond the northern bank rose the picturesque Antelope Hills, bathed in the light of the sunrise. This was deep in Comanche territory, where they did not expect to be attacked. What they were looking at was not just a mobile war camp but a full-scale village, with women and children and buffalo meat drying on racks in front of the tipis. Ford's two hundred thirteen men were now confronting four hundred Kotsoteka warriors.

Ford sent his Indian cohort first, the idea being, as he put it, "to make the Comanches believe that they had only Indians and bows and arrows to contend against."[42]

The ploy apparently worked. The main Comanche chief, Pobishequasso, "Iron Jacket," emerged from the swirling masses of horsemen and rode forward. Iron Jacket was not just a war chief. He was also a great medicine man. Instead of a buckskin shirt he wore iron mail, an ancient piece of Spanish armor. He carried a bow and a lance, wore a headdress decorated with feathers and long red-flannel streamers, and was elaborately smeared with paint.[43] His horse, according to Ford, was "gloriously caparisoned."[44] As he rode forward he summoned his big magic, walking his horse in a circle and then expelling his breath with great force. He was said to be able to blow arrows away from their targets. Bullets and arrows were said to bounce off him; Iron Jacket was said to be invincible. And indeed for a little while he seemed to be. Rangers and Indians shot at him, to no effect. One participant recalled that pistol rounds "would glance off [his armor] like hail from a tin roof."[45] He circled again and moved forward. But now Ford's Indians, who were armed with six-shooters and Mississippi rifles, found their mark. "About six rifle shots rang on the air," wrote Ford. "The chief's horse jumped about six feet straight up and fell. Another barrage followed, and the Comanche medicine man was no more."[46]

The effect was predictable and immediate. The Comanches in the main camp made a brief stand and then fled, demoralized by their chief's broken magic. What followed was a running fight that featured Rangers and their Indian allies with far superior weaponry picking off Kotsoteka riders on the open plain and in the wooded river bottom. The battle extended to an area three miles by six miles, and soon turned into a series of single combats, in which the Rangers with reloadable .45-caliber six-shooters and breech-loading carbines held an enormous advantage of the bow-and-lance-wielding Comanches. The latter did have guns, but they were the old single-shot muskets that could be discharged only once. The Indians fought valiantly. Much of their fighting was meant to try to cover the retreat of their women and children. Women were killed along with the men. Ford makes a point of noting that "it was not an easy matter to distinguish Indian warriors from squaws," meaning that the Rangers did not knowingly kill women. This was not really true. Women could ride as well as the men and were extremely adept with a bow. They were often killed as combatants (as would be true a hundred years later in the Vietnam War), and in any case were always potential combatants. Needless to say, the Tonkawas and Shawnees and other Indians had no such compunctions about killing women. Plains warfare was a fight to the death, always. In the running fight seventy-six Comanches were killed and many more were wounded. The Rangers suffered only two dead and three wounded. The numbers of dead "friendly" Indians were never reported.

Now something very strange happened. Another force of Comanches, as large as or larger than the first, emerged over the ravines and thicket to confront Ford's men. According to legend, it was commanded by Peta Nocona, but there is no hard evidence for that. What followed was ancient, ritual combat, of the sort that few white men had ever seen. Comanches in full regalia rode forth individually onto the plain, screaming taunts at the reservation Indians and daring them to come out in single combat. This they did. "A scene was now enacted beggaring description," wrote Ford. "It reminded one of the rude and chivalrous days of knight-errantry. Shields and lances and bows and head dresses, prancing steeds and many minutias were not wanting to compile the resemblance. And when the combatants rushed at each other with defiant shouts, nothing save the piercing report of the rifle varied the affair from a battlefield of the middle ages. Half an hour was spent in this without much damage to either party."[47]

Then the modern era quickly reasserted itself. The Rangers charged, en masse, guns blazing, and the Comanche line soon broke. There was a running fight of some three miles, ending with no casualties on either side. Ford's horses were exhausted. The Comanches hauled themselves off to lick their wounds.

Ford's fight became known in Texas history as the Battle of Antelope Hills, and it is famous for several reasons. It reasserted the superiority of Texans against Comanches, and underscored the incompetence of the army and the Indian office. It sealed Rip Ford's fame and, most important, proved the lesson that Jack Hays had learned but that had somehow gotten lost over the years. "The Comanches," Ford later wrote to Runnels, "can be followed, overtaken, and beaten, provided the pursuers will be laborious, vigilant, and are willing to undergo privations." Willing, in short, to behave and fight like the Rangers of the late 1830s and early 1840s.

The Battle of Antelope Hills also brought into focus the rather thorny political question of who was better qualified to patrol the borderlands, federals or Texans. On the floor of the U.S. Senate that year Sam Houston had risen to say, with withering scorn, that Texas no longer wanted federal troops at all. "Give us one thousand Rangers and we will be responsible for the defense of our frontier. Texas does not want regular troops. Withdraw them if you please." He was countered by Mississippi senator Jefferson Davis, secretary of war, who reminded Houston of the disciplinary problems the army had experienced with the Rangers in the Mexican War. "If the General had gone further," he retorted, "and said that irregular cavalry [Rangers] always produce disturbance in the neighborhood of a camp, he would have said no more than my experience would confirm."[48]

But Ford's raid had stung the army deeply; it had suggested, or perhaps proven, that Houston was right. Ford had done what no one in the U.S. Army had ever done, which was to pursue Comanches into their home ranges. Thus was the Second Cavalry summoned from its labors in Utah, to make its own march north of the Red River against the Comanches.

The expedition was political from start to finish. Ford's raid had prompted the U.S. Army commander in Texas, the chubby, profane General David Twiggs, to obtain authority directly from army headquarters at West Point to abandon the passive defense policy the army had been forced to put up with since 1849. A punitive force was thus organized at Fort Belknap under the command of the dapper, blond, egotistical Mississippian Earl Van Dorn, who would later find fame as a Confederate major general. With five companies of troops and 135 friendly Indians under the command of the wiry, ambitious twenty-year-old college student Sul Ross, they rode north on September 15, 1858. They were tracking Buffalo Hump, the seemingly indestructible Penateka chief who had refused to go on the reservation and now rode with other Comanche bands. Their Wichita scouts soon found a large village of Comanches next to a village of Wichitas. The Indians were completely unaware of the danger.

The reason they were unaware of danger is that they had just concluded a treaty with a Captain Prince, the commanding army officer at Fort Arbuckle, which was located just to the east. While the intrepid Van Dorn was at Fort Belknap making ready to strike the Comanches a deathblow, Prince was hobnobbing and making peace with the chiefs of the same band—Buffalo Hump, Hair-Bobbed-on-One-Side, and Over-the-Buttes. Neither Van Dorn nor Prince had any idea what the other was doing.[49] Pleased with what seemed to be at least a temporary peace and freedom from worry about attacks like the one Rip Ford had made, the Wichitas and Comanches were feasting, trading, gambling, and generally carrying on. They were completely unaware of the approach of the bluecoats and "friendlies" under Van Dorn and Ross. Several reports on their location and strength were given to Hair-Bobbed-on-One-Side, who considered the matter and concluded that the white man would never attack them having just made a treaty with them. The omens were good. They were safe. They went to sleep.

At dawn the next morning Van Dorn's troops attacked the Comanche village with a vengeance. Ross and his reserve Indians had run off the horses, so most of the warriors were forced to fight on foot. It was more of a massacre than a fight. Two hundred blue-coated troops were in the village, blasting away into the tipis, while the Indians frantically tried, as they always did, to cover the retreat of their families. Seventy Indians were killed, untold numbers wounded. Buffalo Hump managed to escape with most of his warriors. The Rangers lost four killed, and twelve wounded, including Van Dorn with an arrow through his navel and Ross with two bullet wounds. Both men had to stay on the field of battle for five days to recuperate.[50] The army burned one hundred twenty tipis, along with all the Comanche ammunition, cooking utensils, clothing, dressed skins, corn, and subsistence stores. Those who escaped had only the clothing on their back, and many were afoot, since the soldiers had captured three hundred horses, too.[51]

Though what had been perpetrated upon the Comanches amounted to a cruel trick, the army boasted a glorious victory. The Texas press wasn't so sure. One paper expressed the opinion that the effect of what became known as the Battle of the Wichita Village "will, probably, be a cessation of depredations upon the border settlements for a time at least," but insisted that "an end of the war should be the blow followed by active, energetic operations."[52] The latter did not happen anytime soon. On November 5, 1858, barely seven weeks later, Sul Ross himself noted that, since the battle, Comanches had stolen more than one hundred head of horses from settlements in northern Texas. The violent Indian raids of the fall of 1858, which had set off John Baylor's reservation war, came at least in part in reprisal for Van Dorn's attack.[53]

Still, there was clear meaning in both Ford's and Van Dorn's attacks. They were unambiguously offensive, for one thing. They showed a willingness, for the first time, to cross the Red River in pursuit of Comanches, and they showed that such tactics could at least kill Indians. Whether they could stop raiding remained to be seen. They also showed that advances in weaponry, especially the six-shooter and the breech-loading carbine, had radically altered the basic balance of power. When two hundred men could take on and devastate a Comanche force twice their size, there was a lesson to be learned. Jack Hays of course had demonstrated this in 1844 at Walker's Creek. But nobody remembered that now.

Twelve

✦═◆═✦

WHITE QUEEN OF THE
COMANCHES

✦═◆═✦

EVEN IN ONE of the bloodiest years on the frontier—1860—the killing of Martha Sherman stood out. Maybe it was because she had been gang-raped and tortured while she was pregnant. Maybe it was because of her dead baby or because the precise, horrific details of what happened to her, which she herself related in the few days she lived, spread so quickly in Parker, Jack, and other counties. Whatever the case, in the days following the Sherman raid, all hell broke loose. People panicked. They fled the frontier as fast as they could. "The indications are," wrote twenty-eight-year-old schoolteacher Jonathan Hamilton Baker in his diary on November 28, "that our county will soon be depopulated."[1] Caravans were moving. The counties were emptying. Within days of the raid there were a hundred deserted farms in the area. Most of the people west of Weatherford had retreated eastward, leaving, in the words of one rancher, "the extreme frontier post."[2]

Yet not everyone was leaving. A twenty-four-year-old named Charles Goodnight, destined to become one of the most famous cattlemen in Texas and one of the originators of the great cattle drives, rode through the chill, rainy night, recruiting a posse to pursue the raiders. He found eight willing men who met the next morning at the house of an old man named Isaac Lynn, whose daughter and son-in-law had recently been brutally murdered by Comanches. When Goodnight entered the house, he found Lynn "sitting before a large log fire in the old-fashioned fireplace, with a long, forked dogwood stick, on which was an Indian scalp, thoroughly salted. The hair was tucked inside. As he turned it carefully over the fire, the grease oozed out of it. . . . He looked back over his shoulder, bade me good morning, and then turned to his work of roasting the scalp. I do not think I ever saw so sad a face." Since his daughter's death he had become a collector of scalps and asked people to bring him any they had. He roasted them so they wouldn't spoil. Like so many people on the bleeding frontier, he was drowning in hatred and grief.[3]

Goodnight and his men left immediately to track Peta Nocona's raiders. Because the Indians were traveling with one hundred fifty stolen horses, this was easily done. The Comanches, who normally took pains to avoid being tracked, scattering their herds when they came to gravel, rock, or hard ground, were soon well beyond where white men had ever followed them before. And so they had stopped taking precautions and, in Goodnight's words, "were driving in a body." Goodnight and his party had traveled at least one hundred twenty miles across open prairies and swift, cold rivers. It had rained incessantly. They were without food or bedding, and now they realized they were approaching a camp with a large number of Indians, many more than had been with Peta Nocona's raiders. This was Nautdah's village on Mule Creek, the great supply depot and clearinghouse for the frontier raids. Satisfied that they knew where the Indians had gone, and aware that they had no chance against so many of them, Goodnight and his trackers turned back.[4]

A full-scale expedition was quickly mounted. By the time it coalesced at Fort Belknap on December 13, it consisted of forty Rangers, twenty-one army soldiers from the Second Cavalry at Fort Cooper, and some seventy local volunteers, including Goodnight as scout. They were commanded by twenty-three-year-old Sul Ross, the wiry, ambitious young man who had recruited Indian scouts for the Van Dorn expedition while still an undergraduate at Wesleyan University in Florence, Alabama. Ross had fought bravely at the Battle of Antelope Hills and had been gravely wounded and had thus made a name for himself. He had been chosen personally by Governor Sam Houston to replace the incompetent and love-struck Middleton Johnson, under whom Ross had served. Ross's commission would turn out to be a brilliant move for both men and convince people that Houston was doing something about the Comanche problem. Ross would use it as the springboard to a dazzling career. He later became the youngest general in the Confederacy, a popular two-term governor of Texas, and president of the Agricultural and Mechanical College of Texas (now Texas A&M). For the moment, plenty of people hated him, especially John Baylor's rabble-rousers, who saw him as an Indian sympathizer and threatened to hang him if they found him. Ross himself had higher purposes. In a letter written later that contained more than a hint of vainglory, he wrote: "I determined to make a desperate attempt to curb the insolence of these implacable enemies of Texas. . . . I planned to accomplish this by following them into their fastness and carry the war into their own homes where this tribe, the most inveterate raiders on the border, retired with their captives and booty to their wild haunts amid the hills and valleys of the beautiful Canadian and Pease rivers."[5] One can almost hear the campaign speeches and slogans stirring in his brain.

The cavalcade headed northwest in bitter cold, over mesquite prairies scarred by ravines and limestone ridges. This was open country, dun-colored and wintry. The young schoolteacher Baker, who joined the volunteers, later recalled "poor prairie uplands with tolerably good valleys along the creeks where the grass was fine. There was no timber along our route today except small hackberries in the valleys and scrubby mesquite on the prairies."[6] They saw thousands of buffalo. The water of the Big Wichita and Pease rivers was "salty and gyppy," and tasted awful. At night there were heavy frosts; the men wrapped themselves in blankets and buffalo robes and shivered before small fires. They crossed rivers in the tracks of the buffalo, to avoid quicksand.[7] On December 17 came rain, dense fog, and briefly warmer air. On December 18 there were thunderstorms in the night. The next morning Goodnight found a pillow slip with a little girl's belt and Martha Sherman's Bible in it. Why had the Indians made a point of taking the Bible? According to Goodnight, Comanche shields, made of two layers of the toughest rawhide from the neck of a buffalo and hardened in fire, were almost invulnerable to bullets when stuffed with paper. When Comanches robbed houses they invariably took all the books they could find.[8]

On December 19, the Rangers and soldiers from the Second Cavalry, riding out ahead of the volunteers in a long valley bounded by a range of sand hills, spotted the Indian camp Charles Goodnight and his scouts had seen. They were lucky: A blustery norther had come up, of the sort the plains were famous for, and the soldiers' position was concealed by blowing clouds of sand.[9] There were not many Indians in the camp; the five hundred that Goodnight had theorized were no longer there. The few they could see were packing horses and mules and preparing to leave, unaware of the approach of the white men. Seeing this, Ross ordered the army sergeant to circle around to the other side of the camp, to block the Indians' retreat.

Then he and his sixty men attacked what were later determined to be fifteen Indians. Many of the latter were killed before they even picked up weapons. Others fled into the jaws of the trap and were cut down there. Once among them, the men realized that most of the occupants of the camp were women. There were a few old men, too, and a few warriors. In Goodnight's account, the Rangers spared most, but not all, of the women they encountered. The federal troops, meanwhile, killed everyone they encountered, regardless of sex. As Goodnight described it:

> The Sergeant and his men [from the Second Cavalry] fell in behind on the squaws, six or eight in number, who never got across the first bend of the creek. They were so heavily loaded with meat, tent poles and camp equipage that their horses could not run. We supposed they had about a thousand pounds of buffalo meat in various stages of curing. The sergeant and his men killed every one of them, nearly in a pile.[10]

The fight lasted only a few minutes and was more of a butchery than a pitched battle. Participants remembered some interesting details. The few warriors in the camp used their horses for breastworks, standing behind them when they were on their feet, and lying down behind them after they were shot down.[11] In the midst of the struggle, the white soldiers found themselves under attack from fifteen or so dogs from the Indian camp, who tried valiantly to defend their Indian masters. Almost all were shot and killed.

The battle ended in a brief running fight. Ross and Lieutenant Tom Kelliheir rode in pursuit of the last three Indians, who were mounted on two horses. After a mile, they caught up with the single Indian, who rode a splendid iron-gray stallion. Ross was about to shoot when the Comanche, who he could now see was carrying a small child, reined in the horse and, depending on which version you believe, either opened her robe to show her breasts, or cried "Americano! Americano!" She may have done both. In any case, her ploy worked: Ross did not shoot. He ordered Kelliheir to stay with her and the child while Ross took off after the other two riders. He soon caught them and fired his army Colt, hitting the rear rider, who also turned out to be a woman. As she fell, she dragged the main rider to the ground with her. He was a large man, fully armed. From his earlier behavior and the way he had barked commands, Ross had identified him as the main chief, and he looked the part. He was nude to the waist, his body streaked with bright pigments. He wore two eagle plumes in his hair, a disk of beaten gold around his neck embossed with a turtle, broad gold bands on his upper arms, and fawn-skin leggings trimmed out with scalplocks.[12] He managed to land on his feet, seized his bow, and loosed several arrows. The following is Ross's account of what happened next:

> [M]y horse, running at full speed, was very nearly up on top of [the man] when he was struck with an arrow which caused him to begin pitching or bucking, and it was with great difficulty that I kept my saddle, and in the meantime narrowly escaped several arrows coming in quick succession from the chief's bow. . . . He would have killed me but for a random shot from my pistol, which broke his right arm at the elbow, completely disabling him. My horse then became quiet, and I shot the chief twice through the body, whereupon he deliberately walked to a small tree, the only one in sight, and leaning against it began to sing a wild, weird song. . . . As he seemed to prefer death to life, I directed the Mexican boy to end his misery by a charge of buckshot.[13]

Other accounts suggest a slightly more complex drama, in which Ross and the chief conversed through an interpreter, the chief insisting that "when I am dead I will surrender but not before" and even trying to throw a spear at Ross with his good arm. Either way, the Indian was soon dead. A man named Anton Martinez, Ross's manservant who had been a child captive of the Comanches—and who said he had been a slave in Peta Nocona's own family—identified him as Peta Nocona. The final tally: twelve Indians dead, three captured. The third was a nine-year-old Comanche boy. The loss to the Comanches, who were hunkering down into their winter camps, was stunning: sixty-nine pack-mule loads of buffalo meat—something more than fifteen thousand pounds of it—and three hundred seventy horses.[14]

Now Ross rode back to the place where Kelliheir held the woman and her child captive. The woman was filthy, covered with dirt and grease from handling so much bloody buffalo meat. But to Ross's astonishment he noticed that she had blue eyes. And he saw that under the grime her short-cropped hair was lighter in color than Indian black. She was white. Not quite believing what they had found, they took her back to what was left of her village, which the soldiers were busily looting. They were also scalping the dead Indians, men and women alike. By now scalping was the common practice on both sides. Since two men claimed the scalp of Peta Nocona, they decided to split it into two parts.[15]

The "white squaw" was then taken back to where Peta Nocona had been killed. She wept and wailed over his body. The soldiers did not let her stay there. They brought her to the main battlefield, where she was allowed to walk among the mutilated dead, carrying her child. She muttered in Comanche as she went, and wailed loudly only when she came to one young warrior who had white features. When Martinez, who spoke Comanche, asked her who he was, the woman replied cryptically, "He's my boy, and he's not my boy." She later explained that he was the son of another white girl who had been captured by the Comanches and married an Indian. She had died but had asked Nautdah to look after the boy as though he were her own son.

She then told the Mexican how she had come to be there. In Ranger Frank Gholson's account, she was with her two boys—whom the translator identified as Quanah and "Grassnut"—when the Rangers attacked. They fled, along with other women and children. "After I had gone some distance," she told Martinez, "I missed both of my boys. I came back in search of them, coming as near the battle as I could. In this way I was caught. I am greatly distressed about my boys. I fear they are killed."[16] Ross, whose men had killed no one of that description, assured her that they were alive. She continued to weep. This was, after all, the second time in her life that she had seen people close to her massacred and scalped. The second time she had been taken captive by an alien culture whose language she did not speak.

Through Martinez, she told Ross that she remembered that her father had been killed in a battle long ago and that she and her brother had been captured. That and other details convinced Ross that she might be "the long lost Cynthia Ann Parker." With that, she stopped talking. According to Gholson, she also "gave them a lot of trouble trying to escape." At some point Jonathan Baker noticed a tiny, elaborately beaded moccasin on the ground. He picked it up and was looking at it when he noticed that Nautdah was watching him closely. He then realized that the child was missing a shoe. The little girl toddled over to him and he gave her the moccasin.[17] Nautdah lived a hard life, but she had found the time and energy to make this exquisite little shoe. The next day the men burned everything they could not carry, and rode out.

They took her back to Fort Belknap, and thence to Fort Cooper, where she was delivered into the care of the captain's wife. A Ranger named A. B. Mason, who accompanied her on that trip, recalled that after she arrived, she "sat for a time immovable, lost in profound meditation, oblivious to everything by which she was surrounded, ever and anon convulsed as it were by some powerful emotion which she struggled to suppress."[18] Mason wrote a version of what Cynthia Ann told officials at Fort Cooper, in the February 5, 1861, issue of the *Galveston Civilian*. His piece was undoubtedly edited, but this is how he quoted her:

> I remember when I was a little girl, being a long time at the house with a picket fence all around; one day some Indians came to the house. They had a white rag on a stick. My father went out to talk to them, they surrounded and killed him, then many other Indians came and fought at the house; several whites were killed; my mother and her four children were taken prisoner; in the evening mother and two of her children were retaken by a white man. My brother died among the Indians of smallpox, I lived with the Indians north of Santa Fe. I have three children.[19]

She was wrong about her father talking to the Indians—it was her uncle Benjamin. And she was wrong about her brother John dying of smallpox; he was ransomed back to his family in September 1842. But her memory was extremely accurate about everything else. She may have been confused by the fury of the raid, but she remembered it quite clearly. She remembered watching her father die.

Ross sent immediately for Cynthia Ann's uncle Isaac Parker. The women of Fort Cooper, meanwhile, decided to clean the filthy woman up, an enterprise that offered some comic relief amid the tragedy. They found some clothes for her, then got "an old negro mammy" to scrub her down with soap and hot water. Then they combed her hair and let her look at herself in the mirror. "She submitted to all this willingly enough, apparently," wrote Gholson in his memoir, "until she got a good opportunity to get out the door of the place. When this opportunity occurred she made a dive for the door and got past the negro mammy." She then headed for her tent, which was two or three hundred yards away, tearing her clothes off as she ran until she had almost nothing on, followed by the mammy frantically waving a washcloth as three bewildered army wives looked on and the child toddled along after them "with nobody paying much attention to her."[20] Nautdah reached her tent, where she managed to find and put on some Comanche clothing. After that, the army wives gave up trying to pretty her up.

When Isaac Parker arrived, the captive was seated on a pine box with her elbows on her knees and her head in her hands. She paid no attention to the assembled men until Parker spoke her name. With that, she stood, looked directly at him, patted her breast and said "Me Cincee Ann." She repeated it, then resumed her seat. She agreed to answer questions about the raid on

Parker's Fort. She got some of the details wrong, but she remembered correctly that there were five captives, two grown women and three children. Then she was asked to describe Parker's Fort. She responded by using a stick to draw an outline, using dots and dashes. She then drank from the canteen and dribbled water to round out the portrait, which included the stream that ran behind the fort. "Gentlemen," Isaac Parker said, "I actually could not make as good a picture of the old fort as she has made."[21]

The Battle of Pease River, as this very small skirmish came to be known rather grandiosely, has long been regarded by Texans as a major historical event. The return of the legendary white squaw offered what was to whites a completely satisfying ending to the great epic tale. Poor Cynthia Ann, the girl who had descended into pagan savagery, was back at last in the arms of her loving and God-fearing family. For the next century, the amazing tale of Cynthia Ann Parker's Comanche captivity would be taught to schoolchildren in Texas.

There were some interesting sequels to the battle, as well, with enormous implications for the future of the Comanche tribe. Quanah and his brother survived it. After the fight Goodnight realized that two Indians had left on horseback. The young Ranger and ten scouts tracked them to a Comanche camp in the panhandle. Though Goodnight never learned their identity, the riders were almost certainly Quanah and Peanuts.[22] The other child involved in the fight, the nine-year-old Comanche boy, was adopted by Sul Ross and his wife. They named him Pease. He was General Ross's horse tender in 135 civil war engagements, married a former slave, became a respectable citizen of Waco, and died in 1883.[23]

The fight also came to be seen, incorrectly, as the turning point in the war against the Comanches. "Thus was fought the great battle of Pease River," intoned one of the breathless historical accounts of the day, "with the great Comanche chief, Peta Nocona, with a strong force on one side and the brave Captain Ross with sixty Rangers on the other. In the fight the greater part of the warriors were killed, and such a victory never before had been gained over these Comanches."[24] In Ross's own description, the battle takes on nearly mythic proportions. "The fruits of this important victory can never be computed in dollars and cents," he wrote later. "The great Comanche confederacy was forever broken, the blow was decisive, their illustrious chief slept with his fathers and with him were most of his doughty warriors."[25]

This was utter nonsense. Comanche raids in 1864, to take just one year, were the worst in history; 1871 and 1872 were bad years, too. The U.S. Army sent three thousand soldiers against the Comanches in 1874, the largest army ever sent to hunt down hostile Indians. Though Ross had shown great personal courage in his hand-to-hand combat with Peta Nocona, the Indian foes in the Battle of Pease River were mostly women who were shot down while trying to escape on heavily laden horses. "I was in the Pease River fight," wrote H. B. Rogers in a memoir, "but I am not very proud of it. That was not a battle at all, but just a killing of squaws. One or two bucks and 16 squaws were killed. The Indians were getting ready to leave when we came upon them."[26]

In the weeks and months that followed, the "battle" received wide coverage in Texas newspapers. None of them bothered to mention who the victims were. Considering the anti-Indian hysteria of the moment, it is unlikely that anyone really cared. What is interesting was the virtually universal belief among Texans at the time that Sul Ross, the hero of the battle and the future governor, had saved the poor, unfortunate Cynthia Ann Parker from an ugly fate. That belief would color the histories for a long, long time.

We will never know how Cynthia Ann Parker felt in the weeks and months after her capture by Sul Ross. There are so few comparable events in American history. But it was painfully apparent from the earliest days that the real tragedy in her life was not her first captivity but her second. White men never quite grasped this. The event that destroyed her life was not the raid at Parker's Fort in 1836 but her miraculous and much-celebrated "rescue" at Mule Creek in 1860. The latter killed her husband, separated her forever from her beloved sons, and deposited her in a culture where she was more a true captive than she had ever been with the Comanches. In the moments before Ross's raid, she had been quite as primitive as any other Plains Indian; packing thousands of pounds of buffalo meat onto mules, covered from head to toe in blood and grease, literally immersed in this elemental world that never quite left the Stone Age—a world of ceaseless toil, hunger, constant war, and early death. But also of pure magic, of beaver ceremonies and eagle dances, of spirits that inhabited springs, trees, rocks, turtles, and crows; a place where people danced all night and sang bear medicine songs, where wolf medicine made a person invulnerable to bullets, dream visions dictated tribal policy, and ghosts were alive in the wind. On grassy plains and timbered river bottoms from Kansas to Texas, Cynthia Ann—Nautdah—had drifted in the mystical cycles of the seasons, living in that random, terrifying, bloody, and intensely alive place where nature and divinity became one.

And then, suddenly, all of it disappeared. Instead of Stone Age camps aswirl in magic and taboo and scented smoke from mesquite lodge fires, she found herself sitting on taffeta chairs in drawing rooms on the outer margins of the Industrial Revolution, being interrogated by polite uncomprehending white men who believed in a single God and in a supremely rational universe where everything could be explained. This new culture was every bit as alien as the one she confronted after the attack on Parker's Fort. It was as though she had walked yet again through a door into another world, quite as complete as the one she had left and, in all of its mystifying details, completely different.

Isaac Parker quickly satisfied himself that the woman Ross had captured was his long-lost niece Cynthia Ann. He decided immediately that he would take her and her daughter, Prairie Flower, back home with him to Birdville (now Haltom City), just north of Fort Worth. Both of her parents were dead. Silas had of course perished in the raid on Parker's Fort. Her mother, Lucy, had died in 1852 after a life filled with bad marriages (three after Silas), poor health, and a brutal five-year legal battle over her husband's estate.[27] Cynthia Ann's brother Silas Jr. and sister, Orlena, having survived a rough childhood—Cynthia Ann, ironically, probably had a better life—were married and living in Texas. But it was Silas's brother Isaac who decided to take his niece in. (Cynthia Ann's uncle James, the old searcher, was still alive but curiously absent in all of this; perhaps he gave up when he heard that she did not want to be rescued.)

They soon departed, accompanied by the former Comanche captive Anton Martinez, who acted as interpreter, along with two Rangers. They stopped on the way at Fort Belknap, where a more successful effort was made to clean the mother and daughter up, and where Prairie Flower played happily with other children. She was by all accounts a bumptious and "sprightly" child. She was dark-skinned and strikingly pretty. Everyone liked her. Cynthia Ann herself was sturdily built, with short-cropped, medium brown hair; wide-set, striking light-blue eyes; and a mouth that seemed set in anger, or resignation, or both. She was not pretty, nor was she especially unattractive; in calico she looked in most ways like a typical Anglo pioneer woman of the day, a bit stout and rather more worn-looking than her urban counterparts at a comparable age. She was also, recognizably, a Parker. One account put

Parker's Fort: The site of the famous 1836 Indian massacre that resulted in the kidnapping of Cynthia Ann Parker and other family members. This fort was a replica of the original, built in the 1930s. It was rebuilt again and exists today in the town of Grosbeck, Texas.

Jack Hays: He was the greatest Texas Ranger, the one the Comanches and Mexicans feared most, the source of countless legends of the Old West. It was said that before Hays, Americans came into the West on foot carrying long rifles, and that after Hays, everybody was mounted and carrying a six-shooter.

3

Cynthia Ann Parker and her daughter, Prairie Flower: Taken at A. F. Corning's studio in Fort Worth, probably in 1862, the photo became famous on the frontier and beyond. Note her large, muscular hands and wrists.

4

Comanche warriors: Famed photographer William Soule took this photograph in the early 1870s at Fort Sill in southwestern Oklahoma, where the Comanches were brought after their surrender.

5

6

The young Sul Ross: This is the way he looked when he killed Comanche war chief Peta Nocona at the Battle of Pease River and recaptured Nocona's wife, who turned out to be Cynthia Ann Parker. Ross later became governor of Texas.

Ranald S. Mackenzie during the Civil War, 1863 or 1864: The man who would destroy the Comanches and become America's greatest Indian fighter graduated first in his class at West Point in 1862 at the age of twenty-one and by August he was serving in the army in the Second Battle of Manassas. By the end of the war—at the advanced age of twenty-four—he had been promoted to brevet brigadier general.

7

Quanah in 1877: The earliest known photo of him, two years after his surrender. Though he is fully clad in traditional leather and fringe, one can still see how massive his forearms and upper body were. He was considered the most formidable fighter of his generation of Comanches.

8

The onslaught of the hide men: In the 1870s the pursuit of the buffalo became less like hunting and more like extermination. In 1873 a hunter named Tom Nixon killed 3,200 in 35 days. In the winter of 1872 a single hide fetched $3.50. This "rick" of hides awaits shipment from Dodge City.

9

10

Kotsoteka Comanche chief Shaking Hand (Mow-way): On September 29, 1872, Mackenzie destroyed his village in the Texas Panhandle at the Battle of the North Fork of the Red River (or McClellan Creek). Ironically, Shaking Hand at the time was en route to Washington to talk peace with the Great Father.

Isa-tai in middle age: Part medicine man, part con man, and part showman, Isa-tai appeared in 1874 as the Comanches' great savior and messiah. His magic went disastrously wrong at the Battle of Adobe Walls. He later became Quanah's rival in the reservation years.

11

Scalped buffalo hunter, 1868: The Indians hated buffalo hunters and understood that they, more than the bluecoated federal soldiers, were destroying their way of life on the plains. This hunter, photographed by William Soule near Fort Dodge, met the same fate as hundreds of others like him.

12

Quanah and one of his wives: He had eight of them, seven during the reservation period—an unusually high number. Most were quite attractive and not always happy to share their husband.

13

The formal Quanah: Though he refused to give up his long hair, his multiple wives, or his peyote, he happily wore white man's clothes when he traveled or went to town.

14

Star House: Quanah built his magnificent ten-room house in 1890. It boasted a formal dining room and ten-foot ceilings, and was located on a splendid piece of high ground in the shadow of the Wichita Mountains north of Cache, Oklahoma.

15

Quanah and family, ca. 1908: The aging chief and twenty members of his family on the porch at Star House. He had seven wives and twenty-three children during the reservation period, all of whom lived at the house. One of his wives said later that his greatest achievement was managing his own household.

16

Quanah in his bedroom, ca. 1897: A clash of old and new. Note the framed portrait of his mother, Cynthia Ann, and his sister, Prairie Flower, on his left. It was his most cherished possession.

17

Quanah entertaining dinner guests, ca. 1900: In Star House's formal dining room, Quanah entertained guests from Geronimo to General Nelson Miles to Teddy Roosevelt. This room, and the house, still exist in Cache, Oklahoma.

18

Quanah at fifty-eight: While his wealth waned in his later years, his stature in the tribe, and in American society, grew. This shows him at the height of his power, influence, and popularity in 1906.

her at five feet seven inches and one hundred forty pounds, which would have made her a giant among Comanche women. She and her tall, muscular husband must have cut quite a figure in Comanche camps, just as her son Quanah would later on.

They passed through Weatherford—the seat of Parker County, where the worst of Peta Nocona's raids had taken place—and then stopped in Fort Worth, where Cynthia Ann became an instant celebrity. It is not known why the travelers stopped here. Some accounts say it was to have a photograph taken, but the first known photograph of her—a tintype, actually—was not taken until a month later in Austin.[28] Whatever the reason, her arrival caused a great commotion as residents of Tarrant County (who totaled 6,020 that year) clamored to see the famous captive and her child. Her arrival was considered such an important event that the local children were let out of school. They came in groups to gawk at the terrified captives, who were on display in front of a general store in downtown Fort Worth. It was a sort of freak show: Cynthia Ann was bound with rope and set out atop a large box so that everyone could see her. One can only wonder what role her uncle Isaac, politician that he was, played in it. According to one witness:

> She was not dressed in Indian costume but wore a torn calico dress. Her hair was bronzed by the sun. Her face was tanned, and she made a pathetic figure as she stood there, viewing the crowds that swarmed about her. The tears were streaming down her face, and she was muttering in the Indian language.[29]

Texans could not get enough of her. There were many newspaper accounts of her return, all of which were uniformly obsessed with the idea that a pretty little nine-year-old white girl from a devout Baptist family had been transformed into a pagan savage who had mated with a redskin and borne his children and forgotten her mother tongue. She was thus, according to the morals of the day, grotesquely compromised. She had forsaken the virtues of Christianity for the wanton immorality of the Indian. That was the attraction. And all the stories assumed that everything she had done had been forced upon her. That she had suffered grievous mistreatment, had been whipped and beaten and had led a lonely and desperate existence. People simply did not believe that a Christian white woman had gone along with it voluntarily. One paper, the *Clarksville Northern Standard*, observed later that "her body and arms bear the marks of having been cruelly treated."[30] Yet there is nothing to suggest that she was cruelly treated after the first few days of her captivity, as her cousin Rachel Plummer had described them. She was the ward of a chief, later his wife. The scars may have resulted from the practice among Comanche women of cutting themselves in mourning, often on the arms and breasts. Apparently no white people wanted to think too hard about the implications of the lovely mixed-race girl named Prairie Flower, whom her mother obviously adored.

After the carnival interlude in town, the party continued to Birdville. Here Isaac lived in a spacious "double log" cabin that was considered for many years the finest house in Tarrant County. It is not clear exactly what he thought he was going to accomplish with Cynthia Ann and her daughter. Perhaps he was simply doing what he considered to be his family duty. Perhaps he saw himself as her deliverer, imagining the day when Cynthia Ann, grateful and weeping, would embrace Jesus and forsake her savage ways.

Nothing of the sort happened. Cynthia Ann's repatriation was in fact a disaster. She was not only unrepentant. She was actively, and incessantly, hostile to her captors. She tried repeatedly to escape with her daughter, sometimes making it far into the woods and requiring a search party to find her. She was so intent on leaving that Isaac had to lock her in the house when he was away. As her legal guardian, he was empowered to do so. Cynthia Ann was being treated as though she were crazy: An entirely "free" white woman, thirty-three years old and from a prominent family, was being forcibly restrained so that she could not return to her sons and the culture that raised her. Her family believed that, owing to a life in which they assumed she had been sexually abused and beaten and enslaved, she was unable to know what was best for her. Cynthia Ann, meanwhile, always had a clear and quite correct sense of her own interests. Such treatment must have been terrible to endure.

She could not, or would not, speak English, though in any case what she remembered would have been rudimentary. She would sit for hours and hours on the wide porch of Isaac's house weeping and nursing Prairie Flower. She refused to stop her pagan devotions. One of her relatives described her ritual of worship:

> She went out to a smooth place on the ground, cleaned it off very nicely and made a circle and a cross. On the cross she built a fire, burned some tobacco, and then cut a place on her breast and let the blood drop onto the fire. She then lit her pipe and blowed smoke toward the sun and assumed an attitude of the most sincere devotion. She afterwards said through an interpreter that this was her prayer to her great spirit to enable her to understand and appreciate that these were her relatives and kindred she was among.[31]

The family and neighbors retaliated by demanding that Cynthia Ann and Prairie Flower give up wearing Indian clothing and insisting that Prairie Flower be given instruction in Scripture.[32] Cynthia Ann was uncooperative. Things did not go well.

In late January 1861, a little more than a month after the Pease River fight, Isaac Parker took his charges to Austin to try to convince the Texas legislature to give them a pension—a sort of compensation for the hardships they had endured. This was a clever idea, but would require a good deal of political grease, and he was exactly the sort of man who could pull it off. As a lifelong politician and elected official, Isaac knew everyone in the capital. He and Sam Houston, then governor of Texas, were old friends. They had fought together in the War of 1812. Later, Houston had sent Isaac as an emissary to Washington to gather support for the Texas revolution.

The Parkers arrived in Austin on a chilly January day to find the city firmly in the grip of secession fever. Abraham Lincoln had been elected president the previous fall, and anti-Union sentiment in Texas was in full cry. Austin was its center. Throughout the month of January secessionists marched up and down the rutted dirt of Congress Avenue, the city's broad main street that was newly lined with sturdy limestone buildings. It climbed gently from the Colorado River toward the imposing new three-story domed state capitol, which was fronted by marble Ionic columns and a huge portico. The secessionists were in their glory. They were an unruly bunch, carrying torches and signs that condemned Lincoln and his "abolitionist" government. They held parades and marches on a moment's notice. One featured a loud brass band, a long line of carriages containing ladies who fluttered Texas flags, and a boisterous contingent of men on horseback, all led by Ranger Rip Ford, who pranced down the avenue on a white stallion.[33] Texas flags flew everywhere, and there was even talk of a second republic. The air was cold and bracing, and Texans were in a high mood.

The secession convention, which began on January 28, featured an Olympian fight between Governor Houston, who opposed breaking away from the United States, and almost everyone else, who favored it. The old statesman delivered one of the greatest speeches of his career, pleading that "it is not unmanly to pause and at least endeavor to avert the calamity." People listened respectfully to him. And then voted 171–6 in favor of secession.[34] That took place on February 1, 1861. On April 12, Confederate batteries opened fire on Fort Sumter in Charleston harbor, signaling the start of the Civil War.

Into one of these volatile debates came Cynthia Ann Parker, cleaned up and dressed nicely by two prominent Austin women who had taken a special interest in her. They were showing her the splendors of the white man's world. She entered through the massive portico and climbed the stone steps to the gallery on the second floor where she sat and listened to men debate an issue she could not possibly have comprehended in a language she did not remember. Still, she became visibly agitated. She took up her daughter and ran for the door. After she was tackled and brought back—she was always being tackled and brought back in those days—it occurred to her companions that she believed the men on the floor of the legislature were sitting in judgment of her. She thought they were deciding whether or not to put her to death.[35]

Here, too, Cynthia Ann and her daughter were objects of great curiosity. She was "visited by very many," reported one newspaper, which meant that crowds of people came and stared at her. She was visibly distraught. She spoke sparely and only through an interpreter. At one point she stated that she was surprised to discover that the Comanches were not, as she had supposed, the "most numerous and powerful people in the world."[36] Or at least that is what one newspaper reporter heard. While in Austin she sat for a "tintype"—an early type of photograph. The resulting image shows a woman who has clearly been gussied up, though she looks deeply uncomfortable in her new clothes. Her hair is pulled back in what looks like some sort of net. She wears a patterned cotton blouse and a striped skirt and what looks to be a woolen robe clasped at the neck. Her unusually large and work-scarred hands are crossed on her lap. Her gaze is direct, supplicating, and utterly miserable.[37]

Her misery notwithstanding, Isaac's plan worked. Two months after their visit, the Texas legislature voted to grant Cynthia Ann a $100-a-year pension for five years, plus a league of land (4,428 acres). Here, too, she was treated as a special case. The money and land were not to come to her but to be held in trust for her by her cousins Isaac Duke Parker and Benjamin Parker, as though they were the guardians of a minor—or of a mentally infirm adult who was unable to speak for herself.[38]

Back in Birdville, Cynthia Ann continued to be disconsolate living at her uncle Silas's house. She wept; she tried to escape; she refused to cooperate. Nothing changed. And so, in the hope that she might find greater happiness elsewhere and perhaps also to get her out of Isaac's hair, she began a long and strange odyssey through the homes of various relatives that had the ultimate effect of taking her deeper and deeper into east Texas, farther and farther from the Great Plains, and thus from any hope that she could ever be reunited with her people.

The first stop on this journey was the oddest of all. Hearing of her unhappiness with Isaac, Cynthia Ann's cousin William Parker and his wife, who lived two miles south of Isaac, had volunteered to take her in. His generosity seemed innocent enough. But William, as it turned out, was not acting out of charity. He had a very specific and entirely self-serving reason for inviting Cynthia Ann and Prairie Flower to his home.

Shortly after Cynthia Ann and Prairie Flower moved, cousin William sent a letter to a Texan named Coho Smith. Coho's real name was John Jeremiah Smith. His nickname came as the result of being wounded by a lance. *Cojo* in Spanish means "lame." He was one of those marginal, colorful characters who inhabited the Texas frontier in its early days. He recorded his adventures in a book of his own drawings and observations he dubbed his "Cohographs." He was self-educated and fluent in a number of languages, including Comanche. As a boy, he had spent a year as a Comanche captive. At the time he received Parker's letter, sometime in late 1861, he was working as a Confederate cotton agent, though he had also worked as a teacher and cabinetmaker. In the letter Parker explained that Cynthia Ann had come to live with him and begged Smith to come to his house—a distance of 189 miles—to act as translator. He said that he and his wife were anxious to have a conversation with their new guest, who could not speak English. For whatever reason, Smith agreed and soon arrived at the Parker place. When he asked where Cynthia Ann was, Parker replied, "I saw her go out the gate about half an hour ago. Let us go and hunt her up. She is generally moping around here in these woods."[39] They found her a hundred yards from the house, sitting on a log with "her elbows on her knees and her hands to her face." She wore an old sun bonnet. Prairie Flower was playing on the ground. She had constructed a small corral of sticks and was talking to herself in Comanche. William indicated to his cousin that dinner was ready by putting his hand in his mouth. Cynthia Ann shot a sharp, disapproving glance at Smith, then began to follow them back to the house. His wife explained to Smith that "so many people came to see her that it annoyed her. That is why she looked at you so spitefully." She was still a figure of curiosity, still being gawked at.

Back at the house, Smith spoke to her in Comanche. "Ee-wunee keem," he said, which meant "come here." According to Smith, her reaction was immediate and almost violent. "She sprang with a scream and knocked about half the dishes off the table, scaring Mr. Parker. . . . She ran around to me and fell on the floor and caught me around both ankles, crying in Comanche 'Ee-ma mi mearo,' meaning 'I am going with you.' "

Now she came fully alive. Sitting on a chair next to Smith, she held him by one arm "talking all the time to me in Comanche and Spanish, mixing the two languages all the time." Her Spanish was surprisingly good. She would not eat, but kept talking instead. "Oh, don't eat," she said in Comanche. "Let us talk. Oh my friend, do let us talk."

Then she switched to Spanish, and said something that did not make any sense. "I want to go back to my two boys and Billy there has told me by signs that he wants to go to my people also. I said: 'Billy, do you want to go to the Comanches?' He said 'Yes, I do. And that is why I sent for you to interpret, for it is this way.'"

Perplexed, Smith then asked William Parker what she meant. Parker, at length, explained. He told Smith that he had served in the Confederate Army. A union bullet had shattered his thighbone and had partly crippled him. He was not crippled enough, however, to avoid being sent back to the war by the conscription officers he called "dad-blasted heel flies." The prospect terrified him, as did the notion of being hanged or shot as a deserter. Like thousands of other young men in the Confederate states, Parker had rushed to the recruiting posts in 1861 in anticipation of a brief and glorious war. Now he wanted out. He was desperate.

And he had a plan. "I want you to take me and Cynthia Ann to the Comanches," he told Smith. "I can stay with them until this cruel war is over."

The idea was absurd, as though he conceived of the Comanche tribe as a sort of rooming house where he could stay for a few years. Somehow Cynthia Ann had been able to grasp this idea clearly and to comprehend that Smith had been summoned for this reason. The two Parker relatives had obviously found a way to communicate.

Smith, who had no interest in such a venture—for which he, too, could be hanged—offered the weak excuse that there were no horses available. "Horses," Cynthia Ann exclaimed, "that is nothing! There is some first-rate horses running here . . . don't hesitate a moment about the horses. Oh, I tell you, mi Corazon estan llorando todo el tiempo por mis dos hijos. [My heart is crying all the time for my two sons.]" Then, switching back to Comanche, she said: "En-se-ca-sok bu-ku-ne-suwa? [Do you want a heap of horses?]" Then again in Spanish: "No mas lleba mi." [Only take me.] She offered Smith all the girls or wives he wanted. She offered ten guns, ten horses, ten wives. Cynthia Ann's harangue, Smith wrote, continued into the early-morning hours.

When Smith asked why she and "Billy" could not go by themselves, she answered that she thought he would be killed and she would be made a slave. She had an idea that Coho was tougher than William Parker, the cripple and coward. She was probably right. And of course Smith spoke the Comanche language. The next day Parker took Smith out to see his illegal still, which he had built following the directions in a book entitled *One Thousand Things Worth Knowing*, then made one last effort to convince him to help, offering Smith the deed to more than half of his eighty acres. "They will never get me in the army again," he said. "I will suicide first." Smith again refused. He later heard that Parker had managed to find his way to Illinois anyway, and had thus escaped the war. The last thing Smith remembered Cynthia Ann saying was: "Si le doy o mi gene si le doy, todos las muchachas que si quire, pero bonito y buen mosas. [I will give you, or my people will give you, all the girls you want, but pretty and well made]." He refused that, too. It must have broken her heart.

Coho Smith captured Cynthia Ann as no one else has. Other people saw her as sullen, brooding, unresponsive, detached. Despondent. Even crazy, or at least so far sunk in savagery as to be irredeemable. In Smith's account she was smart, aggressive, focused, strong-willed, and intensely practical. She was completely aware of what she wanted and, at least for that brief moment, of how to get it. Her tragedy was that such a woman was utterly helpless to change the destiny that her family had, with the best of intentions, arranged for her.

In early 1862, Cynthia Ann and Prairie Flower moved yet again, this time to the home of her younger brother, Silas Jr. He had also been at the fort when it was raided, along with his three siblings. For some reason the Indians had taken Cynthia Ann and John and had spared Silas Jr. and Orlena. Silas and his wife, Ann, lived with their three children in Van Zandt County, deep in the piney woods of east Texas, twenty-seven miles northwest of Tyler.

If Cynthia Ann had despaired of getting back home when she was living in Birdville, she was now more than a hundred miles east. She was no longer even near the frontier. She must have understood this as they traveled: She was leaving the prairies, heading for the high timber. She must have known she was never getting out.

Life was no better with Silas, who was twenty-eight at the time and stuttered. She did not get along with his wife, who punished Prairie Flower (who was often called Topsannah or Tecks Ann) every time she called her mother by her Comanche name.[40] Cynthia Ann kept trying to escape, walking off down the road with her daughter in her arms whenever she was left alone. (She said she was "going home, just going home.")[41] She often slashed her arms and breasts with a knife, drawing blood. This was probably an act of mourning for the death of her husband. Or it could have been a simple expression of misery. On one occasion she took a butcher knife and cut off her hair.

It was around this time that a photograph was taken of Cynthia Ann and Prairie Flower that would become famous on the frontier and beyond. They had gone "visiting" in Fort Worth in the company of Silas—probably dragged along so she would not escape—and had somehow, perhaps at Silas's urging, landed in the photography studio of a man named A. F. Corning.[42] The result was an exceptional and luminous portrait of mother and daughter. In it, Cynthia Ann wears a plain cotton blouse with a kerchief tied loosely at the neck. Her board-straight, medium brown hair is cropped short (perhaps this was the result of the butcher knife incident). Her eyes are light and transparent, her gaze disarmingly direct. Again we see the large, muscular hands and thick wrists. What is most extraordinary about the portrait, however, is Cynthia Ann's exposed right breast, at which the black-haired, swaddled, and obviously quite pretty Prairie Flower is nursing. There is probably no precedent for this sort of photography on the Texas frontier in 1862. White women were not photographed with their breasts exposed. And even if a photographer had taken such a photo, no newspaper would have published it. This one was different. It became the picture of Cynthia Ann that generations of schoolchildren knew; it is still in wide circulation. The only explanation is that because Cynthia Ann was seen, and treated, as a savage, even though she was as white as any Scots-Irish settler in the south. The double standard is similar to the one *National Geographic Magazine* famously applied in the mid-twentieth century to photographs of naked African women. The magazine would never have considered showing the breasts of a white woman in its pages. This explains part of the fascination with Cynthia Ann: the sense that, though her skin was white, something darker and more primal lurked beneath. In April 1862, Silas joined the Confederate army, leaving his pregnant wife to care for their three children and also to act as jailer for Cynthia Ann and Prairie Flower.[43] Ann soon put a stop to it, and Cynthia Ann and Prairie Flower were shipped off yet again, this time to her sister Orlena, who also lived in the vicinity of Tyler, with her husband J. R. O'Quinn. Mother and daughter were moved to a separate house.[44]

Now, perhaps because of her growing realization that she was never going back to the Comanches, Cynthia Ann began to adjust. The Civil War had taken most of the able-bodied men, leaving the women to pick up the slack. Cynthia Ann began to relearn English, and, in one account, could eventually speak it when she wanted to. She learned how to spin, weave, and sew and became quite adept at it. Her Comanche experience had taught her how to tan hides, and she became known as the best tanner in the county. According to a neighbor:

> She was stout and weighed about 140 pounds, well made, and liked to work. She had a wild expression and would look down when people looked at her. She could use an axe equal to a man and disliked a lazy person. She was an expert in tanning hides with the hair on them, or plaiting or knitting either ropes or whips. She thought her two boys were lost on the prairie . . . this dissatisfied her very much.[45]

Part of this adjustment, too, was her reintegration into the Parker family. Many of her relatives lived nearby, and she saw them with some regularity. She had friends, too, in a sense, at least people she could talk to. She even remembered some of the people from the old days. Every Sunday one of them would take Prairie Flower visiting. The child had learned English quickly and soon spoke it more often than Comanche.[46] She even went to a nearby school. In the account of Cynthia Ann's relative Tom Champion, she had a "sunny disposition" and was "an open-hearted, good woman, and always ready to help somebody."[47] Most others had a different view. She was seen weeping on the porch, or hiding herself from gawkers, who never stopped coming to see the infamous "white squaw." And there was nothing sunny about her refusal to abandon many of her Indian ways, slicing her body with a knife whenever a family member died, and singing her high-pitched, keening songs of Comanche mourning. She had never forgotten, she had only accommodated; she probably stopped believing the Parker family's promises, which they repeated to the end, that she would be allowed to see her sons again. They had always been empty promises. According to T. J. Cates, one of Cynthia Ann's neighbors, she spoke often of the loss of her two sons.

> I well remember Cynthia Ann Parker and her little Taocks [sic]. She lived at this time about six miles south of [the town of] Ben Wheeler with her brother-in-law Ruff O'Quinn, near Slater's Creek. . . . She thought her two boys were lost on the prairie after she was captured. . . . She would take a knife and hack at her breast until it would bleed and then put the blood on some tobacco and cry for her lost boys.[48]

Champion had the same impression. "I don't think she ever knew but that her sons were killed," he wrote. "And to hear her tell of the happy days of the Indian dances and see the excitement and pure joy which shown [sic] on her face, the memory of it, I am convinced that the white people did more harm by keeping her away from them than the Indians did by taking her at first."[49]

Whatever chance she may have had at contentment was destroyed in 1864 when Prairie Flower died of influenza and pneumonia.[50] The little girl's death shattered her. Now there was nothing left of her Comanche life but memories. What her day-to-day life was like in the years after that is largely unknown. The Comanche version is unambiguous: The white men broke her spirit and made her a misfit. She became bitter over her enforced captivity, refused to eat, and eventually starved herself to death.[51] She lived six more years, until 1870, when she died of influenza, which may well have been complicated by self-starvation. A coffin was built for her by relatives; a bone pin was put in her hair, and they buried her in the Foster Cemetery, four miles south of the town of Poyner, which lies between the larger towns of Tyler and Palestine. It is perhaps fitting for someone who had endured so many changes against her will that, before she came to her final resting place, she was buried three times, in three different cemeteries.

Who was she, in the end? A white woman by birth, yes, but also a relic of old Comancheria, of the fading empire of high grass and fat summer moons and buffalo herds that blackened the horizon. She had seen all of that death and glory. She had been a chief's wife. She had lived free on the high infinite plains as her adopted race had in the very last place in the North American continent where anyone would ever live or run free. She had died in deep pine woods where there was no horizon, where you could see nothing at all. The woods were just a prison. As far as we know, she died without the slightest comprehension of what larger forces had conspired to take her away from her old life.

One thinks of Cynthia Ann on the immensity of the plains, a small figure in buckskin bending to her chores by a diamond-clear stream. It is late autumn, the end of warring and buffalo hunting. Above her looms a single cottonwood tree, gone bright yellow in the season, its leaves and branches framing a deep blue sky. Maybe she lifts her head to see the children and dogs playing in the prairie grass and, beyond them, the coils of smoke rising into the gathering twilight from a hundred lodge fires. And maybe she thinks, just for a moment, that all is right in the world.

Thirteen

THE RISE OF QUANAH

THE BATTLE WAS over and the two boys were alone in the bottoms of the narrow Pease River, among cottonwood and hackberry and walnut and rolling sand hills. They would have shivered in the same bitterly cold north wind that spun tornadoes of blown dust about the white soldiers. The boys were young—twelve and ten years old—but not too young to understand the horror that had just befallen them. When the soldiers had first come into sight a great cry of alarm had gone up and both of them—Quanah and Peanuts—had fled the village. Their mother, Nautdah, had been with them. Then, somehow, they had lost her.[1] There was shooting, and screaming, as the soldiers slashed and blasted their way through the village, killing everyone in sight, even the women with their heavily laden pack mules, even the dogs. Then there was silence. Then the boys were alone. Though they may or may not have witnessed the death of their father, Peta Nocona, they almost certainly understood that their mother had not been killed. But they obviously got the general idea that everybody else was dead. So they fled.

A twelve-year-old Comanche boy was not entirely helpless in the wild. He would have been far more competent than a frontier white boy. He would have been, as all Comanche boys were, a superb rider. He would have known how to hunt small game. He would have known how to make fire. He would have known something about gathering edible roots and berries. But by the timetables of Comanche culture, Quanah would not, at that point in his life, have been allowed to participate in battle, and would probably not even have been allowed on a buffalo or deer hunt. He would never have been permitted to stray very far from camp. He would absolutely never have been left alone in the immensity of the southern plains, without food or weapons, and with no sense of where his people were.

What happened next has been unnoticed or uncredited by the main chroniclers of Comanche history, largely because Quanah himself later forcefully denied that he was even at the Battle of Pease River or that his father had been killed there. Both assertions were untrue, and had to do with Quanah's interest in cleansing what would have been a terrible stain on Peta Nocona's record: The Comanches saw Pease River as a fiasco and a disgrace, and it had happened entirely on his watch. Quanah and Peanuts were at the camp because their mother said they were. She was frantic because of it. We also know that two, and only two, riders survived the fight and managed to get away.[2] We know this because Charles Goodnight and ten scouts under his command tracked them from the confluence of the Pease River and Mule Creek to a large canyon near the foot of the Llano Estacado, somewhere between seventy-five and a hundred miles to the west. He never saw their faces, only the tracks of their horses.

Goodnight and his men found a large Indian camp, the ultimate destination of all that buffalo meat and other provisions the soldiers had found on Mule Creek. The scouts were able to get quite close to it. As Goodnight described it:

> The Indians had not seen us approaching, and it is a mystery to me yet why they had not kept a better lookout . . . as the spies [the Indian riders] had reached the camp to report the battle. There were approximately a thousand Indians in this camp. . . . We scoured back up the canyon to where I found a sharp curve. Here we could be seen only in front of this curve. I threw the men into it to wait until dark, fearing we would be discovered and knowing we would have no show to live if we were.[3]

According to Goodnight, Quanah later gave him this version of what happened in the camp:

> When the two Indian guides, who had escaped from the party killed by Ross, had reached the main body of Indians, they reported that there were ten thousand of us. . . . As soon as the main body of Indians could get ready they moved back north where Quanah stated they wintered from the Washita to

the Wichita Mountains. They suffered much from provisions, for they were
entirely north of the buffalo.[4]

Quanah knew all of this unusual detail because *he* was the one who arrived
at the camp to tell them the terrible news and to inform them, with the naïve
exaggeration of a twelve-year-old, that there were *ten thousand soldiers*.[5] Only
a child could have failed to distinguish a tiny, irregular force of Rangers and
bluecoats from a full army division.

But consider what the boy had accomplished. Abandoned in the December wilderness without food, and pursued by a band of men aroused by the
blood sport of the Pease River killings and fully motivated to catch him, he
had managed, with his little brother in tow, to follow the tracks of his fellow
band members, who had left two or three days before, across a wide swath of
the broken, undulating West Texas prairie. He had presumably done at least
part of this at night, to stay ahead of Goodnight, who was in those days one
of the few white men with the ability to track riders through wilderness. Had
the boy made any errors, or not succeeded in finding the village, Goodnight
would certainly have caught him. Goodnight reported that the two riders
had caused a large commotion when they arrived in the Comanche village.
Of course they had. Not only because they carried the terrible news of the
battle, and thus of the loss of the band's food for the winter. But also because
Quanah and his little brother had done something absolutely extraordinary,
nearly unbelievable, even by Comanche standards.

When Quanah was born in 1848, in a tipi near the Wichita Mountains in
what is now southwestern Oklahoma, white men were still a world away.
The Penatekas were being progressively destroyed along the line of settlement in central Texas, but no white men would yet dare to cross the Red
River in pursuit of Comanches. The horrible disease-bearing scourge of the
Forty-niners had not yet swept through on the Santa Fe and other trails. The
buffalo still roamed the plains in their millions.

And in this world, still insulated from the ravages that would come, the
Comanches did what they had always done. They procreated, hunted, and,
most important, made war on other Indian tribes. A few weeks after Cynthia
Ann gave birth to Quanah, warriors in her band—the Nokonis, or Wanderers—left to fight a Navajo war party. Comanche-Navajo enmity went back a
long way, back to the days when the People had swept down from the Wind

River country to challenge the Apaches in New Mexico. These same Navajos, discovering that the village was now vulnerable, attacked. This was an old Indian tactic. But instead of massacring the village and its inhabitants as they had expected to do, the sixteen attackers ran into fierce resistance from the men who had remained behind. The Navajos fled, taking two hundred Comanche horses with them. They were soon tracked down. Three of them were killed, and the horses were recovered. When the victorious Comanches returned, there were four days of joyous singing and dancing, while the scalps of the three dead Navajos were paraded about on a pole.[6] This was Indian life on the plains; it went on all the time, more or less invisible to white men. Had things gone a bit differently, the baby Quanah might have been skewered on a Navajo lance. That of course would have spawned a revenge raid, which would have invited a counterraid, and the stakes of blood vengeance would have gone up all across the plains. Instead, one of the first things Quanah saw was a victory dance.

Quanah's childhood is divided by his father's death and his mother's capture into two strikingly different periods. For his first twelve years, he was the son of a powerful war chief, a man with much influence and many horses, a talented hunter. We do not know many of its details, but in Comanche terms he led a privileged life. The family was apparently happy, and Quanah later claimed many fond memories of his mother and father. So fearful was Peta Nocona that his white wife would be taken from him that when Comancheros or other traders passed through his camp he often blackened her face with ashes and made her hide away.[7] (This partly explains the dearth of Cynthia Ann sightings over the years.)

Quanah grew up the way most Comanche boys did. By the time he was four he would have been riding an old packhorse. By five he managed a pony of his own. By six he was riding young colts bareback, and soon after that he was enlisted to help herd ponies. Like all Comanche boys, he would have become expert at roping and catching horses. From this point onward he spent an enormous amount of time in the saddle; his horse quickly became, as it was for all of the People, men and women, an extension of his physical being.

As he learned to ride, the Comanche boy was initiated into the secrets of weaponry, usually by his grandfather or another elderly male. At six he was given a bow and blunt arrows and taught to shoot. He soon began hunting with real arrows, going out with other boys and shooting birds. In the Comanche culture boys were allowed extraordinary freedom. They did no menial labor of any kind. They did not fetch water or wood. They did not have to help pack or unpack during the band's frequent moves. Instead they roved about in gangs, wrestling, swimming, racing their horses. They would often follow birds and insects, shooting hummingbirds with special headless arrows that had split foreshafts. They shot grasshoppers and ate the legs for lunch. Sometimes they tied two grasshoppers together with a short thread and then watched them try to jump. They would make bets. The first one that fell on its back was the loser. They occasionally played with girls. One co-ed game called Grizzly Bear consisted of a "bear" inside a circle who tried to capture children outside the circle who were protected by a "mother." The children would run into the circle trying to steal some of the bear's "sugar." At night they listened to their elders tell terrifying stories of Piamempits, the Big Cannibal Owl, a mythological creature who dwelt in a cave in the Wichita Mountains and came out by night to eat naughty children.[8]

Quanah would have gone about naked until he was nine years old, except when the weather was severely cold. After that he wore a breechclout, leggings, and moccasins. The leggings often had fringe work, a trademark of the Comanches. In winter he wore a heavy robe made from a buffalo that had been killed in the late fall, when the creature had grown a dark brown winter fur that was up to twenty inches thick.[9] Plainsmen and soldiers claimed that one such robe offered more warmth than four heavy, army-issue woolen blankets.

As a boy approached puberty, life quickly became more serious. These were the high lonesome plains, after all, and his tribe lived a hard and brutal nomadic life where nothing was guaranteed. Skill in hunting was the only real guarantee of survival, and thus he was expected to perfect his skills in archery. The Comanches were known as exceptional archers, both from horseback and on foot. From fifty yards a warrior could reliably hit an object the size of a doorknob four out of five times. From ten to fifteen yards he could shoot a twenty- to thirty-inch arrow with such force that it would drive entirely through the carcass of a two-thousand-pound buffalo if it did not hit bone. A Comanche boy had to learn to make fire: In those years it was done by hand-twirling a firedrill on a soft stick that was surrounded with a gunpowder-laden rag. (In the old days, Spanish moss tinder or birds' nests were used.) He had to learn basic wilderness skills like telling whether an observed animal was heading toward or away from water. (One example was a bird called the Dirt Dauber. If his mouth was empty, the observer knew he was going straight to water.)[10]

With puberty, too, came the rituals that would transform them, in the eyes of the tribe, from boys to men. One of these was the vision quest, a version of which existed in most North American Indian tribes. For Comanches it began with a swim in a river or stream, a form of purification. The young man then ventured out to a lonely place where he would see no one, clad only in breechclout and moccasins. With him he carried a buffalo robe, a bone pipe, tobacco, and fire-making materials. On the way to his secluded spot he stopped four times, each time smoking and praying. At night he smoked and prayed for power. He looked for signs in the animals and rocks and trees around him. He fasted. (Unlike some of the northern plains tribes, there was no self-torture involved.) Usually this lasted four days and nights, but the idea was for the young brave to remain in place until he received a vision. We do not know exactly what the result of Quanah's vision quest was. Later he told of dreaming of a bear. His medicine as an adult was bear medicine, which meant that the bear was the source of his power, his *puha*. Comanche adolescents also sought spirit power in the ritual of the Eagle Dance, in which the warrior-dancers proceeded to a nearby camp to "capture" a girl, usually an actual captive. After they returned, there was singing and drumming and the young men danced, imitating the cry of eagles. The idea was that they were young eagles attempting to leave the nest.[11]

After the Battle of Pease River, Quanah's life underwent a profound and unpleasant change. The comfort and status of being a chief's son vanished immediately. He was an orphan in a culture that did not easily accommodate orphans. At first he was cared for by his father's Indian wife. But she died within the year, leaving him and his brother with no near relatives to care for them. "We were often treated very cruelly," he said later, "as orphans only of Indians are treated." Then Peanuts died, too (of unknown causes). Quanah was left alone. "It then seemed to me that I was left friendless," he recalled. "I often had to beg for my food and clothes, and could scarcely get anyone to make or mend my clothes. I at last learned that I was more cruelly treated than the other orphans on account of my white blood."[12]

In spite of this hardship, Quanah became a full warrior when he was fifteen years old.[13] He was a large, long-limbed boy, much taller and stronger than the average Comanche. As an adult he was a strapping six-footer, nearly a head taller than many of his peers. In later photos the sheer mass of his biceps and forearms is apparent. If he was treated cruelly for a time, that treatment must surely have stopped as he grew into young manhood. Quanah was no one to tangle with. He was also strikingly handsome: fully dark-skinned Comanche but with a classical, straight northern European nose, high cheekbones, and piercing light gray eyes that were as luminous and transparent as his mother's. He somehow looked completely Indian without looking Asiatic, and could have served as a model of how white people thought a noble savage ought to look, not the least because he looked a bit like them. He was a superb archer and an accomplished hunter. As a youth, and as a warrior, he became known for his "careless, daredevil sort of courage, quite in contrast with the stealthy, deadly character of Indian warfare."[14] He was also, as he would prove conclusively later in his life, extremely intelligent.

He was by nature aggressive, forthright, and fearless, and these qualities were on display at a young age. When he was only seven years old, Quanah, who had been given a small piece of meat one night at dinner, challenged an adult guest who had gotten a larger piece, explaining that the situation was unfair. The astonished guest gave the young boy the meat, which he could not finish. His mother, Cynthia Ann, later punished him by cramming the rest of the meat down his throat.[15] There was never anything subtle about Quanah, either in war or in peace. The other thing that distinguished him, in the years after the Pease River fight, was his smoldering hatred of white men. "He wished to avenge the wrong," his son Baldwin Parker wrote later. "He understood, too, that white people were responsible for his father's death."[16]

His first raid was a foray with thirty warriors from a camp in southwestern Kansas. The raiding party rode south, through Oklahoma, all the way to San Antonio. The goal appears to have been horses as opposed to revenge. They indulged themselves in what, for the Comanches, was routine mischief. They stole thirty-eight horses and killed and scalped two unfortunate white men who happened to cross their path. As was often the case after raids, they were pursued by white horsemen. They rode hard for three days and outdistanced them, returning home triumphantly with their large herd and two scalps. A war dance was held in their honor.

Quanah's second raid was more interesting. This time he rode out with sixty warriors from their camp in what is now western Oklahoma. They swept west and south, into New Mexico, ending up on the Penasco River in the eastern part of the territory. At one point they spotted a company of U.S. Army cavalry headed in the other direction. Instead of leaving them alone, which most Comanches would have done without a second thought, the war chief decided it would be a good idea to steal the cavalry's sixty mules. So they did. The cavalry soon followed and caught up with the Indians, who could move the balky mules only so fast. Quanah was dispatched with two other braves to drive the mules into the mountains while the rest of the party took up defensive positions in a rocky pass. A two-hour shooting fight ensued, with no casualties on either side. Night fell and the soldiers retired to their camp while the Indians, as usual, beat a fast pace toward home. They traveled all night, then all day, then all night, finally stopping and sleeping in a circle around their mules. They were so exhausted that when they awoke they found that many of their precious mules had wandered half a mile from camp. When they returned with the captured herd, another glorious war dance was held in their honor.[17]

In 1868, at age twenty, Quanah took part in an extended expedition into Mexico with nine warriors under the command of the Kiowa chief Tohausan, famous from the battle of Adobe Walls in 1864, where his combined forces of Comanches and Kiowas had come remarkably close to defeating a U.S. Army force commanded by the legendary Kit Carson. The Mexican raid was a classic Comanche (and Kiowa) enterprise, one of the ways young, ambitious men traditionally made their names and fortunes. In 1852, Captain Randolph Marcy described the phenomenon that took warriors away for as long as two years:

> Six or nine young men set out upon one of these adventures, and the only outfit they require is a horse, with their war equipments, consisting of bows and arrows, lance and shield, with occasionally a gun. Thus prepared they set out on a journey of 1,000 miles or more, through a perfectly wild and desolate country, dependent for assistance wholly upon such game as they may chance to find. They make their way to the northern provinces of Mexico.[18]

But times had changed. It was now much harder to go blithely adventuring about the American southwest in search of loot and glory. Comanche power was still strong, and still dominant west of the 98th meridian and east of the Rockies and the Grand Cordillera. But it was no longer unchallenged. A line of forts had been thrown up along the San Antonio–El Paso trail whose purpose was both to protect wagon trains but also to disrupt traditional Comanche raiding patterns into Mexico. Fort Stockton, for example, was built near the site of the plentiful icy waters of Comanche Springs, one of the largest springs in Texas and for a hundred years the main way station for raiders traveling to Mexico. In a bone-dry country, the water hole was an important landmark. Now it was useless to Quanah and his fellow braves; they would never drink its clear, chill waters again.

Tohausan's expedition sounds remarkably inglorious. The days of the great and productive Mexican raiding were fast coming to a close. Comanches would never again be allowed to indulge themselves in the bloody, summer-long raids that emptied out whole districts in northern Mexico and left behind burning ruins over whole states, raids that produced hundreds or thousands of captured horses that then moved in long lines northward through Texas along the Comanche Trace. Quanah's war party was out for months. Twice they went two days without water. They nearly starved in Chihuahua. They found Mexican settlements bristling with hostility and only a few horses to steal. Quanah and a friend lost their mules on the long trek back across northern Mexico and Texas. They arrived back at their village on foot. By his own account, the journey was a complete disaster. There were no victory dances to celebrate his return. If he hadn't been so young and carefree and enthusiastic about his life, he might have noticed that time was running out for the Comanches. But this would not be in his thoughts until much later.

In 1868 he took part in some of the Comanche raids into the Texas hill country, raids that history records as extremely, vengefully violent. One was the infamous raid at the Legion Valley settlement, near present-day Llano, where seven captives were killed, including a baby and a three-year-old, and where Minnie Caudle was kidnapped.[19] There is no proof that he took part in what the white people regarded as unthinkable atrocities, but this sort of raiding was in fact what young Comanche men were doing in the waning days of the plains empire, and Quanah himself was known to burn for revenge against the people who killed his father and stole his mother and sister. Their actions amounted to what we would today consider to be political terrorism. There was still status in horse-thieving, to be sure. But all Comanches knew that the one sure way to roll back the frontier was to torture, rape, and kill all of its white residents. Thus, as time went by the raids took on a more purely political character, and with good reason. There was plenty of evidence that such a strategy worked.

Quanah became a war chief at a very young age. He did it in the traditional way, by demonstrating in battle that he was braver, smarter, fiercer, and cooler under fire than his peers. His transformation took place in two different fights. Both happened in the late 1860s, and both have been claimed as the vehicles of his elevation. In one, the raid originated in a camp in the

Llano Estacado. The leader was a chief named Bear's Ear. Quanah himself had grown up mostly with the Nokoni band. But councils before this expedition were held by Hears the Sunrise, who was a chief of the Yamparikas (the Yap Eaters), whose domain was traditionally above the Canadian River. Also present was Milky Way, a Penateka chief who had chosen not to go to the reservation with most of the rest of his band, and who was married to a Yamparika.[20] Such commingling suggests a blurring of band loyalty, and indeed this was happening. From 1868 to 1872, Quanah spent most of his time with the Quahadis, a band that seems to have coalesced out of the Kotsotekas in the 1850s,[21] perhaps out of a desire to remain aloof and pure on the high plains. He also camped a good deal with the Kotsotekas. And his raiding parties were very likely mixed. With the onslaught of whites and the reduction of the hunting ranges, the old geographic separation of bands was disappearing.

Bear's Ear's expedition roared east from the high flat plains, across the palisaded rock headlands and down onto the rolling, broken, and river-crossed plains, and eventually collided with the line of settlement, which had continued to roll eastward like a receding wave: It was farther east than it had been when Peta Nocona raided it in 1860. The raiders struck hard at the ranches and farms in the area of Gainesville (fifty miles north of Fort Worth). They probably killed people though this is not recorded. They managed to steal a large herd of horses, and headed home. They got as far as the Red River when they were intercepted by a force of soldiers that had been dispatched from Fort Richardson (near Jacksboro) to find them.

A bloody fight followed, during which Bear's Ear was killed. As we have seen, the death of the chief, and thus the failure of his medicine, usually turned the tide of battle in favor of the white men. Dispirited and leaderless, the Indians often picked up the chief's body and fled. Not this time. In the absence of Bear's Ear, Quanah took over. "Spread out," he yelled to his warriors. "Turn the horses north to the river." This was a departure from Bear's Ear's original plan. With Quanah urging them on, the Comanches wheeled the herd about and raced over rough ground toward the river. As Quanah retreated with the others, he was pursued by a bluecoat, who fired at him. Instead of spurring his horse harder to get away, Quanah rounded on his adversary and confronted the soldier head-on. He then charged and, like a medieval jousters, the two warriors thundered toward each other, weapons out. The soldier fired his revolver. His bullet grazed Quanah's thigh. Quanah's arrow, meanwhile, found its mark in the man's shoulder. He dropped his weapon, turned his horse, and fled. But Quanah was now exposed to the fire of other soldiers. He dropped down behind his horse in the old Comanche way, and, with bullets singing all around him, raced after his own war party. Somehow they managed to swim with their stolen stock across the river to safety. The white soldiers did not pursue them. That night around the campfire the Comanche war party chose Quanah as their leader.[22]

The other battle took place in the summer of 1869. Quanah, sixty-three other Indians, and "some Mexicans" left camp in Santa Fe. They rode east to cattle ranches located around present-day San Angelo. These would have been the westernmost settlements in the state of Texas in that year, located not coincidentally near the U.S. Army forts Chadbourne (est. 1852) and Concho (est. 1867). As Quanah later told it, he and some of his friends discovered a cowboy camp and a small herd of horses just a few miles from Fort Concho. The Indians hid in rocks and bushes, waited until nightfall, then stampeded the horses, capturing the best ones for themselves. The cowboys fired into the darkness, but hit no one.[23] The Indians continued south, riding by night, into the Texas hill country west of San Antonio, where they killed a man who was driving a team of oxen. News of the shooting traveled quickly through the settlement. Thirty men rode in pursuit of the raiders.

The whites soon caught them, and a battle ensued. According to Quanah, the white men had long-range rifles, probably buffalo guns. The Indians were losing the battle, and they began a retreat. Quanah, however, did not fall back with the rest. He concealed himself in the bushes beside the trail, and when two of the white men rode by he emerged and killed both of them with his lance, a bravura performance that was witnessed by the other warriors. They quickly re-formed and charged, and the Texans were forced into cover. A brief shooting fight followed, with no resolution. The Indians ran out of ammunition, and withdrew. That night, in council on the San Saba River, this war party, too, elected Quanah as their leader.

Quanah's conspicuous bravery on the battlefield meant that he became, at a very young age, one of a small, select group of Comanche men who would lead the tribe's final raiding and military expeditions in the last years of their freedom. Their world was getting noticeably smaller. The following year there were less than four thousand Comanches left in the world. Of those a mere one thousand had refused to go to the reservation.[24]

The most dramatic story of Quanah's early life involves his marriage. He had many wives later in life but none of his unions was ever as dramatic as his marriage to his second wife, whose name was Weckeah. (His first wife was apparently a Mescalero Apache, about whom little is known.) The marriage probably took place in the early 1870s.[25] In any case, the story begins with a familiar premise. Quanah was in love with Weckeah. They had grown up together. She was in love with him. She beaded his moccasins and bow quiver. They wanted to marry. There was just one problem: Her father, Old Bear, opposed it. This was partly because of Quanah's white blood and partly because, as an orphan and thus a pauper, he had no standing in the tribe.[26] Complicating matters was a rival suitor, one Tannap, son of Eckitoacup, who was a wealthy chief. Weckeah did not like Tannap at all.[27] At the heart of Quanah's problem was that most important unit of Comanche wealth: horseflesh. Tannap's father, who owned a hundred horses, offered ten of them for Weckeah's hand in marriage. Quanah could offer only one horse.

Still, Weckeah implored him to try to match Tannap's offer. So Quanah went to his friends and managed to gather up ten horses. He then drove them to Old Bear's tipi and presented them. Unfortunately, Eckitoacup had already heard of his plan and had doubled his offer.

Undeterred, Quanah came up with a new idea. Now he told Weckeah that their only hope was to elope. This was not uncommon in Comanche culture: An impoverished suitor often had no choice but to abscond with the bride. "When a girl learned that a rich suitor whom she did not care to marry was about to propose," wrote Wallace and Hoebel in their classic ethnographic study of the tribe, "she might elope with the man she loved. Couples occasionally eloped when the boy was poor and unable to furnish enough ponies or other articles of value to satisfy the parents of the girl. In such a case the relatives and friends of the boy might supply the necessary ponies to soothe the dishonor suffered by the wife's parents."[28] Quanah had no such family. Which meant that by taking Weckeah he risked death, as did Weckeah. Comanche families could be quite unforgiving about such things, and it was a simple enough matter for a powerful chief like Eckitoacup to recruit an expedition to seek retribution from a young man who had so grossly violated cultural protocols.

But Quanah had something more than simple elopement in mind. Before he and Weckeah left, he recruited what amounted to an insurance policy:

a war party of twenty-one young Comanche warriors. Together they rode south for seven hours, not breaking a trot except when crossing streams.[29] This was as fast as Comanches could travel, and could only have been done with a large number of mounts for each warrior. So fearful were they of what might be pursuing them that they traveled by night for two nights, split up and rejoined a number of times, then split again into units of two, coming together at Double Mountain, near the present town of Snyder in west Texas. They finally stopped on the North Concho River near the town of San Angelo and, as Quanah put it, "went to stealin' horses."

They stayed there for more than a year, during which time Quanah built the camp into his own power base. Their main activity was horse stealing. "We just stole horses all over Texas," according to Quanah. They undoubtably killed people, too. With time, some of his young and daring cohorts returned to their main camp, telling tales of riches and adventure, and Quanah's leadership, returning to the North Concho with their sweethearts or wives, as well as other young men who wanted to ride with Quanah. At the end of the year, Quanah's band numbered several hundred.[30] They owned a large horse herd.

Meanwhile, Weckeah's elopement had not stopped gnawing at Eckitoacup, and he finally decided he would mount an expedition to get her back. By now everyone knew where Quanah was. Eckitoacup rode south with a war party and arrived at the renegade camp on the river. It is not clear what he expected to find, but what he and his warriors found themselves confronting was Quanah's entire band, armed and painted and drawn up for battle. Shocked by the number of warriors, Eckitoacup became alarmed for his own safety. Instead of fighting, he decided to settle: Four leaders from each side met on neutral ground. After much smoking and haggling, a deal was made. Eckitoacup would receive nineteen horses, the pick of Quanah's herd. In exchange Quanah would be granted the right to return to the tribe. (Quanah observed, after the deal was concluded, that he knew a ranch where he could steal nineteen comparable horses in a few hours.) The deal was sealed with a night of feasting and dancing. Because Quanah's band had by this time become too large to be left in peace in that part of Texas, he followed Eckitoacup back home the next day, where he found that he enjoyed new status as a fully fledged war chief.[31]

Fourteen

UNCIVIL WARS

THE YEAR QUANAH became a warrior, 1863, was the bloodiest year in American history, though most of the blood that was shed had nothing at all to do with this ambitious Comanche boy who rode free on the western plains, stealing horses and taking scalps. The agent of death and destruction was the Civil War. That year it was transformed forever from the relatively brief, self-contained, regional conflict most people believed it would be into the malevolent, drawn-out, continent-girding affair that threatened to rip the country permanently apart. Eighteen sixty-three was the year of Chancellorsville and Chickamauga, of Vicksburg and Chattanooga, the year Robert E. Lee marched seventy-five thousand rebel troops clear into Pennsylvania, into the great heartland of the north, where they fought the Union to a grisly fifty-one-thousand-casualty draw at Gettysburg.

The Civil War had very little to do with the western frontier itself. All of its main engagements took place east of the Mississippi River and such action as there was in Texas, Kansas, New Mexico, and the Indian Territory did not involve the free horse tribes. Still, the war managed to tear that frontier apart. It did so not with armies of men and rolling caissons but with simple neglect. Preoccupied with the war, and in any case lacking the money to fight Indians, Union and Confederate governments alike had no choice but to leave the west to its own devices. That meant that, quite suddenly, most of the people who had defended the borderlands in the 1840s and 1850s, from the Rangers to the Second Cavalry to various state militias, were simply gone. The men who won victories with Ford at Antelope Hills, or Van Dorn at Wichita Village, or Ross at Pease River all departed for eastern battlefields. And with them went the knowledge and will to pursue Comanches into their homelands.

In their place rose the state and territorial militias, a sorry lot of inferior soldiers commanded by substandard officers who were ducking the larger war. They were underequipped as well. They provided their own, often atrocious, weapons. Their lead was in short supply and some of their powder was so poor that it "would not kill a man ten steps from the muzzle."[1] They suffered from bad food, alcoholism, epidemics of measles and intestinal ills, and in any event were neither brave enough nor smart enough to win fights with Comanches or Cheyennes or Kiowas. (One regiment, embarking on an Indian pursuit, decided instead to head to another fort and play poker.)

They were preoccupied with other concerns anyway, which included their own miniaturized version of the war. In 1861 the Texas militia moved into Indian Territory, occupied federal forts, and drove the Union troops north into the brand-new state of Kansas. There would be periodic small-scale fighting over the territory for the duration of the war, culminating in the Battle of Honey Springs in 1863, in which three thousand Union troops from Kansas defeated six thousand Texans and Indians. But these events took place well east of the frontier, which remained ignored and undefended.

And this sudden neglect changed everything. Though the bizarrely passive federal policies of the 1850s had opened the way for hundreds of Indian attacks, the decade had in fact closed with a flash of willpower and resolve. Rip Ford's 1858 expedition was a watershed event with few precedents (including what the only Spanish governor to rein in Comanche terror, the brilliant Don Juan Bautista de Anza, had done in his pursuit of Cuerno Verde onto the plains of eastern Colorado in 1779). And while Sul Ross's victory at Pease River in 1860 may not have been quite as glorious as most histories suggest, as a measure of the *taibos'* will to defend themselves it, too, was a conspicuous advance. Indeed, it would have seemed in the late 1850s, as it had seemed in the late 1830s and the late 1840s, that Comanche power was fast on the wane, that the end of their ability to raid unchallenged would soon come to an end, that their days off the reservation were sharply numbered. And yet all that was an illusion. Comanche history must be understood that way, in terms of pulses and counterpulses of power. The pulse of state and federal power in the late 1850s was awesome. Comanches were running for shelter in the fastness of the Llano Estacado. They would soon have been broken. There were not enough of them left for it to be otherwise.

Then the Civil War came, the Texans went off to fight it, and they left their bones in shallow graves all over the South, and the lesson was forgotten again. What is remarkable, in retrospect, is how long it took the Comanches to figure out that border defenses had lapsed, how long it took them to grasp this massive shift in the balance of power. This was partly because both the Union and Confederacy, equally enfeebled in their western zones, were quick to pursue generous new treaties with them. The resulting agreements were versions of the same tired, disingenuous, and ultimately useless promises. But they did delay the inevitable reckoning. The Confederates promised the People gifts and supplies. In exchange the Indians cheerfully agreed to settle on their reservation, learn how to farm, and stop attacking both white and red people, promises they had no intention of keeping. The treaty was signed by the Comanches who lived on the reservation, mainly Penatekas, as well as the chiefs of the wild Comanche bands, including the Nokoni, Yamparika, Kotsoteka, and a remnant of the Tennawish. The Quahadis, magnificently aloof as always, refused to sign anything. The federal government made its own treaty, too, one that simply restated the treaty of 1853, promising the same old annuities and provisions, asking for the same sort of absurd concessions.

The first of the horrors to be unleashed by the demon of neglect had little to do with the white man. These were the Indian-on-Indian wars in the Indian Territory, the land north of the Red River and south of Kansas that would eventually become the state of Oklahoma. Most of the conquered and displaced tribes from the East, South, and Midwest had been relocated there—a process that had begun in the early nineteenth century. In 1830, Congress passed the Indian Removal Act, which forced most tribes to give up all of their lands in the East and Midwest for a supposedly eternal plot of ground in the Indian Territory. By the 1860s the territory had become an intricate patchwork of aboriginal cultures, each with its own designated reserve. The larger reserves had been given to the Five Civilized Tribes (Creek, Choctaw, Cherokee, Chickasaw, and Seminole), as well as to the combined Comanche, Kiowa, and Apache tribes, the Cheyennes and Arapahos, and to the Wichitas and their affiliated tribes (Caddos, Anadarkos, Tonkawas, Tawakonis, Keechis, and Delawares). There were smaller areas for Kickapoos, Sac and Fox, Osages, Pawnees, Pottawotamies and Shawnees, Iowas, Peorias, Quapaws, Modocs, Ottawas, Wyandottes, Senecas, Poncas, and Otos and Missouris. It was, all in all, an astonishing collision of native interests and antagonisms, all jammed together by fiat of Congress on the rolling plains and timberlands north of the Red River.

For many of these tribes, the Civil War was as much of a disaster as it became, eventually, for white farmers in eastern Georgia. The trouble began in 1861, soon after the first shots of the war were fired, when the United States withdrew its troops from Indian Territory.[2] Though there were a few ragtag confederates scattered through the territory, the agrarian tribes were mostly unprotected from the wild horse tribes, who had always hated them for encroaching on their hunting grounds and for what they saw as their fawning accommodation of the white man. With no one to offer the farming tribes even nominal protection, the Comanches unleashed a terrible violence. (These were mostly the wild bands, but Penatekas from the reservation sometimes rode with them.) The Chickasaws were the principal target, though other tribes also fell victim. Comanches raided their farms and settlements just as they raided on the Texas frontier. They rode down upon their foot-bound, house-dwelling, field-tilling victims. Many Chickasaws were driven out of the Indian Territory altogether and into Kansas. Choctaws and Creeks came under Comanche attack, too, as did the Indians of the Wichita Reservation, some of whom had copied the settled, agrarian ways of the civilized tribes with great success. Comanches made short work of their farms, stock, and crops. Whole settlements were butchered, captives taken. It should be noted that the "civilized" Indians were not always easy prey: They were often capable fighters and sometimes got the better of their tormentors.[3]

But Comanche raids were just part of the tragedy. There were also partisan wars between the entrenched tribes. There were "Confederate" Indians and "Union" Indians. Many members of the Five Civilized Tribes were slaveholders, which both angered Union Indians and caused deep rifts within their own ranks. The result was a series of massacres and retaliations, most of which are lost to history. What is known about them suggests that they were brutal and widespread. Cherokee, Creek, and Seminole territories became the scenes of battles between loyalists on both sides. Houses and farms were burned, seedstock and farming tools destroyed or stolen. Large segments of those tribes ended the war hungry and destitute, dependent once again upon the government for their livelihood.[4] In 1862, one hundred Tonkawas were killed in a single attack, part of a wave of such incidents that nearly resulted in their extermination.[5] This was ostensibly because of their cannibalism, which the other tribes deplored, but it was more likely because they had long served the Texans as scouts in their anti-Indian expeditions.[6] The Civil War offered many such opportunities for settling scores.

As in the larger war, there were massive displacements of human beings. In late 1861 a large body of "loyal" Creeks and other tribes under the command of Creek chief Opothle Yahola were attacked repeatedly in the last week of December by a combination of Confederate tribes and Texas cavalry. The terrified Union Indians dropped everything and fled northward. Large numbers of them froze in the bitter cold, and many of their bodies were eaten by wolves. Babies were born naked on the snow and soon died of exposure.[7] According to one report, 700 Creeks and others were either killed in the attacks or froze to death.[8] Once in Kansas, they gathered in a refugee camp where things were scarcely better. Families slept on the frozen ground with only scraps of cloth—handkerchiefs, aprons, and such—stretched on saplings as protection against the plains blizzards. The initial composition of that camp reveals much about what the Civil War did to the Indian territory. It contained 3,168 Creeks, 53 Creek slaves, 38 "free Creek negroes," 777 Seminoles, 136 Quapaws, 50 Cherokees, 31 Chickasaws, and a few Kickapoos. By April the camp held 7,600 refugees that included Kichais, Hainais, Biloxis, and Caddos, all of them utterly dispossessed of everything they once owned.[9]

As the war raged in the east, the white frontier exploded into its own nightmare of killing. The outbreaks had their origins in the north in 1862, with an Indian revolt on the prairie plains of Minnesota. That year the Santee Sioux (the eastern Sioux, also known as Dakota) rose up in rebellion from their reservation along the Minnesota River. They killed as many as eight hundred white settlers, the highest civilian wartime toll in U.S. history prior to 9/11. They made another forty thousand into refugees, who fled eastward in full mortal panic. The violence was extreme, almost mindless, spurred in part by the failure of the federal government to deliver annuities and supplies, and in part by the absence of government troops. Unlike the Texans, most of whom came from pioneer stock and understood the atrocities of Indian and especially Comanche warfare, these Minnesotans were simple yeoman farmers. Most were from Europe. Their reaction was hysterical fear, which only became worse when they experienced what the northern settlers had not yet encountered: the calculated rape and torture of female captives.

When bluecoat volunteers finally crushed the Santee rebellion, angry mobs screamed at the captives in their cages, castrated the few they got hold of, and demanded that the rebels be executed. If President Lincoln had not stepped in, hundreds would have died that way. As it was, thirty-eight were hanged, the largest one-day execution in American history. The following year the tribe was expelled from Minnesota, their reservations abolished.[10] At long last, the Sioux, the great power of the north, were finally colliding with the advancing line of settlements, something that had been happening in Texas since the 1820s.

By late 1863 it had become clear to most of the free-ranging horse tribes on the southern plains that there were no soldiers to stop them. By the summer of 1864 they were riding roughshod into the settlements from Colorado to south Texas, attacking pioneers and soldiers alike recklessly and with little fear of retribution. Huge stretches of land that had been settled as far back as the 1850s became completely depopulated. Comanche attacks virtually shut down the Santa Fe Trail. The overland mail abandoned its stations for four hundred miles. Emigration stopped. Cheyenne raids cut off supplies to the Colorado mining camps, where people were starving. The price of a bag of flour in the isolated town of Denver reached $45. The frontier again rolled backward, in some places between one hundred and two hundred miles, canceling two decades of westward progress.[11] For a brief and terrifying moment the raids appeared to have stalled the very idea that undergirded America's westward boom. Manifest Destiny only worked, after all, if you could conquer and subdue the nation's midsection.

One of the best examples of this new untrammeled violence was the Elm Creek Raid. In October 1864, a force of seven hundred Comanche and Kiowa warriors and three hundred assorted other women, children, and old men under the Comanche chief Little Buffalo rode out from their camp at Red Bluff on the Canadian River.[12] The expedition—the largest mounted to date by these two tribes—crossed the Red River ten miles above Fort Belknap, then attacked a settlement consisting of sixty houses in the creek bottoms just south of the Red. There was nothing to stop them, no fear of Rangers or federal forces, no commanders like Hays or Ford to pursue them. Unlike the Santee Sioux, they were still nomads and thus could hide anywhere on the Great

Plains. They burned and killed, stole cattle and horses, and forced a group of terrified settlers to retreat into a small stockade called Fort Murrah.

At this point the cavalry arrived, though it did not save the day. Quite the contrary. Riding briskly out of Fort Belknap, fourteen state militiamen ran headlong into a swirling body of three hundred mounted warriors. Five of these soldiers died instantly, and several others were wounded. The rest fled for their lives, some riding double on their horses, most of which had been "pincushioned" with arrows and were bleeding profusely. They took shelter at Fort Murrah, and there they cowered with the others, refusing to ride for help. In their place went several less intimidated settlers, who barely made it with their lives. By the time help arrived, the Indians had lost interest and departed. The tally: eleven settlers and five soldiers killed, seven women and children carried off. The perpetrators were not pursued. This sort of raid was duplicated all along the frontier that year. Like many others against the militias, it was not a fair fight.

Such violence called for retribution. In late 1864, Brigadier General James H. Carleton, the ranking U.S. Army officer in the territory of New Mexico, decided to do something about the problem. Carleton was a buttoned-down New Englander, a prig, and a stubborn know-it-all with a large ego and a startling range of talents that included mountain climbing, seed collecting, waltzing, archaeology, military history, boat design, and the study of meteorites.[13] He was deeply offended by the impunity with which the Comanches were attacking his territory. Early that year he and the legendary scout Colonel Christopher "Kit" Carson had conducted a massive campaign against the Navajos in New Mexico, finally cornering them in the Canyon de Chelly, destroying their crops and seizing their stock, and forcing eight thousand of them on to a reservation.[14]

Unfortunately for Carleton, that reservation happened to be located on the margins of Comancheria. It was not long before the western Comanche bands figured out how exquisitely vulnerable their old enemies were in their new location. The Nermernuh swooped down in early-morning raids, attacking Navajo villages, stealing sheep, horses, women, and children, and generally ruining Carleton's well-laid plans.[15] Carleton was further infuriated by the relentless Comanche attacks on army supply caravans on the Santa Fe Trail. These wagon trains contained both the food that would ensure the Navajos' survival and the communications that served as the general's only contact with his colleagues in the east. Carleton had been, in fact, isolated. From where he sat in his Santa Fe office, everything to the east of him seemed chaos and destruction.

In November 1864 he dispatched Colonel Carson on a punitive expedition into the most remote and historically inviolable part of the Comanche heartland, the thirty-five-hundred-foot-high country in the Texas Panhandle, distinguished by its flat, oceanic expanses of grass that were broken by jagged rock canyons, cut by ancient rivers, inhabited by the fiercest and most remote Comanche bands, and pierced only by the Comanchero traders out of New Mexico. Only a few white men had ever been there before, mostly traders. And no Texan, Ranger or otherwise, had ever had the courage to track Comanches onto the Llano Estacado. That had long been considered certain death: Either the trackless, waterless plains would get you, or the Comanches would. It was quite a brave thing for mounted soldiers to cross the Red River, to ascend the austerely beautiful Wichita Mountains in pursuit of the raiders; launching oneself onto the wide-open high plains to the west was more like suicide. Oddly enough, the Comanches, who had heard about Carleton's plan through Comanchero traders, had tried to arrange a truce. A group of ten Comanches and Kiowas led by the Yamparika chief Ten Bears (Paruasemena) had traveled to Fort Bascom in eastern New Mexico for that purpose.[16] But Carleton had ordered the fort's commander to tell them, in no uncertain terms, that "they need not come in with any more white flags until they are willing to give up the stock they have stolen this year from our people, and also the men among them who have killed our people without provocation or cause."[17] The campaign would move forward. Perilous though it was, if there was one man in the country who could actually lead such an expedition, that man was Kit Carson.

Carson was one of the most storied figures in the American West, celebrated in dime "blood and thunder" novels even while he was alive. He was a trapper, hunter, and wilderness scout and one of the first white men to explore the wild lands beyond the 100th meridian. He served as guide for John C. Frémont's famous expeditions into the transmountain west between 1842 and 1846, and became a national hero through Fremont's published reports. Diminutive, taciturn, barely literate, and unimpressive personally, he was nonetheless a dominant figure on the western frontier. He had married several Indian wives, was fluent in a number of Indian languages, and had served as Indian agent in New Mexico. He was also a successful Indian fighter, having led effective campaigns against the Navajo and the Mescalero

Apaches. He had done battle with Comanches in small engagements over the years. He knew what he was doing.

On November 12, 1864, four days after Abraham Lincoln was reelected president and the day after William Tecumseh Sherman burned Atlanta, Carson rode out of his camp on the plains of eastern New Mexico with 14 officers, 321 enlisted men, and a screen of 72 Apache and Ute scouts. The latter were bitter traditional enemies of the Comanches, and they were not frightened, as most white men were, by the appalling emptiness of the buffalo plains. Carson, moreover, did not have to pay them; he simply promised them all the plunder and Comanche scalps they could carry away. Like other white commanders of Indian scouts, he would simply have to live with, and try to rein in, their worst tendencies, which involved torture and rape and wanton killing of noncombatants and other deeds the whites found distasteful. In principle, anyway. The Utes and Apaches also drove the white soldiers to distraction with their war dances—howlingly loud, raucous affairs that often lasted nearly until dawn.

The expedition left in the late fall. That was when the Indians, who tended to rove in fragmented and widely dispersed groups during the spring and summer, headed for their winter camps, where they concentrated in villages whose sun-bleached buffalo-hide tipis snaked for miles along a few favorite streams. Carleton believed that the Comanches and Kiowas were camped on the Canadian River, in the northern part of the Texas Panhandle. That was Confederate territory, of course, though nothing could have been less likely than an encounter with Rebel militias on the high and wild plains. Carson's troops moved eastward through the thin, frosty air, riding through the horizon-spanning, horse-high grass, behind their screens of Indian scouts.[18]

By now it had become so common to find Kiowas and Comanches camping, hunting, and raiding together that their relationship as fellow-travelers deserves a note of explanation. Though it is hard to say exactly why the two tribes had such a deep affinity for each other, they did share common traits. Like the Comanches, the Kiowas had migrated in the seventeenth century from the mountains north down to the buffalo-rich southern plains. Both tribes had found extraordinary power in the horse. Both were exceptional horsemen, even on the plains, where all tribes were excellent riders, and both were exceptionally warlike, even by the brutal martial standards of the plains. They had fought each other for years, and had made a single definitive peace in 1790. There were differences, too. Instead of the Nermernuh's practical, minimalist culture, the Kiowas had elaborate and hierarchical military societies, a rich tradition of art that produced sophisticated pictographs and elaborate chronological calendars, and a far more complex religious mythology that featured a Sun Dance. What they were not was numerous, and that made perhaps the biggest difference. They never exercised the raw power of numbers that the Comanche tribe did. The Kiowas and their subband the Kiowa—or Plains—Apaches (a very small, Athapaskan-speaking tribe) never numbered more than eighteen hundred—a small fraction of Comanche strength at its apogee.[19]

After a twelve-day ride, Carson's scouts finally spotted Comanche and Kiowa lodges just south of the present town of Borger, Texas. That night the men rode silently and in darkness down into the Canadian River valley, under strict orders not to talk or smoke. They dismounted and stood shivering in heavy frost and holding their horses by their bridle reins until the first gray streaks of dawn appeared in the eastern skies.[20] They moved forward at daylight, fronted by their Indian scouts, and dragging with them two Mountain Howitzers, which they had considerable trouble lugging through the tall brown grass and the driftwood along the banks of the Canadian.

These were not incidental pieces of equipment. The howitzers looked like foreshortened, downsized cannon. They were short-barreled, large-caliber guns with large spoked wheels that fired twelve-pound payloads. Their advantage was that they were extremely mobile. They also packed a nasty wallop, especially when used against crowds of people. They fired two main types of ammo: spherical case shot and canister. Spherical case shot consisted of a single round iron shell filled with 82 musket balls packed in sulfur with a small bursting charge of gunpowder. Canister turned the howitzer into the equivalent of a giant sawed-off shotgun, spewing 148 .69-caliber lead musket balls with every shot. The weapons had seen limited use against Indians, notably in the 1862 campaign against the Santee Sioux in Minnesota. No one among Carson's troops knew, as they cursed and dragged the homely little cannon through the tall grass, that the guns would mean the difference between life and death, victory and defeat for the expedition.[21]

At around eight-thirty in the morning on a brilliantly clear and cloudless day, Carson's advance swept into a Kiowa village of 176 lodges. They surprised the Indians, who fought desperately to cover the retreat of their women and children, then fled downriver themselves. There were only a few casualties in this skirmish, among them four blind and crippled old Kiowas who had had their heads cloven with axes wielded by Ute women, who had been brought along, it seems, to help their mates commit what whites might have considered war atrocities. Meanwhile Carson's main force pressed onward toward the much larger Comanche camp, which was located four miles ahead, finally stopping at the ruins of a trading post known throughout the frontier as Adobe Walls. And it was here, around ten a.m., that they engaged some sixteen hundred Comanches and Kiowas. The battle did not last long. The howitzers, which had been dragged to the top of a symmetrical, cone-shaped thirty-foot-high hill nearby, were loaded and fired. Almost instantly, the Comanches and Kiowas who had been charging furiously along the battle line stopped, stood high on their stirrups, and watched as the case shot exploded and then exploded again. No weapon like this had ever been seen on the high plains. The Indians soon had a name for it: "the gun that shot twice." In the account of Captain George Pettis, who was with Carson at Adobe Walls, the hostiles "gazed, for a single moment with astonishment, then, guiding their horses' heads away from us, and giving one concerted, prolonged yell, they started in a dead run for their village. . . . When the fourth shot was fired there was not a single enemy within the extreme range of the howitzers."[22]

Instead of pursuing the fleeing Indians, however, the white men now decided to take a break. Carson's orders might seem perplexing, but his men had been fighting or marching for thirty hours. They relaxed and ate whatever hardtack or raw bacon or salt pork they had stuffed away in their haversacks, drank from what Pettis described as "as fine a running brook of clear cold water as I ever saw on the frontiers," and told stories of the day's heroics. Their horses grazed peacefully in the lush uncropped grasses. Carson's plan was that, after their rest, the men would mount up and move against the Comanche villages and destroy them. This seemed reasonable enough. But as would soon be apparent, it was actually a setup for the sort of slaughter that would take place twelve years later at the Little Bighorn.

Less than half an hour had elapsed when the Indians began again to mass on the open ground in front of the old adobe ruins, and again the soldiers heard the "sharp, quick whiz of the Indians' rifle balls." They also heard something very strange: a bugle blaring periodically from the enemy's ranks, blowing the opposite of whatever the army bugler blew. If the federal bugles sounded "advance," he would blow "retreat." And so on. The Indian bugler was every bit as good as the white buglers, and each time he blew the soldiers would erupt into laughter, in spite of themselves.

The battle resumed at full intensity, and it soon became clear that the Comanches and Kiowas had figured out at least some of the deadly antipersonnel characteristics of the howitzers. The chiefs spread their warriors out. "Their policy was to act singly," wrote Pettis, "and avoid getting into masses." The tactic worked, and the howitzers were only fired a few times. On one of those occasions,

> the shell passed directly through the body of a horse on which was a Comanche riding at a full run, and went some two or three hundred yards further on before it exploded. The horse, on being struck, went head-foremost to earth, throwing his rider, as it seemed, twenty feet into the air with his hands and feet sprawling in all directions.[23]

The Indians meanwhile had mounted a furious attack. Numbers of them had dismounted and were laying down a withering fire from the high grass, while riders swooped along the front, firing their rifles from beneath their horses' necks. Something else was happening, too, as the battle raged into midafternoon, that Carson and his officers could not help noticing. This was the arrival of more and more warriors from the large Comanche village that lay visible downstream on the Canadian River. They came up steadily, in groups of fifty or more. At some point, probably around three o'clock, Pettis estimated that Colonel Carson's modest Second Cavalry was facing an Indian cohort of three thousand, under the command of legendary Ten Bears, the principal Yamparika band chief of the 1860s and a man who had actually been to Washington in 1863 and received a peace medal.[24] (Kiowa chief Tohausan also figured prominently in the battle.) Though Pettis's estimate of enemy force is undoubtedly high—that number would have accounted for most of the Comanche and Kiowa warriors in existence in 1864—the soldiers now began to fear for their own safety. Their supply train, for one thing, was guarded by a mere seventy-five men, and Carson could see large numbers of Indians begin to stream toward his rear.

It was to Carson's credit that at three-thirty p.m., having engaged the Indians for the better part of five hours, he gave the order to fall back. Though his decision was vigorously opposed by most of his officers, who believed their troops should move forward and take the village before them, the Ute and Apache leaders advocated retreat. Carson listened to the Indians. He sent skirmishers out in his front, rear, and on both flanks, and very carefully made his return march, while the Indians continued to attack him on all sides. His idea was to return to the smaller Kiowa village, burn it, then move out. His force reached that village just before sundown. It was full of Indians. Carson was now surrounded by the full Indian force, which meant ten-to-one odds. He ought not to have survived, any more than Custer survived his own deadly, and not entirely dissimilar, blunder years later. That he did is entirely due to the lethal little howitzers. Carson ordered them dragged to the top of a small sand hill near the Kiowa village. And now they boomed forth case and canister, driving the Indians back out of the village and allowing the whites in. They plundered it—the lodges were full of coveted buffalo robes—and then burned it down, while the deadly case shot sung through the twilight air. One round hit squarely amid some thirty to forty Indian riders. Darkness fell and the retreat continued. The Indians followed Carson's men for a while, and scared them into riding almost continuously for four days. But they did not ever renew their attack. They had just fought one of the largest battles ever fought on the Great Plains.

The version of the Battle of Adobe Walls that went into the military records was noteworthy for its complete inaccuracy. The report stated that Carson and his force

> attacked a Kiowa village of about 150 lodges near the adobe fort on the Canadian River in Texas, and, after a severe fight, compelled the Indians to retreat, with a loss of 60 killed and wounded.[25] [Estimates were of 30 killed and 30 wounded.]

Carson had not beaten anyone. He had narrowly avoided the massacre of his own troops, as he himself conceded on more than one occasion. Without the howitzers, "few would have been left alive to tell the tale," he said later. His own losses were not inconsequential: seven dead (six whites and one Indian) and twenty-one wounded (seventeen whites and four Indians). He had retreated under cover of darkness. Captain Pettis later spoke with a Mexican trader who was at the Comanche camp at the time of the battle. Wrote Pettis:

> The Indians claimed that if the whites had not had with them the "guns that shoot twice," referring to the shells of the mountain howitzers, they would never have allowed a single white man to escape out of the valley of the Canadian, and I may say, without becoming immodest, that this was often the expressed opinion of Colonel Carson.[26]

Carson's was not the only punitive expedition launched in 1864. Four days later, and several hundred miles to the north, a former Methodist preacher turned territorial officer named J. M. Chivington presided over the bloodiest, most treacherous, and least justified slaughter of Indians in American history. It would pass into legend and infamy under the name of the Sand Creek Massacre. Cheyennes were the victims.

Chivington was a product of his times. A tall, imposing man with a barrel chest and a thick neck, he had spent much of his time setting up Sunday schools in the Colorado mining camps. In the personnel vacuum left by the onset of war in the east, he had risen to the position of brigadier general in the U.S. Army, commanding a large, unreliable, often drunk gang of second-rate soldiers who constituted the territorial volunteers in Colorado. The Cheyenne and Comanche attacks of the summer and fall had created a feeling of grim panic in the streets of Denver. Citizens were desperate, sometimes hysterical; everyone knew someone who had been attacked or killed. Whatever sympathy the horse tribes may once have inspired was gone. The idea now was to annihilate them, both in retribution for what they had done and to prevent future attacks. Chivington was their champion, and he believed God was on his side. "Damn any man who sympathizes with the Indians!" he said. "I have come to kill Indians, and I believe it is right and honorable to use any means under God's heaven to kill Indians."[27] To encourage recruitment into the volunteer units, he displayed the mutilated corpses of a white family of four next to the enlistment table. He spoke enthusiastically of "taking scalps" and "wading in gore."[28] His instructions to his men, which later became famous, were unambiguous: "Kill and scalp all, big and little. Nits make lice."

At eight o'clock in the evening of November 28, 1864, under a starry winter sky, Chivington and seven hundred territorial troops advanced from Fort Lyon in the Colorado territory, riding in columns of fours. The next morning they attacked the Cheyenne village of Chief Black Kettle—a village that had just made a truce with the white soldiers. But Chivington's purpose was only to kill Indians, and that is what he did. He began by pounding the lodges with the fragmenting shells from four mountain howitzers. And then his men streamed in, many drunk or hungover from the night's drinking, slashing and shooting indiscriminately. At the time of the attack, there were some six hundred Cheyennes in the camp. Of these, no more than thirty-five were warriors. Most of the men were out hunting buffalo. There is little point in describing in detail what happened. Children were shot, point-blank. Babies were bayoneted. Saddest of all was the sight of the Indians huddling around a large American flag that had been draped over Black Kettle's tipi. They gathered and flew white flags and the women opened their shirts so there could be no mistaking their sex, and waited patiently for the soldiers to see that the Indians were friendly and stop the killing. Instead, they were cut down. When the smoke had cleared and the screaming had stopped, three hundred Cheyennes lay dead. All were scalped, and many were mutilated. One man had cut out a woman's private parts and exhibited them on a stick.[29]

The massacre quickly became public, mainly because a number of Chivington's soldiers were disgusted by what had happened and later told their story to the press, but also because the victors had not been shy of bragging about what they had done, of which they were proud, initially at least. Chivington's return to Denver, in fact, was triumphant, the newspapers full of stories praising him. Chivington himself proclaimed that "Posterity will speak of me as the great Indian fighter. I have eclipsed Kit Carson." (Carson responded: "Jis to think of that dog Chivington and his dirty hounds up thar at Sand Creek. His men shot down squaws and blew the brains out of innocent children. You call sich soldiers Christians, do ye?")[30] At a theater in town the Colorado troopers had displayed their trophies for cheering crowds: tobacco pouches made from scrotums, fingers, scalps, purses made from pudenda cut from Cheyenne women.[31] As the details became known, a wave of revulsion swept through the corridors of power and influence in New York, Philadelphia, and Washington. The Sand Creek Massacre would have an enormous and lasting effect on the Indian policy that was made in those places. It is interesting to note, though, that such gut-churning shame and disgust was largely confined to the east. The protest over the killing of women was not echoed by any such sentiments in Indian country, where everyone knew that women were often combatants (they were not, in this case). Nor was there any outcry on the frontier over the use of the mountain howitzers against a sleeping village, as there was in the east.[32] What Chivington had done was what many people in the west, including the regular army, believed had to be done. The army's distaste for Chivington had more to do with style and with the savagery of his raw recruits. He had, after all, attacked a village under truce. Otherwise, it was clear from the reaction on the raw frontier that it was long past the time when it had become morally justifiable to kill Indian women and children.

Fifteen

━━◆═━━

PEACE, AND OTHER HORRORS

━━◆═━━

T HE END OF the Civil War in the spring of 1865 and the collapse of the Confederacy brought final and complete chaos to the frontier. Before there had been at least a pretense of organization. Now there was nothing. The militias disappeared from the federal lands. For a period of months there could be said to be no government at all in Texas, no systems, no authority, no power. It must have seemed to the People that the good old days had returned, that the Great Father's war had done something strange and permanent and magical to remove their old enemies from the borderlands. The Comanche numbers were still small—there were only, we must remind ourselves, maybe four thousand of them out there holding up the advance of western civilization—but a good deal of their old power had come back, and with it had come the old arrogance. Their social organization was still based on warrior status—there was, indeed, no other form of social advancement—their wealth still consisted of stolen horseflesh, and now once again they had the unfettered ability to make splendid war throughout the borderlands, both on whites and Indians.

The weird time warp persisted: As teenagers, Quanah and his peers were living, hunting, and raiding just as their fathers and grandfathers had done, as though hundreds of thousands of white people were not poised to rush headlong into Comanche lands at the first sign of weakness or opportunity. The tribe had a thriving new business, too, to add to selling stolen horses and captives: cattle thieving. These years had seen the beginning of the great cattle operations in Texas. In the west, the Quahadis had transformed themselves into a sort of bovine clearinghouse. They stole cattle from Texas—Charles Goodnight put the number rustled during the Civil War years at an astonishing 300,000 head—and traded them through Comancheros to government contractors in New Mexico, who sold them to the U.S. Army.[1] General Carleton, to be precise. In some cases, they were actually selling Carleton back his own cattle. In exchange, the Comanches received the guns and ammunition—increasingly revolvers and high-quality carbines—that had been deployed against Kit Carson at Adobe Walls. The business was so good that some wealthy Anglo-Americans got into it, furnishing capital to the Mexican traders.[2] Carleton knew all about this ingenious commercial two-step and it made him furious.

What had happened was that the state and territorial militias, the core of frontier defense for four years, had simply melted away. In the Confederacy they were forcibly disbanded. But they disappeared in Union areas as well. There were political and organizational reasons for this. During the war large numbers of volunteers had been raised under the government's emergency powers. These were the troops under the command of Carson and Chivington. With the end of the war few wanted to remain on permanent duty, and thus most of them were now released. The U.S. military, meanwhile, was undergoing a rapid downsizing that by 1866 would draw the total number of troops down to seventy-five thousand, and the eight thousand regulars that Ulysses S. Grant sent to Texas as an army of occupation were entirely concerned with affairs other than fighting Indians. When the governor of Texas later tried to fill this military void with state troops, the federal government refused to allow it. Demilitarizing the South was a priority of the reconstruction era, and Washington was not going to permit rebellious Texas to raise its own armies again. Nor was Congress, groaning under an enormous war debt, inclined to spend money on costly campaigns against a relatively small group of savages who posed no direct threat to the nation.

There was something else, too, that contributed to this lack of will to stop Indian raiding on the western frontier. This was the particular and very strong belief shared by many people in the civilized East that the Indian wars were principally the fault of white men. The governing idea was that the Comanches and other troublesome tribes would live in peace if only they were treated properly, and the farther its devotees were from the bleeding frontier, the more devoutly they believed it. This was the old fight between the army, who knew better, and the "rosewater dreamers" in the Indian office, who called their uniformed adversaries "butchers, sots determined to exterminate the noble redmen, and foment wars so they had employment."[3] As General John Pope later observed, the army found itself in a no-win position. "If successful, it is a massacre of Indians; if unsuccessful, it is worthlessness or imbecility, and these judgments confront the Army in every newspaper and in public speeches in Congress and elsewhere—judgments by men who are absolutely ignorant of the subject."[4] Reports of Chivington's massacre and white atrocities in Minnesota seemed to prove what the army's critics were saying.

The notion that the trouble with Plains Indians was entirely due to white men was spectacularly wrongheaded. The people who cherished it, many of whom were in the U.S. Congress, the Office of Indian Affairs, and other positions of power, had no historical understanding of the Comanche tribe, no idea that the tribe's very existence was based on war and had been for a long time. No one who knew anything about the century-long horror of Comanche attacks in northern Mexico or about their systematic demolition of the Apaches or the Utes or the Tonkawas could possibly have believed that the tribe was either peaceable or blameless. Except in the larger sense, of course. The Comanches had been first on that land, if that counted for anything, and the westering Anglo-Europeans were the clear aggressors. If the *taibos* agreed to stop the advance of their civilization precisely at the 98th meridian, and kept their western settlements bottled up beyond the Rockies, and refused to build transcontinental railroads or permit pioneers to cross the plains on the Santa Fe and Oregon trails, then a lasting peace might have been made with the Comanches. But these same Indian advocates would never have denied the fundamental right of white Americans to fully possess their continent.

Such beatific urges toward peace, combined with relentless and brutal raiding by Comanches in Texas and the Indian Territory led to the last and most comprehensive treaty ever signed by the Indians of the southern plains. The conference that spawned it took place in October 1867 at a campground where the Kiowas held medicine dances, about seventy-five miles southwest of the present site of Wichita, Kansas. The place was known as Medicine Lodge Creek. The participants were members of a U.S. peace commission and representatives of the Comanche, Cheyenne, Arapaho, Kiowa, and Kiowa Apache tribes. The conference was the last great gathering of free Indians in the American West. The event was magnificent, surreal, doomed, absurd, and bizarre, and surely one of the greatest displays of pure western pageantry ever seen. Nine newspapers sent correspondents to cover it.[5]

The council began, as many treaty meetings did, with each side making a great effort to impress the other. The U.S. peace commission, which included the commissioner of Indian affairs and William Tecumseh Sherman, the head of the army in the West, arrived with an entourage so large that it required a wagon train and fifteen or twenty ambulances to transport them. They were accompanied by a splendidly mounted guard of five hundred soldiers in dress uniform, dragging their lethal, snub-nosed mountain howitzers behind them. The white men had brought with them a large quantity of gifts, too, and set up huge mobile kitchens to feed everyone. Soon after they arrived they sent a rush order for additional supplies of fifteen thousand pounds of sugar, six thousand pounds of coffee, ten thousand pounds of hard bread, and three thousand pounds of tobacco.[6] There were an estimated four thousand Indians in attendance, which included one hundred Comanche lodges.[7]

Once the soldiers had drawn up before the Indian camp, something extraordinary happened. It was described by Alfred A. Taylor, later the governor of Tennessee, who covered the council as a reporter, as follows:

> By this time, thousands of mounted warriors could be seen concentrating and forming themselves into a wedge-shaped mass, the edge of the wedge pointing toward us. In this sort of mass formation, with all their war paraphernalia, their horses striped with war paint, the riders bedecked with war bonnets and their faces painted red, came charging in full speed toward our columns. . . .
> When within a mile of the head of our procession, the wedge, without hitch or break, quickly threw itself into the shape of a huge ring or wheel without hub or spokes, whose rim consisted of five distinct lines of these wild, untutored, yet inimitable horsemen. This ring, winding around and around with the regularity and precision of fresh-oiled machinery, approached nearer and nearer to us with every revolution. Reaching within a hundred yards of us at breakneck speed, the giant wheel or ring ceased to turn and suddenly came to a standstill.[8]

This maneuver was enormously impressive to the white people, not least because it amounted to a test of faith. The giant, spinning wheels-within-wheels formation was a trademark of plains warfare, and the sight of it whirling ever closer would have been eerily familiar to the soldiers who sat their horses in that long parade line. There was also a hint of sadness in all of this martial pomp and circumstance, and many who were there sensed it. The very purpose of the council was to end once and for all this sort of behavior, or to render it meaningless and ceremonial. Such an exhibition, indeed, would be witnessed only a few more times before it passed forever into myth and history and phonied-up traveling shows like Buffalo Bill's.

The council opened with a ritual smoking of the peace pipe, and then the commissioners began the proceedings with a good old-fashioned scolding of the assembled horse tribes. The Indians were reminded that, in shameful violation of their treaties, they had been making war on whites. Said Senator John B. Henderson, chairman of the committee on Indian affairs, this "made the hearts of our people very sad." He did note that "we are greatly rejoiced to see our red brethren so well disposed toward peace." What the Great Father wanted, he patiently explained, as though to children, was to give the Indians their own lands away from the white settlements. They would be given tools and seeds. They would be taught how to farm. A carpenter would show them how to build houses. Schools would be built for them to teach them to read. And while they learned these things, the Great Father would also provide $25,000 worth of clothing and other necessary items every year for thirty years. In exchange, the Indians had to cease all hostilities, reside on the lands provided, and promise not to interfere with white roads, rails, forts, or other development.[9]

The Indians were invited to tell their side of the story, which they were eager to do. The first speaker, Kiowa chief Satanta, set the tone for what was to follow. He began by rubbing sand over his hands. He shook hands with the participants in the council circle,[10] then proceeded to tell them that he wanted nothing to do with the white man's notion of peace. He said:

> This building homes for us is all nonsense. We don't want you to build any for us. We would all die. Look at the Penatekas. Formerly they were powerful, but now they are weak and poor. I want all my land even from the Arkansas south to the Red River. My country is small enough already. If you build us houses, the land will be smaller. Why do you insist on this? What good can come of it?

Speaking next for the Comanches was Penateka chief Tosawa (Silver Brooch), who knew a great deal about what happened to horse Indians on the reservation. Speaking in what one observer described as a "calm, argumentative voice," he delivered a blunt condemnation of the plan:[11]

A long time ago the Penateka Comanches were the strongest band in the nation. The Great Father sent a big chief down to us and promised medicines, houses and many other things. A great, great many years have gone by, but those things have never come. My band is dwindling away fast. My young men are a scoff and a byword among the other nations. I shall wait til next spring to see if these things shall be given to us; if they are not, I and my young men will return to our wild brothers to live on the prairie.[12]

The most impressive address of all—indeed, it was a showstopper—came from Ten Bears, the aging Yamparika chief who had battled Kit Carson at Adobe Walls, who gave one of the most eloquent speeches ever made by an American Indian. In its extraordinary evocation of violence, beauty, suffering, and loss, Ten Bears's words astounded the white participants (for whom it was translated). Among his topics, he described his reactions to the 1864 fight, offering a perspective that would have amazed his adversaries, who tended to believe that Indians did not have the same sort of feelings as they did. Before he began his speech, he put on a pair of wire-rimmed spectacles, which made him look strangely bookish, though he was illiterate.[13] "My heart is filled with joy when I see you here," he began,

as the brooks fill with water when the snows melt in the spring; and I feel glad as the ponies do when the fresh grass starts in the beginning of the year. . . .

My people have never first drawn a bow or fired a gun against the whites. There has been trouble between us . . . my young men have danced the war dance. But it was not begun by us. It was you who sent out the first soldier. . . .

Two years ago I came upon this road, following the buffalo, that my wives and children might have their cheeks plump and their bodies warm. But the soldiers fired on us . . . so it was upon the Canadian. Nor have we been made to cry once alone. The blue-dressed soldiers and the Utes came out from the night . . . and for campfires they lit our lodges. Instead of hunting game they killed my braves, and the warriors of the tribe cut short their hair for the dead.

So it was in Texas. They made sorrow in our camps, and we went out like the buffalo bulls when the cows are attacked. When we found them we killed them, and their scalps hang in our lodges. The Comanches are not weak and blind, like the pups of a dog when seven sleeps old. They are strong and far-sighted, like grown horses. We took their road and we went on it. The white women cried and our women laughed.

But there are things which you have said to me which I do not like. They were not sweet like sugar, but bitter like gourds. You have said that you want to put us on a reservation, to build us houses and make us medicine lodges. I do not want them. I was born under the prairie, where the wind blew free and there was nothing to break the light of the sun. I was born where there were no enclosures and everything drew a free breath. I want to die there and not within walls. I know every stream and wood between the Rio Grande and the Arkansas. I have hunted and lived over that country. I live like my fathers before me and like them I lived happily.

When I was in Washington the Great Father told me that all the Comanche land was ours and that no one should hinder us in living upon it. So, why do you ask us to leave the rivers and the sun and the wind and live in houses? Do not ask us to give up the buffalo for the sheep. The young men have heard talk of this, and it has made them sad and angry. Do not speak of it more. I love to carry out the talk I get from the Great Father. When I get goods and presents I and my people feel glad, since it shows that he holds us in his eye.

If the Texans had kept out of my country, there might have been peace. But that which you now say we must live in, is too small. The Texans have taken away the places where the grass grew the thickest and the timber was best. Had we kept that, we might have done the things you ask. But it is too late. The whites have the country which we loved, and we wish only to wander on the prairie til we die.

It was even too late for that, as the Indians knew better than anyone. No free Indians were going to be allowed to wander anywhere. Ten Bears's soaring rhetoric was elegiac, at best. He did not really think the whites were going to offer him anything better than they already had. Though Medicine Lodge was ostensibly a bargaining session, in fact there was no bargaining at all. The whites were issuing a thinly disguised ultimatum. General Sherman, who had participated in the conference as a peace commissioner but actually advocated military operations against delinquent tribes, offered them no comfort or consolation. It was clear to him, though perhaps not yet to the vast herd of public-policy-makers in Washington, that the old solutions no longer applied. The Indians could not be driven away or removed to the West. That had been the old solution, the one employed with the Creeks, Seminoles, Delawares, Iroquois, and other eastern tribes. The Plains Indians resided in the heart of the last frontier, and their land was not simply wanted as a pass-through for trains and wagons heading west. Comancheria itself was coveted by white men. Sherman told the Indians they would have to give up their old ways and learn to become farmers. And there was nothing, they were told bluntly by the man who had overseen carnage on a scale that these Indians could not possibly comprehend, they could do about it. "You can no more stop this than you can stop the sun or the moon," he said. "You must submit and do the best you can."[14]

And so they did, signing what amounted to a gigantic abstraction that was based on notions of property, on cartography and westward migration, and on the larger idea of Manifest Destiny, none of which they would ever completely comprehend. The white man would drag his treaty back to the

Great Father where it would sit among the forests of granite and marble and somehow work its terrible invisible magic. The Indians were not in any way happy about what they were being asked to do. There was nothing good about it, nothing but destruction and degradation on their end, though to most of them it seemed far better to mollify the white man yet again with a treaty (especially one that came with gifts attached) than to refuse and thus unleash warmongers like Sherman. On October 21, 1867, chiefs from all of the tribes put their marks on the treaty, which of course they could not read.[15] They included headmen from the Yamparika (Ten Bears, Painted Lips, Hears a Wolf, Little Horn, Dog Fat, and Iron Mountain), the Nokonis (Horse Back, Gap in the Woods) and Penatekas (Silver Brooch, Standing Feather).[16] As much as a third of the tribe was not represented at the council. Mostly they were Kotsotekas and Quahadis, the two most remote bands who tended to camp together in the Llano Estacado. The Kotsotekas had signed a treaty in 1865, though they never had abided by it. The Quahadis had never signed anything, and never would. That did not matter to the U.S. peace commission: The entire tribe was presumed to have signed the agreement, and they would all be held to it. The band structure of the Comanches no longer mattered to anyone.

Among the unreconstructed elements of the Quahadis who were present at Medicine Lodge was eighteen-year-old Quanah. Why he should have been there is unknown. Quanah's own description sounds quite casual. He had been on the warpath against the Navajo, he said. While staying at a Cheyenne village, he was told that white soldiers were coming to a great powwow and bringing beeves, sugar, and coffee. "I went and heard it," Quanah said later. "There were many soldiers there. The council was an unusual one, a great many rows. The soldier chief said 'Here are two propositions. You can live on the Arkansas and fight or move down to the Wichita Mountains and I will help you. But you must remember one thing and hold fast to it and that is you must stop going on the warpath. Which one will you choose?' All the chiefs decided to move down here [to the reservation]."[17]

For anyone who believed that the Indians were sincere in signing the Medicine Lodge treaty, its implications would have seemed breathtaking. The treaty required nothing less than that the great and unrivaled powers of the middle and southern plains move immediately and en masse to reservations and take up modest new lives, accepting agencies, schools and farms, gov-

ernment teachers, blacksmiths, carpenters, and agricultural instructors, all
of which they had said specifically and repeatedly that they did not want.[18]
They were allowed to leave the reservation to hunt, south of the Arkansas.
But the treaty really meant that they would have to cease fighting and stop
following the buffalo, which in turn meant that they would have to cease
being Plains Indians. They would have to reorder their entire social structure
around a set of values and principles that were still largely unimaginable to
them. The Comanches and Kiowas were to share a 2.9-million-acre reservation in what is now southwestern Oklahoma, north and east of the Red
River and its north fork, south of the Washita, and west of the 98th meridian. This was actually very good land, huntable and arable and with decent
water sources, and it was in traditional Comanche territory and included
Medicine Bluffs and other sacred sites. But it was a tiny fraction of Comancheria, which at its peak held nearly *200 million acres*. Nor did it include by
far the richest of the old hunting grounds, the Texas bison plains. The Cheyennes and Arapahos, meanwhile—only their southern bands—agreed to live
on a reservation immediately to the north of the Comanche reservation.

Seen from the distance of a century and a half, the Medicine Lodge treaty
can seem like a cynical document. But it did not at the time appear that way
to lawmakers in the East, or to the members of the peace commission who
signed it. Their efforts had inspired great hope that this would offer a final
solution to the Indian problem on the southern plains. This belief was held
despite the Indians' stern protestations and the deep skepticism of the army in
the West. After all, the eastern Indians had made the transition to farming life.
The civilized tribes, after the horrendous attrition of the Trail of Tears, had
managed to change. So could the Plains Indians. To many people the treaty
seemed a fair and reasonable solution to an old and intractable problem.

They were mistaken. Instead, Medicine Lodge provided the framework
for the last great betrayal of the Indians by a government that had betrayed
and lied to Native American tribes more times than anyone could possibly
count. The agent of the betrayal was the Office of Indian Affairs, one of
the most corrupt, venal, and incompetent government agencies in American
history. The new era began with the bizarre decision by J. H. Leavenworth,
the appointed agent for the Comanches and Kiowas and a loud proponent
of peace, to locate his agency at Fort Cobb on the Washita River, which was
on the reservation of the Wichitas and affiliated bands, well north of the
Comanche-Kiowa lands. Leavenworth's ill-considered decision introduced

warlike, mounted Comanches into direct proximity with Indians who farmed and lived in houses. As the Civil War years had shown with cruel clarity, this was a very bad idea.

The error was compounded when several thousand Kiowas and Comanches actually showed up at the agency in the winter of 1867–68, precisely what Leavenworth and his bosses wanted. But for some reason they had failed to anticipate that these Indians would need food. Shockingly, Medicine Lodge had not provided for Indian rations, and so the government had nothing to give them. Nor did it have any of the promised annuity goods (and would not until Congress ratified the treaty in the summer of 1868). Leavenworth himself was not to blame, but collectively the white men had made an unforgivable blunder, which meant a crushing failure of the very first post-treaty test of friendship and sincerity.

The Indians were disgusted, and furious. They believed the white men had lied to them. They were also hungry, because it was winter and they had counted on the government food to help them get through the hard season. Leavenworth tried desperately to compensate, issuing all the goods in his possession, using his breeding cattle for food, and even buying goods with unauthorized credit. But those moves were not sufficient to feed the miserable and restive Comanches. So they began to solve their problem the old way: by raiding the Wichitas and other nearby tribes. They stole cattle, horses, and mules, and if anyone got in their way he was killed and scalped. At one point the raids got so bad that the sedentary tribes were forced to stop farming altogether so they could guard their horses, mules, and cattle.

The food crisis was made worse by yet another remarkably shortsighted decision: The Office of Indian Affairs, in its ardor for peace and in its fundamental belief that these Indians were always gentle unless provoked by white men, had prohibited the stationing of troops at the agency. This was yet another catastrophic mistake, which not only gave the Comanches a free hand to ravage the Indian country, but also gave them a secure base from which to conduct their ever more frequent raids into Texas.

Leavenworth, who had strongly supported the peace plan, was soon complaining bitterly. "I recommend that [the Kiowas'] annuities, as well as the Comanches, be stopped, and all confiscated for the benefit of the orphans they have made. The guilty are demanded—according to our treaties—for punishment. And if not delivered up, then let them be turned over to the military . . . to make short sharp work with them."[19] Thus disabused of his old idealism, Leavenworth now had to contend with a thousand surly, disappointed Comanches who were back to their old habits of raiding and stealing and committing atrocities. Unable to bear the strain, he simply walked off his job in the spring of 1868. From May to October, one of the most critical times in the history of relations between Plains Indians and the U.S. government, there was no federal authority at all in the Comanche-Kiowa reservation. Traders and other white men had fled in fear of their lives. The property custodian, the only white person who remained at the agency, could do nothing but keep track of the continuing raids into Texas and count the number of scalps the raiders brought back.[20] It was pure chaos, pure anarchy.

When the goods finally did arrive, they were of abysmal quality. And now the Indians confronted yet another aspect of the Indian office: its corruption. The clothing the Indians had been promised was shoddy and threadbare. The pants all came in one size: large enough to fit a two-hundred-pound man. Few Comanches weighed that much. The hats they received looked like those worn by the Pilgrims. Most of the Comanches ripped the clothes up and used them for other purposes. The food was bad, too. Instead of fresh meat—which had always been their diet—they got rancid bacon or salt pork. They were given a lot of cornmeal, which they detested and fed to their horses.

None of these failures could be blamed on the tangled government bureaucracy. They were the product of the endemic corruption and graft for which the Indian office had justly become infamous by the 1860s. The Indian peace commission of 1867 had been so scandalized by what they found out in the various agencies that they wrote:

> The records are abundant to show that agents have pocketed the funds appropriated by the government and driven the Indian to starvation. It cannot be doubted that Indian wars have originated from this cause. . . . For a long time these officers have been selected from partisan ranks, not so much on account of honesty and qualification as for devotion to party interests and their willingness to apply the money of the Indian to promote the selfish schemes of local politicians.[21]

As time went by, the agents proved stupid as well as corrupt. Ironically, one commodity they were actually proficient at delivering to Comanches and Kiowas was weapons. The Indians had made an eloquent plea for better rifles; without them they could not hunt effectively, they argued, and thus would be more dependent on the government. While this argument had some merit, it was also quite as obviously true that Comanches were attacking Texas homesteads and Wichita farms. Amazingly, the Indian office persuaded the Department of the Interior, in violation of laws against arming Indians, to deliver several tons of arms and ammunition to plains tribes, including Comanches. And these weapons were not shoddy at all. In a day when the standard army issue weapon was still the single-shot rife, the Indian weapons included repeating Spencer and Henry rifles and carbines.[22]

Meanwhile, the heart of the Medicine Lodge treaty—the plan to turn Comanches and other horse tribes from nomadic hunter-gatherers into house-dwelling farmers—was also proving almost completely futile. A few Penatekas, long in captivity, tried to go along with the idea. But in general Comanche men simply refused to have anything to do with farming. When Leavenworth hired a white farmer in the spring of 1868 to demonstrate the planting of seeds, Comanches swooped down and plundered the fields before the crop was ripe. They ate green watermelons, which made them violently ill. The Indians only wanted beef, and eventually forced the agent to spend most of the budget on it, leaving little or nothing available to buy seed and farming tools.

The result of such efforts was to convince most Comanches that they were better off outside the reservation. On June 30, 1869, it was estimated that there were 916 Comanches on the reservation, but none of them were self-supporting farmers. All were living in tipis and subsisting on a combination of their own hunting, the undependable government food and annuities, and raids on Texas and on other tribal reserves. Many drifted off the government land to join the hostile bands in the Llano Estacado. There developed a pattern. In winter, more Comanches would arrive to camp on the reservation and to claim beeves and other food and annuity goods. In the spring they would drift back to the buffalo plains again or join raiding parties headed for the Texas frontier. It was a confusing, highly fluid situation. The one certainty was that, in spite of considerable government effort, Comanches remained Comanches. They had not yet been broken of their old habits.

Such a situation could not endure. The first casualty was the hated Office of Indian Affairs itself. In 1869, Congress did away with it, and in its place put the Indian Bureau, which soon arrived at what seemed like an ingenious compromise. The individual Indian agencies would be run by nominees from the religious community, thus minimizing the possibility of corruption. And if the Indians were converted to Christianity, so much the better. This became known as Grant's "peace policy," and the religious sect selected to oversee the Comanches was an extremely unlikely one: the gentle, peace-loving Quakers

Sixteen

THE ANTI-CUSTER

RANALD SLIDELL MACKENZIE came from one of those prodigiously overachieving eastern seaboard families that seemed connected, in profound and unaccountable ways, to everyone who was anyone in the corridors of power. His grandfather John Slidell was a Manhattan bank president and political power broker in New York City. His uncle John Jr. became the most powerful man in Louisiana politics, a U.S. senator, and the top adviser to President James Buchanan. Mackenzie's aunt Jane married Commodore Matthew Perry, the man who opened Japan to the West. Aunt Julia married a rear admiral. Uncle Thomas became chief justice of Louisiana. His father, Alexander Mackenzie Slidell, who reversed his last and middle names at the request of a maternal uncle, was both a prominent naval commander and a well-known writer of histories and travel books who once had the distinction of being court-martialed for hanging the son of the secretary of war for mutiny. His mother came from splendid bloodlines, too: Her grandfather had been assistant secretary of the treasury under Alexander Hamilton.

Mackenzie thus grew up in elevated society, though his father's death when he was eight put the family in more or less permanent financial difficulty. He was a frail, shy, smallish, unhealthy boy with the pale skin and transparent eyes of his Scottish forebears and a speech impediment that some described as a lisp and others as a slight stutter. He attended Williams

College in Massachusetts, hoping to be a lawyer. But the family's straitened finances would not allow him to finish. After two years he arranged for a transfer to West Point, which paid a salary in addition to providing free education. He matriculated there in 1858.

Against all of his family's expectations, he performed brilliantly, graduating first in his class of twenty-eight cadets. He was considered by many in his class to be "the all-around ablest man in it."[1] He never grew much—as an adult he was a slim five feet nine inches tall (the limit for a cavalryman)—but he lost some of his shyness, made friends more easily, played pranks, and ran with a lively crowd. His talent in mathematics secured him a position as assistant professor while he was still a student. In the tiny, cloistered world of the military academy, he undoubtedly knew the immodest and trouble-prone young man, one class ahead of him, named George Custer, though there are no records of their relationship. The two officers could not have been more different. Custer was exuberant, vainglorious, and outrageous. Mackenzie was dark and complex, deeply private and inwardly turned, and never built for public adulation. Custer was a horrendous student, and the word *able* was not the first that came to mind when people described him. More like "libidinous and alcoholic."[2] When he graduated in 1861, he ranked thirty-fourth out of thirty-four students in his class, having accumulated a class-high of 726 demerits. In spite of these gaping differences, the two men were, oddly, twins of fate. Born less than a year apart, their careers mirrored each other's virtually every step of the way, from their money-strangled ambitions to study law to their West Point days to their heroism and precociousness in the Civil War, where they fought in the same campaigns, and ultimately to their Indian fights in the West. The parallel lines crossed only a few times, the last occurring after the disaster at Little Bighorn, when Mackenzie was sent north to, in effect, clean up Custer's mess.

Mackenzie's graduation in 1862 landed him in the middle of the Civil War, and over the next three years he climbed the ranks with breathtaking speed. He served in the engineer corps at the battles of Manassas (second), Fredericksburg, Chancellorsville, and Gettysburg, receiving brevet promotions that quickly boosted him to the rank of major. (A brevet rank was temporary, often given on the battlefield to increase the officer corps in times of emergency. The idea was to keep the army from becoming, in peacetime, top-heavy with officers.) Still, he was bored by engineering work and longed for command. He finally got it at the battle of Cold Harbor in June 1864, when he was brevetted to lieutenant colonel and given charge of the Second Connecticut Volunteer Artillery. He was twenty-three years old. He soon proved himself to be both dazzlingly competent and almost recklessly brave. At the Battle of Winchester, where Custer also fought, he "seemed to court destruction all day long," wrote one of his soldiers. "With his hat held aloft on the point of his saber, he galloped over the forty-acre field through a perfect hailstorm of rebel lead and iron with as much impunity as though he had been a ghost."[3] At one point a Confederate artillery shell cut the horse he was riding in half. Wounded in the thigh, he bound the gash and kept on fighting.

With just a few months left in the war, he was given his first major command: the cavalry division of the Army of the James. By Appomattox he held the brevet ranks of brigadier general of the regular army and major general of the volunteers, making him the highest-ranking officer in West Point's class of 1862. He was only twenty-four years old. He had been brevetted seven times in less than three years, a pace of promotion almost unheard of in the army and which beat Custer's five brevets, though Custer ended with the same rank.[4] Mackenzie was, moreover, one of Grant's favorites. "I regarded Mackenzie as the most promising young officer in the army," Grant later wrote in his memoirs. "Graduating at West Point, as he did, during the second year of the war, he had won his way up to command of a corps before its close. This he did upon his own merit and without influence."[5]

Something else happened to Mackenzie during the war. Like so many other young men, he hardened. He lost his easy affability, his prankishness, and much of his good humor. This was undoubtedly caused in part by the bloodshed and suffering he witnessed from 1862 to 1865. But it was more directly related to a series of gruesome, debilitating wounds he received and from which he would never fully recover. He was wounded on six different occasions. At Manassas, he was shot with a .50-plus-caliber bullet through both shoulders, a terrible internal wound that should have killed him. He lay where he fell for twenty-four hours before being rescued. He was hit in the leg with an artillery shell (at Winchester), and later wounded in the chest by shrapnel. Another artillery shell took off the first two fingers of his right hand. The pain never left him, and it changed him.

His first command felt the brunt of this change. When he inherited it, the Second Connecticut had been a beaten, neglected, and demoralized unit. After Cold Harbor, Mackenzie drilled them mercilessly and punished them liberally. The men hated him. He was so hard on them that some even plotted to shoot him in the next battle.[6] "By the time we reached the Shenandoah Valley," wrote one of his lieutenants, "he had so far developed as to be a greater terror to both officers and men than Early's grape and canister."[7] At Winchester the regiment fought gallantly; its losses were higher than any other regiment in the fight; the men also witnessed Mackenzie's astounding bravery. After that the talk of mutiny stopped. His men did not like him. Many feared him. But like all men in subsequent Mackenzie commands, they always believed they had a better chance with him in battle than with other commanders. He was not what West Pointers would describe as a martinet. He was neither vain nor arrogant nor capricious. He was just brutally demanding: the boss from hell.

After the war was over, Mackenzie remained in the army, reverting to his actual rank of captain (as did Custer), and building harbor defenses in Portsmouth, New Hampshire. In 1867 he was promoted to colonel and took command of the Forty-first Infantry, a black regiment that soon moved to Texas. He was stationed at various different forts there, and saw his first limited Indian engagements in 1869 and 1870. They were really nothing more than skirmishes. He spent a good deal of his time sitting on courts-martial in San Antonio. In 1871 he got his big break. He was given command of the Fourth Cavalry on the frontier, an event that was a direct consequence of President Grant's increasing impatience with the "peace policy." It was no accident that the man he considered his most aggressive and effective officer was being placed squarely in the path of Comanche war parties.

The record of federal officers on the frontier in those days showed just how lethal the West still was, even for mounted bluecoats. In 1864, Carson had nearly perished against Comanches and Kiowas at Adobe Walls. Van Dorn and Chivington had had their massacres, but the experience of the ebullient and egocentric Captain William Fetterman in 1866 more closely approximated the real risks of western command. Oozing self-confidence and itching to kill savages, Fetterman led eighty men out from Fort Phil Kearney in Wyoming on December 21, under orders to rescue a wagon train of woodcutters that was under attack by Red Cloud's Oglala Sioux. He was warned twice that he should do nothing more than escort the woodcutters back to the fort.

Instead of following those orders, Fetterman plunged ahead looking for Indians to shoot. He spotted a small and vulnerable-looking group of Sioux warriors and pursued them. He soon discovered that they had been put there as bait. He thus rode directly into ambush. Exactly how many Indians took part in the attack is not known. Enough to kill eighty troopers in less than twenty minutes. In his report to his superiors, post-commandant Henry Carrington listed some of the items he found on the battlefield the next day: eyes torn out and laid on rocks, noses and ears cut off, teeth chopped out, brains taken out and placed on rocks, hands and feet cut off, private parts severed. The Oglalas seemed especially annoyed at two men who carried brand-new sixteen-shot Henry repeating rifles. Presumably they had done a good deal of damage. Their faces had been reduced to bloody pulp, and one of the men had been pierced by more than a hundred arrows.[8]

Two years later another army unit was destroyed at the Battle of the Washita, which was in all other ways a massacre of Indians. In November 1868, Colonel George Custer, commanding the Seventh Cavalry for the first time, attacked a Cheyenne village on the Washita River in what is now western Oklahoma. His strategy was the same one that got him killed eight years later. He divided his force, then advanced over unknown terrain against an enemy of unknown strength, and executed a "double envelopment," a maneuver that required overwhelming superiority in numbers. This time he got lucky, at least at first. At dawn, his troopers tore into a small village of fifty-one lodges under Chief Black Kettle, surprising them and sending them fleeing from their tipis. Black Kettle had made the mistake of not believing his scouts, a mistake Custer also made and would soon pay for. Custer's men rampaged through the snowy camp, killing indiscriminately.[9] Women and children who had taken cover under buffalo robes were dragged out of the tipis by Osage scouts and shot. Though Custer reported that he had killed a hundred three warriors, he had actually killed only eleven. The rest were women, children, and old men. The soldiers then looted and burned the village.

Meanwhile a squad of men under Major Joel Elliot, last seen in hot pursuit of Indians, was now missing. It was later learned that they had fallen for the same immemorial trick that had fooled Fetterman. They had ridden after a bunch of Cheyenne boys. At some distance from the village, the boys evaporated and in their place appeared several hundred mounted, armed Indians. The white soldiers then dived for cover in the high grass, thus violating a fundamental principal of defensive combat: They abandoned a clear field of fire.[10] They were mostly shot where they lay. Their bodies were later found on the south bank of the river, frozen and horribly mutilated. It was believed that the Indians who killed them were Arapahos.

What were Arapahos doing near the Cheyenne camp? The answer revealed exactly how lucky Custer had been. Just below Black Kettle's camp, stretching for fifteen miles along the river, was *the entire winter encampment* of the southern Cheyenne and Arapaho tribes. Comanches and Kiowas were camped with them. This disconcerting fact was uncovered when a platoon that had gone downriver to round up horses suddenly found itself encircled by warriors from the lower camps. Beyond the Indians the white men could see hundreds of tipis in the river valley. Laying down a covering fire, they retreated, barely making it back to camp, where they breathlessly told Custer the news. He was alarmed. His men were tired; he was running out of ammunition; the command was alone in subzero weather in a hostile wilderness; and his main supply train had been left lightly guarded many miles away. Realizing now that he could not take the eight hundred captured Indian horses with him, he ordered them all shot. The men used pistols to do it and the scene was gruesome. After being shot the horses broke away and ran in all directions, bleeding onto the snow. Then he retreated. He was so worried about an Indian attack that he marched all night.[11]

One of the Comanches in those lower camps was twenty-year-old Quanah. "When we heard of the fight," he recalled later, "all of our men hurried to the scene but General Custer retreated when he saw so many of us coming. We did not get close enough to fight him. After several skirmishes without results, we returned to our camp and moved out onto the plains."[12] He never explained how he had come to be there, though the Washita was fully within the Comanche heartland.

Custer had only narrowly avoided Fetterman's fate. He had come perilously close to confronting what would have been perhaps the largest group of hostile Indians ever assembled in one place. Later, he would *actually* face the largest group of hostile Indians ever assembled in one place, and he would not be so lucky.

By the time Mackenzie arrived at Fort Concho (in present San Angelo), President Grant's peace policy had been in effect for two years. The idea had been to replace graft, corruption, and indifference in the Indian service with a stern but loving kindness. By putting Quakers in place of the old self-serving agents of the Indian office, Indian trust would be regained. Annuities would be paid on time. Promises would be kept. The Indians would honor the Great Father by coming into their reservations, laying down their weapons, and taking up peaceful new lives as farmers, as specified by the Medicine Lodge treaty. This was devoutly to be wished, especially since nothing like it had ever actually happened. When the Quaker agent Lawrie Tatum arrived at the Comanche and Kiowa agency in 1869, some two-thirds of all Comanches were not on the reservation. They accounted for most of the continuing attacks on settlements in Texas and Mexico.

Almost from the start, the plan was a disaster, less a coherent policy than an invitation to open war. Its most basic problem was that the peace policy rewarded aggression and punished good conduct. The Indians realized that their most violent wars always ended with some sort of treaty, which was always accompanied by many splendid gifts and tokens of friendship and trust. They were thus convinced that the easiest way to get money and goods was, in Tatum's words, "to go on the warpath awhile, kill a few white people, steal a good many horses and mules, and then make a treaty, and they would get a large amount of presents and a liberal supply of goods for that fall."[13] The treaties also typically allowed them to retain any horses and mules they had stolen. When they behaved well and limited their raiding, on the other hand, they got nothing. They were acutely aware of this. In addition, the *taibos* appeared to punish those who were cooperating. In 1868 and 1869 a number of Comanches did come in to the reservation, notably from the Yamparika and Nokoni bands. But because their west Texas brethren kept raiding, all annuities in 1869 were forfeited to pay depredation claims, thus penalizing the "good" Indians, which of course made no sense to any of them.

Worse still, by prohibiting the use of troops in the reservation areas, the government had created what amounted to a sanctuary for Comanche raiding parties. This was probably the most pernicious effect of the peace policy. It meant there was nothing preventing the Indians from coming and going as they pleased, or from using their two-million-acre reserve as a base camp for attacks on the Texas settlements. They could evade cavalry pursuit, and even keep their stolen stock, simply by crossing the Red River. The upshot was that Tatum himself, the pacifist Quaker, became convinced that force would have to be used to get the Comanches to stay on the reservation.

It was into this illogical and decidedly unpeaceful world of the far Comanche frontier that Mackenzie came in 1871. The border was still rolling backward, unmaking decades of progress. Counties west of Fort Worth and on down to Waco and the hill country continued to empty out. The peace policy was, perforce, about to change, and Ranald Slidell Mackenzie would be the instrument of that change. Following the Salt Creek Massacre (where General Sherman had narrowly escaped) and the trial of the Kiowa chiefs who had led it, Mackenzie wrote a letter to Sherman, advocating a large-scale campaign. "The Kiowas and Comanches are entirely beyond any control and have been for a long time. . . ." he wrote. "Mr. Tatum understands the matter. . . . He is anxious that the Kiowas and Comanches now out of control be brought under. This can only be accomplished by the Army. . . . It is not very important who we deal with first, the staked plains people, or those of the reserve."[14] Sherman agreed. Not only to a campaign but to new freedom for the army to pursue hostile Indians north of the border. Nothing had changed officially, but this was the beginning of the end of the peace policy.

And so in the fall of that year Mackenzie, not quite knowing what he was doing yet, and with an indifferent regiment he had not yet had time to remake, marched six hundred men and twenty-five Tonkawa scouts up into Blanco Canyon and made his humbling mistakes and then had sixty-six of his horses, including his own gray pacer, deftly removed from him by Quanah and his midnight raiders. That encounter is worth noting because such Indian behavior was probably without precedent on the plains. Indians habitually avoided soldiers; almost all their battles with army regulars were defensive, including those against Fetterman in Wyoming and Custer on the Washita. Large concentrations of soldiers with long supply trains were a signal to simply disappear, which was usually easy enough. It was the reason so many U.S. troops spent so much time marching and riding about, looking for and not finding Indians. Not finding Indians had been the principal activity of the U.S. cavalry for years in the West. Mackenzie's force was enormous by plains standards: It was the largest that had ever been sent to pursue Indians.

And yet it was directly into the camp of this large assemblage of firepower— the men all were equipped with Colt revolvers and repeating Spencer carbines and several hundred rounds each—that Quanah rode on the night of October 10. He and his men had not simply run off horses on a far perimeter. They had crashed directly into the sleeping area, nearly running over Mackenzie's tent, all the while screaming and shooting and ringing cowbells.[15] Was it the sheer reckless bravery of youth that had led him to do it? Was it desperation? An instinctive defensive response to the presence of so many bluecoats so far out on the buffalo plains, like a man blocking a punch? In later interviews, Quanah said that his plan had been to put the soldiers afoot.[16] If he had succeeded, the result might well have been a disaster of epic proportions for the whites.

They had avoided that disaster by moving quickly in the darkness, amid the panicked horses and the lethal swinging pickets, to recapture most of their mounts. But there were now sixty-six dismounted cavalrymen on the high remote plains of west Texas. And there was not much you could do with such men under those circumstances except order them to march east, back to the supply camp. Humiliated by the repeated blunders his command had made, the man they called Three-Finger Jack and his Fourth Cavalry sorted through the tangled mass of horses, lariats, and picket pins, and set out at dawn on the morning of October 11 to find the Comanches who had attacked them. Mackenzie had no idea then that he had stumbled into not just a Quahadi village, but *the main body of the Quahadi band,* several hundred lodges' worth. Though the principal chiefs of the Quahadis were thought to be Bull Bear and Wild Horse, the village was under the much younger Quanah's command. The remarkable tactics employed during this extended engagement were his and his alone.[17] Meanwhile Mackenzie, snapping the stumps of his fingers irritably—it had already become a defining personal habit—was also completely unaware that he was about to embark upon a rollicking forty-mile chase along a razor edge of the Llano Estacado, the likes of which no western troops had ever experienced.

The day began with yet another blunder by the white soldiers, this one far more serious. Just as the first light began to streak the eastern sky, two detachments of troops searching in the valley for the lost herd came upon a dozen Comanches leading as many horses. Thrilled with their good luck, the men under Captain E. M. Heyl spurred forward, gaining rapidly on the Indians, until they were just within pistol range. The Indians abandoned the animals and appeared to make a run for it, crossing a ravine and climbing onto the higher ground just beyond it, where a butte rose toward the top of the canyon walls. The soldiers, who also numbered a dozen and were now three miles from their camp, followed. As they ascended toward the butte, they could see in the clear light of morning that the Indians they were following had turned on them. And now a much larger force had emerged on the high ground. Heyl had been suckered by the same trick that had fooled Fetterman and Elliot. Suddenly the prairie was "fairly swarming with Indians, all mounted and galloping toward us with whoops and blood curdling yells that, for the moment, seemed to take the breath completely away from our bodies," wrote Carter. "It was like an electric shock. All seemed to realize the deadly peril of the situation."[18] Above them, from the battlements of the canyon walls, came the eerie high-pitched ululation of the Comanche women, looking down at their men and cheering them on.[19]

Again, it was the twenty-three-year-old Quanah riding in front, resplendent in black war paint and bear-claw necklace and armed with a brace of six-shooters. Carter found him terrifying to look at, and, considering Quanah's height and massive upper-body muscles, there is no reason to doubt him. Having sprung the trap, Quanah ordered his warriors to flank and surround the twelve men. The besieged troopers, realizing what was about to happen to them, dismounted and backed slowly toward the ravine, firing as they retreated. Suddenly the seven men with Heyl turned and ran, abandoning their comrades to the Indians. The Indians whooped and came on. The five remaining soldiers, one of whom had been shot in the hand, continued their retreat. As they reached the lip of the ravine, they unlocked their magazines and delivered several volleys, driving the Indians back long enough for them to mount their horses. But as they turned and started toward the ravine, the horse carrying Private Seander Gregg faltered.

Carter gives us an interesting and rare snapshot of frontier battle in the close-quarters fight that followed. Seeing Gregg's problem, Quanah spun and rode quickly toward him, zigzagging his horse and turning Gregg and his stumbling mount into a shield. Quanah's command of his horse was such that Carter and the others could not shoot at him without hitting Gregg. As Quanah closed for the kill, Gregg tried to use his carbine but in his panic failed to pull the lever hard enough, jamming the cartridge. Carter shouted at him to use his six-shooter, but it was too late. Quanah was upon him. He shot Gregg in the head from feet or inches away. It would have been customary for Quanah to scalp the fallen Gregg. But instead he whirled and with the rest of his men galloped away and up the canyon wall. Amazed, Carter turned and saw why. The Tonkawa scouts had crested the ridge; behind them rose the prodigious dust from Mackenzie's main column.

Carter's cool head had saved his men from almost certain death. For his actions in Blanco Canyon that morning he was awarded the Congressional Medal of Honor. He was undoubtedly a very brave man. But he had something else going for him, too, that would bear importantly on the final outcome of the Indian wars: Spencer rifles. Prior to the Civil War the only repeating weapons in military use in America were the six-shot revolvers that Samuel Colt had introduced in the 1840s. But the war had seen the advent of the repeating rifle, most of which were Spencer carbines. For their time, they were technological wonders. They fired .52-caliber bullets from a seven-round magazine, which could be reloaded in one-tenth the time it took to reload a Colt-style revolver and gave the rifles a sustainable rate of fire of *twenty rounds per minute.* They were accurate up to five hundred yards.

The Comanches had nothing at the time of the Blanco Canyon fight to match it.[20] Their main weapons, revolvers and bows, were effective only at short range, generally less than sixty yards. The single-shot muskets they carried, meanwhile, were accurate at longer ranges but were so cumbersome to load—two shots a minute from horseback would have been considered good—that they were mainly used only to fire an opening volley. (Carter noted that most of their muskets were muzzle-loading.)[21] The mismatch was extraordinary. Colonel Richard Dodge observed this huge gap in firepower between whites and Indians. He believed that a horse Indian armed with repeating rifle, "an arm suited to his mode of fighting" was "the finest natural soldier in the world."[22] But Indians carrying repeaters would not appear in numbers until the last days of the plains wars. And even at Little Bighorn, five years later, most of the shots the Indians fired came from bows.

Now that Mackenzie's column had nearly caught up to Quanah's advance guard, the chase began in earnest. Mackenzie outnumbered him and with his superior weaponry enjoyed an enormous tactical advantage, something the Indians, who scrupulously avoided pitched battles against well-equipped bluecoats, were well aware of. They were also defending their village, which included their women and children. And so they ran.

One might think that an entire human settlement consisting of several hundred lodges, with large numbers of women and children and old men, many tons of equipment and provisions and supplies, along with a remuda of three thousand horses and mules, an unspecified number of cattle, and dogs, would be an easy enough quarry. The Comanche village could not hide on the open plains. Nor could it possibly move as fast as a well-mounted and determined force of nearly six hundred men. These things seem obvious enough. This was one of the few times in recorded history where a large number of troops pursued an entire village in open country, and its outcome might have seemed a foregone conclusion. Instead, Quanah gave Colonel Mackenzie an object lesson in one of the most important components of plains warfare down the centuries: escape.

Aware now that they were hunting the whole camp as well as the warriors, Mackenzie's men moved northwest along the Clear Fork of the Brazos, cutting a gentle arc just to the east of the present city of Lubbock. The river ran through a canyon that was sometimes narrow and sometimes opened out into broad valleys broken by ravines and rolling sand hills, and bordered by high, often impassable bluffs. The men saw small herds of buffalo here and there, and at places where the creek widened into lovely, clear pools, enormous flocks of ducks and curlews. This was unmapped terrain, pristine and untouched by white civilization. Every so often they would pass abandoned grass and brush huts, known as wickiups, that were used by the Indian herders.

The highest of the bluffs, on the west side of the canyon, were part of a massive geological formation in west Texas called the "caprock," essentially a long seam of rock that underlies the Llano Estacado and becomes an outcropping just at the point where the high plains give way to the lower, rolling plains. The formation is worth noting because it became a key part of the Indians' evasive maneuvers. Seen from the land below, where Mackenzie's men were, it looks like an enormous shelf, topped by rocky battlements. It rises anywhere from two hundred to a thousand feet above the lower plains. The term *llano estacado* is usually translated as "staked plain." But that is not what Coronado meant when he named it. He meant "palisaded plain," meaning a plain that begins (or ends) in a steep cliff. The caprock runs for several hundred miles.[23]

The men marched steadily through the day in the "stillness and utter solitude of this lovely valley only disturbed by the tramp of our horses' hoofs."[24] They were more than fifty miles from their supply camp, isolated on the absolute edge of the known world, in one of the most dangerous places on the plains for white men. Late in the afternoon they came upon the site of Quanah's village. The Comanches had left in great haste, dragging their enormous load with them, leaving a broad trail up the canyon. Confident now that they were close on the heels of the slow-moving tribe, Mackenzie's column spurred forward, following their twenty-five Tonkawa trackers.

That confidence was short-lived. Soon the trail divided, and then it appeared to cross and recross itself in every direction until the scouts could discern no clear direction. After much parleying with Mackenzie and the other officers, the scouts concluded that Quanah and his band had actually *doubled back* on their pursuers, and had proceeded away back down the trail. Frustrated and chagrined that they had been outfoxed yet again by the Comanches, the Fourth had no choice but to countermarch, bivouacking for the night at the site of the abandoned village.[25]

The next morning the Tonks managed to pick up the trail again, but now the broad traces left by hundreds of lodge poles and thousands of head of stock seemed to do the impossible, climbing hundreds of feet up the nearly vertical canyon wall and over the cliffs of the caprock. Somehow the village was behaving like a small group of riders. And now the soldiers toiled upward through an extremely steep ascent over rock outcroppings and ravines. At the top, they saw something that relatively few white men had ever seen: the preternaturally flat expanse of the high plains, covered only with short buffalo grass. "As far as the eye could reach," wrote Carter, "not an object of any kind or a living thing, was in sight. It stretched out before us—one uninterrupted plain, only to be compared with the ocean in its vastness."[26] The scene was terrifying even for men with experience of the plains. "This is a terrible country," railroad worker Arthur Ferguson had written a few years earlier, "the stillness, wildness and desolation of which is awful. Not a tree to be seen. The stillness too was perfectly awful, not a sign of man to be seen, and it seemed as if the solitude had been eternal."[27] The men noticed something else, too: The temperature was dropping; a norther was starting to kick up. They were at an elevation over three thousand feet, still wearing their summer uniforms. The day before they had basked in the warm sunshine of the cloistered canyon. Now the north wind bit into them, and the short, stiff grass made the task of tracking the Comanches difficult at best.

Again, the column paused while the Tonks tried to figure out where Quanah's village had gone. When they finally found the trail, they realized that, after following the edge of the caprock, it went back over the bluff and down into the canyon. Disgusted, and aware that they had been duped once more, the troopers made the dangerous descent, only to find the same tangled skein of wildly crisscrossing trails, some leading up the valley, some down, and some moving directly across it. The Tonks fanned out again. Now they found that the trail led once again up and over the steep bluffs, this time on the other side of the canyon. Again, the troopers went up through the rocky breaks. For all of their anger and frustration, the men were beginning to feel admiration, bordering on astonishment, at what Quanah's Comanches were able to do. Wrote Carter:

> It was a singularly sharp trick, even for Indians, done of course to blind us and gain time in moving their families of women and children as far as possible out of our reach. Without our own Indian scouts to beat the Comanches at their own native shrewdness, we would have undoubtedly lost the trail and [in] hopelessness abandoned the task.[28]

Whether the Tonks were beating the Comanches, or being successfully tricked time and time again by a commander who knew exactly what he was doing, is a matter of interpretation.

Back upon the Llano Estacado yet again, the troops began to feel the full fury of the norther. Under a darkening sky, the frigid wind cut through their thin uniforms. Many of the men had neither coats nor gloves, and they were now a hundred miles from their supply base. As they moved forward, they caught occasional glimpses of the fleeing band, silhouetted against the horizon. They were closer than they had thought, and as if to underscore that fact Comanche riders suddenly appeared on their flanks, trying to divert them. Mackenzie refused to be distracted. He pressed his column onward toward the village, which in its haste and alarm had begun to throw off all sorts of debris, including lodge poles and tools. Even puppies, which some of Mackenzie's men picked up and placed athwart their saddles. Battle seemed imminent. The Tonks painted themselves and invoked their medicine, the men closed up in columns of fours, the pack mules were closed in and set in herd formation.

Now as if on cue, the leaden skies seemed to descend upon them. What had been a garden-variety norther now turned into what people in west Texas call a "blue norther"—rain, sleet, and snow all mixed together, driven relentlessly by winds up to fifty miles per hour. Darkness was coming on fast, and the moment for decision had arrived: the Fourth Cavalry could either gallop forward into the gathering storm and attack, or break off for the day. Oddly, considering how aggressive Mackenzie was by nature, he decided not to attack. He did this against the advice of his officers. In retrospect, he probably made the right decision. His men were fatigued, his horses worn thin and frail, and unlike the Comanches he had no fresh mounts. The soldiers dismounted, and the storm that had been building up all afternoon now unleashed its full fury. Winds of gale force drove freezing rain, which soon coated the men with ice. It was the sort of night in which a soldier and his horse could easily die. Huge hailstones began to fall, bruising the troopers. They wrapped themselves in what they could find and miserably settled in. Mackenzie himself had brought no overcoat with him. Somebody was kind enough to wrap him in a buffalo robe.

The Quahadis, meanwhile, did not stop. They soldiered on into the teeth of the norther for the rest of the night. One can only wonder what it must have been like. The next day Mackenzie made a halfhearted attempt to follow them but soon gave up. He had chased them more than forty miles (from present-day Crosbyton to Plainview). He was beginning to push the limits of his supplies. The next day, while the troopers were making their descent back into Blanco Canyon, they cornered two stray Comanches in a ravine. For some reason, perhaps out of frustration, Mackenzie insisted on directing the skirmish from the front. He was hit by a barbed arrow that pierced to the bone and had to be cut out. Embarrassed at his own impetuousness, he never mentioned in his official report that he had been wounded.[29] Robert Carter summed up the disappointment he felt in the campaign's end in his memoirs, saying that "it was with the keenest regret and bitter disappointment that the driving of this half-breed Qua-ha-da into the Fort Sill reservation to become later a 'good Indian' could not have been accomplished then by the Fourth Cavalry, instead of its being delayed until more than three years from that date, and then by converging columns operating in four directions."[30] Quanah roamed free, and Mackenzie had missed a glorious opportunity to break the most violent Comanche band in its homeland.

Seventeen

━◆━

MACKENZIE UNBOUND

━◆━

OR THE FREE Comanches in the spring of 1872, Mackenzie's dramatic failure at Blanco Canyon was both good news and bad news. The good news was that one of America's toughest combat officers had been duped and humiliated time and time again by people who knew a great deal more about this sort of warfare than he did. Quanah had outmaneuvered and outnavigated him; Mackenzie's men had stumbled around in darkness and in dead-end arroyos and had their horses stampeded and paid a terrible price. They had been led on a merry chase, not by a highly mobile war party but by an entire village. The bluecoats had nearly perished in a storm that, nevertheless, did not prevent the Indians, young and old, from traveling to safety. Considering that the *taibos* had almost lost all their horses and their supply train, they were probably lucky to be alive.

The bad news, for those who could see it, was that Blanco Canyon marked the beginning of the end of the old empire. The logic was disarmingly simple. Previous military expeditions had violated Comancheria's borders and had introduced the Indians to the idea that their home ranges were no longer completely safe. But they had done nothing to change the basic balance of power. Now, in their deliberate penetration of the heartland, the bluecoat leaders were signaling their intent not just to protect the frontier but to destroy the raiders themselves, to find the wolves in their den and kill them. They were aiming directly at the source of Comanche strength.

And much of that strength was pure illusion, a sort of fantasy propped up by the self-defeating politics of Washington, D.C. In the year 1872 the once-glorious Comanches were really nothing more than a tiny population of overmatched and outgunned aboriginals who happened to occupy an absurdly large chunk of the nation's midsection. That they were able to do so in an era of steam engines, transcontinental railroads, nation-spanning telegraph lines, and armies capable of greater destruction than the world had ever witnessed, was nearly inconceivable. Now, finally, that was going to change. Blanco Canyon meant that the tribe's final ruin was only a matter of time. A few years at most, perhaps months. It meant that there existed both the will to pursue them to the caprock and beyond—embodied in grim warriors like Grant, Sherman, and Sheridan, the men who had destroyed the South—and a commander in Texas who was capable of doing it. The dour, irascible Mackenzie was nothing if not a quick study, and he had just learned a critical lesson in how not to fight Comanches in the Texas Panhandle.

For the moment, however, death came to the frontier as it always had. In the spring of 1872, Comanche and Kiowa raiders swooped down into the Texas settlements as though there were nothing in the world that could possibly stop them. Some of those attacks were made by "reservation" Comanches—Yamparikas, Nokonis, and Penatekas—who used their agency as a refuge. Some were made by the Quahadis, who had never come to the reservation. Others were accounted for by Shaking Hand's Kotsoteka band, which was straddling both worlds. The latter had come into the agency over the winter to get food and annuity goods, and then had moved back out onto the buffalo plains in the spring. Others, from the reservation bands, had followed them. The situation was highly fluid, unsettled, explosive. Many residents of the frontier, especially those in the Palo Pinto country southwest of Fort Worth, thought that 1872 was the worst year ever for Indian raids. A district judge from that area wrote a letter to President Grant that year, begging for relief. He described the worsening horror, and said that

> I might give your Excellency scores of instances of recent date of murder, rape, and robbery which [the Indians] have committed alone in the counties composing my judicial district. It was but a few days since the whole Lee family, three of them being females, were ravished, murdered, and most terribly mutilated. Then Mr. Dobs, Justice of the Peace of Palo Pinto County, was but last week murdered and scalped, his ears and his nose were cut off. . . . Wm. McCluskey was but yesterday shot down by those same bloody Quaker pets upon his own threshold.[1]

Such a description of frontier violence could as easily have come from 1850 as from 1872. News of "depredations" had become so drearily familiar that it could sometimes seem unreal, almost a cliché. It was all horrifyingly real, of course. The terror had been taking place along roughly the same line of longitude in Texas for more than thirty-five years. Like some nightmarish and never-ending war, the front never really moved. No phase of the American Indian wars, beginning in the early 1600s, was remotely comparable.

And now Mackenzie was being unchained and ordered to make it stop. The peace policy still applied to Indians who were on the reservation, and his Fourth Cavalry, staging out of forts in central Texas, was still not allowed to cross the Red River to hunt hostiles. But there was to be death and scorched earth for those who insisted on remaining off the reservation. The problem was, as always, where to find them. In the spring of 1872 a solution presented itself. A captured Comanchero named Polonio Ortiz revealed the existence of a wagon road with plenty of water and grass that ran, east to west, across the Llano Estacado and into New Mexico. This was not only the legendary pass through the desiccated and impassable plains that white men had heard about but never found, it was also the road down which thousands of head of stolen cattle moved from Texas to New Mexico. This was the Comanchero cattle lode, the source of guns and ammunition and food for the still-wild Comanche bands. To discover it meant that they would not only disrupt the illegal cattle trade, they would also find Comanches.

In July and August of 1872, under orders to break up the organized cattle raiding, Colonel Mackenzie and his Fourth Cavalry conducted a series of remarkable, unprecedented explorations. Operating out of a base camp on the Freshwater Fork of the Brazos in Blanco Canyon, he first scouted northward along the caprock, crossing and recrossing from high to low plains as the Quahadis had done. Using the Comanchero Ortiz as a scout, he crossed the southern fork of the Red River (known as the Prairie Dog Town Fork) and into the region of present-day Clarendon. He then turned south again through jagged and harshly beautiful canyon lands and along a route that passed through present-day Turkey, Matador, and Roaring Springs. He did not know it at the time, but this part of Texas, just east of present-day Amarillo, had become the main refuge and sanctuary of the wild Comanche bands. One can imagine how Mackenzie's troops looked: tiny figures in the monumental landscape of east Texas, riding week after week through the searing plains heat and the untracked immensity, their tack creaking and their regimental song on their lips ("Come home John, don't stay long; Come home soon to your own Chick-a-biddy!") The land was pristine, untouched. There was wildlife everywhere, sandhill cranes rising by the tens of thousands from playa lakes, buffalo herds that filled the horizon. Mackenzie found no Indians there, or the cattle trail, but his new understanding of the country, knowledge no white man had ever possessed, would figure heavily in the final battles. In late July Ortiz and other scouts discovered a wide road leading onto the Llano Estacado bearing evidence that large herds of cattle had recently traveled over it.

Mackenzie followed the new trail. He was by this point obsessed with his task, which as he conceived it meant forcing the Comanche and Kiowa outliers onto the reservation. He slept lightly, if at all, staying up late into the night studying scouting and other reports and whatever maps he could get his hands on. He drilled his troops hard. They were already a vastly superior fighting unit to the one he had inherited, not least because of their schooling at Blanco Canyon. His personality was harsher and quirkier than ever. His Civil War wounds, several of which had never properly healed, caused him unceasing pain. Riding for long hours over rough terrain was excruciating. According to Robert G. Carter, who served under him for many years, it was this "almost criminal neglect of his own health" that accounted for a personality that had become "irritable, irascible, exacting, sometimes erratic, and frequently explosive."[2] To the white epithet Three-Finger Jack was added the Comanche names Bad Hand and No-Finger Chief. They were getting to know him. He had a hectoring, badgering sort of personality that would not leave anything or anyone alone. He was hard on everyone around him, harsh in his assessments and almost never generous with praise. That included his reports to his superiors. His reticence to talk about what he had done guaranteed him and his men an obscure place in American history. Mackenzie was not without his good points. He was scrupulously fair, and quick to correct an injustice. He never played favorites and would not tolerate servility or self-seeking.

In the next month he crossed the Llano Estacado twice, by different routes, navigating an area that had never been penetrated by the army. (Carson's trip from New Mexico to Adobe Walls had followed the Canadian River, much farther north.) On his return trip, which traced a route roughly from today's Tucumcari to today's Canyon, just south of Amarillo, he made a brilliant discovery: a plains-spanning trail with access to permanent, high-quality water sources at points no more than thirty miles distant from one another.[3] It was just as Ortiz had predicted. Though Mackenzie had not seen any Indians or cattle—in such enormous spaces the chance had been small anyway—he had penetrated the great mystery of the Llano Estacado, the undiscovered country at the heart of Comancheria. By the end of the trip, the Fourth Cavalry knew all about the weird and quirky world of the high plains: its vicious thunderstorms, killer ant colonies, and raging wildfires; they learned how to use buffalo dung as fuel, and how to find water and navigate through immense flatness. Mackenzie, wrote Wallace,

> had made a highly significant contribution to the exploration and opening of the Great American West. He had found two routes across the treacherous plains. The discovery of the roads and the good water would make it possible to keep the hostile Indians constantly on the run until they would surrender, or all be surprised and captured or killed.[4]

He thought nothing of this accomplishment. He still had work to do. He had heard from the same Comanchero that Kotsoteka chief Shaking Hand's band was camped on the North Fork of the Red River. On September 21, 1872, he turned north. With 222 soldiers and 9 Tonkawa scouts he marched toward the rolling, broken prairie on the eastern slope of the caprock escarpment. At four o'clock in the afternoon of September 29, Mackenzie's force, riding in four-column "echelon," galloped into the middle of a Comanche village of 175 large tipis and 87 small ones on the North Fork, about five miles from the present town of Lefors.

Taken completely by surprise, the Comanches could do little more than run and hide from the bluecoats and their guns. Many died within the first few minutes of battle. Eighty or more of them were cut off and cornered in a ravine. They charged the white battle line several times, and each time were repulsed at great cost. The fight quickly became something more like a shooting gallery. One of Mackenzie's officers, W. A. Thompson, compared it to "a troop of men in line on a stage firing into a crowded theater pit."[5] Many of the Indians ended up in a pool made by a brook that ran through the middle of the camp. Some were there hiding beneath overhanging grass. Most were dead. "So many were killed and wounded in the water that it was red from hole to hole with blood," wrote a white captive named Clinton Smith who fought with the Indians.[6] Many Comanches escaped into the brush of the river bottom. As Mackenzie noted tersely in his report, the battle was over in half an hour. He had to forcibly restrain his Tonkawas from scalping all the dead Comanches.

When the smoke from the black powder had cleared, he had killed fifty-two Indians, and had lost only four of his own. He had taken 124 prisoners—mostly women and children—something that had not happened to Comanches within anyone's memory. It had very likely never happened. Not, at least, since the advent of the horse. Just as important, he had captured three thousand horses, which meant that he had very likely put on foot a good many of those who had escaped. How many got away is not known, just as it is not known how many were in the camp when the bluecoats attacked. The rule was eight to ten people, and two fighting men, per large tipi. If that was true, then a huge percentage of what was left of the Comanches, including reservation Indians, had been camped with Shaking Hand. It would later be learned that members of all five major bands were there, though at the time of the battle Shaking Hand, ironically, was on a train to Washington to meet the Great Father and discuss peace.[7] Just downriver, moreover, was another camp of mostly Quahadis, so close that they could hear the shooting. In Mackenzie's official report, he noted without elaboration that "the lodges were generally burned, and a large amount of other property was destroyed."[8] There would, in any case, be nothing left for the Indians to use.

In historical terms, Mackenzie's victory was stunning. He had achieved it by daring to go where white men had not gone, by using his Indian scouts well, and then by attacking in force the moment he had intelligence of the camp. He had attacked with fury. Unlike Chivington's drunken thugs, though, his men also knew restraint. They had been under orders to try to avoid killing women, children, and old men—Mackenzie was unusually attentive to this, for a western officer—but as he himself noted, many of the people in those categories "were too badly wounded to be moved."[9] And the Tonks had done plenty of damage before he could rein them in. The other side, predictably, had a somewhat different account. Captive Herman Lehmann, who was with the Comanches at the time, wrote:

> We arrived the next day after the fight and found the dead bodies scattered about. I remember finding the body of Batsena, a very brave warrior, lying mutilated and scalped, and alongside of him was the horribly mangled remains of his daughter, Nooki, a beautiful Indian maiden, who had been disemboweled and scalped. The bodies presented a revolting sight. . . . Other bodies were mutilated too, which showed the hand of the Tonkaway in the battle.[10]

Mackenzie had achieved what Plains Indians valued more than anything: surprise. He was learning from them to exploit weakness. That night he took pains to place his captives inside a well-guarded circle of supply wagons. They were amazingly representative of the larger tribe: there were thirty-four Kotsotekas, thirty Quahadis, eighteen Yamparikas, eleven Nokonis, and nine Penatekas, showing just how fluid the exchange between the "reservation" and the "wild" Comanches really was and suggesting that the old band structures were dissolving. (One or possibly two of the Quahadis were wives of Quanah.)

He ordered the pony herd to be taken a mile away from the burned village, and placed the horses under the guard of the one of his lieutenants and the Tonkawas. Incredibly, Mackenzie, so roughly schooled in Comanche horse culture, had made another mistake. He still did not understand Comanches and horses, or the fact that a handful of Tonks were still no match for Comanche riders. After dark, the Comanches made short work of it, stampeding the horses and not only getting most of their own back, but also those of the Tonkawas, who arrived in the main camp the next day looking sheepish and unhappy, leading a small burro.[11] The following night, when the command made another camp eighteen miles distant, the Comanches took back most of the horses that were left. All that remained of the remuda were fifty horses and nine mules.[12] Mackenzie was furious. He would never again make the mistake of believing he could hang on to Comanche horses. According to his sergeant John Charlton, "No effort after that was ever made to hold a herd of wild captured Indian ponies. *They were all shot.*"[13]

For the People, the Battle of the North Fork of the Red River (sometimes called the Battle of McClellan Creek) was a shattering experience. Nothing like this had happened to them before, and the depth of their grief was startling. They were inconsolable. Wrote former captive Clinton Smith, who was with the tribe:

> Every night for a long time I could hear the old squaws crying away out from the camp, mourning for their dead. They would gash themselves with knives, and when they returned to the camp their faces and arms and breasts showed signs of the mutilation which they underwent in their agony.[14]

The worst of it was their utter powerlessness to get the captives back. The Comanches, famous for their arrogance, were abject and helpless in their grief. This was amply shown a few weeks later when Bull Bear, the chief of the wild, unbowed Quahadis and the only chief who had never signed a treaty or reported to the agency, humbly brought his band to the vicinity of Fort

Sill to beg for the release of the women and children. He told agent Lawrie Tatum, known to him as Bald Head, that he had lost the fight with the soldiers, accepted his final defeat, and was now ready for peace. He would come into the reservation, put his children in the white man's school, and become a farmer, as long as he got his women and children back. Bull Bear was lying. His views on the subject were well known. He believed in fighting to the death. But at the moment he just wanted his people released.

He got his wish. In June 1873, one hundred sixteen women and children and a few old men were brought back from their imprisonment at Fort Concho to Fort Sill and returned to freedom. The release did not resolve anything. Soon large numbers of Comanches, including Bull Bear and his Quahadis, were back in their old camps, doing what they had always done. That year they got a reprieve: Mackenzie, who was ready to mount a final campaign against them, was sent instead to the Mexican borderlands to stop the cross-border raiding of Texas settlements by Kickapoos and Apaches. Acting on unofficial orders from Sheridan, Mackenzie and his Fourth Cavalry crossed eighty miles into Mexico—in violation of every conceivable international treaty—and destroyed three Kickapoo Apache settlements.[15] His attack caused an international furor, and he maintained all along the fiction that he had taken the action on his own authority. When one of his men then asked what Mackenzie would have done if he had refused to cross the border, the colonel answered: "I would have had you shot." When he returned in August he had a violent attack of rheumatism that kept him out of the field until January 1874.

It meant that the Comanche problem would have to wait another year.

Eighteen

+—+ ᛟ◈ᛟ +—+

THE HIDE MEN AND THE MESSIAH

+—+ ᛟ◈ᛟ +—+

B UT SOMETHING EVEN worse than the No-Finger Chief haunted the
Comanche nation in the cruel spring of 1874. They were losing their
identity. In the long years of their ascendancy they had always been
a people apart, fiercely independent, arrogantly certain that their pragmatic,
stripped-down spartan ethic was the best way to live. Unlike the Romans,
who had borrowed everything from clothing to art, food, and religion from
cultures around them, the Comanches were aggressively parochial. They
were the world's best horsemen and the unchallenged military masters of the
south plains. They did not need elaborate religious rituals or complex social
hierarchies. They kept their own counsel.

Now, in ways startlingly reminiscent of what happened to the miserable
Penatekas, all that was changing. It began with the bands themselves. Once
the main social units of the tribe, and the principal source of tribal identity,
they were disintegrating, losing their boundaries, merging with other remnants. The captives taken by Mackenzie from what was nominally a Kotsoteka camp represented all five major bands, a level of tribal intermingling
that would have been unimaginable even ten years before.[1] This partly had to
do with sheer numbers. Where, once, thousands upon thousands of Comanches in single, unified bands lived in camps that wound for miles along the
Brazos or Canadian or Cimarron rivers, now groups with blurred affiliations
numbering only in the hundreds huddled together against the harsh empti-

ness of the plains. The idiosyncrasies of language, customs, and folkways that had made each band distinct were vanishing. (Quahadi culture and vernacular, in fact, had begun to dominate.) The end of the bands meant a scarcity of war chiefs and peace chiefs: Increasingly, there were no followers to lead.

There was also the relentless push of the invading culture. Like all Indians before them, the People were being submerged in a sea of the white man's material goods. This was true even of the Quahadis, who had held themselves aloof and apart longer than any others. Where once the tribe lived in the purity of the buffalo and all that it provided, now there were the *taibos'* weapons and cooking tools and sheet metal, his sugar and coffee and whiskey, his clothing and calico. They used his blankets. They ate food boiled in his brass kettles. At the agency they waited quietly to be given his rancid meat, rotten tobacco, and moldy flour.[2]

But it wasn't just the white man's civilization that was corrupting the old Nermernuh. They had also begun to adopt the customs of other tribes. There were many examples of this cultural jostling, to which they were increasingly vulnerable. Their traditional headgear, for example, had been the fearsome, unornamented black buffalo-wool cap with jutting horns, the stuff of nightmares for generations of settlers. Now most of them had taken to wearing the more delicate, streaming feathered headdress of the Cheyennes. (Quanah was among those who had adopted this style.)[3] Comanche burial had been, like so much else in the culture, a simple and practical affair. The body would be carried off to a natural cave, a crevice, or a deep wash and covered with rocks or sticks in no particular arrangement.[4] Now the tribe was adopting the more elaborate, raised scaffold biers of the northern tribes. Soon they would even steal the Kiowas' Sun Dance. They had witnessed the ceremony for decades without caring much about what it was. Now they were less sure that they did not need it.

At the core of their identity, of course, they were hunters and warriors—precisely what the white man wanted to deny them. While the Great Father and his apostles had not yet succeeded in this righteous mission, the thousand or so Comanches who took food and annuities at Fort Sill had already lost their identity as hunters. The men saw this as a form of slavery. What stories could they tell their children or grandchildren if all they did was wait at the reservation to be given food? Or, worse still, became farmers?

The greatest threat of all to their identity, and to the very idea of a nomadic hunter in North America, appeared on the plains in the late 1860s. These were the buffalo men. Between 1868 and 1881 they would kill thirty-one million buffalo, stripping the plains almost entirely of the huge, lumbering creatures and destroying any last small hope that any horse tribe could ever be restored to its traditional life. There was no such thing as a horse Indian without a buffalo herd. Such an Indian had no identity at all.

The first large-scale slaughter of buffalo by white men with high-powered rifles took place in the years 1871 and 1872. There had been a limited market for buffalo products before that. Even as far back as 1825, several hundred thousand Indian-tanned robes had made it to markets in New Orleans.[5] There had been demand for buffalo meat to feed the railway workers building the transcontinental railroad in the 1860s, spawning the fame and legend of hunters like Buffalo Bill Cody. But there was no real market for buffalo hides until 1870, when a new tanning technology allowed them to be turned into high-grade leather. That, combined with a new railhead in Dodge City, Kansas, meant that the skins could be shipped commercially. For hunters, the economics of the new business was miraculous, all the more so since the animals were so stupefyingly easy to kill. If a buffalo saw the animal next to it drop dead it would not flee unless it could see the source of the danger. Thus one shooter with a long-range rifle could drop an entire stand of the creatures without moving. A hunter named Tom Nixon once shot 120 animals in 40 minutes. In 1873 he killed 3,200 in 35 days, making Cody's once outlandish-sounding claim of killing 4,280 in 18 months seem paltry by comparison.[6] Behind the hunters stood the stinking, sweating skinners, covered head to toe in blood and grease and the animals' parasites. Legendary hunter Brick Bond, who killed 250 animals a day, employed 15 such men.[7] Covered wagons waited at Adobe Walls to take the stacked skins to Dodge City. Except for the tongues, which were salted and shipped as a delicacy, the carcasses were left to rot on the plains. The profits, like the mass killing itself, were obscene. In the winter of 1871–72 a single hide fetched $3.50.[8]

Within two years these hunters, working mainly the Kansas plains close to Dodge City, had killed five million buffalo.[9] Almost immediately, they were victims of their own success. By the spring of 1874 the herds on the middle plains had been decimated. The economics of hunting became a good deal less miraculous. As one scout traveling from Dodge City to the Indian territory put it: "In 1872 we were never out of sight of the buffalo. In the following autumn, while traveling over the same district, the whole country was whitened with bleached and bleaching bones."[10] Thus the hunters were forced to move farther from the railheads in search of prey.[11]

So they went south to the Texas plains, where horizon-spanning herds still drifted across the landscape, where they appeared, as historian Francis Parkman observed in 1846, "like the black shadow of a cloud, passing rapidly over swell after swell of the distant plain."[12] The problem was that the Texas Panhandle was 150 miles away from Dodge City, the only place set up to ship hides. To remedy that, and to give the hunters a place to sell their goods, in March 1874 a trading post was built near the Canadian River, only a mile from the Adobe Walls ruins where Kit Carson had battled Comanches a decade before. The place went by the same name and consisted of two stores, a saloon, and a blacksmith shop. Except for the blacksmith shop, which was built of pickets, the buildings were wood-framed, sod-sided, and sod-roofed. The precise type of building materials would soon become extremely important. By June the post was doing a brisk business. Hunters brought in tens of thousands of hides, and traded for weapons, ammunition, flour, bacon, coffee, canned tomatoes, soup, dried apples and syrup, and such sundries as wolf poison and axle grease.[13] The money was beyond their wildest dreams of avarice; it flowed in buckets; the fortunes of Dodge revived, and the slaughter, which everyone knew would result in the extermination of the buffalo within a few years, continued apace.

The hide men were, on the whole, a nasty lot. They were violent, alcoholic, illiterate, unkempt men who wore their hair long and never bathed. The skinners had body odors that defied the imagination. These plainsmen hated the Indians, and not just because they had brown skins. They believed that the Comanches and Kiowas raided and made war not because it was their traditional way but so they could squeeze money and land out of the government. They believed that what the government paid the Indians amounted to blackmail. "They are a lazy, dirty, lousy, deceitful, race," said hunter Emmanuel Dubbs in 1874. "True manhood is unknown, and they hold their women in abject slavery."[14] When they were not eradicating the helpless buffalo from the face of the earth, the hide men congregated in a set of western "hell towns" that had arisen to meet their primitive urges. Outside the Fourth Cavalry outpost at Fort Griffin, for example, an instant town was put up known as "The Flat." It consisted of flimsy, unpainted frame buildings made of lumber that had been hauled several hundred miles. There were sleazy hotels, dance halls, and saloons, prostitutes, gamblers, and cardsharps. In one of the saloons a red-haired poker queen named Lottie Deno held court. Her hired gunmen stood by to kill anyone who questioned her ethics.[15]

Surprisingly, only a few voices cried out against the slaughter of the buffalo, which had no precedent in human history. Mostly people didn't trouble themselves about the consequences. It was simply capitalism working itself out, the exploitation of another natural resource. There was another, better, explanation for the lack of protest, articulated best by General Phil Sheridan, then commander of the Military Division of the Missouri. "These men [hunters] have done in the last two years . . . more to settle the vexed Indian question than the entire regular army has done in the last thirty years," he said. "They are destroying the Indians' commissary. . . . For the sake of a lasting peace, let them kill, skin and sell until the buffaloes are exterminated. Then your prairies can be covered with speckled cattle and the festive cowboy." Killing the Indians' food was not just an accident of commerce; it was a deliberate political act.

The winter of 1873–74 had been a hard one for the People, many of whom were now shifting restlessly between the agency lands and the camps of the wild Comanches in west Texas. Those who stayed on the reservation were cruelly deceived. There was little game there and no buffalo at all. As before, they were forced to live on the white man's rations. As before, much of this promised food simply never arrived and what was given to them was often of shockingly inferior quality. Facing starvation, the Comanches were forced to kill their own horses and mules for food.[16]

These Indians were now victimized by an entirely new phenomenon: organized gangs of white horse thieves, often dressed up as Indians, who preyed with impunity on the Comanche and Kiowa herds. They took the animals to Kansas and sold them. No one pursued them, no one prosecuted them.[17] Cheating the Indians was always a good business. And while that was happening white whiskey peddlers moved freely inside the reservation, illegally selling diluted rotgut in exchange for buffalo robes. It amounted to robbery; the liquor cost little to make, while selling robes was virtually the only way many Indians could make money. Whiskey was becoming a serious problem. Many of the Indians became quickly addicted, and thus desperate to trade anything to get it.

For those Comanches who still raided the borderlands, the winter of

1873–74 was even worse. Mackenzie kept patrols in the field at all times, and those patrols began to have a devastating effect on small raiding parties. In December a group of twenty-one Comanches and nine Kiowas rode south through Texas and crossed the Rio Grande into Mexico. It was a good, old-fashioned raid, and must have warmed their hearts. They killed and took captives and stole horses and suffered no casualties. Then they turned for home, and their luck ran out. At Kickapoo Springs (near present-day San Angelo), they and their string of one hundred fifty horses were intercepted by Lieutenant Charles Hudson and forty-one troopers from Mackenzie's Fourth Cavalry. A hot, ten-minute fight ensued in which nine Comanches were killed and Hudson suffered only one man wounded. The Comanches also lost seventy horses. A few weeks later a Tenth Cavalry patrol under Lt. Col. George Buell engaged a Comanche raiding party near the Double Mountain Fork of the Brazos River, killing eleven. Two weeks later, another raiding party was attacked and another ten Indians killed.[18]

Though the absolute numbers were small, in the desperate, waning years of Comancheria, these were major disasters. The People took the news hard, as did the Kiowas. Kiowa chief Lone Wolf lost his son and his nephew in the fight with Hudson. In his grief, Lone Wolf cut off his hair, killed his horses, and burned his wagon, lodge, and buffalo robes and vowed revenge.[19] He might have been gratified to know that Lieutenant Hudson died that winter, too, killed accidentally by his roommate, who was cleaning a gun. Quanah, who also lost a nephew to Buell's men, would have a far more radical reaction, one that would eventually affect the fate of all Plains Indians.

All of this was terrible news for the People. They went into deep mourning for their lost ones and also, perhaps, for their own lost world. Then, when it did not seem as if things could get any worse, the buffalo hunters arrived in Adobe Walls and began to turn the panhandle into a stinking graveyard. These were frightening times, and there is no reason to believe that the last of the Comanches, defiant on the high plains, did not understand their historical position. They were almost alone now. Most of the Arapahos had given up; they had gone in. The Cheyennes were confused and leaderless. (These were the southern bands of those two tribes.) The Kiowas were riven by political quarrels, deeply split between the idea of surrendering and fighting to the end. There was no one else living outside the territories anymore, not on the south plains. Just a few thousand Comanches who were watching their old world die and losing their identities in the process.

Just at this point, when it seemed that all hope would soon be lost, there arose from the Comanche tribe a prophet. He was very young, but he had a great and towering vision. He had the answer to all of their ardent prayers.

He was called Isa-tai, which was one of those Comanche names that delicate western sensibilities had trouble translating. Sometimes it is given as "rear end of a wolf," which is amusing but inaccurate. Elsewhere it appears as "coyote droppings," "coyote anus," and "wolf shit." But even these were euphemisms along the lines of "Buffalo Hump." The more accurate translation would have been "wolf's vulva," or "coyote vagina," both of which were unprintable until well into the twentieth century.[20]

He was a medicine man, a magician, and probably a con man, too, though there was no question that he believed at least some of what he was preaching. He was a Quahadi, probably around twenty-three years old, a stocky man with a large head, a broad, open face, and a bull neck. In the winter and spring of 1873–74 Isa-tai had established himself as the possessor of an electrifying sort of *puha* that Comanches had never seen before. He claimed miraculous healing powers and the ability to raise the dead.[21] Though he was as yet untested in battle, he maintained that the white man's bullets had no effect on him, and that he could also make medicine that would make others immune, even if they stood directly before the muzzles of the white man's guns.[22] These were impressive things, but not without precedent. Other shamans had claimed the same magic. That year, however, Isa-tai had, in the presence of witnesses, raised from his stomach a wagonload of cartridges, belched it up, and then swallowed it again. On four separate occasions he had—again, in front of witnesses—ascended into the skies, far beyond the sun, to the home of the Great Spirit, remaining there overnight and coming back the next day. Most astonishing of all, when a brilliant comet appeared in the sky, he had correctly predicted that it would disappear in five days.[23] His legend spread throughout the plains. People said that he could control the elements, and send hail, lightning, and thunder against his enemies.

How did he convince people he could do these things? Part of the answer may lie in his abilities as a magician. In one account, he was able to make arrows appear in his hands, as though they had flown there out of the air.[24] This sounds like the sort of sleight of hand that any competent modern magician could do. According to Quaker teacher Thomas Battey, who worked at the time on the Kiowa reservation, Isa-tai had a particular technique for creating the illusion that he was rising into the clouds. He gathered people in a sacred spot, wrote Battey, then "tells them to look directly at the sun until he speaks to them, then to let their eyes slowly fall to the place where he is standing. As they do this they will see dark bodies descend to receive him, with which he will ascend."[25] He would then slip away, and remain concealed until his "return."

But Isa-tai was about more than just magic. He had a vision of a new order on the plains. During his ascent into the clouds, the Great Spirit had endowed him with power to wage final war on the white man—a war that would not only kill many *taibos* but would restore the Comanche nation to its former glory. And this is what he now proposed to the Comanche tribe. That spring he moved among the bands, preaching that if they purified themselves, and stopped following the white man's road, the time of salvation was near.

Then he expanded his evangelism to include Cheyenne, Kiowa, and Arapaho camps. Accompanying him on many of these trips was the charismatic young warrior Quanah, who had considerable battle experience and whose fame as a war chief was spreading across the plains.[26] Together they were a formidable team. Isa-tai was the magic man; Quanah was the tough guy, the tall, battle-hardened warrior with rippling muscles and a startlingly direct gaze, the one you did not want to disappoint. Their pitch had its roots in one of the oldest of Comanche martial traditions: the revenge raid. Isa-tai had lost an uncle in the fight with Lieutenant Hudson, and so he and Quanah had both been grieving since January. Now that spring had arrived, they were ready for revenge. Quanah had always burned for retribution, ever since the *taibos* killed his father and took his mother and sister away. Now Isa-tai's *puha* offered him the chance to wreak it on a colossal scale. Together, over a period of months, they managed to rouse the entire Comanche nation to a frenzy of hope and expectation.

Quanah later recalled his efforts at recruitment: "That time I pretty big man, pretty young man and knew how to fight pretty good. I work one month. I go to Nokoni Comanche camp on head of Cache Creek, call in everybody. I tell [them] about my friend kill him in Texas. I fill pipe. I tell that man: 'You want to smoke?' He take pipe and smoke it. I give it to another man. He say 'I not want to smoke.' If he smoke he go on war path. He not hand back. God kill him, he afraid. "[27] It is evident from this last line that this was not a soft sell. Warriors' courage, patriotism, and manhood were being called into question.

In May, Isa-tai did something that no Comanche leader in history had ever done: He sent runners to all the Comanche bands, on and off the reservation, summoning them to a Sun Dance. This was an extraordinary move for three reasons. First, there had never been a single council attended by all Comanches. Nothing even close to that had ever happened, at least since the tribe migrated south out of the Wind River country of Wyoming. Second, there had never been a single leader, a *paraibo*, with the power to convoke the whole tribe. And third, the Sun Dance was not a tradition of the Comanche tribe and never had been. The People had watched Kiowa ceremonies, but they had little or no idea of what a Sun Dance actually meant or how it was performed.

In spite of this, virtually the entire Comanche people agreed to come, even the sedentary Penatekas. The idea was to unite under this powerful new medicine and drive the whites forever from the plains. In concept it was not unlike Buffalo Hump's great expedition, driven by his vision of white men falling into the sea, which had resulted in the Linnville Raid and the Battle of Plum Creek in 1840. The Sun Dance would thus be the focal point for the Comanche tribe's second large-scale revenge raid against the white man.

The bands gathered in May on the Red River just west of the reservation boundary (near present-day Texola, where I-40 intersects the Texas-Oklahoma border). Though they did worship the sun, and usually blew the first puff of sacred smoke in its direction, they were true animists: power and magic was not concentrated in one or two places (such as a Great Spirit) but diffused throughout the universe. Power could reside in wolves and trees and rock bluffs as much as in the sun. But Comanches were intensely practical people; they were happy to try anything that worked, and Isa-tai was a persuasive man. So they dispensed with the military societies, the fetish dolls, the trained priests, the medicine bundles, the rite of warriors' piercing their breast tendons with thongs and hanging from the lodge pole, and other traditions considered essential by other tribes.[28] They built a medicine lodge of poles and brush and acted out sham battles and sham buffalo hunts. They danced a simplified, practical Sun Dance, and they held a massive party with a good deal of whiskey and feasting and all-night drum playing. They gloried in believing again in the power of Comanches.

In the end, perhaps half of the tribe agreed to follow Quanah and Isa-tai. The exact number, or percentage, is unknown. The Penatekas, by now quite tame and even engaged in some farming, left for the reservation. They were frightened by such talk. Most of the Nokonis left, too, under their chief Horse Back, and many of the Yamparikas went with them. They did so under threat. Quanah's people said they would kill their horses and strand them afoot if they did not go along.[29] Some of the defectors were even threatened with personal violence. The Yamparika chief Quitsquip reported back to Indian agent J. M. Haworth that by night the Comanches were being whipped into a chauvinistic frenzy with whiskey, drumming, dancing, and war talk, only to lapse into confusion and indecision, and presumably hangovers, the next morning. "They have a great many hearts," he told Haworth. "[They] make up their minds at night for one thing and get up in the morning entirely changed."[30] At their war councils, Quanah and Isa-tai promoted their idea of a revenge raid in Texas, starting with the traitor Tonkawas and moving on to a war on the settlements. But the tribal elders had other ideas, and overruled the two young men. Quanah later remembered it this way:

> They said "You pretty good fighter, Quanah, but you not know everything. We think you take pipe first against the white buffalo hunters. You kill white men and make your heart feel good. After that you come back and take all young men and go Texas war path." Isa-tai make big talk that time. [He said] "God tell me we going to kill lots of white men. I stop the bullets in gun. Bullets not penetrate shirts. We kill them just like old women."[31]

So the first target would be the buffalo hunters at Adobe Walls. Then the full fury of the tribe would fall upon the hated Texans and their traitorous allies the Tonks. Armed with their powerful idea, Quanah and Isa-tai now visited the camps of the Kiowas, Cheyennes, and Arapahos to recruit warriors for the attack on the hide men. They had little success with the Kiowas, where, according to one of them, the elders "were afraid of that pipe."[32] Only a few of the tribe agreed to go. They had better luck with the Cheyennes, many of whom were enthusiastic about the expedition, especially with the protection of Isa-tai's medicine. The Arapahos liked the idea but hedged: Powder Face, their main chief, was deeply committed to the white man's road. Only twenty-two of them agreed to go, under the young upstart chief Yellow Horse. The force of two hundred fifty warriors was thus composed mainly of Comanches and Cheyennes. They were clear on three things: that the attack would be made on the buffalo camp forty miles to the west; that it would be made under Isa-tai's protective magic; and that it would be led by the young Quanah, who had impressed everyone with his burning passion and his singleness of purpose.

The raid on the trading post should have been an outright slaughter. The night was warm and sultry and most of the people at the post—twenty-eight men and one woman, scattered among two stores and a saloon—were sleeping outdoors. There was no hotel, no rooms for rent. Those who were under roofs were in buildings whose doors were wide open. Isa-tai knew this from a scouting party he had sent out, and had confidently promised his men that they would sweep down on the *taibos* and club them to death in their sleep. It was a good plan. In principle, anyway. In the early-morning hours of May 26, 1874, the Indians under Quanah's command massed on a high bluff beside the Canadian River. They waited. Among them was the messiah, Isa-tai, stark naked except for a cap of sage stems, and painted completely yellow, as was his horse. Yellow meant invulnerable. Most of the other braves and their horses were painted yellow, too, along with other colors. They all believed, or they would not have been there, that Isa-tai had true *puha*, that they would be immune to the white man's bullets. After all, a man who could ascend into the sky, and who could burp up a load of cartridges, would have little trouble with a small band of the hated buffalo men. The assembled Comanches, Cheyennes, Kiowas, and Arapahos believed that this was a moment of destiny and that their redemption was at hand.

But the massacre of sleeping *taibos* never happened. That was because the owner of the saloon, a transplanted Pennsylvanian by way of Dodge City named James Hanrahan, fired his gun in the middle of the night, waking many of the hunters, skinners, merchants, and drovers. He told his guests, and they apparently believed him, that the loud noise they had heard had been made by the cracking of the ridgepole, the main beam holding up the sod roof of the saloon. Such an event would mean death, injury, or at the very least extreme inconvenience for the people underneath it. Fully awake now, the men then pitched in and spent the rest of the night replacing the ridgepole.

In fact the ridgepole was fine. Hanrahan had invented the story about the roof falling in because he had been informed several days before that the Indian attack was coming and had not wanted to hurt his business and thus hadn't told anyone. When the men had finished their task, Hanrahan, refusing to come clean about the attack but afraid to let anyone go back to sleep, offered them free drinks. At four a.m. Thus many of them were wide awake when the Indian war party swept down from the bluff just before dawn on June 27.

The Indians drove down into the valley with a fury. Quanah recalled later that the horses were moving at a gallop, throwing dust high in the air, and that some of them tripped on the prairie-dog holes, which sent men in feathered headdresses and horses rolling over and over in the semidarkness.[33] At the settlement they crowded around the buildings, firing their carbines at windows and doors. Inside, the buffalo men barricaded themselves as best they could, piled up sacks of grain, and found that they were fairly well protected behind two-foot walls of sod. Sod would not burn, either, which would have offered the Indians an easy victory. The attackers flattened themselves against the walls. Quanah backed his horse into one of the doors, trying unsuccessfully to break it down, and later climbed up on the roof of one of the buildings to shoot down at the occupants. At one point he picked up a wounded comrade from the ground while seated on his horse, a feat of strength that astounded the men inside the buildings. In the early minutes of the fight both sides were using six-shooters. For the white men inside, the fury of the attack was terrifying. The buildings were full of smoke; people were shouting and screaming; the air was full of singing lead. Billy Dixon recalled that "At times the bullets poured in like hail and made us hug the sod walls like gophers when an owl is swooping past."[34]

This is Quanah's own account, filtered through the memory of his friend J. A. Dickson:

> We at once surrounded the place and began to fire on it. The hunters got in the houses and shot through the cracks and holes in the wall. Fight lasted about two hours. We tried to storm the place several times but the hunters shot so well we would have to retreat. At one time I picked up five braves and we crawled along a little ravine to their corral, which was only a few yards from the house. Then we picked our chance and made a run for the house before they could shoot us, and we tried to break the door in but it was too strong and being afraid to stay long, we went back the way we had come.[35]

Three white men had been killed in the early moments of the raid, but the others had managed to hold the Indians off.[36] The flanking fire from the saloon protected the people in the two mercantile buildings, most of whom had been asleep. The whites learned that by poking holes in the sod they could create gun ports for themselves, and thus drive back the Indians from the other side of the wall. The hide men, moreover, were an unusually tough bunch, even by plains standards. In addition to various hunters, skinners, and wagon drivers, they included Billy Dixon, a famous buffalo hunter who would win a Congressional Medal of Honor later that year fighting Indians; William Barclay "Bat" Masterson, a gambler and gunman who later became legendary as the sheriff of Dodge City; "Dutch Henry" Born, later the most feared of the professional horse thieves on the Great Plains; and James "Bermuda" Carlyle, later killed when a posse in White Oaks, New Mexico, tried to arrest Billy the Kid and his gang.[37]

The Indians were driven back. They discovered that, even though many among their ranks had repeating, lever-action rifles, they were yet again at an enormous disadvantage in firepower. Inside those buildings were not just hardened and determined men with considerable experience of violence, cocooned inside thick walls of mud and grass. They also had a virtual arsenal of ammunition and weaponry at their disposal, most notably the brand-new Sharps "Big Fifties," rifles of astonishing power, range, and accuracy that had made the wholesale slaughter of the buffalo possible in the first place. The merchants had whole cases of brand-new Sharps rifles, plus at least 11,000 rounds of ammunition. The Big Fifties were single-shot weapons with octagonal 34-inch barrels that used huge cartridges: .50-caliber, 600-grain bullets driven by 125 grains of black powder. They were so powerful that they could knock down a 2,000-pound buffalo at 1,000 yards. In the hands of the buffalo hunters, they were horrifically effective against horses and human beings. The rifles' ranges were far longer than the Indians' carbines could possibly reach.

By ten o'clock the Indians had retreated from the booming buffalo guns. Quanah, who had also fallen back after heroically fighting at close quarters, had his horse shot out from under him at five hundred yards.[38] He took shelter behind a buffalo carcass, where he was hit by a bullet that ricocheted off a powder horn around his neck and lodged between his shoulder blade and neck. The wound was not serious. Astonished at the range and accuracy of the guns, the Indians retreated yet farther, only to learn that they had still not gone far enough. A group of them had met to plan strategy at a distance of roughly three-quarters of a mile from the trading post. Undeterred, the hunters began to pick them off one by one. A Comanche named Cohayyah who was among them recalled that he was standing with his friends trying to figure out how to rescue their dead when "suddenly and without warning one of the warriors fell from his horse dead." They found a bullet hole in his head. The wind had shifted, and they had not even heard the sound of a rifle shot.[39]

In the distance, Isa-tai sat on his horse, naked and bright ochre, watching the epic failure of his medicine. Nothing he had predicted had come true. The men who were supposed to be slaughtered in their sleep were now dropping Indians on the field like shotgunned mallards. The Cheyennes were angry at him. One of them struck Isa-tai in the face with his riding quirt; another, the father of a young warrior who had been killed, demanded to know why, if the messiah were immune to bullets, he did not go recover the young man's body. As if to emphasize Isa-tai's powerlessness, the man on the horse next to him was shot dead, then Isa-tai's own horse was shot out from under him. His magic may have failed, but the magic of the Big Fifties worked just fine.[40] Killing people three-quarters of a mile away was, by all objective precedent, godlike. Isa-tai's excuse was that the Cheyennes had killed and skinned a skunk the day before the battle, and thus queered his medicine. His people did not really believe him.

The effect on the Indians was devastating. It was not so much the carnage—fifteen were killed that day and many more wounded—as the shocking failure of Isa-tai's medicine. That was the first great demoralizing blow. The second was the wounding of Quanah, who was rescued by his people and brought back out of range of the buffalo guns. As we have seen, the killing or wounding of the leader was almost invariably a signal for retreat. By four o'clock the Indians had given up. The whites emerged from their buildings and collected trinkets and souvenirs. Though the Indians remained nearby for the next several days, taking occasional shots at the sod walls of the trading post, they never attacked again. The battle was over. On the third day Billy Dixon made what became the most famous single shot in the history of the West. A party of about fifteen Indians had appeared at the edge of the bluff, at a distance of probably fifteen hundred yards, or almost a mile. As Dixon recalled, "some of the boys suggested that I try the big '50' on them. . . . I took careful aim and pulled the trigger. We saw an Indian fall from his horse."[41] He was the last casualty of what would become famous in frontier history as the Second Battle of Adobe Walls, where a handful of doughty white men held off a buzzing horde of Indians that has been variously estimated at seven hundred to a thousand, though two hundred fifty is closer to the truth. Astonished and terrified, the rest of the Indians fled.

The rest was anticlimax. The whites, strengthened by the arrival of more than seventy hunters who were now afraid to be alone on the plains, eventually decided it was safe to go about their business. After burying their four dead comrades (one died accidentally) and the scalped Newfoundland dog that had died with the drovers, the whites beheaded the dead Indians and stuck their heads on stakes outside the walls. They placed the thirteen headless bodies on buffalo hides and dragged them away along with the dead horses (the Indians had killed them all), which had begun to reek.

Meanwhile the Indians drifted off, furious, helpless. Once again, bad medicine had been their fatal weakness. They could not help themselves. Reverse the roles to see what might have happened. The whites would have surrounded the buildings and kept up the attack. They would have come by night and caved in the walls. They would have accepted far greater losses to achieve the objective than Indians ever would. Indians never understood the concept of seizing and holding a small piece of real estate, or of calculating the grim cost-benefit ratio of a siege. Failing all this, the white men would have simply starved the Indians out, waiting patiently for them to get so thirsty they would have to choose between dying and fighting.

Though the hide men had escaped Quanah's army with their skins intact, the rest of the frontier wasn't so lucky. After their failure at Adobe Walls, the enraged warriors formed smaller groups and struck blindly in all directions at western settlements from Colorado to Texas.[42] Kiowas under Lone Wolf crossed the border into Texas. Cheyennes and Comanches under Quanah struck first to the east, driving the herd of buffalo hunters' horses, and destroying a wagon train in the Indian territory, then attacking settlements in Texas. Little is known of these raids. Some said Quanah ventured as far north as southern Colorado. He himself later allowed only that, following Adobe Walls, "I take all men, go warpath to Texas."[43] Attacks were made as far north as Medicine Lodge in Kansas. The entire frontier was forced to "fort up."[44] Stages were attacked; stations were burned. Parties of hide men were tortured and killed. Men were staked out on the prairie and women raped and murdered in terrible ways. The Indian outbreak that swept the southern plains that summer killed an estimated one hundred ninety white people and wounded many more. Its effects were immediate. Hide hunting stopped altogether. Hunters and settlers and anyone on the edge of the frontier fled to the protection of the federal forts. Adobe Walls may have failed. But the summer raids accomplished exactly what Isa-tai and Quanah had wanted: massive revenge against the white people that caused panic and terror for a thousand miles. Amid their feelings of rage and frustration, the summer killing must have given them satisfaction. It represented justice to them, the evening of old scores.

Unfortunately for Quanah and Lone Wolf and the others killing white men that summer, their predations also exhausted the last of the white man's patience, and ruined forever the arguments of the peace advocates and pro-Indian humanitarians. On July 26, Grant gave Sherman permission to put the agencies and reservations under military control, thus ending five years of the failed peace policy.[45] On the same day Lieutenant Col. John W. "Black Jack" Davidson, the commander at Fort Sill, ordered all friendly Indians to register and enroll at the agencies by August 3, and to report for a daily roll call. Grant ordered the army to move immediately and in force. All restrictions were lifted on movements of the army. They were at liberty to pursue the Indians to the front porch of the agency at Fort Sill, if necessary, and kill them there. There would be no safe harbor on the reservation, no forgiveness for those who stayed out. The bluecoats were now, as the über-warrior Grant put it simply and bluntly, "to subdue all Indians who offered resistance to constituted authority." The plan, for which an enormous amount of army firepower would be brought to bear, was to hunt them all down.

Nineteen

❖

THE RED RIVER WAR

❖

BY THE LATE summer of 1874 there were only three thousand Comanches left in the world. That was the rough estimate made by the agents at Fort Sill, and it is probably close to the truth. Two thousand of them lived on the Comanche-Kiowa reservation in the southwestern part of what is now Oklahoma. These were the tame Comanches, the broken Comanches. The other thousand had refused to surrender. That group included no more than three hundred fighting men, all that was left of the most militarily dominant tribe in American history.[1] There were also a thousand untamed Southern Cheyennes and a comparable number of renegade Kiowas and Kiowa Apaches. Probably three thousand "hostiles" in all. Eight hundred warriors, at most, on all of the southern plains.[2] Unfortunately for later novelists and filmmakers, they were not arrayed in battle lines on a mesa top, spearheads gleaming in the sun, awaiting the arrival of the bluecoats' main force. There would be no Thermopylae, no epic last stand. This was guerrilla war. As always, the Indians were scattered in various camps and bands. Along with the hostile outliers of the Lakota Sioux, Northern Cheyenne, and Northern Arapaho on the plains north of Nebraska, they were the last of their kind.

Remarkably, these remnants of once powerful tribes all found themselves in the same place: the northern Texas Panhandle. This was not accidental. The panhandle plains were close to the reservations, whose western boundaries were less than a hundred miles to the east. All of the hostiles (even the Quahadis) had camped on the government's land at various times. Some had wintered on the reservations. Many of the apparent "reservation" Indians, moreover, were not, as we have seen, really permanent residents. Indians who docilely queued up to receive federal beef in January might well be raiding the Palo Pinto frontier under the summer moon.

But the best reason to camp in the panhandle was that, in all of the southern plains, there was no better place to hide. In the general vicinity of present-day Amarillo, the dead-flat Llano Estacado gave way to the rocky buttes and muscular upheavals of the caprock, where the elevation fell as much as a thousand feet. Into this giant escarpment the four major forks of the Red River had cut deep, tortuous canyons, creating some of the most dramatic landscapes in the American West. The spectacular Palo Duro Canyon, carved out over the geologic aeons by the Prairie Dog Town Fork of the Red River, was a thousand feet deep, one hundred twenty miles long, between a half-mile and twenty miles wide, and crossed by innumerable breaks, washes, arroyos, and side canyons. This was long the Quahadis' sanctuary. Nestled in the middle of the panhandle plains, an area roughly the size of Ohio, it offered the last free Indians some small chance of delaying the inevitable reckoning with this burgeoning nation of thirty-nine million that was impatient to get on with its destiny.

In August and September the full might of the western army was finally summoned forth to hunt, engage, and destroy what was left of the horse Indians. Sheridan's idea was that the Indians would be harried through four seasons, if necessary. They would be given no rest, no freedom to hunt. They would be starved out. Their villages would be found and burned, their horses taken from them. That this action was probably two decades late was irrelevant now. The will was there, and all editorial opinion in the land supported it.

The final campaign took the form of five mounted columns designed to converge on the rivers and streams east of the caprock. Mackenzie commanded three of them: his own crack Fourth Cavalry was to march from Fort Concho (present-day San Angelo), and probe northward from his old supply camp on the Fresh Water Fork of the Brazos; Black Jack Davidson's Tenth Cavalry would move due west from Fort Sill; and George Buell's Eleventh Infantry would operate in a northwesterly direction between the two.[3] From Fort Bascom in New Mexico, Major William Price would march east with the Eighth Cavalry, while Colonel Nelson A. Miles, a Mackenzie rival and a man destined to become one of the country's most famous Indian fighters, came south with the Sixth Cavalry and Fifth Infantry from Fort Dodge, Kansas. They would rely heavily on Mackenzie's knowledge of the land. In all, forty-six companies and three thousand men took the field, the largest force ever sent against Native Americans.[4] Unlike previous expeditions, including Mackenzie's, they would have permanent supply bases. They would be able to stay in the field indefinitely. In military terms they had other advantages, too, including raw firepower. But the principal, overwhelming edge they had was that their adversaries would be forced to take the field *carrying all their women, children, old men, lodges, horse herds, and belongings with them.*

What followed became known to history as the Red River War. It loomed large in the national consciousness not because it was a real war—it was more of an antiguerrilla campaign—but because of its grand finality. Over the years people had spoken of the last frontier and dreamed of it, but now that romantic idea came fully into focus: *the last frontier.* You could see it, grasp it; the end of the horse tribes' dominion was the end of the very idea of limitlessness, the end of the old America of the imagination and the beginning of the new West that could be measured and divided and subdivided and tamed first by cattlemen and then by everybody else. Within a few years barbed wire would stretch the length and breadth of the plains.

Before that could happen, the Indians had to be found. Even though they were traveling as entire communities, in such a large area the task was still extremely difficult, as Quanah had so brilliantly demonstrated at Blanco Canyon three years before. The five columns stayed in the field for four to five months, crossing and recrossing the various forks of the Red, climbing and descending the caprock, marching and countermarching and following a maddeningly desultory set of trails left by many independent bands of Indians. The soldiers' mad sorties here and there call to mind the Keystone Kops: much frantic pursuit with little to show for it. The Indians may not have fully understood the nature of the campaign against them, but they absolutely understood that they could not beat any of the columns in open battle. So they avoided them, shadowed them; attacked only when they found a small, detached party; or came at night to stampede horses.

It was thus a war with only a handful of major engagements. Colonel Nelson Miles, first in the field, drew first blood. On August 30 he found and attacked a large body of warriors, mostly Cheyennes, near Palo Duro Canyon. His estimates of the enemy force were wildly exaggerated: He claimed to have fought four hundred to six hundred warriors, which is in retrospect completely implausible, then later to have tracked a village containing as many as three thousand people. The latter is purely impossible. In his inflated reports he was one-upping Mackenzie, with whom he had a sharp rivalry, inventing enormous cohorts of the enemy that did not exist. (Mackenzie did not parry; his reports were terse, understated, and made even dramatic engagements sound boring.) In a running, twelve-mile, five-hour fight, Miles killed twenty-five Indians and wounded more, while suffering only two wounded. He burned a large village.[5] In mid-September, William Price encountered a hundred Comanches and Kiowas. A fierce one-and-a-half-hour fight ensued, in which the Indians fought bravely to screen the escape of their families, then withdrew. In October, Buell burned two villages but managed to kill only one Indian. That same month Black Jack Davidson ran down a group of sixty-nine Comanche warriors along with two hundred fifty women and children and two thousand horses. They surrendered to him. In November a detachment of Miles's Fifth Infantry attacked and routed a group of Cheyennes on McClellan Creek. The unnerved Indians broke and fled out on to the plains, leaving most of their possessions behind. The infantry's claims of bravery were somewhat muted when they learned that the Cheyennes could not have returned fire if they had wanted to: They had run out of ammunition.[6] So it went. The campaign played out mostly in dozens of small actions that stretched over the fall, as the bluecoats and Indians played a vast game of hide-and-seek in the breaks below the caprock. The Indians did not lose all the engagements: On November 6, one hundred Cheyennes under their chief Graybeard ambushed twenty-five men from Price's Eighth Cavalry, killing two, wounding four, and forcing the whites to retreat.[7] The war dragged on across the upper panhandle, through a cold, rainy season so muddy and wet that the Indians called it the Wrinkled Hand Chase.

The most important battle—one that was deserving of the name—was fought by Mackenzie's Fourth Cavalry. The converging columns had been his idea in the first place: In theory, the Indians would be driven by one force into another, cornered and destroyed. That was more or less what happened in late September, beneath the spectacular red, brown, white, and ochre battlements of Palo Duro Canyon.

Mackenzie's troops had taken the field on August 23, marching north from Fort Concho in columns of four: 560 enlisted men, 47 officers, 3 surgeons, and 32 scouts—642 in all. They had gone to their old supply camp in Blanco Canyon, on the Freshwater Fork of the Brazos. Then they turned north, up the familiar trail that ran along the razor edge of the Llano Estacado, where Quanah had schooled them three years before in the fine art of escape. The summer had been dry and brutally hot; as the men marched they were enshrouded in a fog of dust. On their first night out, a howling wind sent sparks from their campfires into the desiccated grass, setting it afire and almost destroying their camp. They were used to this now. Because of their experience in the field, and because of Mackenzie's relentless drilling, the Fourth had become the toughest, most seasoned force ever to fight Plains Indians.[8] He was supported by two crack commanders: Captain Eugene B. Beaumont, a veteran of the mauling of Shaking Hand's village on the North Fork of the Red in 1872, who had fought at Gettysburg and had marched with Sherman through Georgia; and Captain N. B. McLaughlin, a Civil War brigadier general who had been the hero of Mackenzie's attack on the Kickapoo village in Mexico in 1873.[9] Because of Mackenzie's intimacy with the terrain—the other commanders followed the roads he blazed during his 1872 expeditions, now known as the Mackenzie Trail—he was given enormous freedom to do what he wanted. "In carrying out your plans," he was informed by his commanding officer in Texas, General C. C. Augur, "you need pay no regard to Department or Reservation lines. You are at liberty to follow the Indians wherever they go, even to the agencies." If the Indians fled to Fort Sill he was "to follow them there, and assuming Command of all troops there at that point, you will take such measures as will ensure entire control of the Indians there."[10]

Mackenzie's troops had scouted for more than a month, fought a few small actions with Comanches who melted away into the canyon lands, and braved torrents of rain that had begun in September and turned the ground into a glutinous mud. Mackenzie was irritable and, as usual, impatient. Riding long distances took a tremendous toll on his shattered body. He drove the men hard, snapping the stumps of his fingers and railing against the conditions that kept his wagon train mired in knee-deep sludge. At dawn on September 25, with his wagons stuck in mud, he left them behind and headed northwest. Walking part of the way to preserve the horses, his men marched twenty grueling miles to Tule Canyon, another starkly beautiful formation etched into the edges of the Llano Estacado, cut by Tule Creek, which flowed north to join the Prairie Dog Town Fork of the Red in Palo

Duro Canyon. At sunset one of his scouts rode in with the news Mackenzie had been waiting for: Up ahead, among the many trails leading crazily off in all directions, there was one very big one, made by about fifteen hundred horses. It led east.

Though his men were bone-weary from the long and muddy march, Mackenzie ordered them back in their saddles. They rode on in darkness, a long dark column moving under a bright harvest moon through thick buffalo grass that muffled the horses' hooves.[11] They followed the trail for five miles, expecting attack at any moment. Mackenzie was aware that his quarry was all around him, silent and elusive as ghosts. When his troops camped for the night, the horses were picketed under a strong guard. The men slept with their boots on and their weapons to hand. Mackenzie stayed in camp the next day, waiting for his supply train to catch up with him. That night, remembering the painful lessons of Blanco Canyon and Shaking Hand's village, and sensing the presence of many Indians, Mackenzie redoubled his precautions. Under his orders, each horse was not only hobbled, meaning that its front legs were tied together, but also cross-sidelined, meaning that forefeet were tied to opposite hind feet. The horses were then secured with thirty-foot, one-inch-thick ropes, which were tied to fifteen-inch iron stakes driven deep into the ground.[12] In addition, "sleeping parties" of twelve to twenty men each were posted around the horse herd.[13] Mackenzie was taking no chances.

As he had expected, the Indians attacked in force that night. The first charge came at ten-thirty. Comanches under the command of Shaking Hand, Wild Horse, and Hears the Sunrise galloped through the perimeter of the camp, firing and yelling, trying to stampede the horses. When this did not work they regrouped and began circling, still hoping to steal the horses. But now they were facing a withering return fire from the horse guards. The Indians withdrew around one o'clock. The next morning, Mackenzie's men rode out of camp to find a line of Comanches on high, level ground. Mackenzie attacked, the Indians retreated. Mackenzie lost only three horses. The only human casualty happened when a Tonkawa scout named Henry shot the horse out from under an elaborately feathered (in northern plains style) Comanche warrior. Henry rode in for the kill, but had forgotten to load his rifle. He was dragged down by his adversary, who began to beat him with his bow. The army troopers, standing nearby and watching, found this amusing. Each time another blow landed on the poor Tonkawa, he pleaded with his friends: "Why you no shoot? Why you no shoot?" Tiring of the joke, one of the soldiers finally shot the Comanche. The Tonk scalped him.[14] The Comanche, of course, knew he was going to die from the moment he lost his horse. While the troopers were snickering, he was fighting his death fight. Such casual cruelty was worthy of a Comanche. It is worth noting that the brave was not carrying a firearm of any kind.

Mackenzie now moved to offense. He ordered the mules loaded with twelve days' rations. Once again he left his supply train—under guard of his infantry and one company of cavalry—then marched southwest, up Tule Canyon. His enemies were no doubt gratified to see him moving away from their camps.

But this was merely a feint executed by a commander who was intimately familiar, as no other white commander was, with the trails through the canyon lands. Mackenzie knew precisely where the Comanche camp was, and was traveling there by the most direct route possible. He had apparently learned of the location of the enemy camp from a captured Comanchero whom Mackenzie had stretched out, presumably painfully, on a wagon wheel. The scouts, riding twenty-five miles out from the main column, had then verified it. The troopers of the Fourth Cavalry held their course until dusk, when the Indians could no longer easily track their movement. They then turned abruptly north, crossing Tule Canyon in the tracks of Mackenzie's 1872 exploration, and headed out across the muddy plains toward Palo Duro Canyon. He marched the men mercilessly through the night over rough terrain, covering the distance in twelve hours.[15] As the sun was just lighting the eastern sky on September 28, the seven companies of the Fourth rode up to the abrupt edge of a yawning chasm in the earth: This was Palo Duro, six miles wide, just below its junction with a half-mile-wide side canyon known as Blanca Cita.

The men crept to the edge of the cliff, where the land fell away in a nine-hundred-foot vertical drop. They were astonished to see below them, stretching for three miles along a stream, five distinct Indian villages consisting of two hundred lodges and a large herd of horses. The white men were looking into the *sanctum sanctorum* of Comancheria. Inside this prodigious scar in the earth caused by ninety million years of erosion was a world unto itself, a graceful canyon split by a meandering river and greened with juniper, hackberry, wild cherry, mesquite, and cottonwood. At the bottom of the gorge was a stream of crystal-clear water that fell from a spring at the canyon's edge.

Though the *taibos* did not know this at the time, camped there were Comanches under a chief named O-ha-ma-tai (the majority of them), Kiowas under Maman-ti, and a small group of Cheyennes under Iron Shirt.

Mackenzie now took what seemed to at least some of his men to be a huge risk. After wandering for a mile along the canyon rim, he discovered a small, precipitous goat trail leading to the canyon floor and into what one of his men later called "the jaws of death."[16] Standing at the head of the tiny trail, he turned to his lieutenant and said simply, "Mr. Thompson, take your men down and open the fight."[17] The men dismounted and, stumbling, slipping, and sliding, one by one eventually reached the bottom.

The risk lay in the exposure of the troops as they came down. It took nearly an hour to get all seven companies down. They got lucky. Maman-ti, the Kiowa chief and medicine man, had consulted the spirits and assured the Indians camped there that they were in no danger of attack from the bluecoats, so they slumbered without sentries that day. Once again their medicine had given away an enormous advantage to the whites. Most of the soldiers reached the valley floor before the Indians realized it. As soon as they spotted the soldiers descending the canyon walls, they responded as they usually did when their village was attacked: They fought fiercely in order to cover the escape of their families. Wrote Sergeant John Charlton:

> [They] attacked us from every quarter, first by dozens, later by hundreds. . . . Many were concealed behind rocks while others were ambushed in the foliage of cedars. . . . The warriors held their ground for a time, fighting desperately to cover the exit of their squaws and pack animals, but under the persistent fire of the troops they soon began falling back.[18]

The troops advanced, with Mackenzie in the lead, through village after village of abandoned Indian lodges. The ground was littered with buffalo robes and dried buffalo meat but also a wide array of white men's goods, evidence of the deep cultural contamination that had seeped into all corners of plains life: army blankets, tinner's snips, stone china, cooking kettles, breech loaders with ammunition, bales of calico, and sacks of flour. The women had evidently gathered these items up in order to save them, then dropped them as they panicked and fled up the canyon on horseback. What ensued was a four-mile running fight, during which four Comanches were killed. But soon the troopers were surrounded by Indians again, who now fired down on them from the canyon walls, a circumstance that suggested they had trapped themselves. "How will we ever get out of here?" one frightened trooper asked, afraid the command could be annihilated. Hearing this, Mackenzie snapped back: "I brought you in. I will take you out."[19] Mackenzie ordered the men forward into the teeth of the attack. His audacity worked: The Indians turned and retreated up the walls of Blanca Cita Canyon, following in the path of their families who had fled earlier.

Mackenzie did not follow. Instead, he turned back and ordered the villages burned. Bonfires roared; the scent of burning buffalo meat filled the air along with the smells of scorched Indian Department flour and sugar. Around three o'clock, his companies climbed back up the canyon walls, this time with 1,424 captured horses. Once up on the high plains again, the five hundred or so men formed a "hollow square," a sort of living corral in which the captured herd was driven along. They marched twenty miles, returning to their supply camp in Tule Canyon at one a.m. The men, who had been awake and in the saddle for thirty-one of thirty-three hours, were exhausted. Sergeant Charlton, who tried to sleep, was awakened by Mackenzie's voice "pitched to that high, fretful key," saying "Wake up, Sergeant! Wake up your men and look after the horses!"[20]

After breakfast Mackenzie gave the best of the horses to his scouts, cut out a few for his own use, and then ordered the others—more than a thousand— shot. Custer had shot horses on the Washita in 1868, but that was mere expediency, since his column was in grave danger of annihilation. Mackenzie now did it as a military tactic, a way to take away the Indians' means of survival. It was a gruesome job, and it took time. The infantry roped the crazed horses and led them into firing squads. As more and more horses were killed, they became harder to handle. The last one was not shot until almost three o'clock in the afternoon. The result was a massive pile of dead horses. They rotted at the head of Tule Canyon, then turned to bleached bones that remained there for many years, becoming both a navigational landmark and a grotesque monument marking the end of the horse tribes' dominion on the plains. Eventually some enterprising person gathered what was left up and sold it for fertilizer. Mackenzie's slaughter of the Comanche horses also spawned a legend. On certain nights, it is said, a phantom herd can be seen galloping through the canyon, riderless, their spectral manes flying in the wind.

Thus ended the Battle of Palo Duro Canyon. Only four Indians had been killed, but Mackenzie had dealt them a devastating blow. No one knows how many of them were camped in the village, but the number of lodges suggests perhaps a thousand. And these Indians now faced a terrible new reality. They were mostly afoot, without shelter, food, or clothing, facing winter on the high plains where the buffalo herds were being quickly thinned out by the hide men. They had been routed, in large number, from their last important hideout. Most of the Indians who escaped through Blanca Cita Canyon that day straggled back to Fort Sill in the following weeks, thoroughly beaten and never to roam off the reservation again.[21]

Sheridan's great campaign was soon over. The hide-and-seek game continued through the winter, with ever fewer Indians as players. A large number of Indians had returned to Fort Sill in the fall. Those who had not were short of food; some were starving to death. In February, Lone Wolf and the last of the Kiowas came in. In March, 825 Southern Cheyennes gave up. Small groups and individuals streamed in continuously. In April the Comanche bands of Shaking Hand, Hears the Sunrise, and Wild Horse surrendered with thirty-five warriors, one hundred forty women and children, and seven hundred horses. They were disarmed, and had their horses and mules taken from them. They were initially put into internment camps west of Fort Sill. Chiefs who had broken treaties or promises were often dealt with harshly. The Kiowa Satanta was sent to a prison in Huntsville, Texas, where he committed suicide by diving headfirst from a second-floor window of the prison hospital. Others were sent by rail to exile in Florida. When the authorities realized how thoroughly broken the horse tribes were, they allowed most of the chiefs to come back. For all of its lack of large-scale drama, Sheridan in his report for 1875 called the Red River War "the most successful of any Indian campaign in this country since its settlement by the whites."

By the end of April there were only a few bands of southern Plains Indians that had not surrendered, by far the largest of which were Quanah's Quahadis. As far as the army could tell, the band had completely disappeared after the Battle of Adobe Walls.[22] There were four hundred of them, including one hundred able-bodied fighting men. In spite of their numbers, and a large horse herd, they had accomplished the signal feat of completely evading the white man's incessant patrols. They had done this by quick and agile movement. They had also stayed well south of the other concentrations of Indians in the panhandle, spending most of their time camped southeast of present-day Lubbock, near the towns of Gail and Snyder, just on the eastern side of the caprock. Mackenzie searched for them twice there, acting on intelligence from captured Kiowas. He had found nothing. He had in fact spent a good deal of time looking for Quanah. In his third and last scouting trip in December 1874 he had spent seventeen days and traveled two hundred fifty-five miles, all in the southern part of the Llano Estacado. His men had trudged through deep snow and ice storms from today's Floydada to Snyder, during which time they had killed exactly three Indians. They did find a fresh trail heading across the high plains to the Mucha-que country, a favorite trading site near today's Gail. Mackenzie followed. He was so sure that he had Quanah's band in his sights that he requested that an immediate detachment of troops be sent from Fort Concho to intercept it. Nothing came of that, either. Bogged down in yet another snowstorm, Mackenzie received a message from Sheridan that his war duties were over. He was to report to Fort Sill and assume command of the Comanche-Kiowa and Cheyenne-Arapaho reservations.[23]

In a later interview, Quanah confirmed that he had in fact spent the entire fall and winter playing cat and mouse with the federals. "Having several hundred good horses," he said, "we kept a good watch for the approach of the enemy, and when we would learn that they were coming in our direction we would quickly move. Several of my men, with our families, kept up that kind of tactic all winter. . . . During that time we were almost continuously going, as the soldiers were after us and many times they were almost upon us."[24] They hunted buffalo when they could, and when they could not eat buffalo or horse meat they reverted to the old Comanche ways of the prehorse days in Wyoming, eating nuts, grubs, and rodents. They most likely traded with Comancheros who had slipped through Mackenzie's blockade. They had a very hard time.

On March 16, 1875, Mackenzie arrived to take command at Fort Sill. By mid-April he was aware that only one large band remained in the wild, and he knew who they were. On April 23 he dispatched a special delegation to try to persuade Quanah to come in peacefully. It consisted of a Dr. Jacob J. Sturm, a self-styled "physician" and translator who had married a Caddo woman, plus three Comanches including the Quahadi chief Wild Horse. They had only a vague idea of where they were going. They headed southwest from Fort Sill, crossed the Red River and traveled along the eastern edge of the caprock. Near the present town of Matador they came upon the small, fifteen-lodge village of the Quahadi chief Black Beard. The emissaries were received cordially, and Black Beard readily accepted Mackenzie's offer to come in peaceably with his fifty Comanches. The winter had been brutally hard. He said he was tired of war, and told the white men where Quanah's camp was. It was "two sleeps" distant. On May 1, Sturm and his group found the camp more or less exactly where Mackenzie had thought it was. Sturm wrote:

On our arrival in camp the Indians rode up from every direction to see who we were and finding we were peace messengers they invited us to alight from our horses, which were taken care of by the squaws while we were escorted to a large tent by the men. Here we divided our tobacco, coffee, and sugar with them which pleased them immensely having had none of the luxuries for a long time.[25]

He spent the next two days in counsel with both Quanah and Isa-tai, who had somehow retained his influence and position in spite of his glaring failure at Adobe Walls. Sturm made an interesting observation about him.

The Medicine Man says he is no chief but admits that he has much influence over his people. . . . He further states that he has not acquired this influence by being a warrior and what influence he has he acquired by kind treatment of his people, never abusing them. He says he has a big heart, loves everybody and every living thing that he never gets mad or strikes even a beast.[26]

Quanah, unexpectedly, was preaching surrender. He had been foremost among the white-man haters; he had burned hottest for revenge for the death of his father, the capture of his mother and sister, and the death of his nephew and other friends and family. He had demonstrated a willful disregard of personal danger at Adobe Walls, and he had spent the early summer killing white people. He had long despised the Comanches who traveled the white man's road. He also understood that he was a half-breed, and that his mother had been a white woman. Now he spoke passionately in favor of taking the white man's road. Parker family legend has it that in order to make his decision, Quanah had gone to a mesa top to meditate. He had begun to pray to the Great Spirit for guidance when he saw a wolf that howled at him and ran off in the direction of Fort Sill. Then saw an eagle, who swooped down at him several times, and flew off to the northeast. He took these as signs that he should surrender.[27] His people agreed. Isa-tai left a pictographic note for thirty men of the band who were out on a buffalo hunt, writing it on buffalo skin and sticking it on a pole, and on May 6, 1875, the entire group left for Fort Sill.

They traveled slowly. Their horses, weakened from lack of food and the harsh winter, were unable to do otherwise. The slowness of the travel lent a sort of wistfulness to the journey. There was a sense that they were performing what amounted to the last rites of freedom. The Comanches hunted every day. They killed buffalo and antelope and wild horses and feasted on food cooked in rock-lined pits. They stopped periodically while women dried and packed meat, the men raced horses, and the children chased prairie chickens. They drank the white man's coffee, loaded with sugar. They danced the old dances. Sturm said that "they make it to be the last Medicine Dance they ever expect to have on these broad plains. They say they will abandon their roving life and try to learn to live as white people do."[28] Strangely, Sturm records no bitterness, no sadness. Perhaps this was simply a failure of imagination. Perhaps the People really had no idea what bean farming or sheep ranching was going to be like, or what it was like to live in a single place in a single dwelling and never move with the spring herds, or what Comanche men would find to do with themselves if there was no hunting or fighting and no way to prove their worth.

At noon on June 2, nearly a month after they left their camp, four hundred seven Quahadis arrived at Signal Station, a few miles west of Fort Sill, and surrendered themselves, their fifteen hundred horses, and their arms to the military authorities of the United States. They were treated well. Unlike the other tribes and bands before them, the warriors were not sequestered, under guard, in a roofless icehouse with a stone floor, where once a day a wagon stacked with raw meat came by, and soldiers threw chunks of it over the walls.[29] The women, children, and old men, meanwhile, were taken off to their appointed campground. At the time there were only fifty holdouts remaining. They were all camped on the reservation.

From the moment of Quanah's arrival, Colonel Mackenzie took an intense interest in him. In spite of his travails with them, Mackenzie admired the Quahadis. When he learned they were coming in, he wrote Sheridan: "I think better of this band than of any other on the reserve. . . . I shall let them down as easily as I can." He did, in fact. The Quahadis were allowed to keep a large number of their horses, and he made sure that no one in Quanah's band was confined in the icehouse or guardhouse at Fort Sill.[30] There are no records of what happened when the two men first met, or what they said to each other. What is known is that before Quanah even arrived, Mackenzie had found out via messenger the identity of his mother and had written a letter, dated May 19, 1875, to the military quartermaster at Dennison, Texas, inquiring about the whereabouts of Cynthia Ann and Prairie Flower. The letter was also published in a Dallas newspaper, and managed to elicit the information that both Quanah's sister and his mother were dead.[31] He had not yet met Quanah, but the letter was the beginning of what history records as a remarkable friendship.

Twenty

FORWARD, IN DEFEAT

THE RESERVATION WAS a shattering experience. It was bad enough that the Comanches, having bent to the white man's will, had to line up meekly to receive his beneficence. Like small, helpless children they were now unable to feed or clothe themselves. But as usual—to layer nightmare upon nightmare—much of this desperately needed welfare never came. The system was both cruel and humiliating: The *taibos* had taken away everything that had defined Comanche existence and offered nothing but crude squalor in its place. From the moment the People arrived, there was only a great yawning void of hunger and desperation and dependency. There was no way out and no way back.[1]

The white man's charity came in two forms: food rations and annuities. The latter consisted of $30,000 worth of goods each year for the combined Comanche and Kiowa tribes. Divided by three thousand residents, that meant $10 per person. The goods included axes, frying pans, thimbles, tin plates, butcher knives, and basic clothing. A lot of it was shoddy, if not completely worthless. The Comanches usually sold it cheap to white men. The beef ration of 1.5 pounds per person per day, on which the Indians mainly survived, turned out to be a bureaucratic and logistical disaster. The beef was issued *on the hoof,* and the government's assumption was that an animal would produce edible food in the amount of 50 percent of its weight. This was a fine notion in a wet, fertile season when there was plenty of grass.

But in winter many of the range-fed cattle lost so much weight that many had value only as hides. Since the reservation's game was nearly hunted out, and the buffalo rarely came into range, and the nonbeef components of the ration (flour, coffee, sugar, salt) were less than half of what a soldier got—when they came at all—many families went hungry. The weekly issue did at least provide a diversion, if a pathetic one. The ration cows would be released from their pens, and then the Comanche warriors, whooping and yelling, would run them down and kill them with bows, arrows, and pistols.[2]

Strange, then, that this despondent, crippled, post-cataclysmic world became the staging ground for the remarkable career of Quanah Parker, as he would insist on being called, the man who became the most successful and influential Native American of the late nineteenth century and the first and only man ever to hold the title Principal Chief of the Comanches. His rise was doubly strange since he had been the hardest of the hard cases, the last holdout of the last band of the fanatical Quahadis, the only band of any tribe in North America that had never signed a treaty with the white man. At the time of his surrender he was twenty-seven years old. He was known as a fierce and charismatic warrior, a true killer, probably the toughest of his generation of Comanches, which was saying something. He had killed many Indians and white people in his short life, a statistic that will remain forever unknown because in the reservation years he quite intelligently refused to address the subject. He had led his own band in the wilderness after his elopement with Weckeah and was famous for having done so; along with Isa-tai he was the most prominent and the fastest rising of the young war chiefs. His surrender to Mackenzie in June 1875 ended such traditional career prospects forever.

But it also marked the beginning of something. His attitude toward his captivity had completely changed by the time he arrived at Fort Sill.[3] He would take the white man's road. He would leave the glories of the free life on the plains behind and he would not look back. Just as important, he would strive to lead his often recalcitrant, retrogressive tribe down that road. That meant the white man's farming and ranching, white man's schools for the children, white man's commerce and politics and language. The void that loomed before the pitiable remnant of the Comanches was for Quanah Parker a grand opportunity. He would remake himself as a prosperous, tax-paying citizen of the United States of America who dressed in wool suits and Stetson hats and attended school board meetings. And he would try to haul the rest of the Comanche nation along with him. In the dreary, hopeless winter of 1875–76, the notion of bourgeois citizen-Comanches was just short of ridiculous; no one would have wanted it anyway. But Quanah saw the future clearly. On the high and wild plains he had been a fighter of jaw-dropping aggressiveness; now he would move just as resolutely from the life of a late Stone Age barbarian into the mainstream of industrial American culture.

Quanah arrived on the harsh shores of the American nation like many other immigrants: in abject poverty. When he reached Fort Sill he had two wives, a daughter, a degree of standing in the tribe, and little more. He was a ration-drawer like everyone else, living in a tipi near the agency, waiting patiently in long lines for food. Whatever wealth he had possessed in the way of horse-flesh was gone. Killing or dispersing Comanche horse herds was an integral part of the whites' economic and military destruction of the Comanche tribe. In both white and Comanche terms, he was destitute.

Quanah was, moreover, only one of a number of chiefs with a claim on band or tribal leadership. There were older leaders like Horseback (Nokoni), Milky Way (Penateka), Shaking Hand (Kotsoteka), Wild Horse (Quahadi), and most especially Hears the Sunrise (Yamparika), all of whom wielded more influence than he did. But he was undeterred. From his first days on the reservation he plotted to advance himself and was not shy about it. Perhaps he had discovered something about his true nature in the days when he and Isa-tai had recruited Indians from five tribes to attack the buffalo hunters, a feat unprecedented in plains history, and one that caused him to be deferred to even by such great chiefs as the Kiowas' Lone Wolf. Up until that disastrous first morning at Adobe Walls, when Isa-tai's magic failed and the buffalo guns roared, they had been stunningly successful.

Quanah understood that the way to power was through the white man and his power to designate and appoint leaders, as it was for the native populations in nineteenth-century British colonies in Malaysia, India, and elsewhere. Thus he cultivated both the Indian agent, the Quaker J. M. Haworth, and the army commander, who from April 1, 1875, until 1877 was the irascible and brutally competent Ranald Slidell Mackenzie. Mackenzie had been surprised to learn of his parentage, and had taken some trouble, starting with his May 19 letter, to find out what had happened to his mother and sister. In one of their early meetings, Mackenzie told Quanah what he had learned, thus shattering Quanah's immemorial dreams of a reunion with his beloved mother.

Still, Quanah had a fierce curiosity about his white family and continued to write, which meant having someone else write, letters seeking information. (Throughout the reservation years, Quanah's apparent level of literacy varied with the educational level of whomever he got to write for him; he sounds alternately like a hillbilly, a pidgin-speaking Indian, and an English professor.) Evidence of his blossoming relationship with his new friend Mackenzie was a letter Mackenzie wrote on Quanah's behalf to Cynthia Ann's eighty-two-year-old uncle Isaac Parker in Fort Worth. In it, he explained to Isaac that Quanah was upset that the Parkers were apparently refusing to acknowledge him as a member of their family, and argued that Quanah "certainly should not be held responsible for the sins of a former generation of Comanches, and is a man whom it is worth trying to do something with."[4] Isaac never replied. The two men met on many other occasions. They lived for a while in close proximity to each other—Quanah in his tipi and Mackenzie in the row of houses that constituted the Fort Sill officers' quarters. Quanah later told Charles Goodnight, after Goodnight complimented him on his manners, that it had been Mackenzie who had taken the time to teach him about white ways.[5] This suggested that the two men spent significant time together. It would have been something to watch the etiquette lessons given by America's greatest Indian fighter to the man who would turn out to be the last Comanche chief.

In a world of sullen, dispossessed Indians, camped disconsolately in tipis in the grassy, rolling hills and stream bottoms around Fort Sill, Quanah made a point of being cheerful, helpful, and cooperative. That was his nature anyway. He was naturally gregarious, the product of an intensely communal society where consensus-building was the most valued political skill and the particular skill that he possessed in abundance. A young war chief's standing was based entirely on his ability to recruit warriors to go along with him on raids and military expeditions. Recruitment and consensus was what the Adobe Walls campaign was all about. Quanah volunteered to bring back several Comanches who had left the reservation to hunt buffalo. He also brought in a brave who was charged with murdering a soldier.[6]

His approach soon paid off. When agent Haworth divided up the tribes into "beef bands" in order to streamline the rationing process, he appointed leaders of each band, and by 1878, Quanah had been named head of the third-largest band. Thus, like a ward boss in Chicago of a later day, he controlled the distribution of goods, and obviously guaranteed his own take. This was his first taste of power in the new political order, and it did not come without consequences. Some of the Comanche leaders despised him and his favored status with the *taibos*. They would force him to fight for whatever power he got for virtually his whole life on the reservation.

Just as important for the new politics of captivity, Quanah agreed to go on a special mission for his new friend Mackenzie. His task: to track down and bring back a small group of renegade Comanches and their families who remained outside the reservation. In July 1877, Quanah set out to find them with two older Comanche men, three women, and several government pack mules loaded with supplies. He carried a white flag and a stern letter from Colonel Mackenzie on army letterhead detailing Quanah's mission and promising severe consequences for anyone who interfered with it. Still, it was an extremely dangerous undertaking. The land to the west of Fort Sill was loaded with buffalo hunters and other cold-eyed men in the hide business who sought revenge on Indians in general and specifically on Comanches. A lightly armed party of six consisting mostly of old men and women would have been easy prey. That Quanah, until his surrender one of the most arrogant warriors of the plains and at the height of his physical prowess, would undertake such a bloodless diplomatic mission with women as his outriders was extraordinary. It showed just how much he had changed his thinking. Or perhaps it showed how much he wanted to impress his new bosses.

Quanah and his party headed westward across the rolling plains, climbed the caprock, and crossed the dead-flat grasslands of the high plains under the scorching summer sun. Near the Texas–New Mexico border he encountered a unit of forty black soldiers from the Tenth Cavalry under Captain Nicholas Nolan, a white man. They were looking for the same group of runaway Comanches, who had apparently attacked some buffalo hunters. The bluecoats were anticipating considerable glory when they caught the renegades and were thus unhappy when they learned of Quanah's commission and of Colonel Mackenzie's plan to give the criminal Indians a free pass back to Fort Sill.[7] Quanah told Nolan that he knew where the Indians were and that he was heading southeast to find them. This was a bald-faced lie, and had its intended effect. Nolan's troops took off in hot pursuit, in the wrong direction. In their haste they also neglected to provision themselves adequately for a trip across the plains in high summer. They soon ran out of water. The men were forced to drink their own and their horses' urine, mixing it with sugar to make it more palatable. They killed and drank the blood of two of their horses. They somehow survived.[8] They never found anybody.

Quanah had no such trouble, either with the searing heat and bone-dry land or in locating the runaway Indians. He found them camped on the Pecos River and met with the men in council over four days, laboring to convince them that they had to give up their lives on the open plains. "Quanah told us that it was useless for us to fight longer, for the white people would kill us all if we kept on fighting," wrote Herman Lehmann, a former captive who had become a full-fledged, battle-hardened Comanche warrior and who was among the renegades. "If we went on the reservation the Great White Father at Washington would feed us, and give us homes, and we would in time become like the white man, with lots of good horses and cattle, and pretty things to wear."[2] This may sound disingenuous: Quanah knew as well as anyone what life on the reservation was like. But there is no reason to doubt his hope or his optimism. His entire career was based on his peculiarly sunny view of the future. He always genuinely believed things would get better, if he could only convince his people to change their old ways. Persuasive as always, and with unmatched credentials as a killer of white men, Quanah won the renegades over. Then he escorted them to their new home, a distance of two hundred fifty miles as the crow flies, across the same potentially lethal plains. Now, of course, his band was far more numerous and therefore much more visible. Quanah took no chances. He traveled by night. He abandoned three hundred horses. There were still several tense encounters with whites, but according to Lehmann, Quanah, speaking broken English, somehow managed to talk his way through.[9]

On August 20, Quanah brought fifty-seven Indians (probably no more than fifteen fighting men) and one white captive (Lehmann) into the reservation.[10] When Lehmann first saw the bluecoats approaching, he panicked. "I was riding a black mare and a pretty swift horse," he wrote in a memoir. "So I turned and rode for life back toward the Wichita Mountains." But as a horseman he was no match for Quanah, who rode him down after four miles and gently persuaded him to return.[11] (Lehmann, who was seventeen at the time, lived with Quanah and his family for three years and considered him his foster father. He was sent back to his mother in 1880.)[12] Mackenzie was impressed that Quanah had been able to get everyone home without bloodshed, and praised the young chief's "excellent conduct in a danger-ous expedition." Leveraging this goodwill—something he was quite good at—Quanah persuaded Mackenzie and Haworth that the renegades should not be sent off to prison in Fort Leavenworth. For that he also earned the gratitude of his tribe.

He won even more political points when he successfully opposed the government's plan to merge the Kiowa-Comanche agency with the Wichita agency, which would have meant a fifty-mile trek for some Comanches just to draw rations. By 1880 he had become the acknowledged leader of the Quahadis and the Indian leader most often consulted by the agent.[13]

For all of his cooperation with the white man, however, and his commit-ment to the new road, Quanah was not yet quite ready to put aside all dreams of the old life. He and others lobbied hard for permission to go on a buffalo hunt. It is not clear whether this was to be one last buffalo hunt or merely the first of several, but in March 1878 a group of Comanches and Kiowas, including some women and children, were finally allowed to go out, unsu-pervised, on a hunt. This was cause for great excitement among the Indians. Perhaps it was the simple urge to validate their own past, or maybe a desire to show their children who they really were. They would ride out again into the great oceanic emptiness that so terrified the *taibos*. They would kill and eat, and use the gallbladder to salt the raw bloody liver, and drink the warm milk from the udders mixed with blood, and it would be, however briefly, like the old days. They rode west from Fort Sill toward the high plains, full of dreams and nostalgia. They understood that the hide hunters had taken a terrible toll on the buffalo. But they had never doubted that there were herds left to hunt.

What they found shocked them. There were no buffalo anywhere, no liv-ing ones, anyway, only vast numbers of stinking, decaying corpses or bones bleached white by the sun. The idea of traveling a hundred miles and not seeing a buffalo was unimaginable. It had not been true at the time of their surrender. Disappointed—perhaps heartbroken might be a better word— Quanah and his cohort pushed deeper into the Texas Panhandle, certainly well beyond where the army and Indian agents had intended them to go. He led them back to the old Quahadi sanctuary, the magnificent rock bat-tlements of Palo Duro Canyon in the upper Texas Panhandle, which had once teemed with bison herds. This, too, was an emotional moment. Most of them, who knew it affectionately as Prairie Dog, had never expected to see it again.

Nor had it ever occurred to them that a white man might now *own* the second-largest canyon in the West. But in the three years since the end of the Red River War an enterprising white man had in fact managed to acquire it. Charles Goodnight—the ranger who had tracked Peta Nocona to the Pease River in 1860 and had later tracked Quanah and his brother to those same canyon lands—was now the sole proprietor of the Palo Duro. He was already one of the more prominent ranchers in the state, having given his name to one of its main cattle highways, the Goodnight-Loving Trail, which he opened in 1866 to bring cattle to markets in New Mexico and Colorado.

On a bitter cold day, with snow on the ground, the Indians entered the canyon, and, still finding no buffalo, started killing Goodnight's cattle. Goodnight rode out to meet them. The intruders were in an ugly mood, having just learned that their sacred canyons now "belonged" to someone else. They put Goodnight and an interpreter in the middle of a circle and asked him what he was doing there. "I am raising cattle," he replied. They then asked, provocatively, did he not know that "the country was theirs." He answered that he "had heard that they claimed the country but that the great captain of the Texans also claimed it."[14] A parley with Quanah followed. When Goodnight asked what his name was, he replied in his broken English: "Maybe so two names—Mr. Parker or Quanah."[15]

Then Quanah asked Goodnight where he came from, a loaded question intended to elicit the answer that he was one of the hated Texans. Comanches always drew a sharp distinction between Texans and everyone else. Texan encroachment, after all, had ended their way of life. Goodnight lied and said he was from Colorado, whereupon the Indians tried to prove him wrong, grilling him about every prominent landmark and river in Colorado. Since he had pioneered the cattle trail to Denver and beyond, he was able to answer all their questions correctly. Satisfied that he was not a Tejano, Quanah said he was ready to make a treaty. "We're ready to talk business," said Quanah. "What have you got?" Goodnight answered: "I've got plenty of guns and bullets, good men and good shots, but I don't want to fight unless you force me. You keep order and behave yourself and I will give you two beeves every other day until you find out where the buffaloes are."[16] Quanah agreed, and thus was a "treaty" made between the legendary Comanche chief and the rancher they called the Leopard Coat Man. (Two generations hence, Texas schoolchildren would be required to study this odd agreement.) Several days later, twenty-five black soldiers under a white lieutenant, who had been summoned by Goodnight, arrived to deal with the Indian threat. Goodnight assured them that the problem had been solved, and the Indians remained camped there another three weeks.

There was one incident where Quanah's inveterate warrior instincts flashed briefly. It is worth noting because there is nothing else in his reservation life that remotely resembled this sequence of events; he really had left just about everything behind; the ill-fated hunt had just seemed like a reasonable idea, a modest gesture to placate people who had lost everything else. Comanches and Kiowas had long been uneasy about black troops, whom they called "buffalo soldiers" because their tight, curly hair reminded them of a buffalo's ruff. They considered them bad medicine and were the only adversaries they would not scalp. After a fight had broken out between the soldiers and the Indians, Goodnight gathered Quanah and the army lieutenant to discuss the problem. The lieutenant told the interpreter that if the Indians did not settle down he would take their guns away. Quanah replied, in Spanish: "You can have the guns." Then he pointed to some lodge poles and said "We will use those on the negroes." The idea was: He would not waste any bullets on the buffalo soldiers, and he would not need anything but the poles to defeat them.[17] This was the old, snarling Comanche arrogance, now consigned to making idle threats. Quanah was never known for it in the reservation years; perhaps this outburst was his last indulgence. He and his party returned to Fort Sill without ever finding a buffalo. Any lingering notions that they could return to their ancient ways, even momentarily, were now forever dispelled. The buffalo were all dead, and the white man owned the sacred canyons.

What really changed Quanah's life on the reservation was the cattle business, which by the late 1870s was transforming the entire western frontier. While the Indian wars raged, the Texas cattle industry, which had its origins in the Spanish missions of the mid-eighteenth century, had been steadily increasing in size. In 1830 there were an estimated 100,000 head of cattle in the state; by 1860 there were between four and five million.[18] Though the Civil War temporarily arrested the industry's development, by the latter 1860s the state was fairly bursting with beef in search of markets. The big northerly drives started in earnest in 1866, taking Texas cattle north to the railheads in Kansas, and grew geometrically with the surrender of the Comanches and Kiowas. Many of these cattle traveled along the Western Trail, which led through Fort Griffin and across the Red River and north to Dodge City.

That trail happened to lead through the heart of the Comanche-Kiowa Reservation in Oklahoma.

Such intrusions were neither innocent nor coincidental. The cowboys would often linger on the reservation, sometimes for weeks, fattening thousands of their cattle on the lush grass that belonged to Indians. The contractors who supplied beef to the reservation also turned their animals out to graze on the Indian lands. None of this was legal, but there were no troops to police it. And many of the big ranchers south of the Red River, facing competition for grazing lands, now coveted the same reservation grass.

The Indians' response to the white incursions was to form what amounted to protection rackets. Quanah was the first to figure out how to make them work. Groups of armed Comanches, not exactly war parties but not terribly friendly, either, patrolled the southern and western parts of their reservation looking for trespassing herds. A drover named Julian Gunter recalled encountering "a large band of Indians" who rode slowly around Gunter's herd. Quanah, who led them, lectured him: "Your government gave this land to the Indian to be his hunting ground," said Quanah. "But you go through and scare the game and your cattle eat the grass so the buffalo leaves and the Indian starves." Sensing what was required, Gunter let Quanah's braves cut six "fat cows" from the herd for themselves and went on his way.[19] On another occasion a cattleman named G. W. Roberson was similarly forced by Quanah "to give him a beef." Roberson explained: "We had to kind of stand in with those scoundrels. If you didn't they come in at night and run your horses off or stampede your cattle. And most any man would rather give them a beef than have them run his cattle off."[20] Some even reported that Quanah was charging fees in the form of a one-dollar tax per wagon and ten cents per head of stock.[21] Once they had paid up, of course, the cattlemen enjoyed the protection of Quanah's men while they crossed the reservation. That "protection" included advice on the best route to follow and on sources of water. Those who did not cooperate made payment in other ways: One outfit lost 295 head to the Comanches on a single drive. Nor was Quanah reluctant to play hardball politics inside the reservation. He was happy to report the Kiowas to the agent for taking cattle from herds heading north and assaulting cowboys while he himself managed to obtain official permission from the agent to practice what amounted to an identical form of blackmail.[22]

But these were mere annoyances. The larger issue was whether or not the Indians should do what everybody else in America did: lease out their

unused grazing lands. In this case, to white cattle outfits. This was a surprisingly controversial question, considering that the Indians were sitting on
top of more than three thousand square miles of prime grazing land. Many
Indians, including most of the Kiowas and a portion of the Comanches,
thought it was a bad idea. They believed it would encourage white men to
take over the land, jeopardizing the Indians' future as stockmen. Such gratu-
itous income from "grass money," moreover, would lead the young men to
become lazy and gamble. The other side, represented by Quanah, saw it as a
legitimate way for Indians to make money off what was happening anyway.
The money could be used to build their own herds. There was plenty of land:
Some two million acres were available, and thirty-five white cattle outfits
were lining up for the privilege.

The question was hotly debated in a political fight that lasted from 1880
to 1884. Quanah soon emerged as the leader of the pro-leasing faction. He
traveled several times to Washington to help build his case. In one of his
audiences with the secretary of the interior, he dismissed the antileasers contemptuously, saying "I cannot tell what objection they have to it, unless they
have not got sense. They are kind of old fogy, on the wild road yet, unless
they have not got brains enough to sabe [sic] the advantage there is in it." His
rivals—Hears the Sunrise, Isa-tai, Lone Wolf, White Wolf, and many Kiowas—meanwhile, denounced Quanah as "bought by the cattlemen."

They were at least partly right. Quanah had been put on the payroll at
$35 a month by one of the leading cattle outfits. The cattlemen, who were
rabid advocates of the leasing of Indian lands, saw him as their spokesman, a
job he performed very well because he believed his tribe's interests were the
same as theirs. The white ranchers also very likely contributed to Quanah's
own growing herd of cattle, and paid for his trips to Washington to counter-
balance the lobbying done in the nation's capital by Hears the Sunrise and
the antileasers, who repeatedly demanded that Quanah be stripped of his
authority as a tribal leader.[23]

On its face, Quanah's arrangement with the stockmen might seem like
simple corruption. But it could only be seen that way against standards that
did not exist on the frontier. Quanah was merely playing the game the way
everyone else did. Almost everyone who was a party to leasing talks had a
substantial conflict of interest. Isa-tai, who opposed leasing, was actually
running his own protection racket for two thousand head of cattle that
grazed continuously on Indian land, as was Permansu, the nephew of the

famous Comanche chief Ten Bears.[24] The Indian agent, the agency clerk, and other agency personnel all had received payments from cattlemen or had vested interests in the outcome. (The agent was eventually fired for his inside dealing.) Four other Comanches were also on the stockmen's payroll, as were several "squaw men" (white men who had married Indian women) on the reservation. Bribes were being paid all around. This was the world in which Quanah was learning to operate: It was his introduction to how business was done in the rawboned American West of the latter nineteenth century, where corners were routinely cut and where conflicts of interest were the rule rather than the exception. Such behavior often resulted in the Indians being cheated or defrauded. No one ever cheated Quanah, as far as we know. He understood the game too well, and was always a step ahead of everyone else, including the white stockmen. He played by the rules as he perceived them to be, and he was as good as most white men at playing the game. He also truly believed that making money off the unused land was best for his tribe.

He was right. He won the fight outright in 1884, when Indians on the reservation voted to approve leasing. Rights to Indian grass were awarded to cattlemen who had been handpicked by him. When asked pointedly by the secretary of the interior whether he had been compensated, Quanah replied: "They have not paid me anything for the lease." That was probably technically true: He was on the payroll long before the lease was negotiated. In the end the Indians got six cents per acre per year on a six-year lease. It was later increased to ten cents an acre. As part of the deal, the cattlemen also agreed to hire fifty-four Indians as cowboys, which could be seen as a form of patronage: Quanah taking care of his own.

After the leases were signed, Quanah worked even harder to establish himself as the principal chief of the Comanches, a title that had never before existed. In the history of the tribe there had been no need for centralized political power, or for a single spokesman of any kind. Now there was. He was appointed to serve as judge on the Court of Indian Offenses, a curious body that dispensed justice that was somewhere between English common law and Comanche tribal tradition. His growing political power was instrumental in preventing the Ghost Dance cult from spreading to Comanches and Kiowas—the same cult that led to the infamous massacre of Miniconjou Sioux at Wounded Knee in South Dakota in 1890—for which he received notice in the national press. The Ghost Dance was driven by an apocalyptic vision of the return of dead Indians and the annihilation or disappearance of whites. Quanah, having witnessed the destructive power of Isa-tai's grand visions at Adobe Walls, opposed it from the start and spoke against it. In a letter to the agent he stated: "I hear the koway [Kiowas] and shianis [Cheyennes] say that there are Indians come from heaven and want to take me and my People and go see to see them. But I tell them that I want my People to work and pay no attention to that. . . . We depend òn the government to help us and no [*sic*] them."[25]

Meanwhile, his own business was prospering. He built up his own cattle herd by gifts from the cattlemen, by outright purchase, and by selective breeding until he was running nearly five hundred head. His new friend Charles Goodnight gave him a prime Durham bull for breeding. He became a supplier to his own people: In 1884 alone he sold forty head to the agency, making $400 on the transaction. He also came to control a pasture of forty-four thousand acres (sixty-nine square miles) that was soon known as the Quanah Pasture, some of which he leased out to cattlemen who paid him directly. He had a hundred-fifty-acre farm that was tended by a white man and two hundred hogs, three wagons, and one buggy.

A few years earlier, in 1886, something else had added to his growing celebrity: James DeShields published the first book about his mother, Cynthia Ann, which received wide circulation in the Southwest. Anyone who was not aware of Quanah's origins now learned about them in minute detail. The book included Quanah's photograph and a description of him that was both flattering and accurate.

> Quanah speaks English, is considerably advanced in civilization, and owns a ranch with considerable livestock and a small farm; wears a citizen's suit and conforms to the customs of civilization—withal a fine-looking and dignified son of the plains. . . . He is tall, muscular, as straight as an arrow; look-you-straight-through eyes, very dark skin, perfect teeth, and heavy, raven-black hair—the envy of feminine hearts. . . . He has a handsome carriage and drives a pair of matched grays.[26]

This was the image—that of a prosperous burger—that Quanah increasingly sought to convey to the rest of the world. For all of his desire to walk the white man's road, however, there were compromises he never made. He wore his hair long and plaited and never cut it. He kept his wives. He was once asked by the Indian commissioner why he refused to get rid of his surplus wives. Quanah replied:

A long time ago I lived free among the buffalo on the staked plains and had as many wives as I wanted, according to the laws of my people. I used to go to war in Texas and Mexico. You wanted me to stop fighting and sent messages all the time "You stop, Quanah." You did not say then "How many wives you got, Quanah?" Now I come and sit down as you want. You talk about wives. Which one do I throw away? You, little girl, you go away, you got no Papa. You, little fellow, you go away. You pick him?[27]

His crowning glory, and the thing he was most proud of, was the extraordinary house he built for himself in 1890. The story behind it is so purely Quanah, so revelatory of the man he was, that it is worth noting. While many others in his tribe had gotten government funding to build the typical $350 shotgun shacks that dotted the reservation, he had been content to live in a tipi, spending his summers outdoors in the traditional Comanche "brush arbor." But by the late 1880s his status in the tribe was such that he needed something better. Something much better. What he wanted, once he had thought about it, was a ten-room, two-story clapboard house, the sort of grand and stately plains home that any white rancher would have been proud to own and that absolutely no reservation Indian had ever owned.

The problem was where to get the money. There were the stockmen, of course, Quanah's old friends like Burk Burnett and Daniel Waggoner who could be counted on to help. Better still, there was the government, which surely owed him *something*. Even better than that was the ploy he eventually concocted. He sent his white tenant farmer and adoptive son, David Grantham,[28] to tell the agent that he wanted a subsidy and that if he did not get it "he will see the stock men and get the money," a curious sort of threat but one that clearly hit its mark. Indian Agent Charles Adams applied to the Indian affairs office for $500 to help Quanah build his house, saying that "he is an Indian who deserves some assistance from the government." He was turned down by Commissioner T. J. Morgan, a staunch Baptist who strongly disapproved of Quanah's polygamy.

Quanah did not give up. He and Adams peppered Washington with more letters, even bypassing Morgan and appealing to his boss, the secretary of the interior. Quanah had almost every ranking person at Fort Sill sign his pleas, including the commandant. He argued that other polygamous Indians had received grants; that a lesser Penateka chief had received funds for a house; that he was being treated unfairly because of an ancient custom of his tribe. He would not agree to jettison his multiple wives, or offer any sort of compromise. This was the quintessential Quanah: hustling, demanding, always looking for an angle, always negotiating yet unwilling to compromise his own principles. Morgan never changed his mind. He wrote: "As it is against the policy of this office to encourage or in any way countenance polygamy, no assistance will be granted Parker in the erection of his house, unless he will agree, in writing, to make a choice among his wives and to live only with the one chosen and to fully provide for his other wives without living with them."[29] Quanah of course refused.

So the privilege of helping to finance Quanah's new home went to the stockmen, after all, mainly to Burk Burnett. They were happy to oblige, though it is not known how much they contributed. Quanah certainly had substantial resources of his own. In 1890, Quanah's new house was finished. It was indeed a ten-room, two-story clapboard affair, and it cost more than $2,000. The interior was finished beaded board, with ten-foot ceilings. There was a formal, wallpapered dining room with a long table and a wood-burning stove. The house sat on a splendid piece of high ground in the shadow of the Wichita Mountains. He later added a wide, colonnaded two-story porch to it and painted enormous white stars on the roof. His home became known as Star House and still stands today, having been moved twice. One of the great, obscure treasures of the American West, it occupies the back lot of a defunct amusement park behind an Indian trading post in Cache, Oklahoma.

The scene at Quanah's splendid new house had no precedent in Comanche history; it could have existed only in the weird half-world of the reservation. No one had ever seen anything like it. He had a total of eight wives (one of them was Weckeah, the woman with whom he had eloped), seven of whom he married during the reservation period. Between them he fathered twenty-four children, five of whom died in infancy. Photographs of his wives taken in the 1880s and 1890s reveal women who are strikingly attractive. Quanah liked women, and somehow managed to keep them even though he infuriated existing wives by constantly courting new ones.[30] In spite of Quanah's arguments to the contrary, multiple wives no longer had a real place in the Comanche culture. Polygamy had been mainly a way of providing extra labor in tanning and processing buffalo. Those days were gone. Quanah had wives now simply because he wanted them and could afford them. His enormous family soon contained white members: two of Quanah's daughters married white men. He adopted and raised two white boys of his own, one of whom he found in a circus in San Antonio and adopted on the spot.[31] He had adopted Herman Lehmann for three years, and Lehmann was so fond of his Comanche family that in 1901 he applied for full status as a tribe member.[32] One young white man, Dick Banks, showed up at Star House just because he wanted to meet Quanah; he was given a bed and invited to stay indefinitely.[33] Family members lived either at the house or in tipis in the front yard, which was surrounded by a white picket fence. Photographs from the era show the place with its double porches literally spilling over with people.

The remarkable scene consisted of more than just his own family. There were always many other Comanche tipis around the house, too. That was partly because of Quanah's unfailing generosity—he fed many hungry Comanches over the years and never turned anyone away.[34] According to people who knew him, feeding members of his tribe was the main use to which he put his private herd. Many sick Comanches came there in order to receive prayers—often related to peyote ceremonies (on which more later)—or, sometimes, in the knowledge that Quanah would handle the funeral arrangements. Most were put in beds inside Star House, which meant that family members slept in the tipis.[35] His reputation as a healer drew white men as well, at least one of whom claimed to have been healed by him.[36]

There was also a constant stream of guests, white and Indian, at his dining room, a formal place with wainscoted and wallpapered walls, a molded tin ceiling, and a dinner table that would seat twelve comfortably.[37] Quanah laid a splendid table. He hired white women to teach his wives how to cook, and for ten years employed a white servant, a Russian immigrant named Anna Gomez.[38] Over the years guests included General Nelson Miles, who had tracked him in the Red River War, his neighbor Geronimo, Kiowa chief Lone Wolf, Charles Goodnight, Commissioner of Indian Affairs R. G. Valentine, British ambassador Lord Brice, Isa-tai, Burk Burnett and Daniel Waggoner, and eventually President Teddy Roosevelt. Though Quanah always refused to talk about his days as a Comanche warrior, he loved to hold forth on tribal politics, or on his frequent trips to Washington. He loved jokes. He dined often with a family named Miller, and at one meal he stated that the white man had pushed the Indian off the land. When Mr. Miller asked how the whites had done this, Quanah told him to sit down on a cottonwood log in the yard. Quanah sat down close to him and said "Move over." Miller moved. Parker moved with him, and again sat down close to him. "Move over," he repeated. This continued until Miller had fallen off the log. "Like that," said Quanah.[39]

By 1890, Quanah's letterhead read "Quanah Parker: Principal Chief of the Comanches," a title he had been permitted by the agent to use. There had never been such a person before in the history of the tribe. There would never be another. He still had rivals, including the perennial second-rater Isa-tai, but the reality, acknowledged by the white man as well as most Comanches, was that he was the main chief. If, as F. Scott Fitzgerald suggested in the early twentieth century, there are no second acts in American lives, then Quanah was an exception to the rule. The lives of most of his fellow tribe members, however, proved Fitzgerald's thesis admirably. That year most Comanche adult males still lived in tipis, wore their hair long as in the prereservation days, spoke little or no English, preferred their medicine men to the white man's doctors, dressed in buckskins and blankets, and continued to condemn agriculture as women's work.

While Quanah prospered, his friend Ranald Mackenzie's life took an abrupt turn into sadness and tragedy. The change did not happen right away. During the years after the Red River War, Mackenzie was one of the most highly regarded officers in the U.S. Army. At Fort Sill he had further distinguished himself. As an administrator he may have been abrupt and easily angered, but he was also firm, fair, and just, and won the respect of Kiowas, Apaches, and Comanches alike. One particular story illustrates his stern and deliberate style of management. In 1876 a group of Comanches had illegally left the reservation, then had quietly returned. Mackenzie found out about it and ordered the chiefs to arrest the offenders. Instead of obeying, they showed up at his office wanting to parley. These were typical Indian tactics: parley, dither for an extended period of time, then find a compromise. Mackenzie listened patiently for half an hour to their harangue, while surreptitiously ordering his men to mount up and prepare for battle. He then rose from his desk, and calmly said, "If you do not bring in the renegades in twenty minutes, I will go to their camps and kill them all." Then he left the room. The renegades were soon delivered.[40]

Sheridan thought so well of Mackenzie that he sent him and his crack Fourth Cavalry veterans north following Custer's defeat at Little Bighorn in June 1876. Less than two months after Custer's demise, Mackenzie assumed command of both the District of the Black Hills and Camp Robinson, the fort that guarded the Red Cloud Sioux Agency. When a large group of Sioux scoffed at Mackenzie's order to return to the reservation, he promptly took eighteen companies and surrounded the Indian village at dawn. Two hundred thirty-nine men surrendered, along with 729 horses.

That winter he was placed in charge of another major campaign: the Powder River Expedition against the Northern Cheyennes and their chief Dull Knife, a group that had taken part in the destruction of Custer's troops. In heavy snow and subzero conditions, Mackenzie with 818 soldiers and 363 Indian scouts attacked Dull Knife's village at dawn on November 25, 1876. They routed the Indians, killing twenty-five and wounding many more and capturing five hundred horses with the loss of only six of his own. In April, Dull Knife, hearing Mackenzie was still after him, surrendered. "You are the one I was afraid of when you came here last summer," he told Mackenzie. Two weeks later Crazy Horse and 889 Sioux surrendered to Mackenzie at the Red Cloud Agency, ending the Sioux and Cheyenne war.[41] The surrender stands as a sort of bookend to the twinned fates of Custer and Mackenzie, the one destined for eternal fame and glory, the other for obscurity and oblivion.

Mackenzie became Sherman and Sheridan's favorite commander in the West, as he had been Grant's favorite young officer in the Civil War. He was the one they sent to deal with difficult situations. In 1877 he was called to the border to subdue bandits. In 1879 and 1881 he went to deal with rebellious Utes in Colorado, issuing an ultimatum to them that resembled the one the Comanches had received at Fort Sill—with equivalent success. He crushed an uprising of Apaches in New Mexico and was so successful in dealing with the Indians in general that the governor and citizens of the state lobbied for his promotion to brigadier general. With former president Grant's enthusiastic help, he got the promotion in October 1881.

But by that time something was already terribly wrong with Ranald Slidell Mackenzie. Soon after his promotion he wrote a letter to his superiors with the odd request for reassignment to a military court or retiring board. The handwriting in the letter was so poor as to suggest that the writer had suffered a stroke. He wanted the soft duty, said the tough-as-nails Mackenzie, because he had suffered "much harder in the last two years than anyone has any idea of."[42] It was the first hint of the calamitous changes that were taking place inside his head.

He was nevertheless assigned to the command of the Department of Texas, based in San Antonio. There, at the age of forty-three, he began a rapid decline. Though he had forsworn alcohol throughout his career, he now began, unaccountably, to drink heavily. His eccentricities, notably his impatience and irritability, increased noticeably. For the first time anyone knew of, he began to keep the company of a lady, the thirty-four-year-old Florida Sharpe, with whom he had fallen in love in the late 1860s while on court-martial duty. (She had then been married to the base's doctor.) On December 9, 1882, the army surgeon began treating Mackenzie for unusual behavior. On December 10 the quartermaster said that he thought Mackenzie was insane. A week later, General Mackenzie became engaged to Mrs. Sharpe, and it became known that he had purchased property in the nearby town of Boerne and had plans to retire there. On December 18 he drank too much and got into a fight with two local citizens. They had no idea who he was, so they beat him senseless and tied him to a cart where he was found the next day. Several days later he was loaded onto a train under the pretext that Sheridan had something important to speak with him about in Washington. On December 29 he was checked in to the Bloomingdale Asylum in New York City. On March 5, an army retiring board declared, over his protests, that he was insane and therefore not fit for duty.

The rest of his life was a steady descent into madness. He remained in the asylum until June, still protesting his forced retirement, when he went to live with his sister at his boyhood home in Morristown, New Jersey. He had plans to revisit Texas and his property in Boerne, but he never moved again. Mrs. Sharpe never spoke of him. His physical and mental health deteriorated; he grew more and more childish until he could no longer make himself understood. He died in a New York hospital on January 18, 1889, at the age of forty-eight.

What caused Mackenzie's madness? There are several theories. For many years it was thought that his condition was the result of syphilis. But this is unlikely. The army knew all about syphilis, dealt with it constantly, and there is no record of Mackenzie ever being treated for it. One historian suggested that his illness was the result of post-traumatic stress disorder, a condition that was unknown at the time. Mackenzie's horrific wounds and central role in many Civil War battles certainly could have produced it, and his irritability, explosive temper, and difficulty forming close relationships are common symptoms. He had also suffered an odd accident back in 1875. In the autumn of that year, he somehow fell off a cart at Fort Sill and injured his head so badly that he was in a stupor for three days. It was said that he became unusually irritable in the days that followed. Finally, there is the more remote possibility that the sunstroke he had suffered as a child had something to do with it. We will never know. His death went virtually unnoticed. Quanah, who was forty at the time, making his way in the new, civilized West that Mackenzie had made possible, must have heard about it, though there is no record of his reaction. The day after Mackenzie's death the following death notice appeared on the obituary page of the *New York Times*:

MACKENZIE—At New Brighton, Staten Island, on the 19th of January, Brig. Gen. Ranald Slidell Mackenzie, United States Army, in the 48th year of his age.

In its brevity and lack of detail, the item suggested a minor military figure, perhaps someone who had won a medal or two in the war, and had then been put out to grass in some lonely outpost of the new empire. There was no news item in the *Times* or any other newspapers with the particulars of his life. The event would have seemed to have no more significance to the casual reader than the passing of a manager in a local dry goods company.

Twenty-one

THIS WAS A MAN

I N 1889 THE U.S. Congress came up with a new and ingenious plan to steal land from the Indians. A three-man panel known as the Jerome Commission was appointed and charged with the task of negotiating with the tribes west of the 96th meridian. Their goal was to secure "the cession to the United States of all of their title." The idea was simple: The Indians would give up their collective, tribal lands. In exchange, each Indian would be allotted a private parcel of land that would be subject to the normal laws of private property. Commissioner David Jerome told the Indians that, instead of a reservation they no longer needed, "now you have the opportunity to sell to the Great Father all that land that you cannot use for homes for his white children."[1] The plan had teeth because of the so-called Dawes Act, passed in 1887, which allowed the president, "whenever he pleases," to require the Indians to give up their reservations for individual allotments. In council at Fort Sill in 1892, the officials smiled and made nice and did not expect much opposition from Indians who undoubtedly could not comprehend either the idea that they would own private property or the sheer magnitude of the proposed transaction, which would affect some twenty tribes and fifteen million acres.

They had not counted on Quanah Parker. He demanded that he be told the specifics of the proposed deal. "I want to know how much will be paid for one acre, what the terms will be, and when it will be paid," he insisted.

Jerome tried to stall, assuring Quanah that he would get his answers "by and by." But Quanah would not be put off. "When will you answer the questions?" he asked. Jerome again refused to answer, and Quanah continued to badger him, explaining that, unlike some other Indians who just wanted some quick cash in their pockets, "I want a thorough understanding. I just want to talk about business. Talk to the point."

The next day he pressed even harder. First he dueled with the commissioners over the size of the allotments. He reminded them that the Treaty of Medicine Lodge had specified three hundred twenty acres per person instead of the one hundred sixty acres they were offering. And he wanted to know how much the government was going to pay for the land that was left over after the Indians each got their one hundred sixty acres. Pressed now, Commissioner Warren Sayre somewhat sheepishly offered up a number: $2 million. The following exchange took place in council.

Quanah: How much per acre?
Sayre: I cannot tell you.
Quanah: How do you arrive at the number of a million dollars if you do not know?
Sayre: We just guess at it.
Quanah: We would like to know how much per acre, because we have heard that some tribes received $1.25 per acre, and the Wichitas received fifty cents per acre and were dissatisfied.[2]

Quanah soon prevailed. The following day, an exasperated Commissioner Jerome, acknowledging that "Yesterday Mr. Parker pushed Judge Sayre hard to tell him how much . . . for one acre," actually provided a figure. He now estimated that the government was offering a little over $1 an acre. When they insisted that the low valuation was partly due to the fact that much of the surplus land was rocky and mountainous, Quanah countered: "I have noticed that coal is burned in such localities, and that iron, silver, and gold are found in such places." Later he added: "The mountains are all supposed to be rocks and the rocks are supposed to be worthless, but the military use them to make houses with. . . ." Thus it went, Quanah hectoring them every step of the way. He was unlike any of the other Indian leaders, who tended to be long-winded, delivering rambling, occasionally poetic complaints that did not address significant issues.

But there was no forestalling the government's plan. The Dawes Act meant that the white man could seize the land by fiat, making the new law a mere formality. In October the Indians signed the Jerome Agreement, which, once ratified, meant that they would get one hundred sixty acres of land apiece and would sell what was left over to the government for $2 million. Quanah's role in the final agreement is not known. He signed it, even though it was not in his interest to do so. He stood to lose more from it than any other Comanche, most notably his forty-four-thousand-acre rent-free pasture, from which he made $1,000 a year.

Quanah also understood the futility of blind resistance. Having nominally agreed to the terms of the Jerome Agreement, he spent the next eight years—the time it took the Senate to ratify it—lobbying hard for changes in its terms. He pushed for a new deal in which the Indians got to keep all of their land; he eventually championed the setting aside of an additional 480,000 acres. With help from powerful supporters in the East, the Jerome Agreement was eventually modified to include this. (The largest chunk of it, 400,000 acres, came to be known as the Big Pasture and was leased to the white cattlemen.)

The agreement became law in 1900. Another thirteen months passed before the reservation was opened. On the eve of the change some fifty thousand "sooners" flooded into the country, scouting their own properties and ignoring Indian property lines. Soldiers from Fort Sill cleared the intruders from the land, but they always came back. They stole the Indians' livestock, and camped on Indian property.

Thus began the Comanches' new lives as owners of property, something they had never wanted and had never really understood. Ten years later, the system had become drearily familiar. Most Comanches leased out their allotments to white ranchers and farmers and simply lived on the lease payments, supplementing them with the $100 or so each received in interest on tribal funds (from the eventual sale of the Big Pasture) and with periodic work picking cotton or harvesting grain. They retained enough land for a house and garden. Few owned any cattle; most kept a horse or two. By Comanche standards, it was an aimless, purposeless existence.[3]

The division of the old Indian lands took away most of Quanah's income. He would never again earn anything near what he made in the 1890s. His unstinting generosity, in fact, would soon make him relatively poor. But this changed very little in his life. His penury coincided with the peak of his power, influence, and celebrity.

The busy and complex scene continued unabated at his house, where he shared his food and his lodging with ever greater numbers of people. His celebrity now attracted people who simply showed up at his house wanting to meet the famous war chief and share his legendary table. But mostly the people who came were local Indians. According to his adopted white son Knox Beall, who later became the translator at the Fort Sill agency:

> My father fed a great many Indians. He had a great herd of cattle and horses in 1890 and when he died in 1911 he did not have many left because he was so generous. When a person became hungry he fed them. He could not stand to see any one of his tribe go hungry.[4]

Robert Thomas, a storekeeper in Cache who knew Quanah well, offers a similar account:

> By 1910, owing to his generosity and kindheartedness, he was a very poor man. A great deal of his own food supplies were given away to his tribe and there were always hundreds of Comanches camped around his home. . . . He was always kind, never speaking ill of anyone.[5]

And this man who once rode free on the high and windy plains had also lived long enough to witness the astonishing technological advances of the late nineteenth and early twentieth centuries. He found it all fascinating. He wanted to try everything. He had one of the first residential telephones in Oklahoma. He bought a car, an old ambulance for which he was ribbed by his friends, who called it a "dead wagon, " and which was apparently driven sometimes by his "bodyguard," a deaf and dumb Comanche named George Washington, whom everyone called Dummie.[6] He had a railroad named after him—the Quanah, Acme and Pacific Railroad, which itself derived from the west Texas town of Quanah—and often rode in the locomotive, blowing the whistle and ringing the bell. He traveled frequently and liked staying in hotels in big cities with their gaslights and modern conveniences. On one of his many trips to Fort Worth, a gaslight nearly killed him. He was sharing a hotel room with his father-in-law Yellow Bear. Before retiring, Yellow Bear "blew out" the gaslight before going to bed, a mistake Indians often made. Before the night was over, he was dead of asphyxiation, and Quanah, who remained unconscious for two days, barely survived.[7]

The events of the year 1908, when he turned sixty, suggested the distance civilization had traveled since his birth on the prairie. That year Teddy

Roosevelt sent his magnificent White Fleet of steel gunships around the world, and Henry Ford introduced the mass-production automobile known as the Model T. That year Quanah himself appeared in the first two-reel western movie ever made: *The Bank Robbery,* filmed near his home in Cache, Oklahoma. He had a bit part. There is something more than a bit surreal, more than one hundred years later, about watching Quanah himself emerge from a stagecoach, pigtails falling down over his shoulders, or ride toward the camera. At this distance, there is simply no reconciling it with the idea of free and wild Comanches on the Llano Estacado.

Quanah also had a curious and noteworthy friendship with Teddy Roosevelt. In March 1905 he rode in an open car in Roosevelt's inaugural parade in buckskins and warbonnet, accompanied by Geronimo, two Sioux chiefs, and a Blackfeet chief. (One of the people who witnessed that event was Robert G. Carter, the officer who had been ambushed by Quanah at Blanco Canyon and who still hated Quanah bitterly and did not understand why someone who had killed so many whites could march in such a parade.)[8] The two men met at a party Roosevelt hosted for the chiefs. A month later, Roosevelt traveled west on a special train to participate in a much-publicized "wolf hunt" on lands belonging to the Comanches, Apaches, and Kiowas in southwestern Oklahoma. His principal hosts were leading cattlemen Burk Burnett and Daniel Waggoner, and the Comanche chief Quanah Parker. This wasn't just fun and recreation: The 400,000-acre Big Pasture where the hunt took place was one of the most hotly contested pieces of land in the West. By virtue of the revised Jerome Agreement, the Indians held title to it and leased it to the likes of Burnett and Waggoner. But a large group of land-hungry whites, supported by Texas congressman James H. Stephens, wanted the government to buy the land and open it for development.

When Roosevelt's train arrived at Frederick, Oklahoma, he was met by a crowd of three thousand and then escorted by a mounted honor guard, which included Quanah, to a speaker's stand in the middle of town. (Quanah said later that he had been afraid someone might try to shoot the president—McKinley had been assassinated four years earlier—and thus had worn a six-shooter for the occasion. The idea is unimaginable today.)[9] Roosevelt made a few brief remarks, then invited Quanah, whom he called "a good citizen," to come up on the stand with him. The two men shook hands, to rousing applause, and then Quanah gave a short speech. There is no record of what he said, but he later told his friend R. B. Thomas that "I got more cheers than Teddy."[10] Roosevelt clearly liked and admired him. "There was Quanah Parker the Comanche chief," he wrote in his description of the wolf hunt (which had bagged seventeen wolves and coyotes) in his book *Outdoor Pastimes of the American Hunter*, "in his youth a bitter foe of the whites, now painfully teaching his people to travel the white man's stony road."[11]

After the wolf hunt, Roosevelt traveled north to visit Quanah at Star House, a truly momentous occasion in tiny Cache, Oklahoma, for which all conceivable pomp and circumstance were brought to bear. Quanah made a point of serving wine (which he never drank) in large goblets, specifically because at the White House Roosevelt had served the Indians wine in small goblets.[12] In his typical fashion, Quanah used the occasion to lobby Roosevelt on Indian issues. The main one was the disposition of the 400,000 acres; Quanah wanted the Indians to retain it. (He eventually lost the battle: Two years later the land was divvied up and sold off, with Comanche children born after 1900 receiving 160-acre parcels; proceeds went into an Indian trust.) Quanah also complained of territorial officers trying to collect taxes from Indians, and of the Indians' terrible unemployment problem. Evidence that Roosevelt listened came in a letter he wrote a few days later to the commissioner of Indian affairs. "My sympathies have been much excited and I have been aroused by what I have seen here, and I am concerned at the condition of these Indians and seeming hopelessness of their future."[13] The wolf hunt and his visit to Quanah are often cited as reasons Roosevelt became determined to create the Wichita Mountains Wildlife Refuge, which today is just north of Quanah's old home.

Quanah remained an active leader, even into his old age. Unhappy with the Indian schools, and finding that his children were unwelcome in the white ones, he put on his broad-brimmed Stetson and wool suit and went lobbying for a new school district. He donated the land, promised that his tribesmen would pay taxes, and got it done. In June 1908 he became head of the school board in the district he had started.[14] He became one of the leading religious figures in the Comanche tribe and the driving force behind the establishment of the peyote religion among the Plains Indians. Peyote is a small, spineless cactus whose ingestion produces visual and auditory hallucinations. It had been used by Comanches as early as the mid-nineteenth century, and the Indians of south Texas had used it as early as 1716. Quanah revived its use and refined it into a meaningful religious ritual that Indians embraced during the grim early days on the reservation. He would preside over all-night rituals, many of which were concerned with the healing of specific people. From his Comanches it spread to Kiowas, Wichitas, Pawnees, and Shawnees before the turn of the century. Between 1900 and 1907 it was adopted by the Poncas, Kickapoos, and Kansas, and subsequently spread throughout the plains and into the Great Basin and deserts of the Southwest. Wrote Wallace and Hoebel: "It was probably the most important cultural contribution of Comanches to the lives of other American Indians."[15] Quanah, who came under fire from time to time for his involvement in these rituals, once defended his religion by saying: "The white man goes into his church and talks *about* Jesus, but the Indian goes into his tipi and talks *to* Jesus." The practice eventually evolved into the entity that became known as the Native American Church.

In spite of his success, and his eventual triumph over his rivals, Quanah's life was never easy. He had to fight to keep prosecutors away from his peyote cult. As he got older he had marital troubles; several of his wives ended up leaving him, perhaps because of his growing financial problems. And he struggled constantly with political rivals in the tribe, including the old medicine quack Isa-tai, who never gave up in his quest to become the principal chief of the Comanches, and the Kiowa Lone Wolf, with whom he once had a fistfight over a boundary dispute.[16] Charges made by Lone Wolf's Kiowa faction, aligned with Isa-tai, in fact, led to a federal investigation of the agency in 1903. The federal agent who investigated, one Francis E. Leupp, not only concluded that Quanah and the agent had done nothing wrong, he had this to say about Quanah:

> If ever nature stamped a man with the seal of headship she did it in his case. Quanah might have been a leader and a governor in any circle where fate might have cast him—it is in his blood. His acceptability to all but an inconsiderable minority of his people is plain to any observer, and even those who are restive under his rule recognize its supremacy. He has his followers under wonderful control, but, on the other hand, looks out for them like a father.[17]

The contrast could not be greater with his more famous neighbor, Geronimo, who had been relocated to Fort Sill from Alabama in 1894. Unlike Quanah, he attracted no crowds and few visitors. Though he was a genius at self-advertising, and made a lot of money selling his signatures, bows and arrows, and such (he reportedly died with $10,000 in his bank account), he was not well liked in Indian country. Hugh Scott, an officer at Fort Sill and a great friend to Indians, described him as "an unlovely character, a cross-grained, mean, selfish old curmudgeon." He drank and liked to gamble, and died from injuries he received by falling off his horse while drunk.[18] The two men's legacies stand very much in contrast even in death. Geronimo is buried in the Apache Cemetery in Fort Sill, whose address happens to be 437 Quanah Road.

Twenty-two

━━◆━━

RESTING HERE UNTIL DAY BREAKS

━━◆━━

Q UANAH NEVER FORGOT his mother. He kept the photograph Sul Ross gave him—the one taken in 1862 at A. F. Corning's studio in Fort Worth, with Prairie Flower nursing at her breast—on the wall above his bed. She had been taken from him when he was only twelve; in a matter of minutes she had disappeared forever into the white man's world. He later learned that she had been unhappy and that she had repeatedly tried to escape to find him. Like her son, she had adapted brilliantly to an alien culture, but she could not do it twice. In 1908 he placed ads in Texas newspapers seeking help in finding her grave. He got a response from a man named J. R. O'Quinn, his first cousin and the son of Cynthia Ann's younger sister Orlena, who told him he knew where to find it. It was Quanah's first contact with his Texas family. Later he heard from another cousin, who invited him to a family function in Athens, Texas, southeast of Dallas. (He would eventually be embraced and celebrated by his Texas family.) Having found his mother, he now lobbied for money to move her grave from Texas to Oklahoma. Persistent and persuasive as always, he convinced his congressman to sponsor a bill authorizing $1,000 to relocate Cynthia Ann's bones. The bill became law in March 1909. He traveled to Texas, met some of his white family, and found the cemetery where she lay. On December 10, 1910, she was reinterred at the Post Oak Mission in Cache. At a ceremony over her grave, Quanah gave a simple speech in his fractured English. "Forty years ago my mother died," he said. "She captured by Comanches, nine years old. Love Indian and wild life so well, no want to go back to white folks. All same people anyway, God say. I love my mother."

He himself had less than three months to live. He had been busy in the fall of 1910 as usual, traveling to Dallas in October for a celebration known as Quanah Route Day at the Texas State Fair. Its purpose was to promote the Quanah, Acme and Pacific Railroad, which ran through the town of Quanah, Texas, just south of the old reservation. Quanah, who rarely turned down a chance to appear in public, drew an overflow crowd. According to a *Dallas Morning News* story from October 25, 1910, "The SRO sign was hung out yesterday afternoon at the convention hall. . . . Every seat was taken and standing room was at a premium. Chief Quanah Parker of the Comanches was, of course, the principal attraction." He was there with his twelve-year-old son, Gussie. Both were dressed in warbonnets, buckskins, and moccasins. He spoke in a voice that was "clear and resonant and distinct to those even in the rear of the hall although his words were occasionally broken and difficult to understand."[1] "Ladies and gentlemen," he began, "I used to be a bad man. Now I am a citizen of the United States. I pay taxes same as you people do. We are the same people now." He spoke of his mother, of stealing Mackenzie's horses at Blanco Canyon. He told the audience about his trips to Washington to "work for my Indians," and about meeting Roosevelt. He was funny and engaging, telling stories he had told many times before. He of course did not mention his career as a raider and killer of white people. In the best American fashion, he had carefully removed the less savory parts from his past. He took the time to deny, once and for all, that his father, Peta Nokona, had died in the battle of Pease River. He was lying, but he had a clear, and forgivable, purpose: He was trying to save his father's reputation. Then he concluded with an odd remark. "Just one more minute, here is one more say. My ways call for money every time they send me to the fair. Two men came to me about a year ago to go to New York City. 'I give you $5,000 for tour six months, to take your family over there.' I say 'No, you put me in little pen. I no monkey.' That is all, gentlemen." Then, as the paper noted, "as the throng crowded forward . . . he took each person by the hand and pressed it and frequently his face was wreathed in smiles."[2] His last comments were, perhaps, a way of saying that he, unlike, say, Geronimo, had limits on how far he would exploit his fame and his heritage. Dignity, he was saying, had its limits. Why he was moved to point that out will remain forever a mystery. As far as we know, they were his last public words.

In February 1911, Quanah was returning by train from a visit to some of his Cheyenne friends, reportedly to seek a cure at a peyote meeting. He knew he was sick. Traveling with his number one wife, the childless To-nar-cy, he rode the train with his head bowed and lips trembling. When he arrived home in Cache, he was taken to his house by his white son-in-law Emmet Cox. He died there on February 23 of rheumatism-induced heart failure.

Word of his death moved like electricity through Oklahoma and Texas, in both white and Indian communities. By morning hundreds had gathered at Quanah's house, with its double porch and bright red roof marked with large white stars. By noon the crowd had swelled to two thousand. Mourners came on horseback and muleback and in farm wagons and buggies and automobiles. There were whites wearing Sunday clothes and Indians in buckskins and blankets. They moved in a long, slow procession to the church, where only a small fraction of them could fit. Those outside sang and prayed. Eventually they all filed past the casket where Quanah lay adorned in his favorite buckskin, his trademark plaited hair falling over his shoulders. At the gravesite, mourners sang "Nearer My God to Thee" and then the casket, draped with brilliantly colored blankets, was lowered into the grave beside Cynthia Ann's.

When his family sorted through his estate, they found there was not much there. He had a few hundred dollars in the bank. His wife To-nar-cy, who was recognized as his widow under Oklahoma law, took the rights to one-third of his land allotment. Wife To-pay, who had two children, aged two and eleven, got the house. His eldest son, White Parker, got the cherished, and now famous, photograph of Cynthia Ann that had hung over Quanah's bed. Otherwise, there were a couple of horses and mules, a coach, a hack, and buggy. He did not have much else. He owed $350, a debt that was covered by the sale of his mules. That was all that remained of the last chief of the Comanches. Except for his house he had what amounted to a nomad's possessions, a sort of symmetry that some Comanches might have appreciated. Four months after his death, the secretary of the interior ordered the Indian superintendent to eliminate the office of chief and instead to create a committee formed of members of the tribes.[3] In later years there were "chairmen" but no *paraibos*.

The Lords of the South Plains, meanwhile, were fast fading into America. That was what aboriginal cultures did if they did not vanish altogether. It would be inaccurate to say that the Comanches adapted well, or that Quanah was a model that the tribe as a whole was prepared or equipped to follow. The first generations of Comanches in captivity never really understood the concept of wealth, of private property. The central truth of their lives was the past, the dimming memory of the wild, ecstatic freedom of the plains, of the days when Comanche warriors in black buffalo headdresses rode unchallenged from Kansas to northern Mexico, of a world without property or boundaries. What Quanah had that the rest of his tribe in the later years did not was that most American of human traits: boundless optimism. Quanah never looked back, an astonishing feat of will for someone who had lived in such untrammeled freedom on the open plains, and who had endured such a shattering transformation. In hard times he looked resolutely forward toward something better. That sentiment appears, obliquely, on his gravestone, which reads:

> *Resting here until day breaks*
> *And shadows fall*
> *And darkness disappears*
> *Is Quanah Parker, the last chief of the Comanches.*

His school-educated daughter probably wrote it, based loosely on a verse in the Song of Solomon, a book of the Old Testament that settlers, among them his forefathers, carried with them into the lethal West, where Stone Age pagans on horseback once ruled the immemorial land. Quanah would have been pleased.

NOTES

━━┅ ≍✦≍ ┅━━

One A NEW KIND OF WAR

1. Robert G. Carter, *On the Border with Mackenzie,* p. 159.
2. Captain George Pettis, *Kit Carson's Fight with the Comanche and Kiowa Indians,* pp. 7ff.
3. Cited in C. C. Rister, ed., "Documents Relating to General W. T. Sherman's Southern Plains Indian Policy 1871–75," *Pandhandle Plains Historical Review* 9, 1936.
4. T. R. Fehrenbach, *Comanches,* p. 494.
5. F. E., Green, ed., "Ranald Mackenzie's Official Correspondence Relating to Texas, 1873–1879," p. 7; this incident is also known as the Wagon Train Massacre, per Fehrenbach, p. 506 (and occasionally as the Warren Wagon Train Massacre).
6. Carter, pp. 81–82.
7. Ernest Wallace and E. Adamson Hoebel, *The Comanches,* pp. 50–55.
8. Ibid.
9. Cited in Herbert Eugene Bolton, *Coronado: Knight of Pueblos and Plains.*
10. Thomas W. Kavanaugh, *The Comanches,* p. 3.
11. Rupert Richardson, *The Comanche Barrier to South Plains Settlement,* p. 156.
12. Carter, p. 149.
13. Ibid., p. 160.
14. Ibid., p. 161.
15. Ibid., p. 176.

Two A LETHAL PARADISE

1. Quanah Parker interview with Charles Goodnight, undated manuscript, Goodnight Papers, Panhandle-Plains Historical Museum, Canyon, Texas.
2. Marshall DeBruhl, *Sam Houston: Sword of San Jacinto,* p. 305.
3. Deed of indenture, November 1, 1835, signed by Juan Basquis for sale of half a league of land to Silas Parker; document in Taulman Archive, Center for American History, University of Texas.
4. Joseph Taulman and Araminta Taulman, "The Fort Parker Massacre and Its Aftermath," unpublished manuscript, Cynthia Ann Parker vertical files, Center for American History, University of Texas, Austin, TX, p. 2.
5. Ibid., p. 247.
6. Bill Yenne, *Sitting Bull,* p. 35.
7. Daniel Parker is given credit for making the first formal proposal to create Ranger companies to protect settlers. His proposal was accepted by the permanent council

of the Consultation of 1835, a committee that directed the affairs of the Texas Revolution, of which Parker was a member. See Margaret Schmidt Hacker, *Cynthia Ann Parker: The Life and Legend,* p. 7; see also Mike Cox, *The Texas Rangers: Wearing the Cinco Peso 1821–1900,* p. 42.

8. Hacker, p. 6.
9. James Parker, *Narrative of the Perilous Adventures,* p. 9.
10. Ibid.
11. Thomas W. Kavanaugh, *The Comanches: A History 1706–1875,* p. 250; see also Cox, p. 49, and Noah Smithwick's account in *Evolution of a State.* He was in the Ranger group.
12. Taulman and Taulman, "The Fort Parker Massacre," pp. 2–3.
13. Rachel Plummer, *Rachel Plummer's Narrative of Twenty-one Months Servitude as a Prisoner among the Comanche Indians,* p. 7. See also Rachel Plummer's other narrative (she wrote two), *Narrative of the Capture and Subsequent Sufferings of Mrs. Rachel Plummer.* General Note: These narratives, plus James Parker's *Narrative of the Perilous Adventures,* form the basis of most accounts of the massacre. There is also an affidavit filed by Daniel Parker and other members of the family shortly after the massacre (Center for American History, University of Texas, Austin), and various other accounts by family members including Quanah's grandson Baldwin Parker's own family-based account of what happened (also at Center for American History archive). Yet another narrative was pieced together by Joseph and Araminta Taulman and is part of their very large archive at the University of Texas in Austin. There is another eyewitness account from Abram Anglin (in Dewitt Baker, ed., *A Texas Scrap Book: Made up of the History, Biography and Miscellany of Texas and Its People* [New York: A.S. Barnes, 1875, reprint 1991 Texas State Historical Assn.]). Additionally there are many newspaper accounts, based on interviews with immediate Parker relatives and descendants, including "Story of the White Squaw," *McKinney Democrat Gazette,* September 22, 1927; "Early Times in Texas and the History of the Parker Family," by Ben J. Parker of Elkhart, Texas (manuscript at Center for American History); J. Marvin Nichols, "White Woman Was the Mother of Great Chief," *San Antonio Daily Express,* July 25, 1909; Ben J. Parker, "Ben Parker Gives Events of Pioneering," *Palestine Herald,* February 15, 1935; for secondary sources it is hard to beat the extensively researched *Frontier Blood* by Jo Ella Powell Exley.
14. Fehrenbach, *Lone Star,* p. 291.
15. This and other architectural details have been wonderfully re-created at Old Parker's Fort in Groesbeck, Texas, built on the site of the original.
16. Plummer, *Rachel Plummer's Narrative,* p. 93.
17. Ibid., p. 93.
18. Daniel Parker, notes dated June 18, 1836, Parker Documents, Center for American History, University of Texas, Austin; see also Hacker, p. 8.
19. Plummer, *Rachel Plummer's Narrative,* p. 95.
20. Exley, p. 44.
21. Ibid., p. 94.
22. Plummer, *Rachel Plummer's Narrative,* p. 9.
23. Parker, *Narrative of the Perilous Adventures,* p. 1.
24. John Graves, *Hard Scrabble,* p. 15.
25. Plummer, *Rachel Plummer's Narrative.*
26. Rachel Plummer, *Narrative of the Capture* (1838), p. 7ff.
27. Ibid.

Three WORLDS IN COLLISION

1. Ernest Wallace and E. Adamson Hoebel, *The Comanches,* p. 12.
2. Alfred Thomas, ed., *Forgotten Frontiers: A Study of the Spanish Indian Policy of Don Juan Bautista de Anza, Governor of New Mexico, 1777–1787, From the Original Documents in the Archives of Spain, Mexico, and New Mexico,* pp. 119ff.
3. Ibid., p. 8; Rupert Richardson, *The Comanche Barrier,* p. 5.
4. T. R. Fehrenbach, *The Comanches,* p. 133.
5. Dorman H. Winfrey and James M. Day, eds., *The Indian Papers of the Southwest,* vol. 1, p. 24.
6. M. Lewis, *The Lewis and Clark Expedition,* p. 30; in Thomas Kavanaugh's book *The Comanches: A History 1706–1875,* he notes that the ethnonym "Padouca" could well have been applied to plains-dwelling Apaches (p. 66). The point, either way, is that in a land where many, many tribes were known and identified, the Comanches of this era were not.
7. George Bird Grinnell, "Who Were the Padouca?" *American Anthropologist* 22 (1920): 248.
8. Kavanaugh, *The Comanches,* pp. 218–19.
9. Ibid., p. 235.
10. George Catlin, *Manners, Customs, and Condition of the North American Indians,* p. 47.
11. W. S. Nye, *Carbine and Lance: The Story of Old Fort Sill,* p. 8.
12. Catlin, pp. 48ff; see also Colonel Richard Irving Dodge, *Our Wild Indians, 33 years' personal experience among the redmen of the great west.*
13. Randolph B. Marcy, *Adventure on Red River: A Report on the Exploration of the Red River by Captain Randolph Marcy and Captin G.B. McClellan,* p. 5.
14. Fehrenbach, *The Comanches,* pp. 30–31.
15. David La Vere, *Contrary Neighbors,* p. 8.
16. Clark Wissler, *The American Indian,* pp. 220ff.
17. Fehrenbach, *The Comanches,* p. 33.
18. Walter Prescott Webb first made this observation in his book *The Great Plains* (p. 53); it has been repeated by others since.
19. J. Frank Dobie, *The Mustangs,* pp. 23ff.
20. Wallace and Hoebel, p. 41.
21. Ibid., p. 24.
22. Fehrenbach, *Lone Star,* p. 31.
23. Dobie, p. 25.
24. Fehrenbach, *The Comanches,* p. 86.
25. Wallace and Hoebel, pp. 35ff.
26. Wissler, p. 220.
27. Fehrenbach, *The Comanches,* p. 126.
28. Wallace and Hoebel, p. 39.
29. Ibid., p. 35; Dobie, p. 69.
30. Athanase de Mézières, "Report by de Mézières of the Expedition to Cadadachos, Oct. 29, 1770," in Herbert E. Bolton, ed., *Athanase de Mézières and the Lousiana-Texas Frontier, 1768–1780,* vol. 1, p. 218.
31. Catlin, pp. 65ff; see also Colonel Richard I. Dodge, *Our Wild Indians.*
32. Dobie, p. 65.
33. Dodge, *The Plains of the Great West,* pp. 401ff.
34. Dobie, p. 48. He is citing an account by Captain Randolph Marcy.
35. General Thomas James, *Three Years Among the Indians and Mexicans,* St. Louis, 1916, cited in Dobie, p. 83.
36. Wallace and Hoebel, p. 46.

37. Richard I. Dodge, *The Plains of the Great West*, pp. 329–30.
38. Ralph E. Twitchell, *The Spanish Archives of New Mexico*, p. 269.
39. Kavanaugh, *The Comanches*, p. 63.
40. Marvin Opler, "The Origins of Comanche and Ute," *American Anthropologist* 45 (1943): 156.

Four HIGH LONESOME

1. Rachel Plummer, *The Narrative of the Capture and Subsequent Sufferings of Mrs. Rachel Plummer*, 1839.
2. T. R. Fehrenbach, *The Comanches*, p. 97.
3. Jo Ella Powell Exley, *Frontier Blood*, p. 133.
4. Plummer, p. 96.
5. Ibid., p. 97.
6. Walter P. Webb, *The Great Plains*, p. 9.
7. Plummer, p. 97.
8. Noah Smithwick, *Evolution of a State or Recollections of Old Texas Days*, p. 113.
9. David La Vere, *Contrary Neighbors*, p. 122.
10. Plummer, p. 97.
11. Ibid., p. 98.
12. Ibid., p. 107.
13. Ibid., p. 108.
14. Herman Lehmann, *Nine Years Among the Comanches, 1870–1879*, p. 155.
15. The scant historical information about Crazy Horse is discussed in some detail in Larry McMurtry's brief but excellent study *Crazy Horse*.
16. See chapter 7 for a fuller explanation of this important phenomenon.
17. Fehrenbach, *The Comanches*, pp. 77ff.
18. Sharon Block, *Rape and Sexual Power in Early America*, pp. 222ff.
19. Ernest Wallace and E. Adamson Hoebel, *The Comanches*, p. 194.
20. Ibid.
21. Ramon Jimanez, *Caesar Against the Celts*, pp. 27ff.
22. Ibid., p. 36.
23. Colonel Richard Irving Dodge, *Our Wild Indians*, p. 59.
24. Ibid.
25. Ibid.
26. Scott Zesch, *Captured*, p 127.
27. John S. Ford, *Rip Ford's Texas*, p. 231.
28. Clinton Smith, op. cit., pp. 69ff.
29. Zesch, p. 79.
30. Clinton Smith, p. 69.
31. Wallace and Hoebel, p. 22.
32. Ibid., p. 25.
33. The only exception was when members of the Penateka band joined U.S. Army forces as scouts during the final campaign against the Quahadis in the Texas Panhandle. They were never combatants.
34. W. S. Nye, *Carbine and Lance, the Story of Old Fort Sill*, p. 7.
35. Rupert N. Richardson, *The Comanche Barrier to South Plains Settlement*, p. 10.
36. Wallace and Hoebel, p. 23.
37. Plummer, p. 113.

Five THE WOLF'S HOWL

1. T. R. Fehrenbach, *The Comanches*, p. 160.
2. Alfred Thomas, ed., *Forgotten Frontiers: A Study of the Spanish Indian Policy of Don Juan Bautista de Anza, from the Original Documents*, p. 58: "As early as 1706 Iribarri reported harrowing details of the inter-tribal conflict that indicated the collapse of Apache civilization northeast of the province."
3. Ibid., p. 58.
4. Herbert E. Bolton, ed., *Athanase de Mézières and the Louisiana-Texas Frontier, 1768– 1780*, vol. 1, p. 34.
5. David La Vere, *Contrary Neighbors*, p. 10.
6. Ernest Wallace and E. Adamson Hoebel, *The Comanches*, p. 12.
7. Hubert H. Bancroft, *History of Arizona and New Mexico* (1889), p. 239.
8. References to this battle appear in several places. First, in a report [Ynforme] dated September 30, 1784, by then Spanish governor of Texas Domingo Cabello y Robles. Second, in Herbert Bolton's 1914 compilation of the writings of noted eighteenth-century Indian agent Athanase de Mézières. p. 25.
9. Fehrenbach, *The Comanches*, p. 138.
10. Richard I. Dodge, *Plains of the Great West*, p. 414. This account came from Pedro Espinosa, a "Mexican Comanche" warrior.
11. La Vere, pp. 30–31.
12. Almost all of what we know about Comanche-Spanish relations comes from official Spanish documents from the era. Two sources are exceptionally thorough: the reports filed by Don Juan Bautista de Anza, translated and compiled by Alfred Thomas in *Forgotten Frontiers*, and the intelligent and insightful reports of Spanish Indian agent Athanase de Mézières, compiled in 1914 by Herbert Bolton in *Athanase de Mézières and the Lousiana-Texas Frontier 1768–1780*. Also helpful and interesting is Ralph Twitchell's edited multivolume compilation *Spanish Archives of New Mexico*.
13. Pedro de Rivera Villalón, *Diario y derrotero de lo camionado, visto y observado en la visita que lo hizo a los presidios de la Nueva Espana septentrional*. Edited by Vito Allesio Robles, Mexico (D.F., Secretaria de la Defensa Nacional, 1946), pp. 78–79 (see Kavanaugh, *The Comanches*, p. 67).
14. Rupert N. Richardson, *The Comanche Barrier to South Plains Settlement*, p. 23.
15. Thomas, p. 58.
16. Ibid., p. 59.
17. Charles Wilson Hackett, ed., *Pichardo's Treatise on the the Limitations of Texas and Louisiana* (Austin: University of Texas Press, 1946), vol. 3, p. 323.
18. An excellent account of Serna's successful 1716 expedition against the Comanches appears in Ralph Twitchell, *Spanish Archives of New Mexico*, vol. 2, p. 301.
19. Kavanaugh, *The Comanches*, pp. 66ff.
20. James T. DeShields, *Border Wars of Texas*, p. 16.
21. William Edward Dunn, "The Apache Mission on the San Saba River; Its Founding and Failure," *Southwestern Historical Quarterly* 17 (1914): 380–81.
22. Ibid., p. 382.
23. Frank Dobie offers an interesting look at the rumors of San Saba gold in his book *Coronado's Children*.
24. Dunn, p. 387.
25. Ibid., p. 389.
26. Ibid., p. 381.
27. Parrilla to the viceroy, *Historia* 95 (June 30, 1757), p. 146.
28. Fathers Banos and Ximenes to the *Guardian*, July 5, 1757, cited in Dunn, p. 401.
29. Fehrenbach, *The Comanches*, p. 201.

30. Thomas, *Forgotten Frontiers*, p. 66.
31. Ibid.
32. By far the best description of this legendary campaign comes from Anza himself, who was both articulate and thorough in his reports to Mexico City. These original documents have been translated and compiled by Alfred Thomas, editor of *Forgotten Frontiers*, see pages 119–42. The Anza writings represent one of the great primary sources of historical material on the relations between the Spanish and the Comanches. Most of my account is taken from these reports.
33. Anza's diary, in Thomas, *Forgotten Frontiers*, p. 136.
34. This estimate came from Sam Houston's commissioner of Indian affairs George V. Bonnell in an article published in 1838 in the *Houston Telegraph and Texas Register*. He apparently got the number from the Comanches, which would make it doubtful indeed. Still, it stands as the only estimate from the era, and later numbers, following the cholera and smallpox epidemics, would seem to bear out a number in that range.

Six BLOOD AND SMOKE

1. It must be noted that General Custer, too, wrote poetry, though Lamar's doggerel was better than Custer's doggerel.
2. Noah Smithwick, *Evolution of a State*, p. 138.
3. James Parker, *Narrative of the Perilous Adventures*, p. 14.
4. Robert M. Utley, *Lone Star Justice: The First Century of the Texas Rangers*, p. 23.
5. Jo Ella Powell Exley, *Frontier Blood*, p. 106 (citing congressional records).
6. Utley, p. 24.
7. "Messages of the President, Submitted to both Houses," December 21, 1838, Lamar Papers, Doc., 948, p. 11.
8. T. R. Fehrenbach, *The Comanches*, p. 310.
9. David La Vere, *Contrary Neighbors*, p. 55.
10. Ibid., p. 310.
11. Donaly E. Brice, *The Great Comanche Raid*, pp. 17–18.
12. La Vere, p. 64.
13. Ibid., p. 20.
14. Mike Cox, *The Texas Rangers: Wearing the Cinco Peso, 1821–1900*, p. 43.
15. Other accounts give different numbers, as usual. John Henry Brown writes that there were fifty-five whites, forty-two Lipans, and twelve Tonkawas. Since Smithwick was actually there, his would seem to be the more credible account.
16. Smithwick, p. 135.
17. Ibid.
18. Cox, p. 69.
19. Ibid.
20. J. W. Wilbarger, *Indian Depredations in Texas*, p. 145.
21. John Henry Brown, *Indian Wars and Pioneers of Texas*, p. 75.
22. Ibid. See contemporary accounts of this whole episode in John Holmes Jenkins, ed., *Recollections of Early Texas: Memoirs of John Holland Jenkins*, and in Noah Smithwick's *Evolution of a State*. Colonel John Moore's report to his superiors concerning the engagement is contained in the *Journals of the Fourth Congress of the Republic of Texas*, vol. 3, pp. 108ff.
23. Cox, p. 75; details on the location of the wound from Charles A. Gulick, Jr., ed., *The Papers of Mirabeau Buonaparte Lamar*, vol. 4, p. 232.
24. Shelby Foote, *The Civil War*, vol. 1, pp. 336ff.

25. Dorman Winfrey and James M. Day, eds., *The Indian Papers of Texas and the Southwest*, vol. 1, p. 105.
26. Mary Maverick, *Memoirs of Mary Maverick*, p. 31.
27. Ibid.
28. Fehrenbach, *The Comanches*, p. 326.
29. Ibid.
30. See Smithwick's account of his three months with Spirit Talker in *Evolution of a State*, pp. 107ff.
31. Ibid., p. 134.
32. William Preston Johnston, *Life of General Albert Sidney Johnston*, p. 117.
33. Maverick, p. 35.
34. Brice, p. 24.
35. Maverick, p. 32.
36. Fehrenbach, *The Comanches*, p. 328.
37. Maverick, p. 36.
38. This account was given in a report from Captain George Howard to Colonel Fisher dated April 6, 1840; it is also mentioned in the memoirs of ranger John Salmon "Rip" Ford.
39. Rupert N. Richardson, *The Comanche Barrier to South Plains Settlement*, p. 51.
40. Ibid.; see also Jodye Lynne Dickson Schilz and Thomas F. Schilz, *Buffalo Hump and the Penateka Comanches* (El Paso: University of Texas at El Paso Press, 1989), p. 18.
41. Thomas Kavanaugh, *The Comanches*, p. 264.
42. Ibid.

Seven DREAM VISIONS AND APOCALYPSE

1. David La Vere, *Contrary Neighbors*, p. 36.
2. Scott Zesch, *The Captured*, p. 34.
3. *Houston Telegraph and Texas Register*, May 30, 1838.
4. La Vere, p. 28.
5. Jodye Lynne Dickson Schilz and Thomas F. Schilz, *Buffalo Hump and the Penateka Comanches* p. 5.
6. Ibid., p. 20.
7. Ibid., p. 9.
8. Ibid.
9. Ibid., endnotes, p. 51.
10. The number of Indians varies according to who is giving the account. A citizen of Victoria, John Linn, who witnessed the attack, estimated six hundred warriors in the raiding party. Ranger Ben McCulloch estimated a thousand Indians. An account in a local newspaper estimated two hundred. I am inclined to believe both McCulloch and Linn, meaning that there were in fact six hundred warriors and the rest were women, boys, and older men. McCulloch, one of the best trackers ever to come out of Texas, cut their trail and would have been quite accurate in assessing the number of horses and riders.
11. John Holmes Jenkins III, ed., *Recollections of Early Texas: The Memoirs of John Holland Jenkins* (Austin, University of Texas Press, 1958), p. 62.
12. John J. Linn, *Reminiscences of Fifty Years in Texas*, p. 340.
13. Donaly E. Brice, *Great Comanche Raid*, p. 30.
14. John Henry Brown, *Indian Wars and Pioneers of Texas*, p. 80.
15. Jenkins, p. 68.

16. Ibid., p. 80.
17. Linn, pp. 341–42.
18. Mike Cox, *The Texas Rangers*, p. 76.
19. Jenkins, p. 64.
20. Brown, p. 81.
21. Mary Maverick, *Memoirs of Mary Maverick*, p. 29.
22. Linn, p. 347.
23. Victor M. Rose, *The Life and Services of General Ben McCulloch*, p. 64 (citing verbatim account of John Henry Brown).
24. Walter Prescott Webb, *The Texas Rangers: A Century of Frontier Defense*, p. 62.
25. Jenkins, p. 68.
26. Linn, p. 343.
27. Schilz and Schilz, p. 23.
28. Brazos, *Life of Robert Hall*, pp. 52–53.
29. Schilz and Schilz, p. 24.
30. J. W. Wilbarger, *Indian Depredations in Texas*, p. 185.

Eight WHITE SQUAW

1. Eugene E. White, *Experiences of a Special Indian Agent*, p. 262.
2. James T. DeShields, *Cynthia Ann Parker: The Story of Her Capture*, pp. 23–24.
3. *Clarksville Northern Standard*, May 25, 1846.
4. Daniel J. Gielo and Scott Zesch, eds., "Every day Seemed to Be a Holiday: The Captivity of Bianca Babb," *Southwestern Historical Quarterly* 107 (July 2003): 36.
5. T. A. Babb, *In the Bosom of the Comanches*, p. 34.
6. Scott Zesch, *The Captured*, p. 45.
7. Babb, p. 22.
8. Gielo and Zesch, p. 56.
9. Ibid.
10. Ibid., p. 57.
11. Zesch, p. 75.
12. Ibid.
13. Ibid., p. 81.
14. Ibid.
15. Ibid., p. 85.
16. Babb, p. 58.
17. Rupert N. Richardson, *The Comanche Barrier to South Plains Settlement*, p. 61; and Thomas Kavanaugh, *The Comanches*, p. 296. Note that Buffalo Hump, Little Wolf, and Santa Anna were all powerful chiefs, and some considered them more powerful than Old Owl or Pah-hah-yuco. My research has shown that, assuming the Wallace/Hoebel model of social organization is right, they would fall more into the traditional category of "war chiefs."
18. Kavanaugh, p. 266.
19. Ibid., p. 297.
20. *Clarksville Northern Standard*, May 25, 1846.
21. Ibid.
22. Letter: P. M. Butler and M. G. Lewis to the Hon. W. Medill, Commissioner of Indian Affairs, August 8, 1848, House Executive Documents No. 1, 30th Congress, Second Session, p. 578.
23. DeShields, *The Story of Her Capture*, p. 30.
24. Butler, and Lewis, p. 578.
25. Joyde Lynne Dickson Schilz and Thomas F. Schilz, *Buffalo Hump and the Penateka*

Comanches, p. 24, and Dorman H. Winfrey and James M. Day, eds., *Indian Papers of Texas and the Southwest, 1816–1925,* vol. 1, p. 266.

26. Richardson, *The Comanche Barrier to South Plains Settlement,* p. 57.
27. Ibid., p. 72.
28. DeShields, p. 28.
29. T. R. Fehrenbach, *The Comanches,* p. 349.
30. David La Vere, *Contrary Neighbors,* p. 120.
31. Ernest Wallace and E. Adamson Hoebel, *The Comanches,* pp. 169–70.
32. Ramon Powers and James N. Leiker, "Cholera Among the Plains Indians," *Western Historical Quarterly* 29 (Fall 1998): 319.
33. Ibid., p. 321.
34. Ibid., pp. 322–23.
35. Richardson, *The Comanche Barrier to South Plains Settlement,* p. 78.
36. Letter: Horace Capron to Robert Howard, Commissioner of Indian Affairs, September 30, 1852, letters received, M234, Roll 858, Texas Agency (cited in Schilz and Schilz, p. 38).
37. Richardson, *The Comanche Barrier to South Plains Settlement,* p. 60.
38. Letter: Robert S. Neighbors to the Hon. W. Medill, Commissioner of Indian Affairs, November 18, 1847, 30th Congress, First Session, Senate Committee Report 171.
39. Kavanaugh, p. 265.
40. Chief Baldwin Parker, *The Life of Quanah Parker, Comanche Chief,* through J. Evetts Haley, August 29, 1930, manuscript, Center for American History, University of Texas, p. 9.
41. Jo Ella Powell Exley, *Frontier Blood,* p. 291 (note).
42. Ibid., p. 139.
43. Ibid., p. 138.
44. DeShields, p. 32.
45. Bill Neeley, *The Last Comanche Chief: The Life and Times of Quanah Parker,* p. 52; also, Cynthia Ann later picked up another nickname: "Preloch." It was not uncommon for Indians to have several names.
46. Randolph Marcy, *Exploration of the Red River of Louisiana in the Year 1852,* p. 37.

Nine CHASING THE WIND

1. James W. Parker, *Defence of James W. Parker Against Slanderous Accusations,* p. 4.
2. Ibid., p. 5.
3. James W. Parker, *The Rachel Plummer Narrative,* entire.
4. W. S. Nye, *Carbine and Lance: The Story of Old Fort Sill,* pp. 35–36.
5. T. R. Fehrenbach, *The Comanches,* p. 224.
6. J. Evetts Haley, "The Comanchero Trade," *Southwestern Historical Quarterly* 38 (January 1935): 38.
7. David La Vere, *Contrary Neighbors,* p. 117.
8. Ibid., p. 123.
9. Jo Ella Powell Exley, *Frontier Blood,* p. 84.
10. Ibid., p. 87.
11. Rachel Plummer, *Narrative of the Capture and Subsequent Sufferings of Rachel Plummer,* pp. 116–17.
12. James Parker, *The Rachel Plummer Narrative,* p. 27.
13. Letter: James Parker to M. B. Lamar, March 17, 1839, in Charles Gulick, ed., *The Papers of Mirabeau Buonaparte Lamar,* vol. 2, p. 494.
14. Ibid.

15. Exley, p. 104. Note that Exley is the sole source on the third child, citing a letter from L. T. M. Plummer to "Dear Nephews" from a private collection.
16. Randolph B. Marcy, *Adventure on Red River,* p. 169.
17. Amelia W. Williams and Eugene C. Barker, *The Writings of Sam Houston, 1813–1863,* vol. 4, pp. 180–81.
18. Exley, p. 177 (citing Confederate records).

Ten DEATH'S INNOCENT FACE

1. Walter Prescott Webb, *The Texas Rangers,* p. 78.
2. This idea is mentioned in Webb's *The Texas Rangers,* but it appeared originally in J. W. Wilbarger's *Indian Depredations in Texas,* originally published in 1889.
3. Walter Prescott, Webb, *The Great Plains,* p. 167.
4. Ibid.
5. Colonel Richard Irving Dodge, *Our Wild Indians,* pp. 418–20.
6. Ibid.
7. Evan Connell, *Son of the Morning Star,* p. 57.
8. Colonel Dodge, *Our Wild Indians,* p. 421.
9. Panhandle Plains Historical Museum exhibit.
10. Colonel Dodge, *Our Wild Indians,* p. 421.
11. David La Vere, *Contrary Neighbors,* p. 35.
12. Ibid.
13. T. R. Fehrenbach, *The Comanches,* p. 298.
14. Ernest Wallace and E. Adamson Hoebel, *The Comanches,* p. 257.
15. Fehrenbach, *The Comanches,* p. 146.
16. Herman Lehmann, *Nine Years Among the Indians,* pp. 47–50.
17. Clinton L. Smith, *The Boy Captives,* pp. 52–53.
18. Mike Cox, *The Texas Rangers: Wearing the Cinco Peso, 1821–1900,* p. 42.
19. Jo Ella Powell Exley, *Frontier Blood,* p. 46.
20. Fehrenbach, *The Comanches,* p. 300.
21. Z. N. Morrell, *Flowers and Fruits in the Wilderness,* p. 86.
22. Mary Maverick, *Memoirs of Mary Maverick,* p. 29.
23. Major John Caperton, *Sketch of Colonel John C. Hays, The Texas Rangers, Incidents in Mexico,* p. 11.
24. Ibid., p. 32.
25. Wallace and Hoebel, p. 258.
26. Captain Nathan Brookshire, Report in *Journals of the Fourth Congress of the Republic of Texas,* vol. 3, pp. 110–11.
27. J. W. Wilbarger, *Indian Depredations in Texas,* pp. 368ff.
28. Colonel Dodge, *Our Wild Indians,* p. 522.
29. James Kimmins Greer, *Colonel Jack Hays: Frontier Leader and California Builder,* p. 35.
30. Wilbarger, p. 74.
31. The photo referred to is in Greer's biography of Hays.
32. Webb, *The Texas Rangers,* p. 67.
33. Caperton, p. 5.
34. Colonel John S. Ford, *John C. Hays In Texas,* p. 5.
35. Caperton, p. 13.
36. Greer, p. 26.
37. Cox, p. 78.
38. Victor Rose, *The Life and Services of Ben McCulloch,* p. 42.
39. Caperton, p. 9.

40. Ibid., p. 10.
41. Webb, *The Texas Rangers*, p 81.
42. Ibid., p. 84.
43. Rose, p. 84.
44. Cox, p. 87 (citing James Nichols Wilson, *Now Your Hear My Horn: Journal of James Wilson Nichols* [Austin: University of Texas Press, 1967], pp. 122–23).
45. Ibid.
46. Wilbarger, p. 73.
47. Caperton, pp. 18–19.
48. Charles Adams Gulick, ed., *The Papers of Mirabeau Buonaparte Lamar*, vol. 4, pp. 234–35.
49. Wilbarger, p. 72.
50. Cox, pp. 82–83; see also Gulick, p. 232.
51. Webb, *The Texas Rangers*, p. 71.
52. Ibid., p. 120.
53. Gulick, p. 234.
54. John E. Parsons, *Sam Colt's Own Record of Transactions with Captain Walker and Eli Whitney, Jr., in 1847*, p. 8.
55. Ibid., p. 9.
56. Cox, p. 93; see also Robert M. Utley, *Lone Star Justice: The First Century of the Texas Rangers*, p. 10.
57. Ford, pp. 18ff. Note that this account comes from Hays himself. He gave it to the *Houston Star*, where it appeared on June 23, 1844, and was later picked up by other papers, including the Clarksville *Northern Standard*.
58. Ford, p. 20.
59. Ibid., p. 21.
60. Parsons, p. 10.
61. Ibid., p 8.
62. Ibid., p. 10.
63. Ibid., p. 16.
64. Ibid., p. 46.
65. Fehrenbach, *The Comanches*, p. 303.
66. Cox, p. 113.

Eleven WAR TO THE KNIFE

1. A. B. Mason, "The White Captive," *Civilian and Gazette*, 1860 (reprint of story in *The White Man*).
2. Jonathan Hamilton Baker, *Diary of Jonathan Hamilton Baker of Palo Pinto County, Texas, Part 1, 1858–1860*, p. 210.
3. Jo Ella Powell Exley, *Frontier Blood*, p. 158.
4. G. A. Holland, *The History of Parker County and the Double Log Cabin* (Weatherford, Tex.: The Herald Publishing Company, 1937), pp. 18, 46.
5. Ibid., p. 46.
6. Hilory G. Bedford, *Texas Indian Troubles*, pp. 70–71.
7. Ibid.
8. Judith Ann Benner, *Sul Ross: Soldier, Statesman, Educator*, p. 38.
9. Ibid., pp. 38ff.
10. J. P. Earle, *A History of Clay County and Northwest Texas, Written by J. P. Earle, one of the first pioneers*, p. 76.
11. Mike Cox, *The Texas Rangers*, p. 164.
12. *The White Man*, September 13, 1860.

13. Cox, p. 162.
14. J. Evetts Haley, *Charles Goodnight: Cowman and Plainsman*, p. 49.
15. Charles Goodnight, *Indian Recollections*, pp. 15ff.
16. Marshall Doyle, *A Cry Unheard: The Story of Indian Attacks in and Around Parker County, Texas, 1858–1872*, pp. 18–19.
17. Ibid., p. 33.
18. Ernest Wallace, *Texas in Turmoil, 1849–1875*, p. 17.
19. Ibid., p. 13.
20. Ibid.
21. Exley, p. 169.
22. Ibid.
23. Walter Prescott Webb, *The Texas Rangers*, p. 142.
24. Ibid., p 147.
25. T. R. Fehrenbach, *The Comanches*, p. 400.
26. Ibid., p. 401.
27. John S. Ford, *Rip Ford's Texas*, p. 222.
28. Wallace, *Texas in Turmoil*, p 18.
29. Fehrenbach, *The Comanches*, p. 402.
30. Ernest Wallace, and E. Adamson Hoebel, *The Comanches*, p. 296.
31. Larry McMurtry, *Crazy Horse*, p. 77, citing Alex Shoumatoff.
32. Wallace and Hoebel, p. 297.
33. Ibid., p. 299.
34. Randolph Marcy, *The Prairie Traveler*, p. 218.
35. Wallace, *Texas in Turmoil*, p. 25.
36. Webb, *The Texas Rangers*, p. 169; Wallace, *Texas in Turmoil*, p. 24.
37. Cox, *The Texas Rangers*, p. 144.
38. Ford, p. 224.
39. Ibid., pp. 223ff.
40. Ibid., pp. 231–32.
41. Cox, p. 146.
42. Ford, p. 233.
43. James DeShields, *Cynthia Ann Parker, the Story of Her Capture*, p. 40.
44. Ford, p. 233.
45. Cox, p. 147.
46. Ford, p. 233.
47. Ibid., p. 235.
48. Cited from Cox, p. 145.
49. W. S. Nye, *Carbine and Lance: The Story of Old Fort Sill*, p. 19.
50. Benner, pp. 29ff.
51. Ibid., p. 32.
52. Ibid.
53. Wallace, *Texas in Turmoil*, p. 24.

Twelve WHITE QUEEN OF THE COMANCHES

1. Jonathan Hamilton Baker, *Diary of Jonathan Hamilton Baker*, pp. 191–92.
2. J. Evetts Haley, *Charles Goodnight: Cowman and Plainsman*, p. 52.
3. Ibid., pp. 50–51.
4. Ibid., pp. 51–52.
5. Cited in Jo Ella Powell Exley, *Frontier Blood*, p. 148.
6. Baker, pp. 202ff.

7. B. F. Gholson, *Recollections of B. F. Gholson,* p. 24.
8. Marshall Doyle, *A Cry Unheard,* p. 35; see also Haley, p. 53.
9. Judith Ann Benner, *Sul Ross: Soldier, Statesman, Educator,* p. 52.
10. Charles Goodnight, *Charles Goodnight's Indian Recollections,* p. 22.
11. Gholson, p. 28.
12. *YA-A-H-HOO: Warwhoop of the Comanches,* narrative in Elizabeth Ross Clarke archives, Center for American History, University of Texas in Austin, p. 66.
13. Hilory G. Bedford, *Texas Indian Troubles,* p. 73; the account also appears in J. W. Wilbarger, *Indian Depredations in Texas.*
14. Ibid., p. 58.
15. Gholson, p. 30.
16. Ibid., p. 34.
17. Baker, p. 204.
18. *The Galveston Civilian,* February 5, 1861.
19. Ibid.
20. Gholson, p. 40.
21. Ibid., p. 44.
22. Amelia W. Williams and Eugene C. Barker, *The Writings of Sam Houston, 1813–1863,* vol. 4, pp. 60–61.
23. Lawrence T. Jones, "Cynthia Ann Parker and Pease Ross, The Forgotten Photographs," *Southwestern Historical Quarterly,* January 1991, p. 379.
24. Bedford, p. 75.
25. Eugene E. White, *Experiences of a Special Indian Agent,* p. 271; letter written by Sul Ross while governor.
26. H. B. Rogers, *The Recollections of H. B. Rogers, as told to J. A. Rickard* (appended to Gholson manuscript), p. 66.
27. Jo Ella Powell Exley, *Frontier Blood,* p. 175.
28. Lawrence T. Jones, "Cynthia Ann Parker and Pease Ross," p. 379.
29. Exley, pp. 170–71, citing an account by Medora Robinson Turner.
30. *Clarksville Northern Standard,* April 6, 1861.
31. Letter: K. J. Pearson, to John D. Floyd, February 3, 1861, Fort Sill Archives.
32. Margaret Schmidt Hacker, *Cynthia Ann Parker: The Life and Legend,* p. 32.
33. Stephen B. Oates, "Texas Under the Secessionists," *Southwestern Historical Quarterly* 167 (October 1963): 167.
34. Ibid., p. 168.
35. James T. DeShields, *The Capture of Cynthia Ann Parker,* p. 71.
36. *Clarksville Northern Standard,* April 6, 1861.
37. Jones, "Cynthia Ann Parker and Pease Ross," p. 380.
38. Exley, p. 175.
39. Coho Smith, *Cohographs,* p. 69. All of the material relating to the Smith-Parker meetings is derived from Smith's own account.
40. Jan Isbelle Fortune, "The Recapture and Return of Cynthia Ann Parker," *Groesbeck Journal,* May 15, 1936, p. 1.
41. Exley, p. 176, citing an article written by Parker family member Tom Champion.
42. Jones, "Cynthia Ann Parker and Pease Ross," p 190.
43. Ibid.
44. Ibid.
45. Hacker, p. 35.
46. Ibid.
47. Exley, p. 178, citing Champion account.
48. Letter: T. J. Cates to the Edgewood *Enterprise,* June 1918.
49. Exley, p. 179.

50. Disinterment Permit, Texas State Department of Health, Bureau of Vital Statistics, dated August 25, 1865.
51. Paul Wellman, "Cynthia Ann Parker," *Chronicles of Oklahoma* 12, no. 2 (1934): 163.

Thirteen THE RISE OF QUANAH

1. This was Cynthia Ann's own account of what had happened. See Judith Ann Benner, *Sul Ross: Soldier, Statesman, Educator,* p. 56.
2. Robert H. Williams, "The Case for Peta Nocona," In *Texana,* Vol 10, 1972, p. 55. Williams makes a superbly argued case for what is fairly obvious anyway, that Quanah's later insistence that he and his father were out hunting during the attack is simply untrue. Quanah did it to protect his father's reputation, and he did not even attempt to set the record straight until 1898, almost forty years after the event. He did it most famously in a speech in Dallas in 1910 shortly before his death. Williams also points out that the two riders who left the battlefield had to be Quanah and his brother.
3. J. Evetts Haley, ed., *Charles Goodnight's Indian Recollections,* pp. 25–26.
4. Ibid.
5. Ibid.
6. Jo Ella Powell Exley, *Frontier Blood,* pp. 183–84; citing untitled manuscript of J. A. Dickson.
7. Ibid., p. 186.
8. Ibid., pp. 199ff.
9. Ernest Wallace and E. Adamson Hoebel, *The Comanches,* p. 81.
10. Charles Goodnight, *The Making of a Scout,* manuscript in Panhandle Plains Historical Museum Archives.
11. Wallace and Hoebel, pp. 178ff.
12. Ibid., p. 183.
13. "Quanah Parker in Adobe Walls Battle," *Borger News Herald,* date unknown, Panhandle Plains Historical Museum Archives, based on interview with J. A. Dickson.
14. Elizabeth Ross Clarke, *YA-A-H-HOO: Warwhoop of the Comanches,* manuscript at Center for American History, University of Texas, Austin, p. 73.
15. Exley, p. 184, citing untitled Dickson ms.
16. Chief Baldwin Parker, *Life of Quanah Parker, Comanche Chief,* through J. Evetts Haley, August 29, 1930, manuscript at Center for American History, University of Texas, Austin.
17. Exley, Dickson ms.
18. Randolph Marcy, *Adventure on Red River: A Report on the Exploration of the Red River by Captain Randolph Marcy and Captain G. B. McClellan,* p. 159.
19. Scott Zesch, *The Captured,* pp. 68–76.
20. Thomas W. Kavanaugh, *The Comanches,* p. 372; Zoe A. Tilghman, *Quanah, Eagle of the Comanches,* pp. 68ff.
21. Kavanaugh, *The Comanches,* p. 481.
22. Tilghman, pp. 68ff.
23. Exley, p. 204, citing untitled Dickson ms.
24. Kavanaugh, *The Comanches,* p. 473.
25. Olive King Dixon, *Fearless and Effective Foe: He Spared Women and Children, Always,* manuscript, Center for American History, University of Texas, Austin.
26. Eugene E. White, *Experiences of a Special Indian Agent,* pp. 276ff. White's account is taken from his conversations with Quanah in later years.

27. The ultimate source of this story is Quanah, but his accounts, passed down to us through three different sources—Eugene White, Olive King Dixon (via Goodnight and Baldwin Parker), and Ella Cox Lutz, Quanah's granddaughter—agree in all important aspects.
28. Wallace and Hoebel, pp. 136–37.
29. White, p. 284.
30. Ibid., p. 286.
31. Dixon, manuscript.

Fourteen UNCIVIL WARS

1. Ernest Wallace, *Texas in Turmoil*, p. 238.
2. David La Vere, *Contrary Neighbors*, p. 169.
3. Ibid., p. 178.
4. Ibid.
5. Ibid., p. 171.
6. T. R. Fehrenbach, *The Comanches*, p. 450.
7. Angie Debo, *The Road to Disappearance: A History of the Creek Indians*, pp. 150ff.
8. Fehrenbach, *The Comanches*, p, 449.
9. Debo, p. 152; also La Vere, p 171.
10. Fehrenbach, *The Comanches*, p. 459.
11. Wallace, p. 244; R. N. Richardson, *The Comanche Barrier to South Plains Settlement*, p. 142.
12. W. S. Nye, *Carbine and Lance: The Story of Old Fort Sill*, p. 35.
13. Hampton Sides, *Blood and Thunder*, p. 308.
14. Thelma S. Guild and Harvey L. Carter, *Kit Carson: A Pattern for Heroes*, pp. 231ff.
15. Sides, p. 368.
16. Thomas Kavanagh, *The Comanches*, p. 398.
17. Letter to commanding officer, Fort Bascom, September 27, 1864; Official Records of the War of Rebellion, series 1, vol. 41, pt. 3, pp. 429–30.
18. Captain George Pettis, *Kit Carson's Fight with the Comanche and Kiowa Indians* (Providence Press Company, Sidney S. Rider [copyright], 1878), p. 3.
19. Mildred Mayhall, *The Kiowas*, p. 161.
20. Pettis, p. 5.
21. David A. Norris, "Confederate Gunners Affectionately Called Their Hard Working Little Mountain Howitzers 'Bull Pups,'" *America's Civil War*, September 1995, pp. 10, 12, 14, 16, 20, and 90.
22. Pettis, p. 9.
23. Ibid.
24. Kavanagh, *The Comanches*, p. 395.
25. Ibid., p. 16.
26. Ibid.
27. 39th U.S. Congress; Second Session, Senate report 156, pp. 53, 74.
28. Dee Brown, *Bury My Heart at Wounded Knee*, p. 86.
29. 39th U.S. Congress; Second Session, Senate report 156, pp. 73, 96.
30. Sides, p. 379.
31. Ibid.
32. Fehrenbach, *The Comanches*, p. 461.

Fifteen PEACE, AND OTHER HORRORS

1. Rupert N. Richardson, *The Comanche Barrier to South Plains Settlement*, p. 157.
2. Ibid.
3. T. R. Fehrenbach, *The Comanches*, p. 484.
4. Abstracted from the *Army Navy Journal* 15, no. 52 (August 31, 1878); cited in Charles M. Robinson, *Bad Hand: A Biography of General Ranald S. Mackenzie*, p. 57.
5. Thomas Kavanagh, *The Comanches*, p. 411.
6. Richardson, p. 151.
7. Kavanagh, *The Comanches*, p. 412.
8. Alfred A. Taylor, account in Chronicles of Oklahoma, II, pp. 102–103.
9. Charles J. Kappler, ed., *Indian Affairs Laws and Treaties* (Washington, D.C., 1903), vol. II, pp. 977ff.
10. Henry M. Stanley, "A British Journalist Reports the Medicine Lodge Councils of 1867," *Kansas Historical Quarterly* 33 (Spring 1967): 282.
11. Ibid., 33:283.
12. Douglas C. Jones, *The Treaty at Medicine Lodge*, pp. 101ff.
13. Stanley, pp. 249–320.
14. Kappler, pp. 977ff.
15. Ibid., p. 982.
16. Richardson, p. 237, note 25.
17. Quanah Parker to Captain Hugh Lenox Scott, 1898, H. L. Scott Material, W. S. Nye Collection, Fort Sill Archives.
18. David La Vere, *Contrary Neighbors*, pp. 183–84.
19. Leavenworth to Commissioner of Indian Affairs, April 23, 1868, 40th Congress, Second Session, Sen. Ex. Doc. No. 60:2.
20. Richardson, p. 161.
21. Lawrence Schmeckebier, *The Office of Indian Affairs, Its History, Activities and Organization*, p. 48; Richardson, p. 164
22. Fehrenbach, *The Comanches*, p. 485.

Sixteen THE ANTI-CUSTER

1. Charles M. Robinson III, *Bad Hand: A Biography of General Ranald S. Mackenzie*, p. 10, citing Morris Schaff, *Old West Point*, pp. 42–43.
2. Evan S. Connell, *Son of the Morning Star*, p. 108.
3. Captain Joseph Dorst, "Ranald Slidell Mackenzie," Twentieth Annual Reunion of the Association Graduates of the United States Military Academy at West Point, June 12, 1889, p. 7.
4. F. E. Green, ed., "Ranald S. Mackenzie's Official Correspondence Relating to Texas, 1873–79," *Museum Journal* 10 (1966): 13ff.
5. U. S. Grant, *Personal Memoirs* (New York: Charles A. Webster and Co., 1885), p. 541.
6. Ernest Wallace, *Ranald S. Mackenzie on the Texas Frontier*, p. 9.
7. Dorst, p. 7.
8. Connell, pp. 128–29.
9. W. S. Nye, *Carbine and Lance*, pp. 63ff.
10. Ibid., p. 67.
11. Ibid., p 69.
12. Jo Ella Powell Exley, *Frontier Blood*, p. 196, citing untitled Dickson manuscript, p. 37.

13. Tatum's second annual report, August 12, 1870, 41st Congress, Third Session, House Ex. Doc. no. 1, vol. 1, 724–729, cited in Rupert N. Richardson, *The Comanche Barrier to South Plains Settlement,* p. 171.

14. Letter: Ranald S. Mackenzie to William T. Sherman, June 15, 1871.

15. Robert G. Carter, *On the Border with Mackenzie,* p. 167.

16. Charles H. Sommer, *Quanah Parker, Last Chief of the Comanches,* p. 43.

17. There is some disagreement about this among historians. Leading Comanche historian Ernest Wallace believes that the command was Quanah's, as does Quanah's principal biographer, Bill Neeley. Evidence to the contrary comes mainly from interviews conducted many years later, and cited extensively in Jo Ella Powell Exley's *Frontier Blood,* with the Comanche warrior Cohayyah, who said that Parra-o-coom (Bull Bear) was the leader at that time. There does not seem to be any disagreement that Quanah led the night raid or that he led the attack on Heyl and Carter.

18. Carter, *On the Border with Mackenzie,* p. 170.

19. Ibid., p. 173.

20. Ibid., p. 175. Carter notes that the Comanches were "poorly armed with muzzle-loading rifles and pistols, lances and bows."

21. Ibid.

22. Colonel Richard Dodge, *Our Wild Indians,* p. 489.

23. Handbook of Texas Online, Texas State Historical Society.

24. Carter, op. cit., p. 187.

25. Ibid., p. 187.

26. Ibid., p. 188.

27. Arthur Ferguson Journal, Utah State Historical Society; cited in Stephen E. Ambrose, *Nothing Like It in the World: The Men who Built the Transcontinental Railroad, 1863–1869,* p. 143.

28. Ibid., p. 189.

29. Wallace, *Ranald S. Mackenzie,* p. 54.

30. Carter, *On the Border with Mackenzie,* p. 194.

Seventeen MACKENZIE UNBOUND

1. Letter: Charles Howard to President Grant, cited in T. R. Fehrenbach, *The Comanches,* p. 515.

2. Robert G. Carter, *On the Border with Mackenzie,* p. 219.

3. Ernest Wallace, *Texas in Turmoil,* pp. 252–53.

4. Ernest Wallace, *Ranald S. Mackenzie on the Texas Frontier,* p. 74.

5. W. A. Thompson, "Scouting with Mackenzie," *Journal of the United States Cavalry Association* 10 (1897): 431.

6. Clinton Smith, *The Boy Captives,* p. 134.

7. David La Vere, *Contrary Neighbors,* p. 194; Scott Zesch, *The Captured,* p. 159.

8. Mackenzie's Official Report, October 12, 1872, "1872, Sept. 29, Attack on Comanche Village," To The Assistant Adjutant General, Department of Texas.

9. Ibid.

10. Herman Lehmann, *Nine Years Among the Indians,* pp. 185–86; Lehmann also notes that Batsena had been using a Spencer carbine, which suggests that the Comanches were finally beginning to trade for some of these weapons. By 1874 they would have many more of them.

11. R. G. Carter, *The Old Sergeant's Story,* p. 84.

12. Mackenzie's Official Report, October 12, 1872.

13. Carter, *Old Sergeant's Story,* p. 84.

14. Smith, *The Boy Captives*, p. 13.7
15. Carter, *On the Border with Mackenzie*, pp. 419ff.

Eighteen THE HIDE MEN AND THE MESSIAH

1. Thomas W. Kavanagh, *The Comanches*, pp. 474ff.
2. Rupert N. Richardson, "The Comanche Indians and the Fight at Adobe Walls," *Panhandle Plains Historical Review* (Canyon, Texas) 4 (1931): 25.
3. Quanah's feathered headdress is on display at the Panhandle Plains Historical Museum in Canyon, Texas.
4. Ernest Wallace and E. Adamson Hoebel, *The Comanches*, p. 150.
5. T. Lindsay Baker and Billy R. Harrison, *Adobe Walls: The History and Archaeology of the Trading Post*, p. 3.
6. Colonel William F. Cody, *The Adventures of Buffalo Bill Cody*, p. viii.
7. Baker and Harrison, p 29; T. R. Fehrenbach, *The Comanches*, p. 523.
8. Baker and Harrison, p. 4
9. James L. Haley, *The Buffalo War*, p. 22.
10. Ibid., p. 26.
11. Ibid., p. 8.
12. Francis Parkman, *The California and Oregon Trails*, p. 251.
13. Baker and Harrison, p. 25.
14. Ibid., p. 41.
15. Fehrenbach, *The Comanches*, p. 523.
16. W. S. Nye, *Carbine and Lance*, p. 188.
17. Thomas Battey, *Life and Adventures of a Quaker Among the Indians*, p. 239; and Baker and Harrison, p. 39.
18. Haley, *The Buffalo War*, p. 51.
19. Ernest Wallace, *Ranald Mackenzie on the Texas Frontier*, p. 119.
20. Kavanagh, *The Comanches*, p. 445; Haley, *The Buffalo War*, note on p. 232.
21. Letter: Agent J. M. Haworth to Enoch Hoag, May 5, 1874.
22. Battey, p. 302.
23. This was Coggia's Comet.
24. Zoe Tilghman, *Quanah Parker, Eagle of the Comanches*, pp. 82–84.
25. Battey, p. 303.
26. Baker and Harrison, p. 44.
27. Quanah interview with Captain Hugh Lennox Scott, 1897, Fort Sill Archives.
28. Wallace and Hoebel, p. 320.
29. Haley, *The Buffalo War*, p. 57.
30. Letter: Agent J. M. Haworth to Enoch Hoag, June 8, 1874.
31. Quanah interview with Scott.
32. W. S. Nye Collection, "Iseeo Account," pp. 58–60, Fort Sill Archives.
33. Quanah interview with Scott.
34. Olive King Dixon, *Life of Billy Dixon*, p. 167.
35. "Quanah Parker in Adobe Walls Battle," *Borger News Herald*, date unknown, Panhandle Plains Historical Museum Archives.
36. Haley, *The Buffalo War*, p. 73.
37. Baker and Harrison, pp. 75ff.
38. Dixon, *Life of Billy Dixon*, p. 186.
39. Baker and Harrison, p. 66.
40. Ibid., pp. 64–66; Dixon, *Life of Billy Dixon*, pp. 162ff.
41. Dixon, *Life of Billy Dixon*, p. 181.
42. Robert G. Carter, *The Old Sergeant's Story*, p. 98.

43. Quanah interview with Scott.
44. Rupert N. Richardson, *The Comanche Barrier to South Plains Settlement*, p. 194.
45. Ernest Wallace, *Texas in Turmoil*, pp. 256–57.

Nineteen THE RED RIVER WAR

1. Thomas Kavanagh, *The Comanches*, pp. 472–74. These are rough estimates. The precise number of Comanches is not known, mainly because it was impossible to tell, on a historical basis, which Indians were on or off the reservation by measuring the number of rations drawn. The best estimate for ration-drawing Indians was 2,643, made in March 1874 by Agent Haworth. Clearly many of those were Comanches who later went back into the wild. Kavanagh analyzes the various estimates of Indian populations from censuses taken in November 1869, December 1870, and March 1874. We know that roughly 650 Comanches were in Quanah's, Black Beard's, and Shaking Hand's bands; that is not counting the Comanches who surrendered in unknown numbers after Palo Duro Canyon.
2. When all the tribes in the southern plains surrendered, the number of adult males was little more than seven hundred; this is my estimate based on that and on the ratio of fighting men to total population in the surrendered tribes; see Rupert N. Richardson, *The Comanche Barrier to South Plains Settlement*, p. 200.
3. Letter: C. C. Augur to Mackenzie, August 28, 1874, in F. E. Green, ed., "Ranald S. Mackenzie's Official Correspondence Relating to Texas, 1873–79," *Museum Journal*, West Texas Museum Association (Lubbock, Texas), 10 (1966): 80ff.
4. Ernest Wallace, *Ranald S. Mackenzie on the Texas Frontier*, p. 124.
5. Nelson Miles to AAG, Dept. of Missouri, September 1, 1874; Mackenzie's Official Correspondence, p. 87.
6. James L. Haley, *The Buffalo War*, p. 193.
7. J. T. Marshall, *The Miles Expedition of 1874–5*, p. 39.
8. Wallace, *Ranald S. Mackenzie on the Texas Frontier*, pp. 125–26.
9. Ibid., p. 131.
10. Augur to Mackenzie, August 28, 1874; Mackenzie Official Correspondence, p. 81.
11. Robert G. Carter, *On the Border with Mackenzie*, p. 484.
12. "Mackenzie's Expedition through the Battle of Palo Duro Canyon as described by a special correspondent of the New York Herald," October 16, 1874, *Museum Journal* 10 (1966): 114.
13. Carter, *On the Border with Mackenzie*, p. 485.
14. Wallace, *Ranald S. Mackenzie on the Texas Frontier*, p. 136.
15. Carter, *On the Border with Mackenzie*, p. 488.
16. John Charlton's account in Captain Robert G. Carter, *The Old Sergeant's Story*, p. 39.
17. Charlton in Carter, *The Old Sergeant's Story*, p. 107, and Wallace, *Ranald S. Mackenzie on the Texas Frontier*, p. 140.
18. Charlton in Carter, *The Old Sergeant's Story*, p. 108.
19. Ibid.
20. Ibid., p. 109.
21. Wallace, *Ranald S. Mackenzie on the Texas Frontier*, p. 139.
22. "Journal of Ranald S. Mackenzie's Messenger to the Quahada Comanches," *Red River Valley Historical Review* 3, no. 2 (Spring 1978): 227.
23. Ibid., p. 229.
24. Jo Ella Powell Exley, *Frontier Blood*, p. 255, citing untitled Dickson manuscript.
25. "Journal of Mackenzie's Messenger," p. 237.
26. Ibid., p. 237.

27. Wayne Parker, *Quanah Parker, Last Chief of the Kwahadi Obeys the Great Spirit,* manuscript.
28. Ibid., p. 239.
29. W. S. Nye, *Carbine and Lance,* p. 229.
30. William T. Hagan, *Quanah Parker, Comanche Chief,* p. 15.
31. Ibid.

Twenty FORWARD, IN DEFEAT

1. Charles M. Robinson III, *Bad Hand: A Biography of General Ranald S. Mackenzie,* pp. 186–88.
2. William T. Hagan, *Quanah Parker, Comanche Chief,* pp. 20–21, Mackenzie to Pope, letter, September 5, 1875.
3. Bill Neeley, *The Last Comanche Chief: The Life and Times of Quanah Parker,* p. 144.
4. Letter: Ranald S. Mackenzie to Isaac Parker, September 5, 1877 (Fort Sill Letter Book).
5. Charles Goodnight, "Pioneer Outlines Sketch of Quanah Parker's Life," *Amarillo Sunday News and Globe,* August 6, 1928.
6. Accounts of both actions are in letters from J. M. Haworth to William Nicholson, August 26, 1877, Kiowa Agency Microform, National Archives; and Colonel J. W. Davidson to Asst. Adjutant General, October 29, 1878, House Executive Document, 45th Congress, Third Session, p. 555.
7. John R. Cook, *The Border and the Buffalo,* pp. 249ff.
8. Neeley, p. 153.
9. Herman Lehmann, *Nine Years Among the Indians,* pp. 186–87.
10. Scott Zesch, *The Captured,* pp. 220–21, citing Haworth and Mackenzie correspondence.
11. Lehmann, pp. 187–88.
12. Ibid., p. 232.
13. Hagan, *Quanah Parker, Comanche Chief,* p. 26.
14. Wellington Brink, "Quanah and the Leopard Coat Man," *Farm and Ranch,* April 17, 1926.
15. Harley True Burton, "History of the JA Ranch," *Southwestern Historical Quarterly* 31, no. 2 (October 1927).
16. Brink.
17. Burton.
18. Walter Prescott Webb, *The Great Plains,* p. 212.
19. Lillian Gunter, "Sketch of the Life of Julian Gunter," manuscript made for Panhandle Plains Historical Association, 1923, Panhandle Plains Historical Museum archives.
20. G. W. Roberson to J. Evetts Haley, June 30, 1926, manuscript in Panhandle Plains Historical Museum archives.
21. Haley, *Charles Goodnight: Cowman and Plainsman,* p. 30.
22. Hagan, *Quanah Parker, Comanche Chief,* p. 31.
23. Council Meeting of May 23, 1884, Kiowas, 17:46, Oklahoma Historical Society.
24. H. P. Jones to Philemon Hunt, interview, June 21, 1883, Kiowa Agency files, Oklahoma Historical Society; George Fox to Philemon Hunt, October 13, 1884, Kiowa Agency files.
25. Quanah Parker to Charles Adams, interview, May 13, 1890, Kiowa Agency files, Oklahoma History Center.
26. James T. DeShields, *Cynthia Ann Parker: The Story of Her Capture,* pp. 78–79.

27. Hugh Lennox Scott, *Some Memories of a Soldier,* p. 151.
28. *Hobart Democrat-Chief* (Oklahoma), August 4, 1925, interview with Knox Beall who said that Grantham was adopted and also Quanah's business adviser.
29. Commissioner T. J. Morgan to Agent Adams, interview, December 18, 1890, Kiowa Agency files, Oklahoma Historical Society.
30. Profile of Charlie Hart by Evelyn Fleming, manuscript, Quanah Parker papers, Panhandle Plains Historical Museum.
31. Knox Beall to R. B. Thomas, interview, November 5, 1937, Indian Pioneer History Project for Oklahoma, Western History Collections, University of Oklahoma; Beall to Bessie Thomas, April 15, 1938.
32. Lehmann, pp. 233–34.
33. Dick Banks to Bessie Smith, interview, Indian Pioneer History Project for Oklahoma.
34. Robert B. Thomas, undated manuscript, Indian Pioneer History Project for Oklahoma, Western History Collections, University of Oklahoma; also Beall to Thomas, November 5, 1937.
35. Anna Gomez to Ophelia D. Vestal, interview, December 13, 1937, Indian Pioneer History Project for Oklahoma, Western History Collections, University of Oklahoma.
36. Letter: Bob Linger to Quanah, March 9, 1909, in Neeley Archive at Panhandle Plains Historical Museum, Canyon, Texas.
37. Star House still exists, in somewhat deteriorated condition, in Cache, Oklahoma. My tour of it included the dining room, which, based on photographs from the early twentieth century, is substantially as it was. The only way to tour it is by inquiring at the old trading post in Cache.
38. Gomez to Vestal, interview, December 13, 1937.
39. Memoirs of Mrs. Cora Miller Kirkpatrick, in Mrs. J. W. Pierce manuscript, Quanah Parker collection, Panhandle Plains Historical Museum, Canyon, Texas.
40. Ernest Wallace, *Ranald S. Mackenzie on the Texas Frontier,* p. 170.
41. Ibid., p. 172.
42. Ibid., p. 190.

Twenty-one THIS WAS A MAN

1. William T. Hagan, *Quanah Parker, Comanche Chief,* p. 65.
2. September 26, 1892, Hearing at Fort Sill, Comanches, Apaches, Kiowas, Quanah Parker Collection, Panhandle Plains Historical Museum, Canyon, Texas.
3. William T. Hagan, *United States-Comanche Relations,* p. 287.
4. Knox Beall to R. B. Thomas, interview, November 5, 1937, Indian Pioneer History Project for Oklahoma, Western History Collections, University of Oklahoma.
5. Robert Thomas, document in Indian Pioneer History Project for Oklahoma, University of Oklahoma.
6. Mrs. J. L. Dupree to Jasper Mead, interview, March 17, 1938; Indian Pioneer History Project for Oklahoma, Western History Collections, University of Oklahoma.
7. George W. Briggs to Eunice M. Mayer, interview, June 17, 1937, Indian Pioneer History Project for Oklahoma, Western History Collections, University of Oklahoma.
8. Robert G. Carter, *Tragedies of Canon Blanco,* pp. 79–80.
9. "Quanah Route Day Draws Large Crowds," *Dallas Morning News,* October 25, 1910.
10. Robert Thomas document, in Indian Pioneer History Project for Oklahoma.

11. T. R. Roosevelt, *Outdoor Pastimes of the American Hunter*, p. 100.
12. Bill Neeley, *The Last Comanche Chief*, p. 220, citing 1985 Neeley interview with Anona Birdsong Dean.
13. Letter: T. R. Roosevelt to Francis Leupp, April 14, 1905, Indian Office Letters Rec'd.
14. Unidentified newspaper story about the school board in Quanah Parker Collection, Panhandle Plains Historical Museum, Canyon, Texas.
15. Ernest Wallace and E. Adamson Hoebel, *The Comanches*, pp. 332ff.
16. *Hobart Democrat-Chief* (Oklahoma), August 4, 1925.
17. Hagan, *Quanah Parker, Comanche Chief*, p. 113.
18. Frank Cummins Lockwood, *The Apaches*, p. 326; Hagan, *Quanah Parker, Comanche Chief*, p. 129.

Twenty-two   RESTING HERE UNTIL DAY BREAKS

1. "Quanah Route Day Draws Large Crowd," *Dallas Morning News*, October 25, 1910.
2. Ibid.
3. William T. Hagan, *Quanah Parker, Comanche Chief*, p. 124.

BIBLIOGRAPHY

BIBLIOGRAPHICAL NOTE

As I hope will be apparent to the reader, much of this book was constructed using a large number of firsthand accounts from the era. When sweeping through three hundred years of history, secondary sources are of course helpful as guides and summaries, but the most valuable resources are always the unfiltered ones. I was extremely fortunate, living in Austin, Texas, to be able to avail myself of the astounding literary and archival materials at the University of Texas libraries, especially the Dolph Briscoe Center for American History, which, in the pursuit of Comanche history, must be regarded as ground zero. Extensive archival materials were also used from the Panhandle Plains Historical Museum archives in Canyon, Texas, and at the Western History Collection at the University of Oklahoma in Norman, Oklahoma. The latter contains the Indian Pioneer History Project, a set of interviews conducted in the 1930s with people whose memories stretched well back into the nineteenth century. I used this heavily in my last chapters on Quanah, and indeed much of what I know about him in the last few decades of his life come from those voluminous interviews. Also extremely useful is Kiowa Agency material at the Oklahoma Historical Society/Oklahoma History Center, which has great detail on Quanah's reservation years. The archives at the Fort Sill museum have regrettably been closed indefinitely to scholars. This required a good deal of hustling on my part to try to find those Comanche materials elsewhere, including the incomparable 1897 Hugh Lenox Scott interviews with Quanah and other items in the W. S. Nye collection. (Many were in the Neely subarchive in Canyon.) Much of my time researching this book was spent at the Briscoe Center, with various rare books, records, dusty archives, and typed and handwritten manuscripts in front of me. (My favorite moment was when several hundred Confederate dollars came fluttering down out of a file full of handwritten manuscripts I was reading. The money looked almost new.)

That and other archival material allowed me to reconstruct the major historical events narrated in the story from authoritative, if not deep, firsthand accounts. These include the events at Parker's Fort and subsequent captivities of family members; the rise of the Texas Rangers including the careers of Jack Hays and Rip Ford (firsthand from Noah Smithwick, Rip Ford, Major John Caperton, B. F. Gholson, Charles Goodnight, and others); the "rescue" of Cynthia Ann Parker, the Council House Fight, Linnville Raid and Battle of Plum Creek, the Battle at Adobe Walls, and the Red River War. The detailed account of the Battle of Blanco Canyon came from men who rode with Mackenzie (Captain Robert G. Carter's "On the Border with Mackenzie" is one of the great documents of the American West). The Red River War was similarly based on contemporary accounts and aided by the wonderful compilation by the West Texas Museum: "Ranald S. Mackenzie's Official Correspondence Relating to Texas," in two volumes, covering the years 1871–79. Captain George Pettis left behind a remarkable blow-by-blow account of Kit Carson's fight with the Comanches in 1860. Primary sources were also used to write some of the early history of the Comanches, most notably the writings of Athanase de Mézières, a Spanish administrator from 1769 and one of the most effective Indian agents of all time, as well as Spanish government reports.

The best descriptions of Texas in the early to mid-nineteenth century come from several contemporaneous sources: Captain Randolph Marcy was a superb and reliable reporter, as were Colonel Richard Irving Dodge and the artist George Catlin. All delivered raw, unvarnished firsthand looks at the unspoiled Indian frontier. Life inside Comanche bands before the reservation period comes alive in the memoirs of a number of captives, including Dot Baab, Herman Lehmann, Clinton Smith, and Nelson Lee. (Though the latter clearly fictionalized some of his story, other parts remain useful.) Other contemporary chronicles, like reservation teacher Thomas Battey's 1875 book *Life and Adventures of a Quaker Among the Indians*, were also quite useful. Mary Maverick's memoir of old San Antonio, including the Council House Fight and the rise of Jack Hays and the Rangers, is indispensable.

For secondary sources, nothing can quite match Ernest Wallace and E. Adamson Hoebel's magisterial ethnography based in large part on ethnological studies from the 1930s: *Comanches: Lords of the South Plains*. Wilbur Nye's *Carbine and Lance: The Story of Old Fort Sill*, and Rupert Richardson's. *Comanche Barrier to South Plains Settlement* were the books that broke the first major ground on Comanche history. The two extant full-length biographies of Mackenzie, Wallace's *Ranald S. Mackenzie on the Texas Frontier*, and Charles M. Robinson III's *Bad Hand*, are well researched and useful. The section on the Comanches in Walter Prescott Webb's 1931 masterpiece *The Great Plains* is what got me interested in the subject in the first place, and his work on the Texas Rangers remains definitive. T. R. Fehrenbach's *The Comanches: Destruction of a People* is well written and remains the modern classic in the field. To these I would add two more current works: William T. Hagan's superb biography of Quanah, which focuses on the reservation years, and Jo Ella Powell Exley's *Frontier Blood*, a solid piece of research centered on the extended Parker clan.

The rest of my research was done by automobile: crossing and recrossing the plains of Comancheria, visiting the marvelous reconstruction of Parker's Fort in Groesbeck, Texas, touring forts such as Richardson, Concho, and Phantom Hill, nearly getting stuck in the ice at Adobe Walls, climbing in the Wichita Mountains, hunting down various battle sites on the Pease River and elsewhere. One of the highlights was finding Quanah's old Star House in an abandoned amusement park in Cache, Oklahoma. It is in moderate stages of decay but everything is still there, including the dining room where Roosevelt and Geronimo once came to dinner (on separate occasions). I have lived in Texas for fifteen years now, and my understanding of the state's peculiar geography, and particularly the geography of the west Texas plains, was an enormous aid in writing this book.

BOOKS

Atkinson, M. J. *The Texas Indians*. San Antonio, Tex.: Naylor Co., 1935.

————. *Indians of the Southwest*. San Antonio, Tex.: Naylor Co., 1963.

Baab, T. A. *In the Bosom of the Comanches*. Dallas: Hargreaves Printing Co., 1923 (second edition of 1912 original).

Baker, T. Lindsay, and Harrison, Billy R. *Adobe Walls, the History and Archaeology of the 1874 Trading Post*. College Station: Texas A&M University Press, 1986.

Bancroft, Hubert H. *History of Arizona and New Mexico*. San Francisco: The History Company, 1889.

Battey, Thomas. *Life and Adventures of a Quaker Among the Indians*. Boston: Lee and Shepard, 1875.

Bedford, Hilory G. *Texas Indian Troubles*. Pasadena, Tex.: Abbotsford Publishing Company, 1966 (facsimile of 1905 original by Hargreaves Printing Co. of Dallas).

Benner, Judith Ann. *Sul Ross: Soldier, Statesman, Educator.* College Station: Texas A&M University Press, 1983.

Bolton, Herbert Eugene. *Coronado: Knight of Pueblos and Plains.* New York: Whittlesey House; Albuquerque: University of New Mexico Press, 1949.

———. *Athanase de Mézières and the Lousiana-Texas Frontier, 1768–1780.* Cleveland, Ohio: Arthur H. Clark Co., 1914.

Bourke, John G. *Mackenzie's Last Fight with the Cheyennes.* New York: Argonaut Press, 1966 (originally published 1890).

Brazos (pseudonym). *The Life of Robert Hall.* Austin: Ben C. Jones and Co., 1898.

Brice, Donaly E. *Great Comanche Raid.* Austin: Eakin Press, 1987.

Brown, Dee. *Bury My Heart at Wounded Knee.* New York: Henry Holt, 1970.

Brown, John Henry. *Indian Wars and Pioneers of Texas.* Austin: State House Press, 1988 (originally published 1890).

———. *The Comanche Raid of 1840.* Houston: Union National Bank, 1933.

Canonge, Elliott. *Comanche Texts.* Norman: University of Oklahoma Institute of Linguistics, 1958.

Carter, Robert G. *On the Border with Mackenzie.* Austin: Texas State Historical Association, 2007 (originally published 1935).

Carter, Captain Robert G. *The Old Sergeant's Story: Winning the West from the Indians and Bad Men in 1870 to 1876.* New York: Frederick H. Hitchcock, 1926.

———. *Tragedies of Blanco Canyon.* Washington, D.C.: Gibson Bros., 1919.

Catlin, George. *Manners, Customs, and Condition of the North American Indians, With Letters and Notes.* London: Henry G. Bohn, 1857, 2 volumes, 9th edition,

Clark, Mary Whatley. *The Palo Pinto Story.* Fort Worth: Manney Co., 1956.

Clark, Randolph. *Reminiscences.* Fort Worth: Texas Christian University Press, 1986 (originally published 1919)

Clark, William P. *The Indian Sign Language.* Philadelphia: L. R. Hamersly, 1885.

Cody, Colonel William F. *The Adventures of Buffalo Bill Cody.* New York and London: Harper & Brothers, 1904.

Connell, Evan S. *Son of the Morning Star.* New York: North Point Press, 1997.

Cook, John R. *The Border and the Buffalo.* Topeka, Kans.: Crane and Co., 1907.

Cox, Mike. *The Texas Rangers: Wearing the Cinco Peso, 1821–1900.* New York: Forge Books, 2008.

Curtis, Edward S. *The North American Indian, Selections.* Santa Fe, NM, Classic Gravure, 1980 (from 1930 original).

Debo, Angie. *The Road to Disappearance, A History of the Creek Indians.* Norman: University of Oklahoma Press, 1941.

DeBruhl, Marshall. *Sword of San Jacinto: A Life of Sam Houston.* New York: Random House, 1931.

DeShields, James T. *Border Wars of Texas.* Tioga, Tex.: 1912.

———. *Cynthia Ann Parker: the Story of Her Capture.* St. Louis, privately printed, 1886.

Dixon, Billy. *The Life and Adventures of Billy Dixon of Adobe Walls.* Guthrie, Okla.: Cooperative Publishing Co., 1914.

———. *The Fight at Adobe Walls.* Houston: Union National Bank, 1935.

Dixon, Olive King. *Life of Billy Dixon.* Austin, Tex.: State House Press, 1987 (originally published 1927).

Dobie, J. Frank. *The Mustangs.* Austin: University of Texas Press, 1934.

Dodge, Richard Irving. *The Hunting Grounds of the Great West.* London: Chatto and Windus, 1878, 2nd edition.

———. *The Plains of the Great West and Their Inhabitants.* New York: G. P. Putnam's, 1877.

Dodge, Colonel Richard Irving. *Our Wild Indians, 33 years' Personal Experience Among The Redmen of the Great West.* New York: Archer House, 1883.

———. *The Indian Territory Journals of Colonel Richard Irving Dodge.* Norman: University of Oklahoma Press, 2000.

Dorst, Captain Joseph. *Twentieth Annual Reunion of the Association of Graduates of the United States Military Academy at West Point.* June 12, 1889.

Dunlay, Tom. *Kit Carson and the Indians.* Lincoln: University of Nebraska Press, 2000.

Edmunds, R. David, ed. *American Indian Leaders: Studies in Diversity.* Lincoln: University of Nebraska Press, 1980.

Exley, Jo Ella Powell. *Frontier Blood: The Saga of the Parker Family.* College Station: Texas A&M Press, 2001.

Fallwell, Gene. *The Comanche Trail of Thunder and the Massacre at Parker's Fort, May 19, 1836.* Dallas: Highlands Historical Press, 1965.

Faludi, Susan. *The Terror Dream.* New York: Metropolitan Books (Henry Holt), 2007.

Farnham, J. T. *Travels in the Great Western Prairies, The Anahuac and Rocky Mountains and in the Oregon Territory.* Poughkeepsie, N.Y.: Killey and Lossing Printers, 1841.

Fehrenbach, T. R. *Lone Star: A History of Texas and the Texans.* Boulder, Colo.: Da Capo Press Edition, 2000 (originally published 1968).

———. *The Comanches: Destruction of a People.* New York: Alfred A. Knopf, 1974.

Foote, Shelby. *The Civil War.* New York: Random House, 1858, vol. 1.

Ford, John Salmon. *Rip Ford's Texas.* Austin: University of Texas Press, 1963 (editor: Stephen B. Oates).

Frazier, Ian. *The Great Plains.* New York: Penguin, 1989.

Gillett, James B. *Six Years with the Texas Rangers.* New Haven: Yale University Press, 1925.

Glisan, Rodney. *Journal of Army Life.* San Francisco: A. L. Bancroft and Co., 1874.

Goodnight, Charles *Charles Goodnight's Indian Recollections.* Amarillo, Tex.: Russell and Cockrell, 1928.

Grant, U. S. *Personal Memoirs of U. S. Grant.* New York: Charles A. Webster & Co., 1886.

Graves, John. *Goodbye to a River.* Houston: Gulf Publishing Company, 1995.

———. *Hard Scrabble: Observations on a Patch of Land.* Dallas: SMU Press, 2002.

Greer, James Kimmins. *Colonel Jack Hays: Frontier Leader and California Builder:* College Station: Texas A&M University Press, 1987.

Grinnell, George Bird. *The Fighting Cheyennes.* Norman: University of Oklahoma Press, 1956 (originally published 1915).

Guild, Thelma S., and Harvey L. Carter. *Kit Carson: A Pattern for Heroes.* Lincoln: University of Nebraska Press, 1984.

Hacker, Margaret Schmidt. *Cynthia Ann Parker: The Life and Legend.* El Paso: Texas Western Press, 1990.

Hackett, Charles Wilson, ed. *Pichardo's Treatise on the Limits of Louisiana and Texas.* Austin: University of Texas Press, 1934.

Hagan, William T. *Quanah Parker, Comanche Chief.* Norman: University of Oklahoma Press, 1993.

———. *United States—Comanche Relations.* New Haven: Yale University Press, 1976.

Haley, J. Evetts. *Charles Goodnight's Indian Recollections.* Amarillo, Tex.: Russell and Cockrell, 1928 (reprinted from Panhandle Plains Historical Review, 1928).

———. *Charles Goodnight: Cowman and Plainsman.* Norman: University of Oklahoma Press, 1936.

Haley, James L. *The Buffalo War: The History of the Red River Indian Uprising of 1874.* Garden City, N.Y.: Doubleday, 1976.

Hamilton, Allen Lee. *Military History of Fort Richardson, Texas,* master's thesis. Lubbock: Texas Tech, 1973.

Hatcher, Mattie Austin. "The Opening of Texas to Foreign Settlement 1801–1821," University of Texas Bulletin, 1927, pp. 53–54.

Hodge, Frederick. *Handbook of American Indians North of Mexico.* New York: Rowman and Littlefield, 1971 (originally published in two volumes in 1907 and 1912).

Holland, G. A. *The History of Parker County and the Double Log Cabin.* Weatherford, Tex.: The Herald Publishing Company, 1937.

Holmes, Floyd J. *Indian Fights on the Texas Frontier.* Fort Worth: Pioneer Publishing, 1927.

House, E., ed. *A Narrative of the Captivity of Mrs. Horn and Her Two Children with That of Mrs. Harris by the Comanche Indians.* St. Louis: C. Keemle Printer, 1939.

Hyde, George E. *Rangers and Regulars,* Columbus, Ohio: Long's College Book Co., 1952.

Jackson, Clyde. *Quanah Parker, Last Chief of the Comanches, a Study in Southwestern Frontier History.* New York: Exposition Press, 1963.

James, General Thomas. *Three Years Among the Indians and Mexicans.* St. Louis: Missouri Historical Society, 1916.

Jenkins, John Holmes, ed. *Recollections of Early Texas: The Memoirs of John Holland Jenkins.* Austin, University of Texas Press, 1958.

Jimanez, Ramon. *Caesar Against the Celts.* Staplehurst, Kent: Spellmount, 1996.

Johnston, William Preston. *The Life of General Albert Sidney Johnston: Embracing His Services in the Armies of the United States, the Republic of Texas, and the Confederate States.* New York: Appleton and Co., 1879.

Jones, Douglas C. *The Treaty at Medicine Lodge.* Norman: University of Oklahoma Press, 1966.

Jones, Jonathan H. *A Condensed History of the Apache and Comanche Indians.* New York: Garland Publishing, 1976 (originally published in 1899).

Josephy, Alvin M., Jr. *The Indian Heritage of America.* New York: Bantam Books, 1969.

Kavanagh, Thomas W. *The Comanches: A History, 1706–1875.* Lincoln: University of Nebraska Press, 1996.

———. *Comanche Ethnography: Field Notes of E. Adamson Hoebel, Waldo R. Wedel, Gustav G. Carlson, and Robert Lowie.* Lincoln: University of Nebraska Press in cooperation with the American Indian Studies Research Institute at Indiana University, © 2008 (from original 1933 study).

Keim, De Benneville Randolph. *Sheridan's Troopers on the Border: A Winter Campaign on the Plains.* Freeport, N.Y.: Books for Librairies Press, 1970 (originally published 1885).

Kenney, M. M. "The History of the Indian Tribes of Texas," *A Comprehensive History of Texas 1685–1897.* Edited by Dudley G. Wooten. Dallas: W. G. Scarff, 1898.

La Vere, David. *Contrary Neighbors, The Southern Plains and Removed Indians in Indian Territory.* Norman: University of Oklahoma Press, 2000.

Lee, Nelson. *Three Years Among the Comanches.* Santa Barbara, Calif.: The Narrative Press, 2001 (originally published 1859).

Lehmann, Herman. *Nine Years Among the Indians (1870–79).* Albuquerque: University of New Mexico Press, 2004 (originally published 1927).

LeMay, Alan. *The Searchers.* New York: Ace Publishers, 1980 (originally published 1954).

Lewis, M. *The Lewis and Clark Expedition.* Philadelphia: J.B. Lippincott Company, 1814 edition, unabridged, vol. 1 (reprinted 1961).

Limerick, Patricia Nelson. *The Legacy of Conquest.* New York: Norton and Co., 1988.

Linn, John J. *Reminiscences of Fifty Years in Texas.* Austin, Tex.: The Steck Company, 1935 (originally published 1883).

Lockwood, Frank Cummins. *The Apaches.* Lincoln: University of Nebraska Press, 1897.

Marcy, Randolph B. *Adventure on Red River: A Report on the Exploration of the Red River by Captain Randolph Marcy and Captain G. B. McClellan.* Norman: University of Oklahoma Press, 1937 (originally published 1853).

———. *The Prairie Traveler: A Handbook for Overland Expeditions.* New York: Harper's, 1859 (1981 reprint by Time-Life Books, New York).

————. *Thirty Years of Army Life on the Border*. New York: Harper and Brothers, 1866.

Marshall, Doyle. *A Cry Unheard: The Story of Indian Attacks in and Around Parker County, Texas, 1858–1872*. Annetta Valley Farm Press, 1990.

Marshall, J. T. *The Miles Expedition of 1874–5: An Eyewitness Account of the River War*. Austin, Tex.: The Encino Press, 1971.

Maverick, Mary. *Memoirs of Mary A. Maverick*. San Antonio: Alamo Printing Co., 1921.

Mayhall, Mildred P. *The Kiowas*. Norman: University of Oklahoma Press, 1962.

————. *Indian Wars of Texas*. Waco, Tex.: Texian Press, 1965.

McMurtry, Larry. *Crazy Horse*. New York: Lipper/Viking, 1999.

Moore, Ben, Sr. *Seven years with the Wild Indians*. O'Donnell, Tex.: Ben Moore Sr. , 1945.

Moore, John H. *The Cheyenne*. Malden, Mass.: Blackwell Publishers Inc., 1996.

Morrell, Z. N. *Flowers and Fruits in the Wilderness*. St. Louis: Commercial Printing Co., 1882, 3rd edition (originally published 1872).

Neeley, Bill. *The Last Comanche Chief: The Life and Times of Quanah Parker*. New York: John Wiley and Sons, 1995.

Neighbours, Kenneth F. *Robert Simpson Neighbors and the Texas Frontier*. Waco, Tex.: Texian Press, 1975.

Neighbours, Robert S. *The Nauni or Comanches of Texas* (in *Information Respecting the History, Conditions, and Prospects of the Indian Tribes of the United States, Office of Indian Affairs*). Philadelphia, 1853.

Neihardt, John G. *Black Elk Speaks*. Lincoln: University of Nebraska Press, 1979 (originally published 1932).

Newcomb, W. W., Jr. *The Indians of Texas*. Austin: University of Texas Press, 1961.

Nye, W. S. *Carbine and Lance: The Story of Old Fort Sill*. Norman: University of Oklahoma Press, 1969 (originally published 1937).

Parker, James, W. *Defence of James W. Parker Against Slanderous Accusations Preferred Against Him*. Houston: Telegraph Power Press, 1839.

————. *Narrative of the Perilous Adventures*. Houston, 1844, self-published.

————. *The Old Army Memories*, Philadelphia: Dorrance and Co., 1929.

————. *The Rachel Plummer Narrative*. Houston: 1839, self-published.

Parkman, Francis. *The California and Oregon Trails: Sketches of Prairie and Rocky Mountain Life*. Chicago: Scott and Foresman, 1911 (originally published 1849).

Parsons, John E., ed. *Sam Colt's Own Record of Transactions with Captain Walker and Eli Whitney Jr. in 1847*. Hartford: Connecticut Historical Society, 1949.

Pettis, Captain George. *Kit Carson's Fight with the Comanche and Kiowa Indians*. Santa Fe: Historical Society of New Mexico, 1908.

Plummer, Rachel. *Rachel Plummer's Narrative of Twenty-one Months of Servitude as a Prisoner Among the Comanche Indians*.

Quaife, Milo Milton. *Kit Carson's Autobiography*. Lincoln: University of Nebrasaka Press (originally published by Bison Books in 1935).

Richardson, Rupert N. *The Comanche Barrier to South Plains Settlement*. Austin, Tex.: Eakin Press, 1996 (originally published 1933).

————. *The Frontier of Northwest Texas 1846–1876*. Glendale, Calif.: A. H. Clark Co., 1963.

Rister, Carl Coke. *Border Captives*. Norman: University of Oklahoma Press, 1955.

————. *The Southwestern Frontier, 1865–1881*. New York: Russell and Russell, 1966 (originally published 1928).

Rivera, Pedro De. *Diario y Derrotero de lo camion ado, visto y observado en la visita que lo hizo a los presidios de la Nueva Espana septentrional*. Edited by Visto Allesio Robles. Mexico D. F.: Secretaria de la Defensa Nacional, 1946.

Robinson, Charles M., III. *Bad Hand: A Biography of General Ranald S. Mackenzie*. Austin, Tex.: State House Press, 1993.

Roe, Frank G. *The Indian and the Horse.* Norman: University of Oklahoma Press, 1962 (originally published 1955).

Roosevelt, T. R. *Outdoor Pastimes of an American Hunter.* New York: Charles Scribner and Sons, 1905.

Rose, Victor M. *The Life and Services of General Ben McCulloch.* Austin, Tex.: The Steck Co., 1958 (originally published 1888).

Ruxton, George F. *Adventures in Mexico and the Rocky Mountains.* London: J. Murray, 1861.

Schaff, Morris. *The Spirit of Old West Point: 1858–1862.* Boston: Houghton Mifflin Company, 1907.

Schilz, Jodye Lynne Dickson, and Thomas F. Schilz. *Buffalo Hump and the Penateka Comanches.* El Paso: University of Texas at El Paso Press, 1989.

Schmeckebier, Lawrence. *The Office of Indian Affairs, Its History, Activities and Organization.* New York: AMS Press, 1972.

Scott, Hugh Lenox. *Some Memories of a Soldier.* New York: The Century Co., 1928.

Sides, Hampton. *Blood and Thunder: An Epic of the American West.* New York: Doubleday, 2006.

Smith, Clinton. *The Boy Captives; Being the True Story of the Experiences and Hardships of Clinton L. and Jeff D. Smith.* San Antonio, Tex.: Cenveo, 2005 (originally published 1927).

Smith, Coho. *Cohographs.* Edited by Iva Roe Logan. Fort Worth: Branch-Smith Inc., 1976.

Smith, F. Todd *From Dominance to Disappearance: Indians of Texas and the Near Southwest, 1786–1859.* Lincoln: University of Nebraska Press, 2005.

Smithwick, Noah. *Evolution of a State or Recollections of Old Texas Days.* Compiled by Nanna Smithwick Donaldson, Gammel Book Company, 1900; reprint, Austin, W. Thomas Taylor, 1995.

Sommer, Charles H. *Quanah Parker, the Last Chief of the Comanches.* St. Louis: 1945, self-published.

Stiff, Colonel Edward. *The Texan Emigrant.* Cincinnati: George Conclin, 1840.

Tatum, Lawrie. *Our Red Brothers and the Peace Policy of President Ulysses S. Grant.* Lincoln: University of Nebraska Press, 1970 (originally published 1889).

Thomas, Alfred B. *Forgotten Frontiers: a Study of the Spanish Indian Policy of Don Juan Batista de Anza, Governor of New Mexico, 1777–87.* Norman: University of Oklahoma, 1932.

———. *A Study of the Spanish Indian Policy of Don Juan Batista De Anza, 1777–78.* Norman: University of Oklahoma Press, 1969 (originally published 1932).

Thompson, R. A. *Crossing the Border with the Fourth Cavalry.* Waco, Tex.: Texian Press, 1986.

Tilghman, Zoe A. *Quanah: Eagle of the Comanches.* Oklahoma City: Harlow Publishing, 1938; Norman: Oklahoma Press, 1940.

Tolbert, Frank X. *An Informal History of Texas.* New York: Harper and Brothers, 1951.

Toole, K. Ross. *Probing the American West.* Santa Fe: Museum of New Mexico Press, 1962.

Utley, Robert M. *Lone Star Justice, The First Century of the Texas Rangers.* New York: Berkeley Books, 2002.

Vestal, Stanley. *Kit Carson: The Happy Warrior of the Old West.* New York: Houghton Mifflin Co., 1928.

Wallace, Ernest. "Final Champion of Comanche Glory," *The Great Chiefs.* Alexandria, Va.: Time-Life Books 1975.

———. *Ranald S. Mackenzie on the Texas Frontier.* College Station: Texas A&M Press, 1993.

———. *Texas in Turmoil.* Austin, Tex.: Steck-Vaughn Co., 1965.

Wallace, Ernest, and E. Adamson Hoebel. *The Comanches: Lords of the South Plains.* Norman: University of Oklahoma Press, 1952.

Webb, Walter P. *The Texas Rangers, a Century of Frontier Defense.* Austin, Tex.: University of Texas Press, 2003 (originally published 1935).

———. *The Great Plains.* Lincoln: University of Nebraska Press, Bison Books, 1981 (originally published 1931).

Weems, John Edward. *Death Song: The Last of the Indian Wars.* Garden City, N.Y.: Doubleday and Co., 1976.

West, G. Derek. *The Battles of Adobe Walls and Lyman's Wagon Train, 1874.* Canyon, Tex.: Panhandle Plains Historical Society, 1964.

White, E. E. *Experiences of a Special Indian Agent.* Norman: University of Oklahoma Press, 1965 (originally published 1893).

Wilbarger, J. W. *Indian Depredations in Texas.* Austin: Pemberton Press, 1967 (originally published 1889).

Williams, Amelia W., and Eugene C. Barker. *The Writings of Sam Houston, 1813–1863,* 8 volumes. Austin: University of Texas Press, 1938–1943, vol. 4.

Winfrey, Dorman H., and James M. Day, eds. *The Indian Papers of the Southwest,* 5 volumes. Austin, Tex.: Pemberton Press, 1959–1966.

Winship, George Parker. *The Coronado Expedition 1540–42.* New York: A. S. Barnes and Co., 1904.

Wissler, Clark. *The American Indian.* New York: Oxford University Press, 1922.

———. *Man and Culture.* New York: Thos. Crowell, 1923.

———. *North American Indians of the Plains.* New York: American Museum of Natural History, 1927.

Yenne, Bill. *Sitting Bull.* Yardley, Pa.: Westholme Publishing, 2008.

Zesch, Scott. *Captured: The True Story of Abduction by Indians on the Texas Frontier.* New York: St. Martin's Press, 2004.

ARTICLES

Anderson, Adrian N. "The Last Phase of Colonel Ranald S. Mackenzie's 1874 Campaign Against the Comanches." *West Texas Historical Association Yearbook* 40 (1964): 74–81.

Brink, Wellington. "Chief Quanah and the Leopard Coat Man." In *Farm and Ranch,* April 17, 1926.

Burton, Harley True. "History of the JA Ranch." In *Southwestern Historical Quarterly* 31 (October 1927): 93.

Clarksville Northern Standard, April 6, 1861.

Clarksville Northern Standard, May 25, 1846.

Dodge, T. A. "Some American Riders." *Harpers New Monthly Magazine,* May 1891, p. 862.

Dunn, William E. "The Apache Mission on the San Saba River, Its Founding and Its Failure." *Southwestern Historical Quarterly* 17 (1914): 379–414.

Fortune, Jan Isbelle. "The Recapture and Return of Cynthia Ann Parker." *Groesbeck Journal,* May 15, 1936, p. 1.

Gielo, Daniel J., and Scott Zesch, eds. "Every Day Seemed to Be a Holiday": The Captivity of Bianca Babb. *Southwestern Historical Quarterly* 47 (July 2003): 36.

Gilles, Albert S., Sr. "A House for Quanah Parker." *Frontier Times,* May 1966, p. 34.

Green, F. E., ed. "Ranald S. Mackenzie's Official Correspondence Relating to Texas, 1873–79." *Museum Journal* (Lubbock, West Texas Museum Association), 10 (1966).

Grinnell, G. B. "Who Were the Padoucas?" *American Anthropologist* 23 (1920): 260.

Haley, J. Evetts. "The Comanchero Trade." *Southwestern Historical Quarterly* 38, no. 3 (January 1935).

Haynes, Francis. "The Northward Spread of Horses Among the Plains Indians." *American Anthropologist* 40 (1938): 428–37.

———. "Where Did the Plains Indians Get Their Horses?" *American Anthropologist* 40 (1938): 112–17.

Hobart Democrat-Chief (Oklahoma), August 4, 1925, Panhandle Plains Museum Archives.

Hunta, J. W. "Nine Years with the Apaches and Comanches," *Frontier Times* 31 (July–September 1954): 251–77.

Jones, Lawrence T. "Cynthia Ann Parker and Pease Ross: The Forgotten Photographs." *Southwestern Historical Quarterly,* June 1990, p. 379.

Mason, A. B. "The White Captive." *Civilian and Gazette,* 1860 (reprint of story in *The White Man*).

Mooney, James. "The Aboriginal Population of America North of Mexico." *Smithsonian Miscellaneous Collections* 80, no. 7 (1928).

———. "Calendar History of the Kiowa Indians." *Seventeenth Annual Report.* Washington, D.C.: Bureau of Ethnology, 1898.

Neighbors, Kenneth. "Battle of Walker's Creek." *West Texas Historical Association Yearbook,* 1965.

Nielsen, Soren. "Ranald S. Mackenzie: The Man and His Battle." *West Texas Historical Assn. Yearbook* 64, p. 140.

Norris, David A. "Confederate Gunners Affectionately Called Their Hard Working Little Mountain Howitzers 'Bull Pups.'" *American's Civil War,* September 1995, pp. 10, 12, 14, 16, 20, and 90.

Oates, Stephen B. "Texas Under the Secessionists." *Southwestern Historical Quarterly* 67 (October 1963): 167.

Opler, Marvin. "The Origins of Comanche and Ute." *American Anthropologist* 45 (1943).

Pate, J'Nell. "The Battles of Adobe Walls." *Great Plains Journal* 46 (Fall 1976): 3.

Pettis, Captain George. "Kit Carson's Fight with the Comanche and Kiowa Indians." *Historical Society of New Mexico* (1908), p. 7.

"Quanah Parker in Adobe Walls Battle." *Borger News Herald,* date unknown, Panhandle Plains Historical Museum Archives, based on interview with J. A. Dickson.

Richardson, Rupert N. "The Comanche Indians and the Fight at Adobe Walls." *Panhandle Plains Historical Review* 9 (1936).

———. "The Comanche Indians and the Fight at Adobe Walls." *Panhandle Plains Historical Review* 4 (1931).

Rister, C. C., ed. "Documents Relating to General W. T. Sherman's Southern Plains Indian Policy 1871–75." *Panhandle Plains Historical Review* 9 (1936).

Roe, F. G. "From Dogs to Horses Among the Western Indian Tribes." *Royal Society of Canada,* Ottawa, 1939, Third Series, Section II.

Stanley, Henry M. "A British Journalist Reports the Medicine Lodge Councils of 1867." *Kansas Historical Quarterly* 33 (1967).

Taylor, Alfred A. "Medicine Lodge Peace Council." *Chronicles of Oklahoma* 2, no. 2 (June 1924).

Thompson, W. A. "Scouting with Mackenzie." *Journal of the United States Cavalry Association* 10 (1897).

Tingley, Donald F. "The Illinois Days of Daniel Parker, Texas Colonizer." *Journal of the Illinois State Historical Society,* no. 51 (1958).

Wallace, Ernest. "David G. Burnet's Letters Describing the Comanche Indians." *West Texas Historical Assoc. Yearbook* 30 (1954).

———. "The Comanche Eagle Dance." *Texas Archaeological and Paleontological Society Bulletin* 18 (1947).

———. "The Comanches on the White Man's Road." *West Texas Historical Assoc. Yearbook* 29 (October 1953).

———. "The Journal of Ranald S. Mackenzie's Messenger to the Kwahadi Comanches." *Red River Valley Historical Review* 3, no. 2 (Spring 1978): 229–46.

———. "Prompt in the Saddle, The Military Career of Ranald S. Mackenzie." *Military History of Texas and the Southwest* 9, no. 3 (1971): 161–67.

Wedel, Waldo R. "An Introduction to Pawnee Archeology." *Bureau of American Ethnography Bulletin,* no. 112, p. 4, map 4.

Wellman, Paul. "Cynthia Ann Parker." *Chronicles of Oklahoma* 12, no. 2 (1934): 163.

West, G. Derek. "The Battle of Adobe Walls (1874)." *Battles of Adobe Walls and Lyman's Wagon Train, 1874.* Canyon, Tex.: Panhandle Plains Historical Society, 1964.

Whisenhunt, Donald W. "Fort Richardson." *West Texas Historical Association Yearbook* 39 (1963): 23–24.

White, Lonnie. "Indian Battles in the Texas Panhandle." *Journal of the West* 6 (April 1967): 283–87.

———. "Kansas Newspaper Items Relating to the Red River War of 1874–1975." *Battles of Adobe Walls and Lyman's Wagon Train 1874.* Canyon, Tex.: Panhandle Plains Historical Society, 1964, pp. 77–78.

Williams, Robert H. "The Case for Peta Nocona." *Texana* 10, no. 1 (1972): 55.

Winn, Mamie Folsom. "History Centers About Cynthia Ann Parker's Home." In *Women Tell the Story of the Southwest* by Maddie L. Wooten. San Antonio, Tex.: The Naylor Company, 1940.

Wissler, Clark. "The Influence of the Horse in the Development of Plains Culture." *American Anthropologist* 16, no. 1 (1914): 1–25.

Worcester, D. E. "Spanish Horses Among the Plains Tribes." *Pacific Historical Review* 14 (December 1945): 409–17.

———. "The Spread of Spanish Horses in the Southwest." *New Mexico Historical Review* 19 (July 1944): 225–32.

Newspaper accounts of Pease River:

Galveston Daily Citizen, December 13, 1860, "Indian News."

Galveston Daily Citizen, January 15, 1861, "Indian News."

Materials pertaining to the Indian attacks leading up to the Pease River Fight:

The White Man, September 13, 1860.

PAPERS, LETTERS, AND OFFICIAL DOCUMENTS

Brown, Marion. *Marion T. Brown: Letters from Fort Sill, 1886–1887.* Austin: The Encino Press, 1970.

Commissioner of Indian Affairs, Annual Reports 1830–1875.

Council Meeting of May 23, 1884, Kiowas, 17:46, Oklahoma Historical Society.

Gulick, Charles Adams, Jr. *The Papers of Mirabeau Buonaparte Lamar,* vols. 2 and 4. Austin: Von Boeckmann-Jones Co., 1924.

Hackett, Charles, ed. *Historical Documents Relating to New Mexico, Nueva Vizcaya, and approaches thereto to 1773 (from TRF).*

House of Representatives Executive Documents, 30th Congress.

Jerome, David. Hearing at Fort Sill with Comanches, Kiowas, and Apaches, September 26, 1892, Panhandle Plains Museum Archives.

Kappler, Charles J., ed. *Indian Affairs Laws and Treaties,* Washington, Government Printing Office, vol. 2, 1903.

Linger, Bob, to Quanah Parker, March 9, 1909, Neeley Archive at Panhandle Plains Historical Museum, Canyon, Texas.

Mackenzie's Official Report, Oct. 12, 1872: "1872, Sept. 29, Attack on Comanche Village," Addressed to the Asst. Adjutant General, Department of Texas.

"Messages of the President, Submitted to Both Houses," December 21, 1838, Lamar Papers, Doc. 948.

Morgan, Commissioner T. J., to Agent Adams, December 18, 1890, Kiowa Agency files, Oklahoma Historical Society.

Parker, Quanah, to Charles Adams, May 13, 1890, Kiowa Agency files, Oklahoma History Center.

Smither, Harriet, ed. *Journals of the Fourth Congress of the Republic of Texas*, vols. 1 and 3.

Ten Bears' Speech at Medicine Lodge Peace Council, 1867. Record Copy of Proceedings of the Indian Peace Commission appointed Under Act of Congress Approved July 20, 1867. Records of the Secretary of the Interior, National Archives, vol. I, pp. 104–106.

Twitchell, Ralph E. *Spanish Archives of New Mexico*, 2 vols. Cedar Rapids, Iowa, 1914.

Wallace, Ernest, ed. *Ranald S. Mackenzie's Official Correspondence Relating to Texas, 1871–73*. Lubbock: West Texas Museum Association, 1967.

Winfrey, Dorman H., and James M. Day, eds. *The Indian Papers of Texas and the Southwest*, 5 vols. Austin: Pemberton Press, 1959–1966.

INDIVIDUAL LETTERS

Augur, C. C., to Mackenzie, August 28, 1874, Mackenzie's Official Correspondence Relating to Texas, *Museum Journal*, vol. 10, 1966 (see books).

Butler, P. M., and M. G. Lewis to the Hon. W. Medill, Commissioner of Indian Affairs, August 8, 1848, House Executive Documents No. 1, 30th Congress, Second Session, p. 578.

Davidson, Colonel J. W., to Asst. Adjutant General, October 29, 1878, House Executive Document, 45th Congress, Third Session, p. 555.

Haworth, J. M., to William Nicholson, August 26, 1877, Kiowa Agency Microform, National Archives.

Jones, H. P., to Philemon Hunt, June 21, 1883, Kiowa Agency files, Oklahoma Historical Society; George Fox to Philemon Hunt, October 13, 1884, Kiowa Agency files.

Leavenworth, J. H., to Commissioner of Indian Affairs, April 23, 1868, 40th Congress, Second Session, Senate Executive Document No. 60:2.

Linger, Bob, to Quanah Parker, letter, March 8, 1909, postmark Cantonment Oklay, regarding peyote.

Mackenzie, Ranald, to W. T. Sherman, June 15, 1871, W. T. Sherman Papers, Library of Congress, Washington, D.C.

Neighbours, Robert S., to the Hon. W. Medill, Commissioner of Indian Affairs, November 18, 1847, 30th Congress, First Session, Committee Report 171.

Parker, James, to Mirabeau Lamar, February 3, 1844, Papers of M. B. Lamar.

Parrilla, Don Diego Ortiz de, to the Viceroy, June 30, 1757 (*Historia*, vol. 95).

Pearson, K. J., to John D. Floyd, February 3, 1861, Fort Sill archives.

To Commanding Officer, Fort Bascom, September 27, 1864, *Official Records of the War of Rebellion*, series 1, vol. 41, part 3.

MANUSCRIPTS AND ARCHIVAL MATERIALS

Anonymous. *Biography of Daniel Parker*. Handwritten manuscript, Center for American History.

Baker, Jonathan Hamilton. *Diary of Jonathan Hamilton Baker of Palo Pinto County, Texas*, Part I, 1858–60. Secured from his daughter Elizabeth Baker, Seattle, Washington, 1932, through Judge E. B. Ritchie, Mineral Wells. By J. Evetts Haley.

Beall, Knox, to R. B. Thomas, November 5, 1937, Indian Pioneer History Project for Oklahoma, Western History Collections, University of Oklahoma.

Beall, Knox, to Bessie Thomas, April 15, 1938.

Caperton, Major John. *Sketch of Colonel John C. Hays, The Texas Rangers, Incidents in Mexico*, *etc.* From materials furnished by Col. Hays and Major John Caperton, MS Center for American History, University of Texas at Austin.

Clarke, Elizabeth Ross. *YA-A-H-HOO: Warwhoop of the Comanches.* Elizabeth Ross Clarke Collection; Narrative, Center For American History, University of Texas.

Dixon, Olive King. *Fearless and Effective Foe, He Spared Women and Children Always.* Manuscript, Olive King Dixon Papers, Research Center, Panhandle Plains Historical Museum, Canyon, Texas.

Dupree, Mrs. J. L., to Jasper Mead, March 17, 1938, Indian Pioneer History Project for Oklahoma, Western History Collections, University of Oklahoma.

Earle, J. P. *A History of Clay County and Northwest Texas. Written by J.P . Earle, one of the first pioneers, Henrietta , Texas,* November 15, 1900 (J. P. Earle Collection, Center for American History), manuscript.

Fleming, Evelyn. Profile of Charlie Hart. Manuscript, Quanah Parker papers, Panhandle Plains Historical Museum.

Ford, Colonel John S. (late adjutant of Col. Hays). *John C. Hays in Texas.* Manuscript, John Salmon Ford Papers, Center for American History, University of Texas at Austin.

Gholson, B. F. Recollections of B. F. Gholson; Services of A. G. Gholson (father) 1835–1860; and B. F. Gholson, Ranger, 1858–1860, told to J. A. Rickard. Typed manuscript at Center for American History.

Gomez, Anna, to Ophelia D. Vestal, December 13, 1937, Indian Pioneer History Project for Oklahoma, Western History Collections, University of Oklahoma.

Goodnight, Charles. "The Making of a Scout." Manuscript, Panhandle Plains Historical Museum.

———. *My recollections and memories of the capture of Cynthia Ann Parker.* Manuscript, Charles Goodnight Papers, Research Center, Panhandle Plaines Historical Museum, Canyon, Texas.

———. *Quanah Parker Interview with Charles Goodnight,* undated. Charles Goodnight Papers, Research Center, Panhandle Plains Historical Museum, Canyon, Texas.

Gunter, Lillian. "Sketch of the Life of Julian Gunter." Manuscript made for Panhandle Plains Historical Association, 1923, Panhandle Plains Historical Museum archives.

Hatfield, Charles A. P. *The Comanche, Kiowa, and Cheyenne Campaign in Northwest Texas and Mackenzie's Fight in the Palo Duro Canyon, Sept. 26, 1874.* Typescript, Panhandle Plains Historical Society, Canyon, Texas.

Indian Pioneer History Project for Oklahoma. Western History Collections, University of Oklahoma (interviews from the 1930s).

Kirkpatrick, Mrs. Cora Miller. Memoirs, in Mrs. J. W. Pierce manuscript, Quanah Parker collection, Panhandle Plains Historical Museum.

Nohl, Lessing. "Bad Hand: The Military Career of Ranald Slidell Mackenzie, 1871–1889." Ph.D. diss. University of New Mexico.

Parker, Chief Baldwin. *The Life of Quanah Parker, Comanche Chief,* through J. Evetts Haley, August 29, 1930. Manuscript at Center for American History, University of Texas, Austin.

Parker, Wayne. *Quanah Parker, Last Chief of the Kwahadi Obeys the Great Spirit.* Manuscript, Quanah Parker Collection, Panhandle Plains Historical Museum, Canyon, Texas.

Roberson, G. W., to J. Evetts Haley, June 30, 1926. Manuscript in Panhandle Plains Historical Museum archives.

Rogers, H. B. *The Recollections of H. B. Rogers, as told to J. A. Rickard* (appended to Gholson manuscript).

Scott, Captain Hugh. Interview with Capt. Hugh Scott, 1897. Hugh Scott Collection, Fort Sill Archives, Lawton, Oklahoma, also partly available through Neeley Archive at Panhandle Plains Historical Museum, Canyon, Texas.

Thomas, Robert B. Undated manuscript, Indian Pioneer History Project for Oklahoma,

Western History Collections, University of Oklahoma; also Knox Beall, op. cit. November 5, 1937.

Unidentified newspaper story about the school board in Quanah Parker Collection; Panhandle Plains Historical Museum.

Wallace, Ernest, Papers. "The Habitat and Range of the Comanche, Kiowa, and Kiowa-Apache Indians." Manuscript, Southwest Collection, Texas Tech, Lubbock.

Zimmerman, Jean Louise. "Ranald Slidell Mackenzie." M.A. thesis. University of Oklahoma, 1965. Western History Collections, University of Oklahoma.

INDEX

♦ A Scribner Reading Group Guide

Empire of the Summer Moon
S. C. Gwynne

INTRODUCTION

Empire of the Summer Moon is a stunning historical account of the forty-year battle for control of the American West and of one of its most remarkable narratives: the century-spanning saga of the pioneer woman Cynthia Ann Parker and her half-white son Quanah, who became the last and greatest chief of the Comanche.

TOPICS AND QUESTIONS FOR DISCUSSION

1. In chapter four, Gwynne compares the Comanche warriors to the Celts, and later, in chapter five, to the Spartans. Both were war-driven cultures that prided themselves on being more fearless than their opponents. Can you think of any other historical cultures that remind you of the Comanche? Do you think it is fair to identify this tribe solely based on their ability to wage and win wars?

2. A journalist by trade, Gwynne maintains impartiality throughout the book. Although it is difficult not to sympathize with the Comanche and their ultimate fate, they were notorious for their extreme violence toward all who stood in their way. How are you able to reconcile the savagery of the tribe with their nobility? Does this moral dichotomy even need to be reconciled, or is it wrong to apply modern standards of ethics to the Comanche?

3. John Coffee Hays, nicknamed "Capitan Yack," was one of the first military officers to successfully adopt the Indian style of warfare and briefly managed to level the battlefield against the Comanche. Hays and the Texas Rangers of the 1830s and 1840s created a blueprint for success that was then forgotten for decades until Ranald Mackenzie and others relearned it. Do you think if the Hays style of fighting had been adopted immediately, the struggle would have lasted as long as it did? Why or why not?

4. The story of Quanah and his second wife, Weckeah, is a wonderful anecdote that displays the courage and determination for which Quanah would later be famous. What other qualities do you think made Quanah such a great leader? Was he at a disadvantage for being from

a mixed heritage? Or did this quality play a role in his rise through the Comanche ranks?

5. Cynthia Ann Parker's story is a fascinating case study in cultural assimilation. The true tragedy of her life was her second stint in captivity following her "escape" from the Comanche (p. 181). Why do you think Cynthia Ann Parker had so much trouble reassimilating into "white" culture? Do you think Sul Ross would have brought her back as a captive had he known the final outcome?

6. Ranald Mackenzie is presented as a counterpoint to the infamous George Custer in chapter sixteen. Mackenzie proved himself at West Point, then in the Civil War, and he won more than his fair share of battles against the Comanche. Considering this, why do you think history remembers Custer rather than Mackenzie?

7. Consider how history would have changed if the Spanish and French had been more successful in fighting the Comanche. If the Comanches hadn't repelled the Spanish and French advancement, would America have become the country it is today?

8. Isa-tai—a medicine man, a magician, and a con man according to Gwynne (p. 264)—was both a blessing and a curse to the Comanche. Together, he and Quanah rallied the warriors necessary to spring a revenge raid on the Texans. Although Quanah is remembered as the last great Comanche chief, how much do you think Isa-tai contributed to Quanah's status? Would Quanah have been able to rally as many warriors into battles without Isa-tai? Do you think Quanah and the Comanche would have ultimately been better off without Isa-tai?

9. Surprisingly enough, Quanah was able to adapt to reservation life. Still, he lived as only a Comanche would be allowed to, with eight wives and twenty-four children. As Gwynne writes, Quanah "existed . . . in the weird half-world of the reservation" (p. 302). What do you make of Quanah's peaceful surrender and his "second life" on the reservation? Were you surprised by his ability to balance both his captivity and his role as an assertive Comanche leader?

10. The scene toward the end of the book when Quanah and his fellow Comanche are allowed off the reservation for a buffalo hunt is heartbreaking. There are no buffalo to be found, and they are reduced, instead, to hunting cattle. This poignant failed attempt to recapture a vital piece of Comanche identity just a few years after surrender begs

the following questions: Would the Comanche have been forced to give up their way of life even if they had not engaged in war? Would they eventually have been rendered obsolete because of their inability and unwillingness to adapt to the ever-modernizing world around them?

11. Did you know the true origin of the phrase Comanche Moon before reading *Empire of the Summer Moon*? What other misconceptions about the Comanche or the history of the West did Gwynne help to dispel with this book?

12. In the final chapter of the book, Gwynne writes about Quanah's legacy: "The contrast could not be greater with his more famous neighbor, Geronimo" (p. 314). He goes on to explain that while Geronimo was not well liked by Indians on the reservation and died a drunk and a gambler, Quanah is remembered as one of the last great Indian chiefs. Do you think we will still remember Quanah one hundred years from now? What do you think his lasting legacy will be?

ENHANCE YOUR BOOK CLUB

1. Listen to S. C. Gwynne talk about the research that went into *Empire of the Summer Moon* and his writing process in an interview he did with Terry Gross on NPR's *Fresh Air*. You can download a podcast for free from iTunes or read the transcript on NPR's website. The episode originally aired on June 23, 2010, and is called "Comanche Nation: The Rise and Fall of an 'Empire.'" Or, visit http://www.npr.org/templates/story/story.php?storyId=127930650 to listen.

2. Schedule a screening with your book club of one of the handful of movies devoted to the Comanche Indians. The most critically acclaimed is Budd Boetticher's *Comanche Station*. Another movie, *Comanche,* a 1956 offering from George Sherman, features an actor playing the role of Quanah Parker. There is also a 2010 documentary produced by the History Channel titled *Comanche Warriors*. John Ford's *The Searchers* is one of the greatest westerns ever made and is based on the stories of Cynthia Ann Parker and her uncle James.

3. If you really want to run your book club in true Comanche style, prepare a feast of buffalo meat! There are a number of great cookbooks devoted to buffalo meat recipes, as well as numerous websites. Comanche Buffalo.com is a good place to start. If possible, purchase meat that is grass fed and organic. Be thankful that you don't have to skin the hide yourself to prepare the meat!

Turn the page for an excerpt from
S. C. Gwynne's new book

HYMNS

of the

REPUBLIC

Coming from Scribner in
hardcover and ebook in
fall 2019

Chapter One

THE END BEGINS

ABRAHAM LINCOLN: By spring 1864 it was clear
that the nation's fate hinged on the president's success
or failure at the November polls.

Washington, DC, had never, in its brief and undistinguished history, known a social season like this one. The winter of 1863–64 had been bitterly cold, but its frozen rains and swirling snows had dampened no spirits. Instead a feeling, almost palpable, of optimism hung in the air, a swelling sense that, after three years of brutal war and humiliating defeats at the hands of rebel armies, God was perhaps in his heaven, after all. The inexplicably lethal Robert E. Lee had finally been beaten at Gettysburg.[1] Vicksburg had fallen, completing the Union conquest of the Mississippi River. A large rebel army had been chased from Chattanooga. Something like hope—or maybe just its shadow—had finally loomed into view.

The season had begun as always with a New Year's reception at the Executive Mansion, hosted by the Lincolns, then had launched itself into a frenzy whose outward manifestation was the city's newest obsession: dancing.

Washingtonians were crazy about it. They were seen spinning through quadrilles, waltzes, and polkas at the great US Patent Office Ball, the Enlistment Fund Ball, and at "monster hops" at Willard's hotel and the National.[2] At these affairs, moreover, *everyone* danced. No bored squires or sad-eyed spinsters lingered in the shadows of cut glass and gaslight. No one could sit still, and together all improvised a wildly moving tapestry of color: ladies in lace and silk and crinolines, in crimson velvet and purple moire, their cascading curls flecked with roses and lilies, their bell-shaped forms whirled by men in black swallowtails and colored cravats.

The great public parties were merely the most visible part of the social scene. That winter had seen an explosion of private parties as well. Limits were pushed here, too, budgets broken, meals set forth of quail, partridge, lobster, terrapin, and acreages of confections. Politicians such as Secretary of State William Seward and Congressman Schuyler "Smiler" Colfax threw musical soirees. The spirit of the season was evident in the wedding of the imperially lovely Kate Chase—daughter of Treasury Secretary Salmon P. Chase—to Senator William Sprague. Sprague's gift to Kate was a $50,000 tiara of matched pearls and diamonds. When the bride appeared, the US Marine Band struck up "The Kate Chase March," a song written by a prominent composer for the occasion.[3]

What was most interesting about these evenings, however, was less their showy proceedings than the profoundly threatened world in which they took place. It was less like a world than a child's snow globe: a small glittering space enclosed by an impenetrable barrier. For in the winter of 1863–64, Washington was the most heavily defended city on earth. Beyond its houses and public buildings stood thirty-seven miles of elaborate trenches and fortifications that included sixty separate forts, manned by fifty thousand soldiers. Along this armored front bristled some nine hundred cannons, many of large caliber, enough to blast entire armies from the face of the earth.[4] There was something distinctly medieval about the fear that drove such engineering.

The danger was quite real. Since the Civil War had begun, Washington had been threatened three times by large armies under Robert E. Lee's command.[5] After the Union defeat at the Second Battle of Bull Run in August 1862, a rebel force under Lee's lieutenant Stonewall Jackson had come within twenty miles of the capital while driving the entire sixty-thousand-man Union army back inside its fortifications, where the bluecoats cowered and licked their wounds and thanked heaven for all those earthworks and cannons.[6]

A year and a half later, the same fundamental truth informed those lively parties. Without that *cordon militaire*, they could not have existed. Washington's elaborate social scene was a brocaded illusion: what the capital's denizens desperately wanted the place to be, not what it actually was.

This garishly defended capital was still a smallish, grubby, corrupt, malodorous, and oddly pretentious municipality whose principal product, along with legislation and war making, was biblical sin in its many varieties. Much of the city had been destroyed in the War of 1812. What had replaced the old settlement was both humble and grandiose. Vast quantities of money had been spent to build the city's precious handful of public buildings: the Capitol itself (finished in December 1863), the Post Office Building, the Smithsonian Institution, the US Patent Office, the US Treasury, and the Executive Mansion. (The Washington Monument, whose construction had been suspended in 1854 for lack of funds, was an abandoned and forlorn-looking stump.)[7]

But those structures stood as though on a barren plain. The Corinthian columns of the Post Office Building may have been worthy of the high Renaissance, but little else in the neighborhood was. The effect was jarring, as though pieces of the Champs-Élysées had been dropped into a swamp. Everything about the place, from its bloody and never-ending war to the faux grandiosity of its windswept plazas, suggested incompleteness. Like the Washington Monument, it all seemed half-finished. The wartime city held only about eighty thousand permanent residents, a pathetic fraction of the populations of New York (800,000) and Philadelphia (500,000), let alone London (2.6 million) or Paris (1.7 million).[8] Foreign travelers, if they came to the national capital at all, found it hollow, showy, and vainglorious. British writer Anthony Trollope, who visited the city during the war and thought it a colossal disappointment, wrote:

> Washington is but a ragged, unfinished collection of unbuilt broad streets. . . . Of all the places I know it is the most ungainly and most unsatisfactory; I fear I must also say the most presumptuous in its pretensions. Taking [a] map with him . . . a man may lose himself in the streets, not as one loses oneself in London between Shoreditch and Russell Square, but as one does so in the deserts of the Holy Land . . . There is much unsettled land within the United States of America, but I think none so desolate as three-fourths of the ground on which is supposed to stand the city of Washington.[9]

He might have added that the place smelled, too. Its canals were still repositories of sewage; tidal flats along the Potomac reeked at low tide. Pigs and cows still roamed the frozen streets. Dead horses, rotting in the winter sun, were common sights. At the War Department, one reporter noted, "The gutter [was] heaped up full of black, rotten mud, a foot deep, and worth fifty cents a car load for manure."[10] The unfinished mall where the unfinished Washington Monument stood held a grazing area and slaughterhouse for the cattle used to feed the capital's defenders.[11] The city was both a haven and a dumping ground for the sort of human chaff that collected at the ragged edges of the war zone: deserters from both armies, sutlers (civilians who sold provisions to soldiers), spies, confidence men, hustlers, and the like.

Washington had also become the nation's single largest refuge for escaped slaves, who now streamed through the capital's rutted streets by the thousands. When Congress freed the city's thirty-three hundred slaves in 1862, it had triggered an enormous inflow of refugees, mostly from Virginia and Maryland.[12] By 1864 fifty thousand of them had moved within Washington's ring of forts. Many were housed in "contraband camps," and many suffered in disease-ridden squalor in a world that often seemed scarcely less prejudiced than the one they had left. But they were never going back. They were never going to be slaves again. This was the migration's central truth, and you could see it on any street corner in the city. Many would make their way into the Union army, which at the end of 1863 had already enlisted fifty thousand from around the country, most of them former slaves.

But the most common sights of all on those streets were soldiers. A war was being fought, one that had a sharp and unappeasable appetite for young men. Several hundred thousand of them had tramped through the city since April 1861, wearing their blue uniforms, slouch hats, and knapsacks. They had lingered on its street corners, camped on its outskirts. Tens of thousands more languished in wartime hospitals. Mostly they were just passing through, on their way to a battlefield or someone's grand campaign or, if they were lucky, home. Many were on their way to death or dismemberment. In their wake came the seemingly endless supply trains with their shouting teamsters, rumbling wagon wheels, snorting horses, and creaking tack.

Because of these soldiers—unattached young men, isolated, and far from home—a booming industry had arisen that was more than a match for its European counterparts: prostitution. This was no minor side effect of war. Ten percent or more of the adult population were inhabitants of Washington's demimonde. In 1863, the *Washington Evening Star* had determined that the capital had more than five thousand prostitutes, with an additional twenty-five hundred in neighboring Georgetown, and twenty-five hundred more across the river in Alexandria, Virginia. That did not count the concubines or courtesans who were simply kept in apartments by the officer corps. The year before, an army survey had revealed 450 houses of ill repute.[13] All served drinks and sex. In a district called Murder Bay, passersby could see nearly naked women in the windows and doors of the houses. For the less affluent—laborers, teamsters, and army riffraff—Nigger Hill and Tin Cup Alley had sleazier establishments, where men were routinely robbed, stabbed, shot, and poisoned with moonshine whiskey. The *Star* could not help wondering how astonished the sisters and mothers of these soldiers would be to see how their noble young men spent their time at the capital.[14] Many of these establishments were in the heart of the city, a few blocks from the president's house and the fashionable streets where the capital's smart set whirled in gaslit dances.

This was Washington, DC, in that manic, unsettled winter of 1863–64, in the grip of a lengthening war whose end no one could clearly see.

OF ALL THE PARTIES, gatherings, and balls that season, none would be as indelibly etched into the memories of Washingtonians as a public reception at the White House on the wet, blustery night of Tuesday, March 8. President Lincoln held two such receptions a week—known in the day as levees—where he and his wife, Mary, would stand in the doorway to the Blue Room and greet all comers. The president would shake hands, in a manner that reminded people of someone sawing wood, and say "How do?" and perhaps a few more words, then visitors would be passed along to Mary Lincoln, who greeted them in turn. The Tuesday reception was the more formal one. According to a reporter who was there, the well-dressed attendees were as usual "pour[ing] through the drawing rooms into the great East Room, where they circulate in a revolving march to the music of the Marine Band, stationed in an adjoining room."[15]

Except that this night was different. At about nine thirty, Lincoln was at his usual perch, wearing a collar one size too large, a badly tied necktie, and his habitual expression of bemused melancholy, when a sudden noise and commotion arose at the entrance to the room.[16]

From the small crowd at the door, which had sorted itself into a double file, now emerged a man with a slender build, slightly stooped shoulders, mild blue eyes, and an unexceptional beard, wearing the uniform of a Union soldier.[17] When Lincoln saw him, all sadness vanished from the president's face, and he rushed toward the man.

"Why, here is General Grant!" Lincoln exclaimed. "Well, this is a great pleasure, I assure you!"[18]

As the crowd gaped, the two men chatted amiably, if somewhat awkwardly, for a moment—the stork-like Lincoln was fully eight inches taller than Grant and had to stoop to engage him—whereupon Grant was passed to Secretary of State William Seward, who then presented him to the first lady. As word of the visitor's arrival traveled rocket-like through the Blue Room and into the crowded East Room, utter pandemonium broke loose. A genteel riot ensued, driven by wild cheers and applause so uninhibited that Secretary of the Navy Gideon Welles found it "rowdy and unseemly."[19] As one observer described it, "Laces were torn, crinoline mashed." Within minutes, Seward and his charge, Ulysses S. Grant, war hero of the west and the great hope of the Union, were swallowed by the great surge of the crowd.[20]

As the crowd's behavior suggested, this was no casual visit. Grant had come to Washington because he had just been promoted by act of Congress to a rank—lieutenant general—that had been held only twice in American history, once by George Washington and once by Winfield Scott, hero of the Mexican-American War. In both cases, the commission was honorary. Thus the modest and unassuming Ulysses S. Grant, known to his army friends as Sam, the antithesis of pomp, circumstance, and military grandeur, was about to become the first full-blown three-star general in US history.[21]

The immediate impetus for the promotion had been his victory at Chattanooga, Tennessee, in November, where he had broken General Braxton Bragg's siege and then sent Bragg's forty-thousand-man Confederate army reeling in retreat, thus confirming what Abraham Lincoln had been thinking anyway: that Grant, among a crowded field of often timid, indecisive, and incompetent Union commanders, was the best choice to win the war. But Chattanooga was merely Grant's most recent trophy of war. In 1862 he had swallowed a twelve-thousand-man rebel army whole at Fort Donelson, Tennessee, refusing to offer any terms but *unconditional surrender.* Those words, with their strange, cold, insistent rhythm, had passed immediately into American legend. At Vicksburg, Mississippi, in 1863 he had shocked the nation again by capturing another entire Confederate army, this time containing thirty thousand men. Nor had his attitude toward surrender grown more charitable. When the opposing general had politely suggested a negotiating session to hammer out terms of surrender to "save the further effusion of blood," Grant replied, "The useless effusion of blood you propose stopping by this course can be ended at any time you may choose by an unconditional surrender of the city and the garrison." This was more of the same music that had sounded at Fort Donelson, bright and dissonant, and it was like nothing anyone had ever before heard. Where other commanders temporized and hesitated, Grant simply put his head down and hammered forward, like a battering ram.

A good deal more was attached to Grant than these three victories—including a drinking problem that had gotten him dismissed from the army, his questionable performance at the Battle of Shiloh, and a bizarre episode of anti-Semitism in 1862—but for now only the winning mattered. Few people of consequence, in the winter of 1863–64, argued against the promotion of "Unconditional Surrender" Grant, the Union general who won. He was the implacable force, the irresistible power from the mysterious west, where the soldiery had not formed a habit of losing.

At Lincoln's request Congress had promoted Grant, and now, in March, he had been summoned by Secretary of War Edwin Stanton to Washington to accept his new commission as head of all Union armies. Traveling with his thirteen-year-old son, Fred, his close aide John Rawlins, and another officer, Grant had made his way by boat from Louisville to Cincinnati, then by train to Washington, arriving at the station on the afternoon of March 8. He was one of the most celebrated men in the Western World at that moment, and the focus of fierce, often obsessive, national interest. He was probably more popular in the North than Lincoln himself. Grant was so famous that his full-length portrait, field glasses in hand and flanked by a demolished rebel cannon, hung in a committee room in the Capitol.[22] His likeness was featured on patriotic posters. Oceans of printer's ink had been expended describing his battlefield victories.

But few people in the east knew what he looked like, a problem compounded by his not looking like much at all. He had grown up in Ohio, which was very much part of "the west" in the middle nineteenth century. Though he had attended West Point in New York State, he had been to Washington exactly once in his life and had spent his entire military career, including the Civil War, in the Midwest, the far West, or Mexico.

His arrival in the late afternoon of March 8 was almost comically unceremonious. Due to a logistical error, no one had met his train at the station. To all appearances, he was just another sunburned soldier in an army hat and linen duster, stepping off a passenger car, looking blankly around him for whoever had been appointed to greet him. Thus stranded, Grant's small group took a carriage to the office of army general-in-chief Henry Wager Halleck, in the hope of seeing a familiar face. But Halleck was not there. The group then proceeded to Halleck's residence, but he was not there either. Having failed three times to find anyone who might welcome him, Grant decided he would just go on to Willard's hotel, where he had been told rooms had been reserved for him and his party.

The difference between Grant's arrival and the arrival, nineteen months earlier, of the Union's leading general George McClellan in Washington following his craven defeat in the Seven Days Battles, east of Richmond, is worth noting.[23] The caravan bearing the baggage of McClellan and his staff consisted of twenty-five six-foot-by-nine-foot wagons, painted dark brown and varnished to a high gleam. The wagons were each drawn by four matched bay horses—both their color and manes had been deliberately coordinated for effect—and each driven by two black attendants in immaculate blue livery. On the side of each wagon, in large gold letters, was the inscription BAGGAGE. HEADQUARTERS. ARMY OF THE POTOMAC. McClellan had arrived like an imperial pasha with one hundred horses and fifty attendants; Grant with only his son and a light suitcase.[24] The lordly McClellan had turned out to be an embarrassment, a timid general who had to be coaxed, cajoled, shamed, and threatened into fighting Confederates and who finally had to be gotten rid of.

Grant's ordeal of anonymity was not quite over. He arrived at Willard's, quietly checked in as "U. S. Grant and son, Galena, Ill.," and, still unrecognized, came down to dinner with Fred.[25] In the dining room the lightning bolt finally struck. After whispers, more whispers, and a rising commotion, a nearby gentleman banged on his table with a dinner knife, rose, and announced that he had "the honor to inform [the diners] that General Grant was present in the room with them." The crowd of diners rose to their feet, and soon thunderous cheers were rolling through the room. "My father arose and bowed," Fred Grant recalled later, "and the crowd began to surge around him; after that, dining became impossible; and an informal reception was held for perhaps three quarters of an hour; but as there seemed to be no end to the crowd assembling, my father left the dining room and retired to his apartments."[26] Word of Grant's arrival spread quickly. Former secretary of war Simon Cameron soon came to collect him and give him a proper escort to Lincoln's reception, two blocks away.

What Grant faced inside the East Room made the disturbance at Willard's seem tame. He was greeted by more booming cheers, but now the possibility that he might be trampled seemed quite real. Secretary of State Seward solved the problem by having Grant climb up onto a sofa, where, in the description of *Sacramento Daily Union* reporter Noah Brooks,

> he could be seen, and where he was secure, at least for a time, from the madness of the multitude. People were caught up and whirled into the torrent which swept through the Great East Room. . . . Many got up on sofas, chairs, and tables to be out of harm's way or to get a better view of the spectacle. It was the only real mob I ever saw in the White House. For at least once, the President of the United States was not the chief figure in the picture. The little, scared-looking man who stood on a crimson-colored sofa was the idol of the hour.[27]

At least sixty minutes passed before Lincoln and a flushed and perspiring Grant were able to hold a conversation.[28] In the meantime the people had gotten a glimpse of Grant and were thrilled by what they saw: a plain and modest man whose clear and impassive blue eyes showed both confidence and determination, a man free of the cant and hollow grandeur that had marked some of his predecessors.[29] With his immense gifts of command and his humble manner, he managed to be transcendently American.

As a westerner—that was how he thought of himself—Grant had learned to despise the intrigue, corruption, infighting, pettifoggery, and personality-driven politics of Washington. Instinctively, he wanted nothing to do with the place. The regular army had enough of all that anyway. He was a straight-ahead fighter, not someone who bent with political winds. He wanted to be measured by battlefield results. Everyone around him agreed with him that he needed to stay away from Washington—both as a place and as an idea. John Rawlins wrote, of his boss's Washington visit, "I am doing everything I can to get him away from here."[30] Grant's sidekick and sometime political conscience William Tecumseh Sherman had advised him, in his letter congratulating him on his promotion, "Do not stay in Washington. . . . For God's sake and for your country's sake, come out of Washington!"[31]

Now, in the presence of the great Lincoln, Grant was vouchsafed a clear view as to why. Though Lincoln had just met Grant, the president was already stage-managing the events of the next day, when Grant would officially accept his new commission. The president spoke to Grant as though the little general might have trouble understanding how such complicated adult matters worked, as one would to a bright middle schooler.

"I shall then make a very short speech to you," Lincoln said, "to which I desire you to make a reply . . . and that you may be properly prepared to do so I have written what I shall say—only four sentences in all—which I will read from my MS. as an example which you may follow and also read your reply, as you are perhaps not as much accustomed to speaking as I, myself—and I therefore give you what I shall say that you may consider it and form your reply." If this wasn't quite patronizing enough—perhaps it had momentarily escaped Lincoln that managing the Union armies in the western theater, from the Alleghenies to the Mississippi River, might require some presentational skills—he then went on to tell Grant exactly what he was to say:

> There are two points that I would like to have you make in your answer, 1st, to say something which shall prevent or obviate any jealousy of you from any of the other generals in the service, and 2nd, something which shall put you on as good terms as possible with this Army of the Potomac.[32]

At the ceremony the next day Lincoln read his statement, praising and promoting Grant, and then Grant made his own little speech, which must have entirely lived up to Lincoln's dismal expectations: choppy, disjointed, and delivered in what one observer called a "struggling" fashion. Grant had scribbled it down in pencil on a half sheet of notepaper and seemed to have trouble reading his own writing. "Mr. President, I accept this commission with gratitude for the high honor conferred, with the aid of the noble armies that have fought on so many fields for our common country." And so on. He managed to say little, and, perhaps not coincidentally, *nothing at all of what his boss had told him to say.* Lincoln's secretary, John G. Nicolay, noted dryly at the time that Grant "had either forgotten or disregarded entirely the president's hints to him of the night previous."[33]

Grant took Sherman's advice and got the hell out of Washington as soon as he could. He turned down a dinner invitation from Lincoln, saying, "Dinner to me means a million dollars a day lost to the country," which appealed to Lincoln's fiscal instincts. He also told Lincoln that he had "become very tired of this show business," which also pleased the president, who was by then tired of grandstanding generals. Grant made a brief excursion to Brandy

Station in northern Virginia to visit the Army of the Potomac and its commander, General George G. Meade—where brass bands greeted Grant in pouring rain—then took a train to Nashville, where he met with his friend Sherman, to whom he handed command of all of the Union armies in the west.[34]

When Grant returned east a few days later, it was not to Washington, DC, but to a small town in Virginia called Culpeper Court House. As general in charge of all Union armies, he would not, as his predecessor Major General Henry Wager Halleck had, make his headquarters in the political rat's nest of Washington. Grant would be at the front. Camped across the Rapidan River from him, just a few miles away, was the single most potent military force on the North American continent, the Army of Northern Virginia, commanded by the other towering military genius of the Civil War, a man whom Grant had never faced on a battlefield. Grant's mission was simple yet unprecedented in a war that had until now favored conquering real estate instead of armies, cities instead of people: destroy Robert E. Lee. In Grant's attempt to do that he would unleash, in just a few months, a storm of blood and death that beggared even the killing fields of Gettysburg and Chancellorsville. He would find himself in a world of bitterness, violence, hatred, and retribution that would make the early years of the conflict look innocent and honorable by comparison. He and Lee would soon remake the war into something that neither the country nor its hardened veterans had ever before seen.